ON THE BLISSFUL I
WITH NIETZSCHE &

CW01095207

What are the blissful islands? And where are they? This book takes as its starting-point the chapter called 'On the Blissful Islands' in Part Two of Nietzsche's *Thus Spoke Zarathustra*, and its enigmatic conclusion: '*The beauty of the Superman came to me as a shadow*'. From this remarkable and powerful passage, it disengages the Nietzschean idea of the Superman and the Jungian notion of the shadow, moving these concepts into a new, interdisciplinary direction.

In particular, *On the Blissful Islands* seeks to develop the kind of interpretative approach that Jung himself employed. Its chief topics are classical (the motif of the blissful islands), psychological (the shadow), and philosophical (the *Übermensch* or superman), blended together to produce a rich, intellectual-historical discussion. By bringing context and depth to a nexus of highly problematic concepts, it offers something new to the specialist and the general reader alike. So this book considers the significance of the statue in the culture of antiquity (and in alchemy), and investigates the associated notion of self-sculpting as a form of existential exercise. This Neoplatonic theme is pursued in relation to a poem by Schiller, at the centre of which lies the notion of self-sculpting, thus highlighting Nietzsche's (and Jung's) relationship to Idealism. Its conclusion directly addresses the vexed (and controversial) question of Nietzsche's relation to Plato.

This book's main ambition is to provide a cross-cultural, interdisciplinary reading of key themes and motifs, using Jungian ideas in general (and Jung's vast seminar on *Zarathustra* in particular) to uncover a dimension of deep meaning in key passages in Nietzsche. Engaging the reader directly on major existential questions, it aims to be an original, thought-provoking contribution to the history of ideas, and to show that Zarathustra was right: *There still are blissful islands!*

This book will be stimulating reading for analytical psychologists, including those in training, and academics and scholars of Jungian studies, Nietzsche, and the history of ideas.

Paul Bishop is William Jacks Chair in Modern Languages at the University of Glasgow. His previous publications include *Carl Jung* (Reaktion, 2014), *Reading Goethe At Midlife* (Spring Journal Books, 2011), *Analytical Psychology and German Classical Aesthetics*, 2 vols (Routledge, 2007–2008); and, as editor, *The Archaic: The Past in the Present* (Routledge, 2012) and *Jung in Contexts: A Reader* (Routledge, 1999).

'This is outstanding! Over many years, Paul Bishop has opened an academic shuttle of the highest quality between luminaries of German culture, such as Goethe, Schiller and Nietzsche, and study of the *oeuvre* of C.G. Jung. It is clear that mutual benefit has arisen from this monumental project, now running into several books and numerous papers. The writing is erudite, witty and limpid. And the writing is also profoundly psychological, for Bishop is no ordinary academic. He brings an emotional sensibility and sensitivity to his work, for example in the sections on ecstasy and asceticism. Bishop shows us that scholarship and the vicissitudes of everyday life are often not that far apart.'

— **Andrew Samuels**, Professor of Analytical Psychology,
University of Essex, UK

'In this study, Paul Bishop returns to the ancient problem of paradise lost and shows Jung's solution. A rigorous reflection on humanity's haunting dream of perfection and a paradise never to be regained.'

— **Murray Stein**, author of *Minding the Self*
(Routledge, 2014)

'With Jung as the most exciting reader of Nietzsche, and Nietzsche the most haunting prophet of epochal change, more than ever does the twenty-first century need the work of Paul Bishop, eminent authority on Germanic Romanticism's reincarnation in Jungian psychology. *On the Blissful Islands* brings together classical traditions of this realm of the dead, with Jung's under-researched notion of 'the shadow' and Nietzsche's less-comprehended 'superman'. In a superb flourish of aesthetical exploration, the book generates new approaches to personal and societal transformation and change. Moreover, this fascinating study extends significance beyond disciplinary boundaries. *On the Blissful Islands* speaks to artists and scholars, students and cultural theorists as well as being essential reading for those seeking to deepen their knowledge of Jung, Nietzsche, German culture and European Romanticism.'

— **Susan Rowland**, Chair, MA Engaged Humanities,
Pacifica Graduate Institute, USA

'Paul Bishop is the foremost interpreter of Jung's Germanic heritage to the English-speaking world. An alchemist of scholarship, he transmutes even the most recondite and mercurial of intellectual material into luminous, exhilarating prose. In the present book, drawing above all on Goethe, Nietzsche, and Jung, he undertakes a profound amplificatory meditation on the themes of the shadow, the blissful islands, sculpting, and much besides, to explore – to activate – contemporary possibilities of self-transformation and embodied mystical realisation. Overflowing with intellectual treasure, this book is a war chest for the embattled humanities.'

— **Professor Roderick Main**, University of Essex, UK

ON THE BLISSFUL ISLANDS WITH NIETZSCHE & JUNG

In the shadow of the superman

Paul Bishop

Routledge
Taylor & Francis Group

LONDON AND NEW YORK

First published 2017
by Routledge
2 Park Square, Milton Park, Abingdon, Oxon OX14 4RN

and by Routledge
711 Third Avenue, New York, NY 10017

Routledge is an imprint of the Taylor & Francis Group, an informa business

British Library Cataloguing in Publication Data
A catalogue record for this book is available from the British Library

Library of Congress Cataloging in Publication Data
Names: Bishop, Paul, 1967- author.
Title: On the blissful islands with Nietzsche and
Jung: in the shadow of the superman / Paul Bishop.
Description: Milton Park, Abingdon, Oxon: New York, NY: Routledge, 2017.
Identifiers: LCCN 2016023524 | ISBN 9781138791619 (hardback : alk. paper) |
ISBN 9781138791626 (pbk. : alk. paper) | ISBN 9781315762692 (ebook)
Subjects: LCSH: Nietzsche, Friedrich Wilhelm, 1844–1900.
Also sprach Zarathustra. | Superman (Philosophical concept) |
Shadow (Psychoanalysis) | Jung, C. G. (Carl Gustav), 1875-1961. | Plato.
Classification: LCC B3313.A44 B57 2017 | DDC 193--dc23
LC record available at https://lccn.loc.gov/2016023524

ISBN: 978-1-138-79161-9 (hbk)
ISBN: 978-1-138-79162-6 (pbk)
ISBN: 978-1-315-76269-2 (ebk)

Typeset in Bembo
by Out of House Publishing

'Do you want us to consider in what way
such men will come into being
and how one will lead them up to the light,
just as some men are said to have gone
from Hades up to the gods?'
'How could I not want to?'
(*The Republic*, 521 c)

Upon this I was as it were awaked out of a sleep,
and I saw, and my sleep was sweet to me.
(Book of Jeremiah, 31: 26)

I wouldn't drink a glass of beer with a Superman.
(Jung, Seminar on Nietzsche's *Zarathustra*)

CONTENTS

FIGURES

ACKNOWLEDGEMENTS

The idea for this book arises from preparation for a paper, the Inaugural David Holt Lecture given on 6 May 2009 at the University of Essex. I am grateful to the Centre for Psychoanalytic Studies for inviting me to give that lecture, and to the College of Arts of the University of Glasgow for allowing me research leave in the second semester of 2012–2013, during which I was able to take up work on this project again.

This book focuses, although by no means exclusively, on Nietzsche and Jung, and I should like to acknowledge the support and encouragement of colleagues working on these thinkers. On the Nietzschean side, I am indebted to conversations with Keith Ansell Pearson, Rebecca Bamford, and Nick Martin; while by telling me that Nietzsche was wrong about Plato, Alan Cardew set me off on a trail of thought for which he cannot be held responsible. Equally, on the Jungian side, I am indebted to conversations with Martin Liebscher, Sonu Shamdasani, Gerhard Schmitt, Leslie Gardiner, Roderick Main, David Burniston, Lucy Huskinson, Terence Dawson, and Christiane Ludwig, Diane Zervas Hirst, and Maggie Stanway; and, most recently, Peter Kingsley. I am grateful to Bruno Gransche of the Fraunhofer-Institut für System- und Innovationsforschung for email conversations about Goethe and Nietzsche. For help and assistance with this book from commissioning through to production, I would like to thank (at Routledge/Taylor & Francis) Kate Hawes, Susannah Frearson, Rebecca Hogg, and Kristina Siosyte; and (at Out of House Publishing) Aimée Feenan and Katie Finnegan. I am very grateful to Thomas Murray for his help in sourcing an image of a tjurunga. And I should like to thank Urs Niffeler, Zentralsekretär of Archäologie Schweiz, for assisting me with an enquiry about painted stones (or *galets coloriés*).

Finally (and, as the Germans like to say, *last but not least*), I am indebted to my students, for having allowed me to share in their discovery, despite the inevitable restrictions of today's university modern languages curriculum, of at least part of the intellectual and cultural heritage that is, by rights, theirs.

The support of Helen Bridge lies, as always, beyond any possible form of acknowledgement.

ABBREVIATIONS

Jung

CW   C.G. Jung, *Collected Works*, ed. Sir H. Read, M. Fordham, G. Adler and W. McGuire, 20 vols, London: Routledge and Kegan Paul, 1953–1983. Cited with volume and paragraph reference.

PU   C.G. Jung, *Psychology of the Unconscious: A Study of the Transformations and Symbolisms of the Libido: A Contribution to the History of the Evolution of Thought*, tr. B.M. Hinkle, intr. W. McGuire, London: Routledge, 1991. Cited with paragraph reference.

MDR   *Memories, Dreams, Reflections: Recorded and edited by Aniela Jaffé*, tr. R. and C. Winston, London: Fontana, 1983. Cited with page reference.

SNZ   C.G. Jung, *Nietzsche's "Zarathustra": Notes of the Seminar given in 1934–1939*, ed. J.L. Jarrett, 2 vols, London: Routledge, 1988. Cited with volume and page reference.

RB   C.G. Jung, *The Red Book: Liber Novus*, ed. S. Shamdasani, tr. M. Kyburz, J. Peck, and S. Shamdasani, New York and London: Norton, 2009. Cited with page reference.

Nietzsche

BW   *Basic Writings of Nietzsche*, ed. and tr. W. Kaufmann, New York: Modern Library, 1968.

KSA   F. Nietzsche, *Sämtliche Werke: Kritische Studienausgabe*, ed. G. Colli and M. Montinari, 15 vols, Berlin and New York; Munich: de Gruyter; Deutscher Taschenbuch Verlag, 1967–1977 and 1988. Cited with volume, fragment number, and page reference.

KSB   F. Nietzsche, *Sämtliche Briefe: Kritische Studienausgabe*, ed. G. Colli
          and M. Montinari, 8 vols, Berlin and New York; Munich: de
          Gruyter; Deutscher Taschenbuch Verlag, 1975–1984. Cited with
          volume and page reference.

Goethe

HA   J.W. von Goethe, *Werke* [*Hamburger Ausgabe*], ed. E. Trunz, 14
          vols, Hamburg: Wegner, 1948–1960; Munich: Beck, 1981.
          Cited as *Werke* [HA]. *Briefe*, ed. K.R. Mandelkow, 4 vols,
          Hamburg: Wegner, 1962–1967. Cited as *Briefe* [HA]. Cited with
          volume and page reference.

Schiller

NA   F. Schiller, *Werke: Nationalausgabe*, ed. J. Petersen and G. Fricke,
          N. Oellers and S. Seidel, im Auftrage des Goethe- und Schiller-
          Archivs, des Schiller-Nationalmuseums und der Deutschen
          Akademie, 43 vols, Weimar: H. Böhlaus Nachfolger, 1943ff.
          Cited with volume and page reference.

Schelling

SW   F.W.J. von Schelling, *Sämtliche Werke*, ed. K.F.A. Schelling, 14 vols,
          Stuttgart and Augsburg: Cotta, 1856–1861. Cited with volume
          and page reference.

Plato

CD   Plato, *The Collected Dialogues of Plato including the Letters*, ed.
          E. Hamilton and H. Cairns, Princeton, NJ: Princeton University
          Press, 1989. Cited with page reference.

Bible Editions Used

DRV   *Douay-Rheims Bible Edition of the Holy Catholic Bible* [revised Bishop
          Richard Challoner] *with a Comprehensive Catholic Commentary*,
          ed. Leo Haydock [1859 edition], Duarte, CA: Catholic Treasures,
          2006.

JB   *The Jerusalem Bible*, ed. A. Jones, London: Darton, Longman &
          Todd, 1966.

NJB   *The New Jerusalem Bible*, ed. H. Wansbrough, London: Darton,
          Longmann & Todd, 1985.

PREFACE

E.T.A. Hoffmann's remarkable tale, 'The Sandman', one of his *Night Pieces* (1817), has caught the attention of many, including Sigmund Freud.[1] (In the Jungian tradition, another work, *The Golden Pot*, has received detailed attention from one of the earliest exponents of Jungian thought, Aniela Jaffé.[2]) As a child, Nathanael comes to associate the nightmarish figure of the Sandman, used by the old woman who acts a nurse to his younger sister to frighten them, with Coppelius, the nasty lawyer who visits his father to carry out ghastly alchemical experiments. One evening, he sees what his father and Coppelius are up to — and he faints.

As an adult, Nathanael relives this experience on two levels: through Coppola, the salesman who sells him a telescope, and Olimpia, the woman — who turns out to be a robot — for whom he has conceived an erotic attraction. These two levels fuse, and the nightmare returns when he sees Olimpia's eyes lying on the ground — and goes insane.

After he has recovered, Nathanael falls in love with and resolves to marry his childhood sweetheart, Clara, a completely different (and altogether more sensible) woman than Olimpia. One day, on the way to his home town, they climb the tower of the town hall and look out from the top at the view. At this point, for the second time the nightmare returns — and all the various timelines and motifs converge. 'Look', says Clara, looking into the distance, 'what's that funny little grey bush coming toward us?' Nathanael looks down through Coppola's telescope — and looks at Clara. For the second time, Nathanael becomes insane: he tries to throw Clara down from the tower, while below, Coppelius looks on. 'Don't worry; he'll come down of his accord', Coppelius says, before Nathanael finally jumps to his death.

Thanks to Hoffmann's clever construction of this text, we never know whether Nathanael has discovered some terrible fact about himself, or whether he is simply a pathological case; or whether he has seen into the fundamental nature of reality, and this has driven him mad. An important clue lies in an apparently insignificant detail in a description of the town before he and Clara decide to ascend the tower:

> At noon they were going through the streets. After making several purchases they found that the lofty tower of the town hall was throwing its giant shadows across the market place. "Come", said Clara, "let us go up to the top once more and have a look at the distant hills."[3]

Here subtly, o so subtly, Hoffmann lets us know that something is wrong, and drops a hint that should alert us to the fact that something terrible is about to happen. For this final scene is set at noon; at noon, when the sun is at its zenith. *And yet the tower of the town hall is throwing a giant shadow.*

In this tale the terror is not simply to be found in the nightmare story of the Sandman who comes to little children, and throws handfuls of sand into their eyes, so that their eyes jump out from their sockets, all bloody; in the apparition of the men's faces without eyes, while Coppelius threatens to remove Nathanael's eyes for his and his father's experiments; or in the discovery that the object of his erotic desires, Olimpia, is in fact an automaton, whose eyes fall out. The terror is also there in this tiny, apparently insignificant, detail, that proves that not everything in the world is as it should be: *for at midday, no object ever casts a shadow.*

In Hoffmann's tale, the shadow is a problem: it is there, when it should not be, and this is the essence of the shadow, as Jung understood it in an archetypal sense. For Jung, the shadow was one of the motley group of figures that constituted, in his view, the collective unconscious: the anima and the animus, the great mother and the wise old man, the child and the trickster, and the more difficult-to-grasp archetypes of the spirit (*Geist*), of rebirth, and the self. And — the shadow.

In the classic exposition of Jungian psychology offered by Jolande Jacobi, another of Jung's earliest followers, in 1942, the shadow is the first of the archetypes one encounters on the path of the individuation process. (The second, on this account, is the anima — if one's a man — or the animus — if one's a woman; then the old wise man — or the *Magna Mater*, and finally, the self.[4]) Of course, this is a simplification; albeit a useful one in orientating oneself around the timeless, spaceless realm that is the collective unconscious.[5] As an instance of the old wise man, Jacobi cites the example of Nietzsche, who 'fully identified himself with the figure of Zarathustra'.[6] And about Nietzsche, and about Zarathustra, Jung himself had had more — much more — to say in his five-year-long seminar about Nietzsche's *Thus Spoke Zarathustra* from 1934 to 1939.

In the physical world, as in the psychological, a shadow is brought about through a projection: by the tower of a town hall, say, when the sun is at a certain angle; or by a false idea which casts a darkness into our perception of the world. What does, in psychoanalytic terms, darkness mean? According to Jung, day and night, or light and dark, are synonyms for consciousness and unconsciousness. In pagan mythology and legend, the 'main feat' of the hero is 'to overcome the monster of darkness'.[7] Or, in Judeo-Christian terms, 'the coming of consciousness was probably the most tremendous experience of primeval times', for with it 'a world came into being whose experience no one had suspected before'.[8] In the famous words in the Biblical account of the Creation in the Book of Genesis, 'God said, "Let there be light!". And there was light'. (That, of course, was day 1; on day 2, God separated the upper waters from the lower, but as the alchemical philosopher, Gerhard Dorn [c. 1530–1584], pointed out, on the evening of that day God neglected to say, as He did on the evening of every other day of Creation, that what He had done 'was good'. For in separating the upper from the lower, Dorn argued, God had created the *binarius*, the cause of 'confusion, division, and strife'.[9] One might also think, however, that there is something 'diabolical' or problematic about the earlier — the primordial? — binary of light and dark ....)

For Jung, 'the shadow personifies everything that the subject refuses to acknowledge about himself and yet is always thrusting itself upon him directly or indirectly',[10] and one of the ways in which the individual copes with this projection of the shadow onto himself is to project the shadow onto other people. And, in Jungian analytical circles, the projection of the shadow onto others is frequently adduced as a cause of interpersonal conflict or social unrest. 'We still attribute to the other fellow', Jung says, 'all the evil and inferior qualities that we do not like to recognize in ourselves, and therefore have to criticize and attack him, when all that has happened is that an inferior "soul" has emigrated from one person to another', or as he chillingly says: 'The world is still full of *bêtes noires* and scapegoats, just as it formerly teemed with witches and werewolves'.[11] At the time of the Cold War, when Europe, Germany, and Berlin were all split between East and West, the Tenth International Congress for Analytical Psychology was held in West Berlin on 2–9 September 1987; its proceedings were published as a collection of papers under the dramatic title, *The Archetype of Shadow in a Split World*.[12] What, one is prompted to ask, really brought down the Berlin Wall? Was it Gorbachev? Was it the demonstrating crowds on the streets? Or was it a change in the archetypal constellation?

In E.T.A. Hoffmann's story, the tell-tale sign that something is wrong comes in the fact that the shadow is there, when in fact it should not be. This might prompt us to ask: Must there always be a shadow? Is a shadow always something bad? And can we understand the shadow, not as a projection of something from the past, but as the way that something in the future will look but which we cannot correctly perceive in the present?

Crystallization

In his autobiographical work, *Poetry and Truth* (*Dichtung und Wahrheit*), Goethe offers an account of the composition of his celebrated novel, *The Sorrows of Young Werther*. In part, the genesis of the novel owed something to Goethe's own love for Charlotte Buff, engaged at the time to her future husband, Johann Christian Kestner; in part, it owed something to the suicide of Goethe's friend in Wetzlar, Karl Wilhelm Jerusalem. In 1772, Jerusalem shot himself, frustrated because of his love for Elisabeth Herd, a married — and unattainable — woman. When Kestner,

Charlotte Buff's fiancé, sent Goethe an account of Jerusalem's last hours, the letter provided Goethe with an immediate source of inspiration. In *Poetry and Truth*, Goethe tells us:

> All at once I heard the news of Jerusalem's death, and on the very heels of the general rumour there followed the most exact and detailed description of the occurrence. At this moment I found the plan for *Werther*. From all sides the whole thing crystallized into a solid mass, just as water in a bucket, when at the freezing point, can be immediately changed to firm ice by the slightest shock.[13]

Goethe's image of crystallization in this passage might be, as has been pointed out, bad physics;[14] but it is good psychology.

For there are moments in life where things do crystallize, where they do — as the etymology of the word suggests, form a *krustallos*: they turn into ice, i.e., they take on a form, they assume a *Gestalt*. Jung uses precisely this image when, in the prologue to *Memories, Dreams, Reflections*, he tells us that his 'inner experiences', his 'dreams and visions', were 'the *prima materia*' of his scientific work, or 'the fiery magma out of which the stone that had to be worked was crystallised' (*MDR*, 18). As always, we should pay attention to the language Jung uses here, for in this passage two different processes are simultaneously at work. On the one hand, out of the fiery magma (or, in German, *feurig-flüssiger Basalt*, 'fiery-liquid igneous rock') something is crystallizing, it is becoming *auskristallisiert*; on the other, the very product of that crystallization, something solid, something stony, is itself in need of further labour and attention: it is something that has to be worked, something that has to be *worked out* — it is a stone, that has to be 'worked' (or, in German, *der zu bearbeitende Stein*).

This book is about the working or *die Bearbeitung* of a particular stone, because this image of working on a stone itself serves as a point of crystallization for a number of ideas and concerns. Tellingly, Jung himself was an accomplished worker of stone, a talented sculptor. In England in the 1920s, and later in his garden in Küsnacht, Jung carved a figure out of wood, then stone: he called it (or rather, we are told, his unconscious named it) Atmavictu, or 'breath of life'. Throughout his life, Jung concerned himself with artistic activity: working away in the years surrounding the First World War on his *Red Book*, and carving a number of statues for his 'tower' in Bollingen.

Jung's tower at Bollingen, currently not accessible for the general public to visit, remains a special place.[15] According to *Memories, Dreams, Reflections*, whenever Jung experienced a lack of creativity, he painted a picture or hewed stone. As early as 1920, Jung had carved two wooden figures, reminiscent of the Telesphorus-like mannikin he had made as a child, later having one (the figure he called Atmavictu, 'the breath of life') reproduced in stone and placing it in the garden of his house in Küsnacht (*MDR*, 38–39). In his later years, working with stone proved to be what he called '*ein rite d'entrée*' for the thoughts and works that followed this activity. In fact, it has been claimed that everything Jung wrote in 1957 — that is, '*The Undiscovered Self (Present and Future)*', '*Flying Saucers: A Modern Myth*', and '*A Psychological View of Conscience*' — 'grew out of' the stone sculptures that Jung made after the death of his wife, Emma Jung, on 27 November 1955 (*MDR*, 198–199). These sculptures and carvings included various reliefs, among them a bear rolling a ball and a woman milking a mare, a bull, and a laughing trickster.[16]

At the end of the path near the boat-house there is a small pillar, carved in stone, dedicated to Attis, the beautiful shepherd of Phrygia who, unfaithful to the goddess Cybele, was driven by her into a state of madness and transformed into a fir tree.[17] And there is the Bollingen Stone, which features various inscriptions: on one side, a Latin verse by a medieval alchemist, Arnaldus de Villa Nova (c. 1235–1311); facing the front, a little hooded figure carrying a lantern, a Telesphorus from the cult of Asclepius, and three Greek inscriptions from Heraclitus, the Mithras liturgy, and Homer; on the third side, facing the lake, a selection of Latin inscriptions from various alchemical texts (*MDR*, 253–254). 'The stone', we read in *Memories, Dreams, Reflections*, 'stands outside the Tower', of which it constitutes 'the explanation'. It is, we are told, 'a manifestation of its occupant, which nevertheless remains incomprehensible for others' (*MDR*, 255).

'The beauty of the superman came to me as a shadow'

The French philosopher and sociologist Henri Lefebvre (1901–1991) opens his study of Hegel, Marx, and Nietzsche with three quotations from each of these thinkers: a passage from the introduction to Hegel's *Science of Logic* (1812): 'The system of logic is the realm of shadows [...] to dwell and labour in this shadowy realm, is the absolute culture and discipline of consciousness'; a passage from Marx's doctoral thesis of 1841: 'The theoretical consciousness, when liberated, becomes practical energy, steps forth as will out of the realm of shadows, and turns against the earthly reality which exists independently of it'; and the following enigmatic passage from Nietzsche's *Thus Spoke Zarathustra*: 'I will complete [my statue]: for a shadow came to me — the most silent, the lightest of all things once came to me! The beauty of the Superman came to me as a shadow'.[18] In this study, Lefebvre uses the motif of the REALM OF SHADOWS as one around which to constellate these three thinkers, and his comments on Nietzsche towards the end of his opening chapter reveal what Lefebvre sees as essential to Nietzsche's philosophy:

> [Nietzsche's] life and thought had one meaning, one goal: to say what is unsayable, to grasp what is ungraspable, to think what is unthinkable, to fathom the unfathomable, to realize the impossible: to transform "the real", itself moribund or already dead, into a new life. The poet wanted to attain redemption by means of what was closest to hand, so close that it is unsayable, unthinkable, unfathomable: the body. "There is more reason in your body than in your wisdom", says Zarathustra. But what did Nietzsche do if not dream his body and proclaim in a loud voice the dream of this body? His

promethean (titanic) effort to live the agony and the death of the modern world by transmuting (metamorphosing) its exhausted values and its reality into complete self-destruction, toward what did this lead him? Toward the Superhuman.[19]

Of his various commentators (including Heidegger, Leo Strauss, and Gilles Deleuze), no one is more alert to the ambiguity of the concept of the Superman than is Henri Lefebvre — with the possible exception of Jung.

Very early on in his seminar, Jung interpreted the superman as Nietzsche's 'formulation for the self' (*SNZ* 1, 60). He reiterated this idea on several occasions (e.g., *SNZ* 1, 568 and 725), but later he appeared to retract it, saying: 'When we say that by his concept of the superman Nietzsche meant the self, it is a mere assumption and not even a valid one; he did not mean the self as we understand the concept' (*SNZ* 1, 925). For Jung, it was important to grasp that Nietzsche did not understand the superman as 'a higher, more differentiated sort of man', but rather as something 'far more complicated' (*SNZ* 1, 71), as 'a coming attitude, a new spirit' that would 'fill the human form and make over our hitherto prevailing world and culture' (*SNZ* 1, 90).

Just how complicated became clear in the course of Jung's seminar, where time and again he grappled with the concept of the superman. In one remark, Jung talks about the superman in a way that demonstrates his understanding of this concept as the outcome of a dialectic of destruction and creation:

> There is a will to self-destruction in the heart, which leads finally to the Superman. The heart wills the drive towards the destruction of that lame and tame and despicable being called Man, the most contemptible of all things to Nietzsche — the thing which should be overcome.
>
> (*SNZ* 1, 93)

If it is the case that 'the Superman can only live through the destruction of Man as he is' (*SNZ* 1, 93), Jung emphatically understood this in an existential, not a political, sense.

For this reason, Jung found in alchemy a congenial vocabulary in which to talk about the kind of existential change (or, if one will, the kind of spiritual transformation) in which he was interested. For Jung, in alchemical philosophy 'the original condition of man was represented by chaotic pieces of elements that found themselves together with no order, quite incidentally', and then 'by the process of fire they were melted together, producing, it was assumed, a new spiritual development' (*SNZ* 1, 105). While acknowledging that Nietzsche 'knew nothing' of alchemy, this transformational strain in his thought was, Jung argued, entirely alchemical: *through Nietzsche*, something was trying to articulate itself (just as, when he was working on his own version of *Zarathustra*, his *Red Book*, Jung believed something had been expressing and articulating itself through *him*). With references to those quintessential Zarathustrian motifs, lightning and madness, Jung writes that 'while [Nietzsche] was speaking of the lightning or the madness, something in himself was reached: the unconscious was beginning to stir', and so Nietzsche 'tried to formulate what is actually happening in the collective unconscious of modern man, to give words to that disturbance' (*SNZ* 1, 104).

Later on, Jung came to link the motif of the superman to another key idea in *Zarathustra*, the great noontide. For Jung, this noontide is at once a great world-historical moment, as well as an individual-historical moment, inasmuch as he associates the great noontide with the crisis that, in his view, takes place about half-way through the life of the individual — the so-called 'midlife crisis'.[20] In his seminar of 2 November 1938 Jung offers the following psychological reading of *Zarathustra* in general and the chapter in Part Four called 'At Noontide' in particular:

> Nietzsche is looking forward with a sort of mystical hope that this fire, this noontide, will come. He often speaks of the noontide, the great mystical hour. [...] In the chapter called "Noon-tide" you will see that that is the hour of the complete revelation of Zarathustra. [...] Nietzsche's evangel is *Zarathustra*, the message to the world of the superman, the idea that man, this human world, should develop to the superman. [...] He wrote *Zarathustra* when he was thirty-eight or thirty-nine, the midday of life; *Zarathustra* is the experience of noontide, the great transformation that takes place at 36. [...] So noontide means the perfect, complete consciousness, the totality, the very *comble* and summit of consciousness, and that of course is the superman, the man with an absolutely superior consciousness.
>
> (*SNZ* 2, 1380–1381)

Here we see Jung tentatively advancing a new, and very different, conception of the superman: not as an individual, not as a member of a new kind of species (or as Jung whimsically put it, 'the man of tomorrow whose tail is a bit shorter or whose ears are no longer pointed, a man who looks like a Greek god or something of the sort'), not as an embodiment of the self, but as *a state of consciousness*. Elsewhere Jung calls this a state of 'superconsciousness' (*SNZ* 1, 839), of which the superman is the symbol (*SNZ* 2, 925).

This book takes as its starting-point a passage in Nietzsche's *Thus Spoke Zarathustra* and tries to develop an *explication de texte* in the same spirit that Jung, in his *Psychology of the Unconscious* (1911–1912; a more exact translation of the original title would be *Transformations and Symbols of the Libido*), offered a comparative, associationist, and amplificatory style of reading of Miss Miller's dreams and numerous works of world literature. Looked at in one way, it aims to expand the insights from its author's earlier attempts to situate Jung in his intellectual-historical context: in relation to Nietzsche in *The Dionysian Self* (1994), in relation to Goethe in *Analytical Psychology and German Classical Aesthetics* (2007 and 2008), as well as to explore (together with co-author R.H. Stephenson) the relation between Goethe and Nietzsche in *Friedrich Nietzsche and Weimar Classicism* (2005). Looked at in another way, it wants to develop an approach previously advanced by its author in 'The Superman as Salamander: Symbols of

Transformation or Transformational Symbols?', a short paper which has provoked some surprisingly supportive and positive comments and responses.[21] In short, this study proposes a blend of three main topics — classical (the motif of the blissful islands), psychological (the shadow), and philosophical (the *Übermensch* or superman) — to produce a rich, intellectual-historical discussion that brings context and depth to a nexus of highly problematic concepts.

It does so in the conviction that the validity of Jung's thought can be tested not just in the clinician's consulting room but in the seminar room and lecture theatre too. (Not to mention, by the same token, in the pub or on public transport — increasingly the locations where it is perhaps easiest to put 'research questions' to the test …). And it does so in the belief that not only is there an important *aurea catena* in the German tradition that links Goethe, Nietzsche, and Jung, but that the central linking element in that intellectual-historical, artistic–conceptual chain, is the notion of CHANGE — of TRANSFORMATION. For there are two kinds of change or transformation, and it is important to distinguish between them.

On the one hand, there is the kind of change proposed by Nietzsche, when he writes in his poem, 'On High Mountains' (*Auf hohen Bergen*), 'You'll have to change to stay akin to me' (*Nur wer sich wandelt, bleibt mit mir verwandt*),[22] a line that finds a reprise in Stefan George's prophetic maxim that 'the master of the future will be whoever can transform himself' (*Und Herr der Zukunft wer sich wandeln kann*), Jung's remark in *Mysterium coniunctionis*, 'All true things must change and […] only that which changes remains true' (*Es scheint, daß alles Wahre sich wandelt und daß nur das Sich-Wandelnde wahr bleibt*) (*CW* 14 §503), and Wolfman Biermann's celebrated remark, 'Only if you change can you remain true to yourself' (*Nur wer sich ändert, bleibt sich treu*).

On the other hand, there is another kind of change, with which this *real* change is easily confused: a Machiavellian kind of change that wants to change everything just a bit — so that nothing really changes at all. (Precisely this sort of pseudo-change is promoted by Tancredi, the young aristocrat in Tomasi di Lampedusa's novel *The Leopard*, when he says: 'If we want things to stay as they are, everything will have to change').[23] Isn't this second kind of change the kind of change with which, all too often, in our personal and professional lives, we are confronted? Instead, the kind of deep, profound, structural change in which Jung (and the tradition behind him) is interested, is as necessary (indeed, urgent) as it is elusive (indeed, hidden or concealed) …

Notes

1 See Freud's paper, 'The Uncanny' (1919), in *Standard Edition of the Complete Psychological Works*, vol. 17, ed. and tr. J. Strachey, London: Hogarth Press, 1955, pp. 217–256. The story itself is available in E.T.A. Hoffmann, *The Best Tales of Hoffmann*, ed. E.F. Bleiler, New York: Dover, 1967, pp. 183–214. For a more recent discussion, see T. Dawson, 'Enchantment, Possession, and the Uncanny' in E.T.A. Hoffmann's "The Sandman"', *International Journal of Jungian Studies*, 2012, vol. 4, no. 1, 41–54.

2 See A. Jaffé, *Bilder und Symbole aus E.T.A. Hoffmanns Märchen "Der goldne Topf"*, Zurich: Daimon, 1990.

3 Hoffmann, *Best Tales*, p. 213.

4 J. Jacobi, *The Psychology of C.G. Jung*, London: Kegan Paul, Trench, Trubner, 1942, pp. 102–123.

5 For discussion of the shadow by Jung, see the chapter entitled 'The Shadow' in *Aion* (1951) in *CW* 9/ii §13–19; and his political essay, 'The Fight with the Shadow' (1946), in *CW* 10 §444–457.

6 Jacobi, *The Psychology of Jung*, p. 116.

7 Jung, 'The Psychology of the Child Archetype' (1940), in *CW* 9/i §284.

8 Jung, 'The Psychology of the Child Archetype', *CW* 9/i §284.

9 Dorn, 'De tenebris contra naturam, et vita brevi', in *Theatrum chemicum*, vol. 1; cited in Jung, 'Psychology and Religion: The Terry Lectures' (1938/1940), in *CW* 11 §104, fn. 47; cf. 'A Psychological Approach to the Dogma of the Trinity' (1942/1948), in *CW* 11 §180. I am grateful to Gerhard Schmitt for drawing Jung's discussion of Dorn to my attention.

10 Jung, 'Conscious, Unconscious, and Individuation' (1939), in *CW* 9/i §513.

11 Jung, 'Archaic Man' (1931; 1933), in *CW* 10 §130.

12 M.A. Mattoon (ed.), *The Archetype of Shadow in a Split World: Tenth International Congress of Analytical Psychology*, Einsiedeln: Daimon, 1987.

13 *From My Life: Poetry and Truth*, Part Three, Book 13, in J. W. von Goethe, *From My Life: Poetry and Truth: Parts One to Three*, ed. T.P. Saine and J.L. Sammons, tr. R.R. Heitner [Goethe Edition, vol. 4], New York: Suhrkamp Publishers, 1987, p. 430.

14 B. Duncan, '"Emilia Galotti lag auf dem Pult aufgeschlagen": Werther as (Mis-) Reader', *Goethe Yearbook*, 1982, vol. 1, 42–50 (p. 49, fn. 2). See also W. Kayser, 'Die Entstehung von Goethes "Werther"', *Deutsche Vierteljahrsschrift für Literatur und Geschichte*, 1941, vol. 19, 430–447.

15 I remain grateful that I was given permission by Jung's son, Franz Jung, to visit the tower at Bollingen on a hot afternoon in 1992.

16 Pictures of these sculped figures can be found in D. Rosen, *The Tao of Jung: The Way of Integrity*, New York: Viking Arcana, 1996, pp. 129, 130, 142, 144, 145, 149, 154.

17 See *Meetings with Jung: Conversations Recorded by E.A. Bennet During the Years 1946–1961*, London: Anchor Press, 1982, p. 107.

18 H. Lefebvre, *Hegel – Marx – Nietzsche: Le royaume des ombres*, Tournai: Castermann, 1975, p. 7.

19 Lefebvre, *Hegel – Marx – Nietzsche*, pp. 56–57.

20 For further discussion of the notion of the midlife crisis, see P. Bishop, *Reading Goethe at Midlife: Ancient Wisdom, German Classicism, and Jung*, New Orleans, LA: Spring Journal Books, 2011.

21 P. Bishop, 'The Superman as Salamander: Symbols of Transformation or Transformational Symbols?', *International Journal of Jungian Studies*, March 2011, vol. 3, no. 1, 4–20.

22 See 'On High Mountains' (F. Nietzsche, *Basic Writings of Nietzsche*, ed. and tr. W. Kaufmann, New York: Modern Library, 1968, pp. 432–433). For further discussion, see P. Grundlehner, *The Poetry of Friedrich Nietzsche*, New York and Oxford: Oxford University Press, 1996, p. 70.

23 G.T. di Lampedusa, *The Leopard* [1958], tr. A. Colquhoun, London: Vintage, 2007, p. 19.

1

ON THE BLISSFUL ISLANDS

In the Shadow of the Superman

> The form of a work of art always has something casual about it. The sculptor
> can add or leave out many little details — just as the pianist can. Everything
> has to be arranged so that it has an effect: i.e., that life has an effect on life.
> (Nietzsche, *Fragments from the Notebooks*, 1877; *KSA* 8, 22[82], 393;
> cf. *'Human, All Too Human'*, vol. 1, §171)

In the fourth part of Friedrich Nietzsche's philosophical-lyrical masterpiece, *Thus
Spoke Zarathustra* (1882–1884), its central protagonist — named after the ancient
Persian founder of Zoroastrianism — encounters a figure he had met earlier in
Part Two, a gloomy and doom-laden prophet, usually understood to represent the
German philosopher, Arthur Schopenhauer (1788–1860). 'Everything is empty,
everything is one, everything is past', so this prophet teaches, and from the surrounding hills the echo resounds: 'Everything is empty, everything is one, everything is past!'[1] If, in Part Two, this figure had made Zarathustra 'sad and weary',
in Part Four his intervention is no less dramatic. For he makes Zarathustra listen
out for 'the sound of rushing and roaring aris[ing] from the depths', for 'a long,
protracted cry, which the abysses threw from one to another', for 'a cry of distress and a human cry'.[2] *What* is this cry? It is a cry of distress, and it is crying for
Zarathustra: 'This cry is meant for you', the prophet tells Zarathustra, 'it calls to
you: Come, come, come, it is time, it is high time!'[3] *Whose* is this cry? It is the
cry of the higher man, crying for Zarathustra; and his cry strikes Zarathustra with
nothing less than 'horror'.

Listening intently to the sound of this cry, the prophet looks away from
Zarathustra, and then he turns back to him: 'in a scornful voice' the prophet tells
Zarathustra that he does not look like a happy man, and the prophet goes on to
deny any possibility of happiness:

Happiness — how could man find happiness with such buried men and hermits! Must I yet seek ultimate happiness upon blissful islands and far away among forgotten seas?

But it is all one, nothing is worth while, seeking is useless, and there are no blissful islands any more![4]

So speaks the prophet, repeating his gloomy message. In the wake of his earlier encounter with this figure, Zarathustra had gone for three days without food or drink, he had had no rest and had spoken to no one: then, falling into 'a deep sleep', he had had a remarkable, if unsettling, dream, which one of his disciples had interpreted for him.[5] Similarly, in this second encounter, Zarathustra is moved to a reaction and a response: in this case, he becomes energized and declares: 'No! No! Thrice no! [...] I know better!', and he insists: 'There still are blissful islands!'.[6] As well as deciding to embark on his search for the Higher Man, whose cry he has just heard, Zarathustra contradicts the gloomy prophet and affirms the existence of the blissful islands. So *what* are the blissful islands? And *where* are they?

What and Where are the Blissful Islands?

According to the Greek poet Hesiod, the blissful islands are located in the furthermost part of the Western ocean at the end of the earth; here the souls of the dead heroes are allowed to retire, 'an abode apart from men' and 'at the ends of the earth'.[7] In Homer, the blissful islands are called the Elysian fields, and in book 4 of *The Odyssey* the prophetic sea-god Proteus tells Menelaus that 'the immortals' will send him to 'the Elysian plain / And the end of the earth, where blond Rhadamanthys' — the wise king who serves as one of the judges of the dead — 'is', a place where 'the easiest living exists for men', for 'no snow is there, not much winter, and never rain', but 'clearly blowing breezes of the West Wind / Does Oceanos always send on to put a fresh breath in men'.[8] For Pindar, there is only one island, not many, but it remains just as blissful:

> But they who endure thrice over
> In the world beyond to keep their souls from all sin
> Have gone God's way to the tower of Kronos; there
> Winds sweep from the Ocean
> Across the Island of the Blessed. Gold flowers to flame
> On land in the glory of the trees; it is fed in the water,
> Whence they bind bracelets to their arms and go chapleted
>
> Under the straight decrees of Rhadamanthys,
> Whom the husband of Rhea, high throned above all,
> Our great father, keeps in the chair of state beside him.
> They say Peleus is there, and Kadmos,
> And his mother with prayer softening Zeus' heart
> Carried Achilles thither,

Who felled Hektor, Troy's unassailable
Tall column of strength, who gave death to Kyknos
And the Aithiop, Dawn's child.[9]

And in the dialogues of Plato, we find a series of allusions to these islands, notably in the *Gorgias*, where Socrates relates the following myth. 'In the days of Cronus', he tells Callicles, 'there was this law about mankind, which from then on has prevailed among the gods', that 'the man who has led a godly and righteous life departs after death to the Isles of the Blessed'; the souls that Rhadamanthys sends straight to these Isles being those of anyone has 'lived in piety and truth', but especially 'the soul of a philosopher'.[10] And in the *Republic*, in the allegory of the cave, those who attain 'the [greatest] knowledge', win 'the vision of the good', and experience 'the contemplation of essence and the brightest region of being', are said by Socrates to believe that 'while still living they have been transported to the Islands of the Blessed'.[11] (So while, in the early dialogue, the blissful islands are projected into the future life, in the later dialogue they are in some sense attainable in the present.)

In Virgil, the great Roman poet of the Augustan period, the blissful islands likewise function in the Latin epic, *The Aeneid*, as a major reference point. In book 6, Aeneas (accompanied by his guide, the sibyl of Cumae, Deiphobe) undertakes a journey to the underworld, passing through Hades and proceeding on to the blissful islands or the Elysian fields:

> [...] They took their way
> Where long extended plains of pleasure lay:
> The verdant fields with those of heav'n may vie,
> With ether vested, and a purple sky;
> The blissful seats of happy souls below.
> Stars of their own, and their own suns, they know.[12]

Virgil not only describes the blissful islands, he tells us how their inhabitants spend their time, mentioning some of them by name — Orpheus, the ancient Greek musician and poet, here presented as a priest of Apollo; Teucer, the ancient king and ancestor of the Trojans; and some of his descendants, such as Ilus, the grandfather of Priam, and his brother, Assaracus, the grandfather of Anchises, as well as Dardanus, said here to be the founder of Troy:

> Their airy limbs in sports they exercise,
> And on the green contend the wrestler's prize.
> Some in heroic verse divinely sing;
> Others in artful measures led the ring.
> The Thracian bard, surrounded by the rest,
> There stands conspicuous in his flowing vest;
> His flying fingers, and harmonious quill,
> Strikes seven distinguish'd notes, and sev'n at once they fill.
> Here found they Teucer's old heroic race,

Born better times and happier years to grace.
Assaracus and Ilus here enjoy
Perpetual fame, with him who founded Troy.
[…]
Some cheerful souls were feasting on the plain;
Some did the song, and some the choir maintain,
Beneath a laurel shade, where mighty Po
Mounts up to woods above, and hides his head below.[13]

Teucer, Ilus, Assaracus, and Dardanus — all warriors, but in a commentary on this passage, the English Neoplatonist Thomas Taylor (1758–1835) was swift to emphasize that Virgil's lines should be understood in an intellectual or a spiritual sense.[14]

In the sixth century, Olympiodorus the Younger of Alexandria (c. 495–570) — a Neoplatonist philosopher and in fact the last pagan to maintain the Platonic tradition in Alexandria — wrote a commentary in the *Gorgias*. In it he notes the identity of the blissful islands and the Elysian fields, as well as their meaning: 'The philosophers liken human life to the sea, because it is disturbed and concerned with begetting and salty and full of toil', but 'islands rise above the sea, being higher', so 'that constitution which rises above life and over becoming is what they call the Isles of the Blessed', Olympiodorus explains, illustrating his point with reference to the heroic figure of Hercules, who 'performed his final labour in the western regions' — 'he laboured against the dark and earthly life, and finally he lived in the daytime, i.e., in truth and light'.[15] This is to say nothing of references in Flavius Philostratus's *Life of Apollonius of Tyana* (where the blissful islands are said to be off the coast of Libya),[16] in Plutarch's *Life of Sertorius* (where they are called the Atlantic Islands, and could be Madeira and Porto Santo),[17] and in the *Natural History* of Pliny the Elder (where they are identified with the Canary Islands).[18] These islands are 'blissful' because it is here that those who are 'blessed' live; and because those who are 'blessed' live on them, these islands are 'blissful'.

So there is a rich pre-classical and classical tradition that stands behind the image of the blissful islands as one finds it in Nietzsche's *Zarathustra*.[19] (The same tradition clearly also stands behind such other works as the novel *Ardinghello and the Blissful Islands* [1787] by Wilhelm Heinse [1746–1803], and its spirit informs such paintings by Arnold Böcklin [1827–1901] as 'The Fields of the Blessed' [1877] and 'The Islands of the Living' [1888].) It is to this tradition, as well as to his use of it, that Nietzsche surely gestures when, in *Ecce Homo*, he describes his memories of Wagner's villa in Tribschen as 'a distant isle of the blessed'.[20]

Now one of the reasons for Nietzsche's choice of this image could be that he had his own 'blissful island' — Ischia, at the northern end of the Gulf of Naples. When, in 1883, an earthquake destroyed the towns of Casamiccola and Lacco Ameno, at the same time as Nietzsche was finishing work in the second part of *Zarathustra*, he wrote in a letter to his friend, Heinrich Köselitz: 'The fate of Ischia has distressed

FIGURE 1.1 Franz Nadorp, *Goethe's Ankunft im Elysium*; *König-Ludwigs-Album*, Munich: Piloty & Loehle, Nr. 173.

me more and more; and apart from everything that concerns every person, there is something about that closely involves me personally, in its own dreadful way. This island was so much on my mind: when you have read Zarathustra II to the end, it will become clear to you *where* I looked for my "blissful islands"'. Referring to the chapter entitled 'The Dance Song', he added: '"Cupido dancing with the girls" is immediately comprehensible only in Ischia: (the Ischians say "Cupido"). Hardly had I finished my work than the island fell apart'.[21]

Leaving aside the autobiographical (and, indeed, psychoanalytic) connotations of the topos of the blissful islands,[22] a third reason for Nietzsche's choice of this image is precisely because of those significant classical associations found in Hesiod, Homer, Pindar, and elsewhere, which are (like so much else in *Thus Spoke Zarathustra*) assumed to be part of the background knowledge of the reader and simply taken for granted. Moreover, in the second part of Nietzsche's epic work, Zarathustra had delivered an entire speech on the subject of the blissful islands, before he then went and actually visited them in person. (It is on the blissful islands that Zarathustra dances, cupid-like, with the girls in a green meadow, and sings a song to Life, as Nietzsche reminds us in his letter to Köselitz.[23])

In the first chapter of Part Two, entitled 'The Child with the Mirror', Zarathustra announces his wish to set sail: 'I want to sail across broad seas like a cry and a shout of joy, until I find the Blissful Islands where my friends are waiting — / And my enemies with them! How I now love anyone to whom I can simply speak! My enemies too are part of my happiness'.[24] Subsequently, the chapter entitled 'On the

Blissful Islands' — a moving discourse delivered before his journey begins or when Zarathustra is already embarked[25] — opens with the following arresting image:

> The figs are falling from the trees, they are fine and sweet; and as they fall their red skins split. I am a north wind to ripe figs.
>
> Thus, like figs, do these teachings fall to you, my friends: now drink their juice and eat their sweet flesh! It is autumn all around and clear sky and afternoon.
>
> Behold, what abundance is around us! And it is fine to gaze out upon distant seas from the midst of superfluity.
>
> Once you said "God" when you gazed upon distant seas; but now I have taught you to say "Superman".[26]

This important passage recapitulates *in nuce* the 'action' of the prologue to *Thus Spoke Zarathustra*: namely, the proclamation — in fact, the taking-for-granted — of 'the death of God',[27] and the concomitant announcement of the doctrine of the 'superman' — of the *Übermensch*, the 'human-who-is-more-than-(just)-human', the human who is not 'human, all-too-human'.

The notion of the superman has been much understood: indeed, there is much in its formulation that would appear to invite misunderstanding. Yet the term, properly understood, is one of great urgency for our age. As Michel Onfray has glossed the term, the superman or the *Übermensch* represents:

> the individual who understands the tragic nature of reality, because he understands the mechanism of the eternal return of all things under the sign of the same; as a consequence, emancipated from the question of free will which he knows is an illusion, he understands there is no other solution than to consent to this tragedy, to love it; henceforth, he attains joy …[28]

Yet is even this definition correct? For in what sense is the *Übermensch* really an individual at all?

After all, as Sheridan Hough has suggested, 'the Übermensch is above all some sort of ideal, a "goal" the free spirit restlessly moves toward' and as such 'not an ideal for everyone, but only for those exceptional individuals who are his rightful genealogical predecessors'; she concludes that 'there is not a discrete character called the Übermensch' and 'in fact the name "Übermensch" designates a particular dimension of the experience of the free spirits'.[29] Correspondingly, as Herbert Theierl has also argued, Nietzsche 'demands a "going-under" [*"Untergang"*], in order that the "superman" [*"Übermensch"*] come into being', giving rise to the conclusion that both terms, 'going-under' and 'superman', refer to one and the same thing, namely to 'a mystical expansion of consciousness, which is experienced as redemption'; correspondingly, the 'superman' refers, not to an individual, but to 'a state of mystical ecstasy' …[30]

In the passage cited above we see how, tellingly, Nietzsche mixes classical and Christian imagery: classical, because its subject is the blissful islands, an essentially pagan motif; Christian, because much of the imagery alludes to a passage from the Book of Revelation. In his vision on Patmos — itself a kind of blissful island in the middle of the Aegean Sea, or at any rate an island — of the end of the world, John the Apostle and the Evangelist sees the stars falling from the heavens, 'as the fig-tree casteth its green figs when it is shaken by a great wind' (Apocalypse 6: 13). In turn, this passage echoes the apocalyptic imagery of the prophet Nahum — 'All thy strong holds shall be like fig-trees with their green figs: if they be shaken, they shall fall into the mouth of the eater' (Nahum 3: 12), which itself expands an image found in the earlier prophecies of Isaiah — 'all the hosts of the heavens [...] shall fall down as the leaf falleth from the vine, and from the fig-tree' (Isaias 34: 4). In his great prophetic book, Jeremiah records Yahweh's threat against Judah: 'Gathering, I will gather them together [...]: there is no grape on the vines, and there are no figs on the fig-tree, the leaf is fallen' (Jeremias 8: 13); relates his vision of 'two baskets full of figs', a warning addressed to King Zedekiah (24: 1–10); and, in his letter to the exiles, conveys Yahweh's anger with those who in remain in Jerusalem: 'I will make them like very bad figs, that cannot be eaten, because they are very bad' (29: 17). Elsewhere, in the gospels, a ripening fig-tree is used as a symbol for the proximity of the Kingdom of Heaven (Matthew 24: 29–31; Mark 13: 28–32; Luke 21: 29–33); Nathanial, one of the disciples, receives his call while he sits under a fig-tree (John 1: 48–50). But why, as a passionate advocate of atheism, would Nietzsche choose to use an image that echoes the Christian bible? Because, in his eyes, Zarathustra ushers in the end of the Christian (conception of the) world.

For Nietzsche, the 'death' of God — first announced in *The Gay Science*, §25, and taken for granted as an unargued assumption by Zarathustra (Prologue, §2) — is the prelude to and precondition for the advent of His successor, the superman. At the end of Zarathustra's discourse entitled 'On the Blissful Islands', the figure of the superman returns — or, more precisely, the *shadow* of the superman comes to him:

> Ah, you men, I see an image sleeping in the stone, the image of my visions! Ah, that it must sleep in the hardest, ugliest stone!
>
> Now my hammer rages fiercely against its prison. Fragments fly from the stone: what is that to me?
>
> I will complete it: for a shadow [*ein Schatten*] came to me — the most silent, the lightest of all things once came to me!
>
> The beauty of the Superman came to me as a shadow [*Des Übermenschen Schönheit kam zur mir als Schatten*]. Ah, my brothers! What are the gods to me now![31]

This astonishing passage has three main thematic elements: the image of SCULPTING A STATUE, the arrival of the superman as a SHADOW, and the theme of BEAUTY. Elsewhere, I have highlighted the aesthetic significance of (self-) sculpting in this passage, and its alchemical overtones.[32] Here, in this chapter and the next, however, I want to focus on another set of questions relating to the shadow in this text. What is the beauty of the superman? What is the shadow of the superman? And why does the beauty of the superman come to Zarathustra *as a shadow*?

This is not an easy set of questions to answer, and to try and answer them leads us straight into the central concerns of an intellectual tradition that saw itself, in key respects, as a reaction and a response to the problems posed by Nietzsche — the Jungian tradition. In his seminars on *Thus Spoke Zarathustra*, held in Zurich over a number of years between 1934 and 1939, C.G. Jung offered a remarkable commentary on Nietzsche's main work, which can help us understand the psychological dynamic at work in Nietzsche's text. In the rest of this chapter, I shall examine what Jung has to say about this passage in his seminars, and highlight some related discussions in some of Jung's other works. Our analysis, informed by the amplificatory style of reading developed by Jung,[33] will involve consideration of a wide range of intertexts, including Neoplatonism (ancient and Renaissance), Patristic theology and mysticism, and the German classical tradition of Goethe and Schiller. Indeed, it is with a reading (in Chapter 3) of a major poetic text by Schiller that our interpretation of this passage from Nietzsche's *Zarathustra* will reach its next stage, before concluding (in Chapter 4) with an analysis of Nietzsche's relationship to Platonism and Neoplatonism.

Jung's Reading of 'On the Blissful Islands'

In his long-running seminar on Nietzsche's *Zarathustra*, Jung devoted no fewer than five sessions to the chapter entitled 'On the Blissful Islands', discussing it in the final seminar of the Winter Term 1936 on 4 March 1936, and again in the early seminars of the Spring Term 1936 on 6 May, 13 May, 20 May, and 27 May 1936. Even allowing for Jung's tendency to digression, this substantial discussion amounts to a clear recognition of the importance of the material in this chapter.

When he came to this chapter's final paragraphs, cited at the outset of our discussion above, Jung interpreted them as follows. First, he associates the description of the superman (more precisely, the shadow of the superman) as 'the most silent, the lightest of all things' with St Athanasius's account in his biography of St Anthony of the life of the desert anchorites. If someone comes with 'a great noise singing psalms or preaching sermons, they should know that this must be the devil', but 'stillness' is associated with the Holy Spirit.[34] At first sight, it seems surprising that Jung associates the 'stillness' and 'silence' of the shadow of the superman with the Holy Spirit, but it becomes less so if one remembers that, for Jung, 'God is dead but He reappears in the idea of the Superman' (*SNZ* 2, 951).[35]

Second, Jung reads the word 'shadow' in two ways. In the immediate context, he sees in it a suggestion of how the superman is 'unsubstantial like a shadow' — 'the idea of an unsubstantial image, as unsubstantial as a shadow', and thus 'a foreshadowing, an anticipation' (*SNZ* 2, 953 and 955). In this respect, Jung says, 'the beauty of the Superman appears to Nietzsche as a sort of anticipation, *a shadow that falls upon his consciousness'* (*SNZ* 2, 955; my emphasis). Mysteriously, Jung adds that, as such, 'this is very genuine, one of the most genuine things in Zarathustra' (*SNZ* 2, 955). While differentiating this sense of the word 'shadow' from its more technical use in analytical psychology, Jung nevertheless believes its psychological sense is applicable here.

'Nietzsche's idea of the Superman', which Jung equates with 'the term of *the self*', would 'naturally' appear 'under the cloak of the shadow', inasmuch as it appears 'in what it is rejected', and in this sense is assimilable to the alchemical idea of the *lapis philosophorum*, or 'the stone of greatest price, [...] the corner-stone first rejected by the builders' (*SNZ* 2, 953). There are important links between the *lapis philosophorum* and the biblical tradition of 'the stone rejected by the builders'.[36] It also plays a significant role in Patristic sources too.[37] Prior to this Patristic tradition, Socrates describes the dialectic as 'set above all other studies to be as it were the coping stone'.[38] And for the alchemical equivalent of the Petrine metaphor, 'Be you also as living stones built up, a spiritual house' (1 Peter 2: 5), one might recall Gerard Dorn's injunction, 'transform yourselves into living philosophical stones!' (*transmutemini de lapidibus mortuis in vivos lapides philosophicos!*).[39] In this alchemical-cum-psychological sense, 'the things which we think the least of, that part of ourselves which we repress perhaps the most, or which we despise, is just the part which contains the mystery' (*SNZ* 2, 953). As a result, 'when you can accept yourself in your totality, then you have brought together the four elements — all the parts of yourself have come together from the four corners of the earth' (*SNZ* 2, 953). Not for the first time — and certainly not for the last — Jung places great emphasis on the notion of *totality*.

Thus there is a psychological imperative to engage with what Jung calls 'the inferior man', or 'the shadow', and, for Jung, the entire drama of *Zarathustra* lies in the failure on Nietzsche's part to engage with this part of the self. To be sure, the notion of the self as a totality plays an important role in Nietzschean and Jungian thought alike, but at this point we should note that, on two occasions in his seminars, Jung is directly asked by a member of his audience: why does the beauty of the superman come to Zarathustra *as a shadow*? On both occasions, Jung equivocates. In his seminar of 20 November 1935, he said that 'we cannot take that so literally', because Nietzsche 'might use that word without any such psychological connotations as we attribute to it' (*SNZ* 1, 703); and on 27 May 1936, he restated this point, arguing that 'we mustn't be deceived by the word; our use of the term *shadow* has a very different meaning' (*SNZ* 2, 953). It is interesting that, both times, Jung — not exactly famous for his terminological exactitude or his precision of expression — gets hung up on a point of vocabulary, and that he avoids closer engagement with the actual statement itself made by Zarathustra. True, we should not simply equate the 'shadow' of the superman with the Jungian concept of the shadow. Yet Jung's seminars on *Zarathustra*, and analytical psychology more generally, can nevertheless provide us with the conceptual apparatus to explain why, at the end of his discourse on the blissful islands, Zarathustra tells us that 'the beauty of the Superman' comes to him — 'like a shadow'.[40]

For the question never asked by Jung or by the other members of his seminar is surely this: not why does the beauty of the superman come to Zarathustra *as a shadow*, but why is it *the beauty* of the superman that comes to him in this way? In other words, why is it that what comes to Zarathustra as a shadow is not simply the superman, but *the beauty of the superman*?

The Beauty of the Superman

For now, let us answer the first of these questions in terms derived directly from Nietzsche's work. On this account, the superman is beautiful, because he — or she (the term in German, *der Übermensch*, is grammatically, but not conceptually, gendered) — stands in opposition to the ugliest man. Beauty is the opposite of ugliness, so the superman, who is beautiful, is the opposite of the ugliest man. But who, then, is *he*?

Now the various commentaries available on *Thus Spoke Zarathustra* interpret the figure of the ugliest man in various ways: for some, he is Socrates,[41] for some, he is a representation of the atheist,[42] while for others he represents 'the "all-too-human" in humanity in general and in Nietzsche in particular'.[43] If we turn to those unpublished notes that appeared as *The Will to Power*, we find an extensive gloss on what, for Nietzsche, ugliness itself means:

> The ugly, i.e., the contradiction to art, that which is excluded from art, its No — every time decline, impoverishment of life, impotence, disintegration, degeneration are suggested even faintly, the aesthetic man reacts with his No. The effect of the ugly is depressing: it is the expression of a depression. It takes away strength, it impoverishes, it weighs down—[.][44]

For Nietzsche, there is a performative aspect to ugliness; it can serve as a kind of test for how much one can endure; but it is also a kind of anti-performance, which inhibits, disables, and drags everything down to its own level:

> The ugly suggests various things; one can use one's states of health to test how variously an indisposition increases the capacity for imagining ugly things. The selection of things, interests, and questions changes. A state closely related to the ugly is encountered in logic, too: heaviness, dimness. Mechanically speaking, equilibrium is lacking: the ugly limps, the ugly stumbles: antithesis to the divine frivolity of the dancer.[45]

By contrast, as Nietzsche tells us and as we see on several occasions in the work, Zarathustra 'is a dancer'.[46]

(Nietzsche's comments on ugliness are line with Plato's critique of ugliness, as found in the *Symposium*. Here Diotima tells Socrates that 'we cannot be quickened by ugliness, but only by the beautiful', for 'ugliness is at odds with the divine, while beauty is in perfect harmony'. According to Diotima, 'beauty is the goddess of both fate and travail, and so when procreancy draws near the beautiful it grows genial and blithe, and birth follows swiftly on conception', but 'when it meets with ugliness it is overcome with heaviness and gloom, and turning away it shrinks into itself [...] and still labours under its painful burden'.[47])

Within the narrative economy of *Zarathustra* itself, however, there is a plain and direct answer to the question about the identity of the ugliest man: he is 'the murderer of God'.[48] That is, he is someone who murdered God, because he could not endure the existence of someone who saw him — who saw him *and saw his ugliness*.[49] In the preface to the second edition of *The Gay Science*, Nietzsche played with the idea that God can see everything in a short, but telling, parable: '"Is it true that God is present everywhere?" a little girl asked her mother; "I think that's indecent" — a hint for philosophers!'.[50] There, his discussion was lewd and rude; here, it takes on a much darker tone, involving the business — the very ugly business — of murder; in fact, the murder of God.

Yet, even though the ugliest man is an 'unutterable creature',[51] he is not without potential; he is ugly, true, but he is not entirely useless. For, inasmuch as he despises himself, he loves himself, and Zarathustra sees in him 'a great lover and a great despiser', and Zarathustra loves 'the great despisers'.[52] Inasmuch as the ugliest man, as a man, is something that must be 'overcome', Zarathustra even wonders if the ugliest man could even perhaps be the higher man. It is the higher man — not the superman, but a man on the way to becoming a superman, or with the potential to do so — whose 'great cry of distress' he hears at the beginning of Part Four, animating the action of this final part. And in a chapter entitled 'The Intoxicated Song', Zarathustra takes the ugliest man by the hand and, guiding him outside, shows him his 'nocturnal world' — 'the big, round moon and the silver waterfalls by his cave'. For the sake of this *one* day, so the ugliest man responds, he is — for the very first time — content to have loved his whole life.[53] He is indeed a man with great potential.

In this way, through his discourses and in his conduct, Zarathustra fulfils the very goal that Nietzsche had set for himself in *The Gay Science*, where he expressed the wish 'to make the thought of life even a hundred times more appealing'.[54] From the artists (or so Nietzsche says elsewhere in that work) one should learn to 'make things beautiful, attractive, and desirable for us [*schön, anziehend, begehrenswert*] when they are not'.[55] For this reason, Nietzsche opens Part Four of *The Gay Science*, placed under the patronage of St Januarius, the martyr saint of Naples whose blood is said miraculously to liquify — to come alive — on his feast-day, with a new year's resolution. 'I want', Nietzsche promises himself, 'to learn more and more to see as beautiful what is necessary in things; then I shall be one of those who make things beautiful'.[56]

The significance of the figure of the ugliest man did not escape Jung, who first commented on this figure in his major work of 1921, *Psychological Types*. In the context of his discussion of Schiller and the problem of types, Jung remarked that the unveiling of the ugliest man had been reserved for our age and for Nietzsche (*CW* 6 §208). (The simultaneity implied here between Nietzsche's age and Jung's is significant: Nietzsche matters for Jung, because Nietzsche's problems became Jung's problems and, by extension, they have become ours, too.) Further on, in his discussion of the type-problem of poetry, Jung expanded on this remark: the 'icono-clastic revolt' against the conventional moral atmosphere, he explained, and 'the acceptance of the ugliest man' had led, in Nietzsche, to the 'shattering unconscious tragedy' presented in *Thus Spoke Zarathustra* (*CW* 6 §322). Intriguingly, in this first exploration of the figure of the ugliest man, Jung declared that, in Nietzsche's work, Zarathustra discovers, in the ugliest man, his own shadow (*CW* 6 §706); thus we find, for the first time, a link being drawn between the figure of the ugliest man and the motif of the shadow. Hence, (and foregrounding his concern with the relation between typology and psychological dynamics) Jung concluded that, in the figure of the ugliest man, we find a striking example of the suppression of the antithesis (*CW* 6 §829).

Over a decade later, in his seminars on *Zarathustra* Jung returned to his analysis of the mysterious, ambiguous figure of the ugliest man. Here he suggested (although without explaining any further) that the rope-dancer in the market-place, whom Zarathustra encounters in the Prologue, is later 'resurrected' as the ugliest man (*SNZ* 1, 141); he argued further that the ugliest man could be interpreted to be a sort of miserable Christian (*SNZ* 1, 143). Later, Jung claimed that the ugliest man is just as much the 'divine man' as the superman is (*SNZ* 1, 336), while in a subse-quent seminar, in which he delivered an entire excursus on ugliness, he remarked that Nietzsche had, in fact, rejected the ugliest man (and what he stood for) (*SNZ* 1, 564–565). That is to say, Nietzsche rejects the ugliest man as 'the man that makes for growth', or in other words 'the inferior man, the instinctive collective being' (*SNZ* 1, 620).

In subsequent remarks, we find once more the hint that there is a link between the figure of the ugliest man and the motif of the shadow. According to Jung, 'the shadow incarnates in the ugliest man', and because of his inflation, Nietzsche rejects him (*SNZ* 1, 702). Even more explicitly, Jung claims that 'what we call the "shadow", the inferior man, appears in the form of the ugliest man' (*SNZ* 1, 703). Hence, we can understand the ugliest man as a culmination of 'the small, incom-plete, imperfect things', which Nietzsche (as a philosopher? as a person?) has a ten-dency to 'wipe […] out' and, in the 'definite form' or 'special figure' of the ugliest man, rejects and 'condemn[s] to hell wholesale' (*SNZ* 1, 990).

Having repeated his view that 'the inferior man comes up in the form of the ugliest man' (*SNZ* 2, 1004), Jung observed, as part of another lengthy excursus (this time on the function of religion), that, by maligning religion as 'false values or fatuous words', we are 'rejecting the ugliest man in ourselves', so that by 'reviling the truth in which the inferior man believes and in which he is rooted', we 'uproot ourselves' (*SNZ* 2, 1014). For Nietzsche 'cannot convince one of the tremendous advantages of being outside the walls of the Church if one is threatened by the madhouse' (*SNZ* 2, 1012) — as Jung sagely remarks. To summarize Jung's analysis in *Psychological Types*, expanded in his *Zarathustra* seminar: *with Nietzsche, Zarathustra discovers, in the ugliest man, his shadow.*

Now although Jung blithely and unproblematically equates the ugliest man with Zarathustra's shadow, in fact these figures in Nietzsche's work are (apparently, at least) quite separate. After the gloomy prophet, the two kings, the leech-ridden, leech-bitten conscientious man of the spirit, the sorcerer, the last pope, the ugliest man, and then the voluntary beggar, the final figure whom Zarathustra meets while wandering in his mountains, looking for the higher man whose cry he heard, is his own shadow. As Sheridan Hough explains, 'the image of a person and his shadow is an important emblem of the free spirit's psychic division', a division into 'his "self and other self"', a division that affords 'a useful opportunity for self-reflection' inasmuch as 'it allows that person to examine and consider a shifting variety of auto-images'.[57]

This figure of the shadow is an intertextual one in at least two respects. Earlier, in Part Two, in the chapter entitled 'Of Great Events', a ship's crew lands on an island with a volcano, not far from Zarathustra's blissful islands. The captain and his men are startled to see a figure flying, like a shadow, through the air, towards the vol-cano: 'Just look!', says the old steersman, 'there is Zarathustra going to Hell!'[58] The appearance of the flying man coincides with the disappearance of Zarathustra; five days later, he re-appears again, and he relates his encounter with the fire-dog who lives in the volcano.[59] When told by his disciples about the sailors, the rabbits, and the flying man,[60] Zarathustra reminds them — and the reader — of a further intertextual reference. 'Surely you have heard something', he asks them, 'of the Wanderer and his shadow?',[61] alluding to the title of the third part of *Human, All Too Human*.[62] (In its turn, this title refers to an earlier poem, 'The Wanderer', a text replete with autobiographical allusions, notably to Nietzsche's friendship with Erwin Rohde.[63])

What have Nietzsche's philosophical and literary critics made of the figure of the shadow? For R.J. Hollingdale, the shadow is a representation of the freethinker;[64] for Laurence Lampert, it is someone who has followed Zarathustra's teachings, and become a nihilist, but not a cheerful nihilist;[65] while for Stanley Rosen, it is 'the dark side of the prophetic mission who frightens and displeases Zarathustra by his ghostly appearance'.[66] Before pursuing any further the connections between Nietzsche and Jung in respect of the figure of Zarathustra's shadow, we should consider the problem of the shadow itself, examining what Jung says elsewhere in his *Zarathustra* seminars about the shadow, and what he says about the shadow in his works as a whole and in a text from 1946 in particular.

The Shadow and the Dark Side

How can one best approach the dark subject of the shadow in Jungian thought? One way might be through the understanding of the shadow in traditions that are different from, but cognate with, the Jungian tradition. For instance, in his magisterial philosophical masterpiece, *Der Geist als Widersacher der Seele* (1929–1932), variously translatable as *The Spirit as Adversary of the Soul* or *Mind as Opponent of Psyche*, the phenomenologist and vitalist Ludwig Klages (1872–1956) explored the significance of the shadow in the 'Pelasgian world-view'. What is the Pelasgian world-view?

By this Klages meant the outlook of the ancient pre-historical people of whom Hesiod, Homer, and Thucydides had written and whose existence had been 'rediscovered' in the nineteenth century by the historian Johann Jakob Bachofen (1815–1817). This originary perception of reality attributed to appearances these three main characteristics: bodilessness, shape, and transformability. All three qualities can be found in the ancient conception of the shadow. For, as Klages writes:

> Even someone who has never been touched by a "classical education" would surely be inclined to think of crowds of *shadows*, when he thinks of the realm of the dead and the underworld, and might then, via the memory of ghost stories, begin to wonder and to come to the conclusion that precisely *permeability* possesses a power that eludes something substantial. In so doing he would have embarked on a path that leads out of the world of things and into the world of appearances, even if it remains uncertain whether, when the road forks, he would follow the deep blue path into the sea of images or the pale path into the intermediate realm of phantoms. Between both of them extends the symbolism of the shadow.[67]

As usual, Klages had at his disposal an entire range of examples from classical and anthropological sources to support his argument. According to a Tongan legend, for instance, the crew of a boat that reached Bolutu, the island of the gods and heroes (in other words, another kind of 'blissful island') reported they had discovered that individuals there simply walk straight through houses, trees, and chieftains. The same had been recounted by a hunter from the Algonquian tribe of Native Americans, who had been transported in a state of ecstasy to the realm of the dead. And from classical literature Klages cited the famous descent to Hades undertaken by Odysseus in book 11 of the *Odyssey*. 'As phantoms and shadows, untouchable by a living person, the souls of the dead swarm around the blood-filled sacrificial pit of Odysseus on the edge of Hades', as Klages comments; 'because they are shadows, the "shades" are shadowless'.[68]

Although the shadow is ghost-like and bodiless, it stands in a close relation to the earth and to night, the means by which the telluric powers (as Klages calls them) manifest themselves as maternally protective and as guarding the past. Accordingly, such linguistic expressions as a 'canopy of foliage' or 'the cathedral of a forest' hint at the practice, found among some Estonian tribes, of offering sacrifices to the shadows of sacred trees, or the custom according to which some sacred groves of the Estonians included the ground covered by their shadow, within which no twig was allowed to be broken or no leaf plucked, and where the dead were usually buried. In the ancient Greek city of Priene, the most solemn oath that could be sworne by its women was 'by the shade of the oak', prompting Bachofen to remark: 'What stands taller than the tree of the gods is the primordial shadow, from the dark womb of which it arises, to which the dead return and by which the women [...] swear in their most sacred oath'.[69] Accordingly, the shadow in its function as a guardian of a grave belongs to what Klages termed the 'elementary thoughts' of humankind.[70]

On the basis of these anthropological investigations, Klages came to a surprising, and radical, conclusion. 'If the state of awareness in thinking contemplation [*denkendes Schauen*] is more similar to our dreaming than to our waking state, not from its individual bearer's dozing lack of openness to the physical external world but thanks to the depth of his relation with the characteristics of the latter's *phenomena*', he argued, 'then dream images and visions must share in one and the same *reality* as the causes of perception, from which they should nevertheless be sharply distinguished', and for this reason, he concluded, 'they can in principle intervene just as decisively in how one leads one's life as can what happens in the course of the day'.[71] Hence, in the words of the ghost of Clytaemenestra, spoken at the beginning of Aeschylus's *Eumenides*, 'For the mind asleep hath clear vision, but in the daytime the fate of mortal men cannot be foreseen'.[72]

Klages's discussion of the shadow and the dream can be read as a modern reformulation of an ancient approach to the entire problematic of the shadow, found in the Hermetic and Kabbalistic traditions. Now one of the most well-known of the Hermetic texts is 'Poimandres, or The Vision', a chapter in the *Corpus Hermeticum*, a collection of tracts (originally translated by Marsilio Ficino) of Greco-Egyptian wisdom texts from the second and third centuries. These texts, presented in the form of a dialogue between the master and a disciple, are traditionally attributed to Hermes Trismegistus (or 'thrice-great Hermes').[73] In this text, part of what is otherwise called *The Divine Pymander*, we find not just an account of how divine wisdom was revealed to Hermes, but a description of the creation of the world. In this description, we learn of how, having been created, humankind seeks knowledge of the world in a way that mirrors the creativity that had brought it into being:

> Learning well their essence and sharing in their nature, the man wished to break through the circumference of the circles to observe the rule of the one given power over the fire. Having all authority over the cosmos of mortals and unreasoning animals, the man broke through the vault and stooped to look through the cosmic framework, thus displaying to lower nature the fair form of god. Nature smiled for love when she saw him whose fairness brings no surfeit [and] who holds in himself all the energy of the governors and the form of god, for in the water she saw the shape of the man's fairest form and *upon the earth its shadow*. When the man saw in the water the form like himself as it was in nature, he loved it and wished to inhabit it; wish and action came in the same moment, and he inhabited the unreasoning form.[74]

On this account, the shadow functions as a token of the divine, and as a symbol of humankind's dual nature: 'Nature took hold of her beloved, hugged him all about and embraced him, for they were lovers', and 'because of this, unlike any other living thing on earth, mankind is twofold — in the body mortal but immortal in the essential man', for 'even though he is immortal and has authority over all things, mankind is affected by mortality because he is subject to fate; thus, although man is above the cosmic framework' — and, in this sense, he is an *Overman* or *Superman* — 'he became a slave within it', and 'lover and sleep are his masters'.[75]

Subsequently, in the Neoplatonic tradition, we find this idea taken up in, for example, the first book of *On the Theology of Plato* by the fifth-century Greek Neoplatonist philosopher, Proclus (412–485). Here Proclus takes a passage from the *First Alcibiades*, a text ascribed to Plato, to set out the task for the soul in terms of a mystic ascension. To begin with, Proclus sets up a parallel between the rites of the ancient Mysteries and the processes that occur within the soul, rendering those cultic rites internal to the individual:

> Indeed, Socrates in the [*First*] *Alcibiades* rightly observes, that the soul entering into herself will behold all other things, and deity itself.[76] For verging to her own union, and to the center of all life, laying aside multitude, and the variety of the all manifold powers which she contains, she ascends to the highest watch-tower of beings. And as in the most holy of the mysteries, they say, that the mystics at first meet with the multiform, and many-shaped genera [i.e., evil daemons] [...], but on entering the interior parts of the temple, unmoved, and guarded by the mystic rites, they genuinely receive in their bosom divine illumination, and divested of their garments [...] participate of a divine nature; — the same mode, as it appears to me, takes place in the speculation of wholes.[77]

Continuing this parallel, Proclus explores how the soul abandons 'the shadows and images of beings' to return to its own essence, but it can only so by means of 'the images of wholes':

> For the soul when looking at things posterior to herself, beholds *the shadows and images of beings*, but when she converts herself to herself she evolves her own essence, and the reasons which she contains. And at first indeed, she only as it were beholds herself; but, when she penetrates more profoundly into the knowledge of herself, she finds in herself both intellect, and the orders of beings. When however, she proceeds into her interior recesses, and into the adytum [holy of holies, inner sanctum] as it were of the soul, she perceives with her eye closed, the genus of the Gods, and the unities of beings. For all things are in us psychically, and through this we are naturally capable of knowing all things, by exciting the powers and *the images of wholes* which we contain.[78]

Once again, the shadow functions as a token of something that lies beyond the material world of representation. And yet, rightly understood, contemplation of shadow and of image can become a spur to a higher kind of knowledge, typically conceived in terms of the ascent of the soul:

> And this is the best employment of our energy, to be extended to divine nature itself, having our powers at rest, to revolve harmoniously round it, to excite all the multitude of the soul to this union, and laying aside all such

things as are posterior to *the one*, to become seated and conjoined with that which is ineffable, and beyond all things.[79]

We find an analogous set of ideas in the Kabbalistic tradition, a set of esoteric teachings that emerged from the Jewish mystical tradition in the twelfth and thirteenth centuries in southern France and in Spain.

In a Kabbalistic reading of verse 26 of the first chapter of Genesis, one commentator — Arthur Dyot Thomson — interprets the Hebrew text for 'Let us make man in our image' to mean 'like us in form and understanding, in shape and in thought', one word in particular signifying 'an image or design taken from the shadow of the body':

> Moses considers man as the shadow of God, or rather of the Gods, and consequently as obliged to follow these luminous or starry deities. Matter, according to Moses, coexists with the Gods, and therefore these deities necessarily act upon it and follow it everywhere, just as their light necessarily illuminates it and contends for it against the empire of darkness. He also considers the Gods, or the God who is the Gods, as bound to man in the same way as a shadow is to a body, and this is why God requires the love and trust of man, which otherwise would be unnecessary to Him.[80]

Thomson looks for support for this reading from other biblical texts — and from ancient Egyptian iconography:

> This is why those covenants are made which are apparently so unequal as between God and man, and this is why the Prophecies and Psalms so often speak of the protecting and salutary shadow of the Deity, and of his wings under the shadow of which man will find security. This what the Egyptian artists symbolically represented by the winged globe, which was always carved over the entrance to the temples. This symbol seemed to cover with its protecting shadow the faithful who entered the temple to offer the homage of their love to God.[81]

The image of the winged globe, of which numerous examples can be found,[82] returns in Nietzsche's *Zarathustra*: instead of the combination of golden disk, bird of

FIGURE 1.2 Egyptian winged globe, in Karl Richard Lepsius, *Denkmäler der Aegypter und Aethiopier*, Leipzig: Nicolai, 1849, vol. 3, pl. 3b.

prey, and serpent, we have the icon of the eagle and the snake — 'an eagle sweeping through the air in wide circles, and from it was hanging a serpent [...] coiled around the eagle's neck' — and the parting gift with which Zarathustra's disciples present him — 'a staff, upon the golden haft of which a serpent was coiled about a sun'.

For Thomson, the Egyptian and Jewish traditions alike have something important to teach us:

> Man therefore, being formed after the shadow of the Gods, is in some sort that shadow itself, and has a share in the Divine attributes, that is, in thought, in a reasoning soul, resolution, the act of reasoning, and the power of creating ruling, and governing, as his name [i.e., Adam] indicates.[83]

Hence the religious — indeed, existential — significance of art in general and sculpture in particular, for at the root of art lies *the shadow*:

> In the dramatic representation of the creation of man in the mysteries, the Aleim [i.e., Elohim] were represented by men who, when sculpturing the form of an Adamite being, of a man, traced the outline of it on their own shadow, or modelled it on their own shadow traced on the wall. This is how the art of drawing originated in Egypt, and the hieroglyphic figures carved on the Egyptian monuments have so little relief that they still resemble a shadow.[84]

Here we should note two points in relation to these passages and their argument. First, when the Canadian-born occultist and historian of mysticism Manly P. Hall (1901–1990) cites this passage in his *Secret Teachings of All Ages* (1928) in the context of a chapter on the Kabbalistic keys to the creation of Man, he discusses the ritualism of those early Jewish mysteries in which the creation was re-enacted. In those mysteries, Hall writes, Adam is endowed with the unusual facility of spiritual generation: 'Instead of reproducing his kind by the physical generative processes, he caused to issue from himself — or, more correctly, to be reflected upon substance — a shadow of himself', a shadow which he then 'ensouled' so that it 'became a living creature'.[85] There is thus an important link (and Nietzsche understood this well) between, on the one hand, the shadow, and, on the other, creation, creativity, and self-creation.

Second, Thomson himself goes on to cite from an encyclopedic work by the Roman historian, Pliny the Elder, whose views on the blissful islands we have already cited above. In his *Natural History*, Pliny offers an account of the origin of painting:

> The question as to the origin of the art of painting is uncertain, and it does not belong to the plan of this work. The Egyptians declare that it was invented among themselves six thousand years ago before it passed over into Greece — which is clearly an idle assertion. As to the Greeks, some of them say it was discovered at Sicyon, others in Corinth, but all agree that it began with tracing an outline round a man's shadow, and consequently that pictures were

originally done in this way, but the second stage when a more elaborate method had been invented was done in a single colour and called mono-chrome, a method still in use at the present day. Line-drawing was invented by the Egyptian Philocles or by the Corinthian Cleanthes [...].[86]

Thomson notes that such drawings can be seen at Naqda (known in classical antiquity as Ombos) and at Medinet Habu. He points out that the name Philocles means 'he who loves — renown, glory', and Cleanthes means 'the artificer of glory, of that which causes glory and renown', and concludes that these two names should be understood as 'an allegorical translation of two words which has relation to the art of hierography in Egypt'.[87]

So, on Pliny's account, the shadow lies at the beginning of painting; but, according to Pliny, it also lies at the beginning of sculpture:

> Enough and more than enough has been said about painting. It may be suitable to append to these remarks something about the plastic art. It was through the service of that same earth that modeling portraits from clay was first invented by Butades, a potter from Sycion, at Corinth. He did this owing to his daughter, who was in love with a young man; and she, when he was going abroad, drew in outline on the wall the shadow of his face thrown by the lamp. Her father pressed clay on this and made a relief, which he hardened by exposure to fire with the rest of his pottery; and it is said that this likeness was preserved in the shrine of the Nymphs until the destruction of Corinth by Mummius.[88]

What these passages from Pliny and from such commentators as Thomson and Hall demonstrate is that there exists an important art-historical and symbolic link between the SHADOW and ART. It is a link which, in Chapter 3, we shall pursue in greater detail. For now, however, let us return to the notion of the shadow as it is understood by Jung.

Jung on the Shadow in his *Zarathustra* Seminars

In Jung's seminars on Nietzsche's *Zarathustra*, the figure of the shadow emerges as a significant archetypal theme of this work as a whole. But as one might expect with the format of a seminar, Jung's interpretation emerged over a series of different occasions: rather than finding one, single authoritative statement, we have to be alert to the cumulative picture that builds up across the weeks, the months, and even the years. For instance, when one of the seminar members suggested that the 'great contempt' of which Zarathustra speaks in the Prologue can be explained because 'all the noble ideals, the most desirable precious things', are 'only the compensation for the shadow', Jung enthusiastically confirmed that Nietzsche was really looking for 'the dark things that lurk behind all these beautiful virtues, as if they surpassed all the good mankind could desire' (*SNZ* 1, 76). Indeed, it was this search that led Nietzsche (or so Jung argued) to believe that 'the greater reality is in the darkness and not in those ideas of beauty and light' (*SNZ* 1, 76).

We shall return to the theme of darkness, but at this point we should remember that, in 'On the Blissful Islands', Zarathustra specifically says *the beauty of the superman came to him as a shadow*: in other words, there is no disjunction for Zarathustra between, on the one hand, beauty, and, on the other, shadow, i.e., darkness. So an explanation of the relation between beauty and shadow still very much remains a desideratum at this stage of our discussion.

Elsewhere in his seminar, Jung interprets the figure of the tightrope-walker as the shadow (*SNZ* 1, 113–114), and the buffoon as the 'active shadow' (*SNZ* 1, 115–116 and 122) — as a representation of the 'demoniacal forces of the shadow' (*SNZ* 1, 115 and 123), or the shadow of the shadow, so to speak. Working with the assumption that, in the scene in the market-place, there is a 'prophecy' or an 'anticipation' of Nietzsche's fate, i.e., his collapse into insanity (*SNZ* 1, 115 and 125; cf. *SNZ* 1, 162–163), Jung argues that 'the rope-dancer is Nietzsche himself in his own form or in the form of Zarathustra', and 'the buffoon is the shadow that holds divine power, the power over death and life' (*SNZ* 1, 128).[89] If we fail to realize 'the destructive powers of the shadow', Jung told his audience, it appears 'in a particularly dangerous way' (*SNZ* 1, 125), as a 'terrible jester' (*SNZ* 1, 124), for if 'the god is dead' and thus 'appears in the shadow', then 'the negative qualities of the shadow become the armor of a new and terrible god' (*SNZ* 1, 128). 'Behind the shadow', there lies 'a much greater power' (*SNZ* 1, 127), and in Jung's view 'the demoniacal power of the buffoon is due to the fact that, being with the shadow, it is activated by the superior power of the wholeness of the self' (*SNZ* 1, 124), understood as the 'totality of conscious and unconscious' (*SNZ* 1, 125 and 127). The shadow of the shadow, then, is the self.

Six sections in *Zarathustra* proved to be particularly significant in Jung's unfolding analysis of the figure of the shadow. To begin with, in the figure of the camel, the first of the stages in the 'three transformations' of the spirit described in Zarathustra's opening discourse, Jung sees a symbol of acceptance of 'one's own negation', or in other words, the shadow (*SNZ* 1, 257). That said, Jung criticizes Nietzsche for his neglect in *Zarathustra* of the unconscious (*SNZ* 1, 391), although he acknowledges that, in another sense, Nietzsche 'already knew' of the unconscious, inasmuch as he was 'aware of the shadow' (*SNZ* 1, 405). In a passage that reads as if it were almost confessional, Jung laments the fact that 'we cannot get rid of ourselves': 'We carry our body, and our shadow and everything else is as it always has been', and 'we can only hope to become balanced between light and shadow — that is practically all we can hope for, no more' (*SNZ* 1, 433).[90] That the shadow is a major problem in itself, as well as something to do with a stage of our project of self-realization, is evident from the following remark: 'The shadow is so strong that you can be honestly in doubt as to what you really are' (*SNZ* 1, 389).

In the chapter of *Zarathustra* entitled 'On Reading and Writing', Jung finds evidence for a 'disidentification' with the shadow, with the result that Nietzsche 'leaves behind the heaviness and fear and darkness which would make him human, and so separates himself from humanity' (*SNZ* 1, 506). For, as Jung went on later to explain, 'whoever creates light must also create shadow, and whoever creates shadow creates also light; whatever is created must have two faces — for one is positive, and for another it is negative' (*SNZ* 1, 581). As a result, human beings 'are never perfect' — 'they may have wonderful and idealistic purposes but they cannot create anything without the black substance included' (*SNZ* 1, 581).

In a line from 'On the Way of the Creator', when Zarathustra tells his disciples: 'Solitary man, you are going the way to yourself! And your way leads past yourself and your seven devils!',[91] Jung interpreted the figure of the solitary man as someone who was on the path to the self. For it is 'on the way to the self', Jung suggested, that the solitary man will meet 'his own opposition', or 'the shadow'; in this case, 'a powerful shadow', since it is expressed as 'seven devils' (*SNZ* 1, 721). We can detect an important link between this solitary man, on his path to the self, and the figure of the superman (at the end of the path?), if we consider the relation of the self and the superman to the shadow. At one point Jung even makes explicit this connection between the superman, the shadow, and the self:

> As the Superman is most definitely not a shadow, he is dreaming of a Superman who is a friend of the self, yet without a shadow. But if he should try to identify or unite with the self, he would come across the shadow and it would interfere. When the shadow does interfere later, he does not recognize it. There is the tragedy. For his shadow is the reality of his ordinary self, which would not allow such a union through identification.[92]
>
> (*SNZ* 1, 703)

Interpreting Zarathustra's words from 'Of the Way of the Creator', 'You must be ready to burn yourself in your own flame: how could you become new, if you had not first become ashes?',[93] Jung referred back to Nietzsche's earlier work, his *Untimely Meditation* on 'Schopenhauer as Educator', §1, and pointed to three intertexts (the Gnostic myth of the soul; a text from the apocryphal New Testament; and a *logion* of Heraclitus). For Jung, Zarathustra's words remind us of the inevitability that 'anyone who seeks the self is forced into that fight with the shadow, with the other side of himself, his own negation; and that will be a catastrophe in which the ordinary man is as if destroyed: he becomes ashes' (*SNZ* 1, 722).

The shadow is problematic for many reasons, not least because of its persistence. Whatever we do, wherever we go, our shadow is always there, too. On another occasion in his seminar Jung makes the following observation:

> Our shadow is the last thing that has to be put on top of everything, and that is the thing we cannot swallow; we can swallow anything else, but not our own shadow because it makes us doubt our good qualities.
>
> (*SNZ* 2, 1090)

Is it ever possible to accept our own shadow? Or, to put it another way, is there such a thing as the acceptance of the inferior man (*SNZ* 2, 1090)? The inferior man is, like taxes and death, always with us, but Jung drives home this point when he remarks that 'the inferior man will come back with a vengeance as soon as he has a chance' (*SNZ* 2, 1091). And why does he come back with a vengeance? Because, as Jung reminds us, 'anything unconscious that lives with us is invariably projected' (*SNZ* 2, 1100). So to the extent that we are not aware of our shadow-side or our inferior nature, we project it; to the extent we are aware of it, we are ashamed. This is the problem of the shadow.

From the discourse of Zarathustra entitled 'Of the Tarantulas', Jung derives the image of the tarantula, the hairy arachnid that provokes such an instantaneous reaction of revulsion on the part of those whom it encounters. For Jung, the tarantula of which Zarathustra speaks is 'an aspect of the shadow in [Nietzsche] himself' (*SNZ* 2, 1113). He told his audience that 'you will see how the shadow comes back at Nietzsche with a vengeance: that is the tragedy of *Zarathustra*' (*SNZ* 2, 1114). In his interpretation of this chapter, Jung offered one of his most elaborate and coherent accounts of the psychodynamic structure at work in *Zarathustra*. 'Having constructed a figure like Zarathustra', he told his audience, Nietzsche 'is bound to construct the counter figure; Zarathustra casts a shadow',[94] for 'in the wake of Zarathustra follows the grotesque parade of evil figures, dwarfs and demons and black snakes that all together make up Zarathustra's shadow' (*SNZ* 2, 1322).

Yet this shadow-forming process is an inevitable part of the project of becoming the self, or in Jung's formula (echoing Zarathustra's words):[95] 'For the love of mankind and for the love of yourself — of mankind in yourself — create a devil' (*SNZ* 2, 1322). By creating a devil, one creates a means to engage with the problematic figure of 'the inferior man in [oneself], [one's] shadow', for 'if one doesn't accept the inferior man, one is liable to become mad[,] since the inferior man brings up the whole collective unconscious', because 'nothing in the unconscious is isolated — everything is united with everything else' (*SNZ* 2, 1356).

Hence the shadow is at once a personal *and* a collective problem: since 'each figure [...] expresses always the whole, and it appears with the overwhelming power of the whole unconscious', so the shadow represents 'the whole collective unconscious', because 'with the shadow you get the whole thing' (*SNZ* 2, 1356–1357). In Jung's eyes, the drama of *Zarathustra* enables us to watch — as it were from a distance, in horror, and with bated breath — how a psychological problem can constellate itself and resist resolution. 'When Nietzsche is afraid of his shadow or tries to cope with it', Jung maintained, 'it means that he himself, alone, has to cope with the terror of the whole collective unconscious, and that makes things unwieldy' (*SNZ* 2, 1357).

In the following lines from 'Of the Virtue that Makes Small', where Zarathustra, speaking to himself, enunciates the principle, 'Always love your neighbour as yourselves — but first be such as *love themselves* — / such as love with a great love, such as love with a great contempt!',[96] Jung finds 'a formula of how to deal with the shadow, of how to deal with the inferior man' (*SNZ* 2, 1367). As a formula, it is paradoxical; it is a call for a kind of *coniunctio oppositorum* internal to the individual, and Jung expands on this formula as follows: 'It is simply impossible to love the inferior man such as he is, to do nothing but love him; you must love him with great love and also with great contempt', and 'that is the enormous difficulty — to bring the two things together in the one action, to love yourself and to have contempt for yourself', 'but there you have the formula of how to assimilate your shadow' (*SNZ* 2, 1367).[97] The solution to a paradox — the shadow is an individual *and* a collective problem at one and the same time — is, not surprisingly, itself a paradox …

Finally, in the course of discussing the chapter entitled 'Of the Spirit of Gravity', Jung detects in the imagery of flight and weightlessness evident in Zarathustra's discourse a direct expression of the shadow: 'The shadow speaks here as an eagle', Jung maintains, 'so when the shadow puts on wings and becomes a bird, when the shadow is liberated, it is an independent, autonomous thing, and it swoops down on Nietzsche and takes him up into another world' (*SNZ* 2, 1466, cf. 1468). Jung also assimilated this figure of 'the shadow, the inferior man' as 'a bird that […] may swoop down upon Nietzsche, sweep him off his feet and carry him away' to the buffoon that had jumped over the tightrope-walker in the Prologue (*SNZ* 2, 1468).[98]

At the same time, however, Jung insisted on detaching the line, 'One must learn to love oneself with a sound and healthy love, so that one may endure it with oneself and not go roaming about',[99] from the problem of Nietzsche's shadow and demanded it be read as 'an impersonal truth' (*SNZ* 2, 1472).[100] So when Zarathustra goes on to say that 'to *learn* to love oneself is no commandment for today or tomorrow', but this art is rather 'the finest, subtlest, ultimate, and most patient of all',[101] Jung enthusiastically agrees: 'One could call it a great art, and I should say a great philosophy because it is the most difficult thing you can imagine, to accept your own inferiority' (*SNZ* 2, 1478).[102] But what Zarathustra does, Nietzsche himself could not do, or so Jung argued: 'The fact that Nietzsche reviles the shadow shows to what extent he is already identical with it, and his vituperation is really a means of separating himself from it' (*SNZ* 2, 1475).

To summarize: for Jung, all of the chapters in Part Three of *Zarathustra* 'deal with the problem of the inferior man, or the shadow', but Nietzsche had first 'met' the shadow in the encounter between the tightrope-walker and the buffoon in the Prologue (*SNZ* 2, 1457). According to Jung, Nietzsche does not merely reject the shadow, he 'reviles' it, reviling not just 'the inferior man in himself', but also 'the shadow in the masses, the collective man' (*SNZ* 2, 1457–1458).

At various points in his seminars, Jung sought to sustain this analysis with references to biographical anecdotes about Nietzsche, gleaned from contemporary biographies[103] or from what he himself had heard. For instance, he related a story about how, in one of his lectures, Nietzsche noticed how a young man was following his exposition about Greece and Graecia Magna with particular interest, and after the lecture invited the young man to accompany him to Greece. Worrying about the cost of such a journey, the young man suddenly looked crestfallen, which was misunderstood by Nietzsche and deeply wounded him (*SNZ* 1, 16–17; cf. *SNZ* 2, 1361). (In Jung's view, this episode showed how 'the young man represented the shadow', or 'that mediocre little fellow whom Nietzsche always disregarded', illustrating how 'Nietzsche could not see the real reason, because that is what he never counted in his life' [*SNZ* 2, 1362].)

Then again, Jung claimed that he knew an old lady who had supported Nietzsche financially, although he never realized it, demonstrating how 'those mediocre people' whom Nietzsche was always reviling were 'the ones who provided for his daily life' (*SNZ* 2, 1362, cf. 961). Within the economy of Nietzsche's life, Jung suggested, these figures functioned as a kind of collective shadow, supporting Nietzsche, yet rejected by him.

Along similar lines, Jung told a tale about an episode recorded by Clara Gelzer-Thurneysen (1858–1919), married to a German classical scholar, Heinrich Gelzer, Professor of Ancient History at Heidelberg and later Professor of Classical Philology and Ancient History at Jena; she was also a close friend of Nietzsche's sister (*SNZ* 1, 255–256 and 609–610). Clara recalled how Nietzsche had once told her at a dinner party: 'I recently dreamed that my hand, which was resting in front of me on the table, suddenly acquired a glassy, transparent skin; I saw clearly into its bone structure, into its tissue, into its muscles. Suddenly I saw a fat toad sitting on my hand and at the same time I felt the irresistible urge to swallow the animal. I overcame my terrible revulsion and gulped it down'. On hearing this, his dining partner laughed — well, what else was she meant to do? — but Nietzsche's response cannot have made the situation easier for her to deal with: '"And you laugh at that?" Nietzsche asked with terrible seriousness and kept his eyes, half questioning, half sad, fixed on the woman sitting next to him'.[104]

For Jung, this frog or toad represented for Nietzsche 'the inferior man living in the swamp or mire'; so when, in 'Of the Three Metamorphoses', the camel asks: 'What is the heaviest thing?', and Zarathustra replies: 'To wade into dirty water when it is the water of truth, and not to disdain cold frogs and hot toads',[105] Jung interpreted this as showing that Nietzsche feels 'the connection with that primitive man', because he was going to 'face again the conflict with the interior man' (*SNZ* 1, 256). In that unsettling exchange with Clara Thurneysen over dinner, the toad functioned as 'the expression of the loathsomeness of life, or the lower man', and inasmuch as it was 'a poisonous creature', it was 'the quintessence of what the world did to Nietzsche' (*SNZ* 2, 610).

What did Clara Thurneysen herself think? According to her intrepretation of the dream, Nietzsche 'experienced the transparency of his hand as a great suffering, from which he could only be healed if he swallowed down a living toad' — which seems rather to miss the point. If she had read the *Viridarium Chymicum* (*The Chemical Pleasure-Garden*), a seventeenth-century collection by Daniel Stolz von Stolzenberg (1600–1660) of emblems by, among others, Michael Maier (1568–1622) and Johann Daniel Mylius (c. 1583–1642), then she might have connected the dream with a picture attributed to Avicenna, depicting in a conjunction of sorts two of the animals found in Nietzsche's *Zarathustra*. In this emblem, from the talons of an eagle in flight a chain descends to the earth, where it is fastened to the back legs of a toad. *Bufonum terrenum Aquile conjunge volanti, / In nostra cernes arte magisterium*, 'Connect the earthly toad with the flying eagle, / And thou shalt understand the secret of our art', runs the verse accompanying this emblem.[106] (In fact, Michael Maier incorporated this emblem into his coat of arms, where the toad and the eagle are linked by a golden chain — that is, by the *aurea catena* or the 'marvellously interconnected chain', as Maier calls it in his *Hymnosophia* [or *Hymn to Wisdom*], linking the heart with gold, gold with the sun, and the sun with God.[107] (A similar emblem, depicting 'an eagle which flies up to heaven on its two wings', but finds itself 'weighed down by a stone tied to one of its feet', is described in Giordano Bruno's *Heroic Frenzies*.[108])

Jung, of course, *had* read the *Viridarium Chymicum*, and on his account of this emblem the eagle represents 'the spirit' or 'mind', 'a flying thought-being that consists of breath', while the toad — or, by analogy, the serpent — is 'an utterly chthonic animal' (*SNZ* 2, 1412). In other words, in line with Jung's complementaristic vision that underpins the entirety of his thought, we need the higher *and* the lower, we need the light *and* the dark — the spirit *and* the shadow [...] For there is something paradoxical about light: as Bertrand Vergely has explained, 'if there is nothing to act as a screen to stop light and to create a luminous side and a dark side, no object is visible', and so, 'bathed in light, one is not illuminated but in the dark'.[109]

Hence, in Vergely's view, the ancient Greeks' keen sense of the shadow is evidenced by the existence of such diurnal gods as Apollo and such nocturnal

FIGURE 1.3 *Avicenna, an Arab*, from Daniel Stoltzius von Stoltzenbart, *Viridarium Chymicum: The Chemical Pleasure-Garden*, 1624.

goddesses as Artemis, and by the contrasting aspects of certain gods, able to dispense evil and good alike. (One thinks, for instance, of the complementary relationship between Dionysos as worshipped in Corinth and Sikyôn, where his light aspect was celebrated as Dionysos Lysios, the 'Liberator' or 'Deliverer', and his dark aspect as Dionysos Bakcheois, the 'Crier'.) In this paradoxical relationship of light and dark, Vergely detects something symbolic about the human condition, arguing that in any human life there is always a moment in which individuals must confront their shadow. 'At night', he says, 'when the moon or a street light shines on us and we see our shadow on the ground, we see what our silhouette looks like, since the shadow projected on the ground is like an image reflected in a mirror'.[110]

So much, then, for the paradox of light and shadow and for Jung's analysis in his *Zarathustra* seminar of the problem of the shadow in relation to Nietzsche. But what does Jung have to say, if anything, about the specific context of our discussion: the passage where Zarathustra tells us that *the beauty of the superman came to him as a shadow*? To answer this question, we must not be afraid of the dark and we shall have to keep thinking, even (and perhaps especially) if we would rather not, about the shadow.

Jung on the Shadow

To gain some purchase on the questions we have asked — why, in the discourse in 'On the Blissful Islands', does the beauty of the superman come to Zarathustra *as a shadow*? and why is it *the beauty of the superman* that comes to him? — let us step back for a moment from Jung's seminar on Nietzsche's *Zarathustra* and his discussion there of the blissful islands and of the shadow. What does Jung, more generally, understand by the term 'the shadow'?

If we consult the entry on the 'shadow' in *A Critical Dictionary of Jungian Analysis*, it points us in the direction of Jung's most direct definition of this term given in *The Psychology of the Transference* (1946): put simply, the shadow is 'the thing someone has no wish to be' (*CW* 16 §470).[111] As always with Jung, however, and as the *Critical Dictionary* realizes, the concept of the shadow covers manifold complexities and subtleties.[112] In a sense, the question of the shadow leads us into the very heart of Jung's thinking, inasmuch as he once observed (in the conclusion to his Eranos lecture on 'Transformation Symbolism in the Mass' [1942; 1954]) that 'it does not seem to have occurred to people that when we say "psyche" we are alluding to the densest darkness it is possible to imagine' (*CW* 11 §448).

In an account of the shadow, originally given in a lecture delivered to the Schweizerische Gesellschaft für Praktische Psychologie in Zurich in 1948, and subsequently included in *Aion* (1951), Jung describes the shadow as a 'moral problem' (*CW* 9/ii §14), linking it to 'emotion' (understood, not as an activity of the individual, but as something that happens to the individual) (*CW* 9/ii §15) and associating it with the phenomenon of 'projection' (*CW* 9/ii §16). As regards this final point, Jung's argument is as follows: unable to acknowledge 'the dark aspects of the personality' (*CW* 9/ii §14), let alone 'assimilate [them] into the conscious personality'

(*CW* 9/ii §16), the unconscious projects these aspects on the others around the individual.

As Jung puts it, projections 'change the world into the replica of one's own unknown face', and ultimately the projection of the shadow leads to 'an autoerotic or autistic condition', in which the individual 'dreams a world, whose reality remains unattainable' (*CW* 9/ii §17). (In passing, one should note that, in contrast to the accusation frequently levelled at it, Jungian psychology is greatly concerned with the 'real world'.) The very negativity projected by the individual onto the world is (incorrectly) interpreted by the individual as the malevolence of the world, setting up a vicious circle that 'isolates the subject from its environment' to an ever greater degree (*CW* 9/ii §17). (Jung appears, in common with much of the psychoanalytic tradition, to exclude the possibility that the world really *is* malevolent in its intentions …) In the following paragraph Jung describes in considerable detail the mechanism that alienates the individual self from the world, and the individual self from the individual self:

> It is often tragic [*tragisch*] to see how blatantly a person bungles his or her own life and the lives of others yet remains totally incapable of seeing how much the whole tragedy [*die ganze Tragödie*] originates in himself or herself, and how he or she continually feeds it and keeps it going. Not *consciously*, of course — for consciously he or she is engaged in bewailing and cursing the faithless world that recedes further and further into the distance. Rather, it is an unconscious factor which spins the illusion that veil his or her world [*ein unbewußter Faktor, der die welt- und selbstverhüllenden Illusionen spinnt*].[113]
>
> (*CW* 9/ii §18)

(Hull's translation elides two different processes: the illusions spun, web-like, by the conscious, veil both the world — *and* the self.) In his seminars on *Zarathustra*, as we saw above, Jung detects precisely this tragedy unfolding in Nietzsche.

Another of Jung's most sensitive discussions of the problem of the shadow can be found in his earlier short paper, 'Problems of Modern Psychotherapy', first published in *Schweizerisches Medizinisches Jahrbuch* in 1929 and reprinted in *Seelenprobleme der Gegenwart* (1931). Here Jung speaks persuasively, not just of the need to engage with one's shadow, but of the need for the shadow *tout court*. For in this paper Jung compares psychoanalysis as 'the rediscovery of an ancient truth' to a particular praxis: to 'catharsis', or cleansing — 'a familiar term in the classical rites of initiation' (*CW* 16 §134). These rites of initiation formed the heart of the great Mystery cults of the Greco-Roman world, including the Orphic, Isiac, Samothracean, Dionysian, Mithraic, and preeminently the Eleusinan Mysteries celebrated every year as part of the cult of Demeter and Persephone at Eleusis, just outside Athens in Greece.[114]

Concomitantly, in 'Problems of Modern Psychotherapy' Jung contrasts analysis with the 'meditation' or 'contemplation' of yoga, describing the aim of analysis as 'to observe the sporadic emergence, whether in the form of images or feelings, of those dim representations which detach themselves in the darkness from the invisible realm of the unconscious and move *as shadows* before the inturned gaze' (*CW* 16 §134). After all, one might add, what else were the visions contained in Jung's *Red Book* than the transcription of what his 'inward gaze' witnessed?[115] This inner work brings about a 'return of the repressed', as 'things repressed and forgotten come back again', only a return that is — if the term is not too inappropriate — 'managed' and hence benign (*CW* 16 §134).

And so, just as 'the beauty of the Superman' comes to Zarathustra 'as a shadow', so the 'shadow' — 'the inferior and even the worthless' — returns to the individual, as 'a gain in itself, though often a painful one', because — paradoxically — the shadow gives the individual 'substance and mass' (*CW* 16 §134). The shadow provides 'substance and mass', for, as Jung asks: 'How can I be substantial without casting a shadow?' 'If I am to be whole', he continues, then 'I must have a dark side, too'; moreover, 'by becoming conscious of my shadow I remember once more that I am a human being like any other'. But by remembering that he or she is 'a human being like any other', i.e., that he or she is (as Nietzsche would say) 'human, all-too-human' (*menschlich, all-zu-menschlich*), the individual becomes — paradoxically again — *more* than 'a human being like any other', i.e., he or she becomes a superman (*Übermensch*).

In particular, Jung pays a tribute, albeit a qualified one, to Freud, describing Freudian psychoanalysis as 'a minute elaboration of man's shadow-side unexampled in any previous age' (*CW* 16 §145). Thanks to Freud's 'pioneer work', Jung adds, we have learned that 'human nature has its black side' — as do 'its works, its institutions, and its convictions' (*CW* 16 §146). Indeed, it turns out that 'our purest and holiest beliefs rest on very deep and dark foundations' (*CW* 16 §146). Although Jung cunningly refers to the interpretation of the Last Supper in terms of primitive totemism by the French archaeologist Salomon Reinach (1858–1932),[116] thus overlooking Freud's (re)statement of this position in *Totem and Taboo* (1913),[117] much of what Jung here attributes to Freud's insight can be found in Nietzsche (especially in his *On the Genealogy of Morals*).[118]

Jung goes on to say in this paper that it would be 'an imperfection in things of beauty' (and, likewise, 'a frailty in humankind'), if beauty (or if humankind) allowed itself to be 'destroyed' by 'a mere shadow-explanation' (*CW* 16 §146). Thus it does not diminish 'radiant things' to interpret them 'from the shadow-side', even at the risk of 'trampling them in the sorry dirt of their beginnings' (*CW* 16 §146). To underscore the importance of this point, Jung repeats it: 'To suppose that the radiant things are done away with by being explained from the shadow-side' is, he declares, 'our mistake'. For darkness is not opposed to light, it is complementary to it: 'Shadow pertains to light as evil to good, and vice versa' (*CW* 16 §146).[119]

In a paper first given at an Eranos conference entitled 'Archetypes of the Collective Unconscious' (1934; 1954), Jung described the confrontation with one's own shadow in the following dramatic terms:

> Whoever goes to himself risks a confrontation with himself. The mirror does not flatter, it faithfully shows whatever looks into it; namely, the face we never

show to the world because we cover it with the *persona*, the mask of the actor. But the mirror lies behind the mask and shows the true face.

(*CW* 9/i §43)

What is this face? What is it we cover with the mask of the *persona*? It is *the shadow*, and so 'this confrontation is the first test of courage on the inner way', for it is 'a test sufficient to frighten off most people', because 'the meeting with ourselves' belongs to 'the more unpleasant things that can be avoided as long as one can project everything negative into the environment' (*CW* 9/i §44). (Here again we find the familiar psychoanalytic theme that the problem never lies with other people, but with ourselves.) Correspondingly, Jung continues, 'if we are able to see our own shadow and can bear knowing about it, then a small part of the problem has already been solved: we have at least brought up the personal unconscious' (*CW* 9/i §44). According to Jung, 'the shadow is a living part of the personality and therefore wants to live with it in some form', it is something that 'cannot be argued out of existence or rationalized into harmlessness' (*CW* 9/i §44). As such, the shadow is a problem that is 'exceedingly difficult', yet nevertheless, 'the account has to be settled sooner or later' (*CW* 9/i §44).

The encounter with the shadow is, on Jung's account, something remarkably paradoxical, while at the same time intensely liberating. 'The shadow is a tight passage, a narrow door', Jung says, echoing Matthew (7: 14), one whose 'painful constriction no one is spared who goes down to the deep well' (*CW* 9/i §44). But, he continues, 'one must learn to know oneself in order to know who one is' (*CW* 9/i §44). (The famous injunction of the Delphic Oracle, 'Know thyself', is thus not a simple injunction, but rather the outline of an entire programme and a monumental task …[120]) And in return for this labour Jung promises a great reward, for 'what comes after the door is, surprisingly enough, a boundless expanse full of unprecedented uncertainty […]' (*CW* 9/i §45).[121] Or so the version by R.F.C. Hull in the *Collected Works* reads, but due to a mistranslation it is easy to misread this passage, which is in fact characterizing the state of life after death (or, in the original German, *was nach dem Tode kommt*).

Yet equally, however one renders this qualifying phrase, the entire passage could be read as a reference to the Neoplatonic concept of the One, which is beyond all determination, for Jung characterizes this 'boundless expanse' as having 'apparently no inside and no outside, no above and no below, no here and no there, no mine and no thine, no good and no bad'; it is 'the world of water, where all life floats in suspension; where the realm of the sympathetic [nervous] system, the soul of everything living [*der Seele alles Lebendigen*], begins', it is a place 'where I am indivisibly this *and* that; where I experience the other in myself and the other-than-myself experiences me' (*CW* 9/i §45).[122] Is the (psychological) encounter with the shadow but a prelude, then, to the (contemplative or mystical) encounter with the One?

So perhaps it is not surprising that, in a paper written as a preface to two further Eranos lectures, entitled 'Introduction to the Religious and Psychological Problems of Alchemy' (1943), Jung placed a religious framework around his discussion of the encounter between the patient and the shadow. For, in addition to projecting the shadow onto one's fellow human beings, another strategy is to 'cast' one's 'sins' onto a divine mediator by means of *contritio* or *attritio* ('perfect' or 'imperfect' repentance) (*CW* 12 §36). In a footnote, Jung observed that, when confronting some people with their 'blackest shadow', the use of religious terminology 'comes naturally', since only it is 'adequate' to those circumstances when one is faced with 'the tragic fate' (*des tragischen Schicksals*) that is, in Jung's view, 'the unavoidable concomitant of wholeness' (*CW* 12 §36, n. 17). On the face of it, *this* kind of tragedy is very different from the kind that, on his account, befell Nietzsche.

Five years later, in his lecture of 1948 included in *Aion* (1951), Jung wrote that 'it is quite within the bounds of possibility for a person to recognize the relative evil of his nature, but it is a rare and shattering experience for him or her to gaze into the face of absolute evil' (*CW* 9/ii §19). Yet is there such a thing as absolute evil? Maybe by 1948 Jung thought there was (and, given world-historical events in the 1930s and 1940s — the Second World War, the Holocaust, the dropping of the atomic bomb — he could easily be forgiven for thinking so).[123] But in 1943 Jung had written that 'evil needs to be pondered just as much as good', for 'good and evil are ultimately nothing but ideal extensions and abstractions of doing', and 'both belong to the chiaroscuro of life [*zur hell-dunkeln Erscheinung des Lebens*]' (*CW* 12 §36). For Jung, good and evil are not just complementary, but each is a dialectical co-implicate of the other: 'In the last resort there is no good that cannot produce evil and no evil that cannot produce good' (*CW* 12 §36).

In 1954 Jung related the shadow to another archetypal figure, the trickster. What in his *Adversus haereses* (I, ii, 1) the Church Father Irenaeus of Lyons called *umbra* or 'shadow' is, Jung suggested, closely related to a certain trickiness of the shadow, reflected in 'gaffes', 'slips', and '*faux pas*' (i.e., parapraxes), while carnival customs can be interpreted as 'remnants of a collective shadow figure'; it is from this 'numinous collective figure', he argued, that the personal shadow is, in part, descended (*CW* 9/i §469). So the trickster-figure, he believed, was both a collective shadow figure, 'a summation of all the individual inferior traits of character in individuals', *and* a parallel of the individual shadow (*CW* 9/i §484–85).

This overlap between the personal and collective allows us to appreciate how the shadow — although, by definition, a *negative* figure — has 'certain positive traits and associations', almost as if it were hiding 'meaningful contents under an unprepossessing exterior'. Consequently there exists a close relation between the shadow and, on the one hand, the anima as the archetype of meaning (cf. *CW* 9/i §66) and, on the other, the archetype of the wise old man (*CW* 9/i §485). (To those who complain that all the different archetypes are starting to merge into one, Jung replies that his concepts are not 'intellectual formulae', but 'names for certain areas of experience'…)

Nevertheless, we gain a sense of just how important Jung considered the shadow to be when he discerns in the trickster and the shadow alike a soteriological function. 'Only out of disaster', he maintained, 'can the longing for the saviour arise', and the disaster he had in mind was 'the recognition and unavoidable integration of the shadow', something so 'harrowing' that only a saviour can 'undo the tangled web of fate' (*CW* 9/i §487). On the individual level, the problem posed by the shadow is answered by the anima, that is, 'relatedness'; on the collective level, it is answered by the 'development of consciousness', liberating us from imprisonment in *agnoia* ('unconsciousness') (*CW* 9/i §487–488). In both cases, then, the shadow (in its collective, mythological, as well as individual form) contains within it the seed of an *enantiodromia*, a conversion of something into its opposite.[124]

Having surveyed Jung's evolving discussion of the shadow in his writings between 1929 and 1954, let us turn to a work that provides a particular insight into the nature of the shadow and examine it more closely. For the concepts and images of *The Psychology of the Transference* (1946) offer us an interpretative key to understand Nietzsche's text and to answer the questions we have asked about it.

The Function of the Shadow in the *Rosarium philosophorum*

The Psychology of the Transference is based on an analysis of the sequence of woodcuts in the first edition of a sixteenth-century alchemical treatise, *Rosarium philosophorum sive pretiosissimum donum Dei* (or *The Rosary of the Philosophers*), originally published in Frankfurt in 1550 as the second volume of *De Alchimia Opuscula complura veterum philosophorum*. The richly illustrated text of the *Rosarium philosophorum* is generally recognised to be one of the most important works in the tradition of European alchemy, and Jung's analysis of it is as extensive as it is profound.

Now the process of psychoanalysis, as Jung understood it in *The Psychology of the Transference*, turns out to map with extraordinary accuracy onto the work of the late medieval alchemist. On this account, the realization on the part of the patient that he or she 'has a shadow', and that 'his [or her] enemy is in his [or her] own heart', constitutes the starting-point of the therapeutic process (*CW* 16 §399). Similarly, in alchemy, 'an integral part of the work is the *umbra solis*' — i.e., the sun's shadow — 'or *sol niger*' — i.e., black sun — 'of the alchemists, the black shadow that everyone carries with him [or her], the inferior and therefore hidden aspect of the personality' (*CW* 16 §420).[125] This 'hidden aspect' is described by Jung as 'the weakness that goes with every strength, the night that follows day, the evil in the good' (*CW* 16 §420); and in a footnote he compares the individual's reaction to this knowledge with a line from the *Aurora consurgens*, a fifteenth-century alchemical treatise allegedly written by Thomas Aquinas.

In the first parable of this work, entitled 'Of the Black Earth', the writer sees from far away a great black cloud that descends on the earth, covering it and his soul, prompting him to reflect that 'there is health in my flesh' and (in the part quoted by Jung) 'all my bones are troubled before the face of my iniquity' (*a facie iniquitatis meae conturbata sunt omnia ossa mea*),[126] a phrase which in turn echoes the biblical psalm, 'my sin has left no health in my bones'.[127] While this response is associated with 'the danger of falling victim to the shadow', precisely this danger brings with it 'the possibility of consciously deciding not to become its victim' (*CW* 16 §420). Here, then, is a reason why *des Übermenschen Schönheit*, 'the beauty of the Superman', comes to Zarathustra 'as a shadow': it brings with it danger, but with it, this danger brings the opportunity to face one's enemy — i.e., one's shadow — and, by integrating one's shadow, the chance to make oneself a complete human — i.e., *to make oneself beautiful*.

For, as Jung emphasizes further on in *The Psychology of the Transference*, the psychoanalytic-cum-alchemical *opus* involves the confrontation of the naked Sol (or sun) with the naked Luna (or moon), of masculine with feminine, of *agens* (or active force) and *patiens* (or passive element): as such, it is 'a union in the spirit' (*CW* 16 §451) that involves (in the words of this chapter title) 'the naked truth'. In line with the 'axiom of Maria', an alchemical precept attributed to the third-century alchemist, Maria Prophetissa,[128] according to which 'one becomes two, two becomes three, and out of the third comes the one as the fourth', the process envisaged by Jung illustrates this principle in reverse: the 4 (the two elements, each of which contains its opposite, i.e., $2 \times 2 = 4$) has become a 3 (the two elements, plus 'the spirit descending from above' — the dove as an attribute of the goddess of love and a symbol of *amor coniugalis* — [*CW* 16 §451, incl. fn. 7], i.e., $2 + 1 = 3$), prior to the *coniunctio* of the two (*CW* 16 §451). Read psychologically, this final stage involves 'a stark encounter with reality, with' — as Jung tellingly puts it — 'no false veils or adornments of any kind', as the individual now stands forth as he or she 'really' is, displaying what had been hidden 'under the mask of conventional adaptation', i.e., the shadow.

Hence, the final stage involves the raising-to-consciousness of the shadow and its integration with the ego, or what Jung describes as 'a move in the direction of wholeness' (*CW* 16 §452). Jung affirms the paradoxical nature of this development when he states that 'assimilation of the shadow *gives a person a body*, so to speak' (*CW* 16 §452; my emphasis). What this means is that 'the animal sphere of the instinct' as well as 'the primitive or archaic psyche' are 'no longer repressed by fictions and illusions' and becomes conscious (*CW* 16 §452). The danger is that the shadow is not 'harmless', for it brings with it 'the archaic psyche' and 'the whole world of the archetypes', saturating the conscious mind with 'archaic influences' (*CW* 16 §452). But the opportunity it brings is equally immense: the chance to move 'in the direction of *wholeness*', and Jung gives us an explicit definition of what he means by this term: 'Wholeness is not so much perfection as completeness' (*CW* 16 §452).

At this point, we might note the significance for Jung of totality or completeness: and his conception of *beauty as wholeness*, found in Neoplatonism and informing the aesthetics of German classicism, constitutes the central meeting-point between these two traditions and the school of analytical psychology. In his *Letters on the Aesthetic Education* of 1795, Friedrich Schiller tells us how the material drive [or *Stofftrieb*] and the formal drive [or *Formtrieb*] give rise, through a process of mutual subordination, to a third drive, the ludic drive (*Spieltrieb*), which in turn, through a synthesis of both drives, brings about beauty. Schiller's aesthetic theory is exactly in line with the argumentational structure of the 'axiom of Maria', as the mutual subordination of the two drives ($2 \times 2 = 4$) gives rise to a third drive

(2 + 1 = 3) which, combining the two drives (1 + 1 = 2), brings forth the one
(1 = 1), or the unity of beauty.

As part of his analysis of the sequence of woodcuts in the first edition of the
Rosarium philosophorum, Jung describes as 'a primordial image that runs through
the whole of alchemy' the story of how 'the Original Man (Nous)' — i.e., mind
or intellect — 'bent down from heaven to earth and was wrapped in the embrace
of Physis' — i.e., nature or the physical world (*CW* 16 §456). (As well as running
through the whole of alchemy, the story of the fall of divine intellect into the
material world is also a central theme in Neoplatonism.) This image of *nous* and
physis embracing each other finds expression, so Jung further explains, in the 'sexual
fantasies' that colour the transference in analysis, as well as in the 'frank eroticism'
of the images of alchemical *coniunctio* (*CW* 16 §460). According to Jung, 'male and
female inevitably constellate the idea of sexual union as the means of producing
the 1, which is then consistently called the *filius regis* or *filius philosophorum*, the
king's son or the philosopher's son (*CW* 16 §404). For Jung, the meaning of the
relationship of Sol and Luna, the alchemical king and queen, is clear: it is nothing
other than 'man's longing for transcendent' — here's that word again — 'wholeness' (*CW* 16 §456). Jung draws our attention to the fifth figure of the *Rosarium
philosophorum*, which depicts the *coniunctio* as the coitus of the alchemical king and
queen (see Figure 1.4a), and to the lines accompanying it attributed to Merculinus
(aka Merlinus or Mercurius):

> White-skinned lady, lovingly joined to her ruddy-limbed husband,
> Wrapped in each other's arms in the bliss of connubial union,
> Merge and dissolve as they come to the goal of perfection:
> They that were two are made one, as though of one body.

(a)

FIGURE 1.4a *Rosarium philosophorum*, showing the *coniunctio*, in *Artis auriferae*, vol. 2,
Basel: Waldkirch, 1593, pp. 575–631.

(b)

FIGURE 1.4b *Rosarium philosophorum*, showing the immersion, in *Artis auriferae*, vol. 2, Basel: Waldkirch, 1593, pp. 575–631.

Whereas, in the earlier pictures in the sequence of the *Rosarium philosophorum*, Jung detects the presence of 'the uniting symbol' (i.e., the device consisting of five flowers, the fifth of which is brought by the dove that descends from the quintessential star) (see *CW* 16 §410 and §451), in this fifth picture 'the partners have themselves become symbolic' (*CW* 16 §462). First, each represents two elements (the masculine and the feminine, the light and the dark, the right and the left, consciousness and the unconscious); second, when united into one, their union represents, says Jung, the 'integration of the shadow'; and finally, when 'the two together with third become a whole' (as the lines of Merculinus suggest), then the 'axiom of Maria' is fulfilled. The representation in the previous picture, depicting the immersion in the bath, of the Holy Spirit by the symbol of the heavenly dove (see Figure 1.4b) has, in the union of the alchemical king and queen, disappeared but, so Jung argues, 'to make up for that, Sol and Luna themselves have become spirit' (*CW* 16 §462).

Whatever the goals and ambitions of alchemy really were, and what kind of truth it might actually contain, we cannot say; but it is evident from Jung's interpretation of alchemy that he sees it as expressing a complex relation between the mind and the body, between the intellect and the senses. While presenting spirit and body in opposition, alchemy does so merely to distinguish them: in fact, as Jung is acutely aware, it insists on their reciprocal relationship and mutual interdependence. *Nous* might fall into *physis*, but *physis* needs *nous* in order to ascend: not, to be sure, to leave the physical realm entirely behind, but to transform the physical world into something richer, more profound — more spiritualized.

Given this interrelationship of spirit and body, intellect and senses, *nous* and *physis*, it is perhaps not surprising that Jung, in an earlier part of *The Psychology of the Transference*, had identified as 'the last and greatest work of alchemy' a work of literature to which, time and again, he always returned — to Goethe's poetic drama (or dramatic poem), *Faust*. For in this text, Jung claimed, Goethe was doing something that, while far removed from the laboratory world of jars, retorts, and fiery salamanders, could nevertheless be described as *alchemical*. According to Jung, in *Faust* Goethe was really describing 'the experience of the alchemist who discovers that what he has projected into the retort is his own darkness, his unredeemed state, his passion, his struggles to reach the goal' or, in other words, 'to become what he really is, to fulfil the purpose for which his mother bore him, and, after the peregrinations of a long life full of confusion and error, to become the *filius regi[u]s*, son of the supreme mother' (*CW* 16 §407).

Consequently, Jung suggested, an important forerunner of *Faust* was the *Chymical Wedding*, a work published in Strasbourg in 1616 and attributed to Christian Rosencreutz, but really written by the German theologian Johann Valentin Andreae (1586–1654). The work is presented as having been composed by the founder of the Rosicrucian Order in 1459, a foundational year in the history of Freemasonry, and Jung maintains that this work had 'assuredly' been known to Goethe (*CW* 16 §407).[129] Now, this intertextual connection made by Jung between the allegorical romance of the *Chymical Wedding* and the poetic epic of Goethe's *Faust* explains the persistent and significant allusions to *Faust* made by Jung throughout *The Psychology of the Transference* (see *CW* 16 §386, §398, §406): all three texts are concerned, one way or another, with the question of transformation.

Goethe's 'Sacred Yearning' (*Selige Sehnsucht*)

When Jung turns to discuss the alchemical *coniunctio* itself, he does not cite *Faust*, but another work, in its own way equally famous, by Goethe: the poem, from a collection published as *West-östlicher Divan* (or *West-Eastern Divan*) (1819; 1827), entitled *Selige Sehnsucht* (or 'Sacred Yearning').[130] Its third stanza runs as follows:

> No more are you held in capture
> Darkly over-shadowed waiting [*In der Finsternis Beschattung*],
> You anew are torn by rapture
> Upwards to a higher mating [*Auf zu höherer Begattung*].[131]

What are these mysterious lines about? In Jung's eyes, these lines are an expression of what is going on in the *unio mystica* between the alchemical king and queen, or Sol and Luna; in the integration of the shadow; and in the two together with the third becoming a whole. So the 'real meaning' of this episode, or so Jung would have us believe, is what Goethe refers to in his poem as 'higher copulation' — that is to say, 'a union in unconscious identity, which could be compared with the primitive, initial state of chaos, the *massa confusa*, or rather with the state of *participation mystique* where heterogeneous factors merge in an unconscious relationship' (*CW* 16 §462).

A confirmation (of sorts) of Jung's reading can be found if we consider the opening and penultimate stanzas of this poem:

> Tell it no one, only sages,
> For the crowd derides such learning,
> Life I seek through all the ages
> Which for death in flames is yearning.
>
> [...]
> From no weight of distance tiring
> You're in spellbound flight held fast,
> And you are, the light desiring,
> Moth, in fire consumed at last.
> [...].[132]

For here we find, prior and subsequent to the 'higher copulation' that takes the moth or butterfly, the symbol of psyche, to the point of death (and, implicitly, beyond), a moment of intense desire for light, for luminosity, for the flame, of a kind that recalls the ideal of contemplative union between the soul and the One proposed in his Enneads by the third-century Neoplatonist, Plotinus. In its contemplation of the Good or the One, says Plotinus, the soul 'has all the vision that may be — of itself luminous now, filled with intellectual light, become pure light, subtle and weightless', for it has 'become divine, is part of the eternal that is beyond becoming', and even 'like a flame'.[133] Consonant with Goethe's later poem, Plotinus stresses the erotic aspect of this vision, in which the soul may 'feel a rapture within it like that of the lover come to rest in his love'.[134]

Precisely this Neoplatonic dimension of love may be found in the sixteenth-century treatise on the philosophy of love and on love as a means of mystical descent, *The Heroic Frenzies* (*De Gli Eroici Fuori*) (1585) by the Renaissance philosopher, Giordano Bruno (1548–1600), in a verse that might even have served as a source for Goethe in his poem.[135] In this dialogue between two interlocutors, Tansillo explains that philosophical lovers are accompanied by Love who is 'two-fold', and who teaches them 'to contemplate the shadow of the divine beauty', as illustrated in the verse:

> If the butterfly wings its way to the sweet light that attracts it, it is because it knows not that the fire is capable of consuming it. [...] In the light, at the fount, in the bosom of my love's light, I see the flames [...].

Such a lover, says Tansillo, is 'guided by a most keenly felt and only too lucid frenzy, which makes him love that fire more than any other consideration', for 'this fire is the burning desire for divine things'.[136] (This Platonic-inspired understanding of erotic love, according to which a love of the beautiful leads to the love of Beauty itself, is developed in further verses by Bruno.)

At the same time as looking back to the Renaissance, the imagery of Goethe's poem reaches forward to the nineteenth and twentieth centuries. To the nineteenth, for the text surely inspired Nietzsche's short poem, 'Ecce Homo', in the opening poetic prelude to *The Gay Science* (1882):

> Yes, I know from where I came!
> Ever hungry like a flame,
> I consume myself and glow.
> Light grows all that I conceive,
> Ashes everything I leave:
> Flame I am assuredly.[137]

(The following remark in the preface to the second edition [1887] serves as a gloss on this text: 'Life — that means for us constantly transforming all that we are into light and flame'[138].)

And it reaches even further forward to the twentieth century, for Goethe's poem informs the poetics of the French thinker Vladimir Jankélévitch (1903–1985) in an important respect, for it surely lies behind a well-known passage in his book, *Quelque part dans l'inachevé* (1978). (This book, a collection of dialogues with Béatrice Berlowitz, takes its title from a phrase by Rilke, *etwas Unabgeschlossenes*, found in the discussion in his Worpswede essay of the German Impressionist painter Hans am Ende (1864–1918), whose work Rilke compares to music.[139]) One of the starting-points of Jankélévitch's reflections is a phrase by Henri Bergson (1859–1941), where Bergson talks about how philosophical insight or intuition consists in 'something simple, infinitely simple, so extraordinarily simple that the philosopher never manages to say it' (*En ce point est quelque chose de simple, d'infiniment simple, de si extraordinairement simple que le philosophe n'a jamais réussi à le dire*).[140] 'And that is why he has been speaking for the whole of his life' (*Et c'est pourquoi il a parlé toute sa vie*), Bergson adds, prompting Jankélévitch in turn to comment that 'intuition discloses itself and interrupts the sterile coincidence between the individual and himself', explaining that 'what is itself immediate, must, in order to become communicable, assent to a minimum of mediation'.[141] To illustrate his point, Jankélévitch uses the following example:

> The artist plays with what is immediate like the butterfly does with the flame. A game that is acrobatic and perilous! To know the flame intuitively one must not only see how the little tongue of fire dances, but unite inwardly with the fire; to join with the image the existential sensation of being burned. The butterfly cannot help getting as close to the flame as possible, to come within an inch of its scorching heat and, literally, to play with fire; but if, desirous to know even more, it ends up by making the unwise decision to penetrate the flame itself, what will remain of it but a pinch of ash? Whether to know the flame from outside while remaining ignorant of its heat, or whether to know the flame itself by being consumed within it, whether to know without being or to be without knowledge — that is the dilemma.[142]

In a discussion of this passage, the French philosophical commentator Raphaël Enthoven has summarized its thesis as follows: Jankélévitch is arguing that 'artists turn the innate fragility of language into a "dangerous game" to which the weightiness of philosophy, the distance between the word and the thing, is unable to stake a claim'. For Enthoven, 'every great thought is summed up, at some time, in poetry, every beautiful philosophy finds its most accurate translation in a narrative that does away with its clumsiness, which gives soles of wind to its leaden-footedness, which replaces the linear exposition of an argumentation with the brilliance of a metaphor'[143] — characteristics of the very kind of writing in which Nietzsche sought to engage, of course.

For Jankélévitch, this epistemological or existential dilemma faced by the butterfly (and hence by the artist) is one that is susceptible only to aesthetic resolution, for only through or in art is something akin to a miracle achieved. Jankélévitch is thinking of a specific piece of music here, the symphonic poem *La Mer* by Debussy, but he emphasizes that his remarks apply to the aesthetic in general:

> But the miracle — and this miracle is just as much that of writing or of art in general — is that music, more artistic and above all more agile than the butterfly, remains as it were suspended above the chaos, ready to sink into formless noise and into the stupidity of imitative sound effects; on the point of no longer being anything, it succeeds *in extremis* in carrying off its acrobatic act of pulling-up sharp.[144]

Jankélévitch's discussion of the function of art highlights the aesthetic message contained within Goethe's poem. And this aesthetic message is just one of several possible ways of reading the poem, as Serge Meitinger has pointed out.[145]

For instance, it can be read in a Christian way (i.e., 'die as a perishable body, and become an eternal soul!'); it can be read in an evolutionary way (i.e., 'die as an individual in order to become as a species!'); or it can be read in an idealist way (i.e., 'die as an individual and temporal particularity in order to become as a general and eternal idea of Humankind!'). Equally, the poem can be read in an aesthetic, in an ethical, and in a mystical, 'spiritualist', or Hermetic way, and although Meitinger presents and categorizes these readings in this order, describing them as 'the three degrees of an initiation, of an inner purification', one could (in line with the argumentation presented in this book) re-arrange them in a different order. Consequently, one would have the mystical-'spiritual'-Hermetic reading (i.e., 'die as a solitary soul to become a spirit communicating with all the others in the World Spirit!'); then, the ethical reading (i.e., 'die as a man of desire to become a man of form, placed within the limitations of the law!'); and finally, the aesthetic interpretation (i.e., 'die as an object, as a sensory and sensual being in order to become form!').

Within this schema, the different readings of the poem involve a set of different kinds of renunciation. The mystical experience is invested with the gestures of earthly love in order to exalt the highest possible kind of union, involving a kind of metaphysical renunciation that it is difficult to conceive. Yet one can understand this type of renunciation as being in line with a moral one, by means of which the desiring individual accommodates himself or herself to the moral law. Thus the 'daimonic' and undisciplined forces limit and master themselves in a process of interior discipline that leads to the individual becoming more perfectly formed.

This process becomes clearer when we examine the reading that proposes an interpretation of the poem in terms of aesthetic transmutation. On this reading, as formulated by Meitinger, the message of the poem is as follows: 'Let the sensible, sensual object (or being) be elevated by an act of intellection which consumes it and subsumes it under a form!' The intellectual operation which performs an act of abstraction consumes in some sense what is sensory about the object and turns it into something intelligible: but the object is subsumed, not under a *concept*, but under a *form*, thus preserving something of its sensory qualities, which are constructed and structured by the intelligible model, without losing itself in pure abstraction.

Thus what is sensory *becomes form* through this momentary and necessary death, brought about by the flame of abstraction. (Correspondingly, the aesthetic principle — namely, that every feeling sensation must be thought and every thought, felt — dictates the inverse: that every pure intelligible must die to become, in its turn, subject to *form*: a *form*, by definition, always partaking of the sensory world.) Reordering these readings (the mystical, the ethical, and the aesthetic) prompts us in turn to consider another question: does the aesthetic stand above the mystical, or does the mystical stand above the aesthetic? In a sense, this is the question that runs throughout Meitinger's reading of Goethe's *Selige Sehnsucht* (and that runs throughout the entirety of our consideration of Nietzsche and Jung). After all, as Meitinger notes, this multiplicity of possible readings of *Selige Sehnsucht* in no way exhausts the meaning of the poem, which finally reveals itself as an allegory in itself, its own interpretative ashes being ceaselessly reborn as *form* …

The fact that Jung chooses at this point in *The Psychology of the Transference* to adduce this text by Goethe should, however, also give us reason to pause. For the word that rhymes in these lines with 'higher copulation', *höhere Begattung*, is precisely the word 'over-shadowing', *Beschattung*. Goethe's poem is about light, love, life — all experienced to the highest possible intensity — but also about shadow and darkness, 'Darkly over-shadowed waiting' (*umfangen / In der Finsternis Beschattung*), and concludes on the prospect, in the absence of the belief in and practice of 'die and become' (*Stirb und werde!*), of becoming 'just a dismal guest / In earth's dark unseeing' (*nur ein trüber Gast / Auf der dunklen Erde*). Is there a link between the shadow (*Schatten*) of the beauty of the superman (*des Übermenschen Schönheit*) and the 'overshadowing' (*Beschattung*) of *Selige Sehnsucht*? And if so, what is it?

At this point, we may wish to pause. Fifteenth and sixteenth-century alchemical texts? The poetry of Johann Wolfgang von Goethe? Twentieth-century French philosophy of aesthetics? Have we not moved a long way away from Nietzsche's *Zarathustra* and the discourse 'On the Blissful Islands'? In some senses — chronological ones — yes, we have; in other respects — imagistic, conceptual, intertextual — no, we have not. After all, surely there is an allusion to the title of *Selige*

Sehnsucht in the title of a chapter in Part Three of *Zarathustra*, entitled *Von der grossen Sehnsucht* (or 'Of the Great Longing')?[146] Indeed, the word *Sehnsucht* recurs repeatedly in *Zarathustra*: in his Prologue, when Zarathustra declares: 'I love the great despisers, for they are the great venerators and arrows of longing [*Pfeile der Sehnsucht*] for the other bank. [...] I love him who loves his virtue: for virtue is will to downfall and an arrow of longing [*ein Pfeil der Sehnsucht*]. [...] Alas! The time is coming when man will no more shoot the arrow of his longing out over mankind [...]';[147] in 'Of the Land of Culture', when Zarathustra laments: 'Alas, whither shall I climb now with my longing? [*Ach, wohin soll ich nun noch steigen mit meiner Sehnsucht!*]';[148] at the conclusion of his vision of the shepherd and the snake in 'Of the Vision and the Riddle', where Zarathustra confesses: 'And now a thirst consumes me, a longing that is never stilled. / My longing for this laughter consumes me [*nun frisst ein Durst an mir, eine Sehnsucht, die nimmer stille wird. / Meine Sehnsucht nach diesem Lachen frisst an mir*]';[149] and in 'Of Old and New Law-Tables', when Zarathustra announces in §2, 'Thus from out of me cried and laughed my wise desire, which was born on the mountains, a wild wisdom, in truth! — my great desire with rushing wings [*Meine weise Sehnsucht schrie und lachte also aus mir, die auf Bergen geboren ist, eine wilde Weisheit wahrlich! — meine grosse flügelbrausende Sehnsucht*]', and in §28, 'What of fatherland! Our helm wants to fare *away*, out to where our *children's land* is! Out, away, more stormy than the sea, storms our great longing [*Was Vaterland! Dorthin will unser Steuer, wo unser Kinder-Land ist! Dorthinaus, stürmischer als das Meer, stürmt unsre grosse Sehnsucht! —*]'.[150] And in 'Of the Three Evils', Nietzsche explicitly creates a pun on Goethe's phrase when he speaks, not of *selige Sehnsucht*, but *selige Selbstsucht* — 'glorious selfishness'.[151]

Indeed, the conclusion of Zarathustra's discourse in 'On the Blissful Islands' becomes susceptible to a more 'spiritual' interpretation when Goethe's poem, *Selige Sehnsucht*, is regarded as functioning as an intertext. For in Goethe's poem there is also an allusion to a theological tradition, in which the image of the 'overshadowing' of Mary at the conception of Christ (as found in the gospel account) is regarded as an indication of the indwelling of the Holy Spirit.

The 'Overshadowing' of Mary: Indwelling of the Holy Spirit

What would it have been like to be present at the Annunciation? What was this miraculous encounter between Gabriel and Mary really like? (Then again: when exactly did it take place? According to ancient tradition, the Annunciation took place on 25 March, the day on which the liturgical feast of this great mystery is celebrated, but also the date to which ancient martyrologies assign the creation of Adam, the fall of Lucifer, the immolation of Isaac, the passing of Israel through the Red Sea, and the Crucifixion of Christ; according to some authorities, it took place at the hour of midnight; according to others, in the ninth hour, i.e., from two to three in the afternoon.)

For one answer to the question: 'what was the Annunciation really like?', we can turn to the *Mystery Sonatas* (sometimes called the *Rosary Sonatas*) by the

Bohemian-Austrian composer Heinrich Ignaz Franz von Biber (1644–1704), in which there is a remarkable acoustic depiction of the Annunciation, the first 'mystery' in this cycle.[152] In the praeludium, we hear the rustling of wings as Gabriel floats in front of Mary, over a long pedal note in D; when he addresses her, the bass moves down to a low A; and when he speaks to her a second time, the bass moves, this time from a low A to a high B flat. In the aria and variations, centred on a bass theme of ten notes, we hear Mary's consent to God's plan; while in the astonishing finale, a final phrase of three descending thirds (high D, B flat; middle D, B flat, low D, B flat) represents the Trinity, descending in its Third Person, the Holy Spirit: and a high, shivering trill offers a musical depiction of the precise moment of Christ's conception.

Biber's musical picture follows faithfully the account as it is found in the Gospel of St Luke:

> And in the sixth month, the Angel Gabriel was sent from God into a city of Galilee, called Nazareth, to a virgin espoused to a man whose name was Joseph, of the house of David; and the name of the virgin was Mary. And the Angel being come in, said to her: Hail, full of grace, the Lord is with thee: Blessed art thou among women. But she having heard, was troubled at his saying, and thought with herself what manner of salutation this should be. And the Angel said to her: Fear not, Mary, for thou hast found grace with God: Behold thou shalt conceive in thy womb, and shalt bring forth a Son, and thou shalt call his name, Jesus. […] And Mary said to the Angel: How shall this be done, because I know not man? And the Angel answering, said to her: The Holy Ghost shall come upon thee, and the power of the most High shall overshadow thee. And therefore also the Holy which shall be born of thee, shall be called the Son of God. […] And Mary said: Behold the handmaid of the Lord, be it done to me according to thy word. And the Angel departed from her.
>
> (Luke 1: 26–31, 34–35, 38)

In St Luke's account of the Annunciation, the archangel Gabriel appears to Mary and, after his angelic salutation, he tells her of how the Incarnation is to come about: 'The Holy Spirit will come upon you, and the power of the Most High will cover you with its shadow' (Luke 1: 35, NJB). Here the image of the shadow, *et virtus Altissimi obumbrabit tibi* (as the Latin Vulgate has it), recalls several earlier episodes in the biblical story: first, the cloud as a manifestation of divine presence that guides the Israelites through the desert (see Exodus, 13: 22; Exodus 14: 19–20); second, the cloud that descends upon the mountain in the theophany on Mount Sinai (see Exodus, 19: 16; 20: 19–21); and third, the cloud that covers the Tent of Witness (see Exodus 40: 32). In line with this third episode, we are to understand that Mary represents the new Ark of the Covenant. (For there are significant parallels between the manifestation of the visible Presence of Yahweh, the Shekhinah Glory, manifests itself in the Holy of Holies — 'The cloud covered the tabernacle of the testament, and the glory of the Lord filled it' [Exodus 40: 32; cf. 3 Kings 8: 10] — and the 'overshadowing' of Mary — 'The Holy Ghost shall come upon thee, and the power of the most High shall overshadow thee'.)

Not surprisingly, Luke's account prompted much reflection and comment from Patristic commentators in the Orthodox and Catholic traditions.[153] In Greek, the word for 'overshadow' is *episkiasei*, the same word for a cloud that is used in the account of the Transfiguration of Jesus (Luke 9: 34; cf. Matthew 17: 5; Mark 9: 7). But what, in the context of the Annunciation, does the term imply? According to the Flemish Jesuit and biblical exegete, Cornelius a Lapide (1567–1637), the metaphor of overshadowing is susceptible to explanation in at least eight different ways.

First, the term 'overshadow' means to produce a body — and hence a shadow — within. In his *Moralia in Job*, St Gregory the Great (c. 540–604) reasoned that 'a shadow is formed by light and body', and so 'because the Incorporeal Light was in her womb to be made corporeal, to her, who conceived the incorporeal for corporality, it is said, *The power of the Highest shall overshadow thee*; i.e., the Incorporeal Light of the Divine Nature shall in thee take the corporeal substance of Human Nature'. In other words, 'because a shadow is caused in no other way than by a light and a body', 'the incorporal Light assumed a body in her womb'.[154] Similarly, in his *Homilies on Joshua*, the Church Father Origen (c. 184/185–c. 253/254) contrasts this first 'coming of Christ in lowliness' with his other, 'expected in glory', citing the words of Jeremiah in his *Lamentations* in relation to 'this first coming in the flesh', 'The breath of our mouth, Christ the Lord, is taken in our sins, to whom we said: Under thy shadow shall we live among the Gentiles' (Lamentations 5: 20).[155] For Origen, we are to understand how 'many things are dimly shadowed at his first coming, the completion and even perfection of which will be consummated by the second coming'.[156]

Second, for St Ambrose (c. 340–397) in the fifth of his *Homilies on Psalm 118*, the shadow refers to this present, mortal life — a shadow of the true life of eternity — given by the Holy Spirit to Christ.[157] Third, for several writers the image of the shadow makes a point about sexuality. For Ambrose, the passage in the First Epistle to the Corinthians where St Paul recalls that 'our fathers were all under the cloud, and all passed through the sea: and all in Moses were baptized, in the cloud, and in the sea' (1 Cor. 10: 1–2) could be read, in conjunction with Gabriel's announcement of how the Holy Spirit overshadowed Mary, to refer to 'a good cloud which cooled the fires of carnal passions'.[158] For St Gregory in his *Moralia in Job*, the shadow referred to 'this cooling of the soul', to 'the cooling of the mind from the heat of carnal thoughts',[159] while for St Augustine in his letter to Dardanus, a former Prefect of the province of Gaul, the shadow was a testament to the sinlessness of Christ's conception, for the Virgin Mary 'burned with no heat of this concupiscence in conceiving her holy offspring under such a shadow'.[160]

Fourth, in *Quaestiones Veteris et Novi Testamenti*, traditionally attributed to St Augustine (354–430) (but now ascribed to Ambrosiaster, the anonymous writer of a commentary on the Epistles of St Paul), Gabriel's announcement can be read as meaning that, in overshadowing Mary, the Most High would adjust itself to her, as a shadow adapts itself to a body, for no human weakness could contain its full force and power.[161] Fifth, in his treatise *On the Trinity*, St Hilary of Poitiers (c. 300–c. 386) explained the effect the overshadowing had on the Virgin herself: for while 'the Holy Ghost, descending from above, hallowed the Virgin's womb, and breathing therein […] mingled Himself with the fleshly nature of man', the power of the Most High 'overshadowed' Mary, 'lest through weakness of the human structure failure should ensue'. This remedy was achieved by 'strengthening her feebleness in semblance of a cloud cast round her', so that 'the shadow, which was the might of God, might fortify her bodily frame to receive the productive power of the Spirit'.[162] (Further on in this chapter of his treatise, Hilary emphasized the special nature of 'the glory of the conception':

> The inward reality is widely different from the outward appearance; the eye sees one thing, the soul another. A virgin bears; her child is of God. An Infant wails; angels are heard in praise. There are coarse swaddling clothes; God is being worshipped.[163]

Consequently, the Magi have to abandon their 'mystic rites of vain philosophy', in order to accede to a *true* mystical vision.

Sixth, in his *Oration of the Nativity of Christ*, St Gregory of Nyssa (c. 335–c. 395), the youngest of the Cappadocian Fathers, suggests that, as we recognize an object from its shadow or its silhouette, so we recognize Christ's divinity from his humanity. In his gloss on the 'ineffable words' about the overshadowing of Mary, Gregory exclaims:

> Oh, that blessed womb, which on account of its exceeding purity attracted to itself the good things of the soul! […] "Christ" is "the power of God, and the wisdom of God." Thus, the Wisdom of the Most High God, which is Christ, takes form in her virginity through the coming of the Holy Spirit. For, just as a shadow assumes the same shape as the body that precedes it, so also the character and the traits of the Divinity of the Son will be manifested in the power of Him Who is to be born, the image, seal, adumbration, and effulgence of the Prototype being shown through His display of miracle-working.[164]

Seventh, on the account of Cornelius Jansen (1585–1638) and Francisco de Toledo (Toletus) (1532–1596), the phrase about the overshadowing means that the power of the Most High shall embrace Mary and make her fruitful, as a man 'overshadows a woman' and makes her fruitful through the act of generation, an interpretation Cornelius a Lapide rejects as 'too crude' and 'immodest to chaste ears'.[165] (In the context of Goethe's poem, *Selige Sehnsucht*, however, such a reading is by no means too crude or immodest.)

Finally, Cornelius a Lapide himself suggests that the phrase 'to overshadow' means that the power of the Most High will cover Mary 'as with a veil', i.e., it will 'secretly work a mighty, mysterious operation in her', for it will be so mysterious that no one, neither a man nor an angel, can 'penetrate into' or 'comprehend' it:

> For in the Old Testament the invisible, incomprehensible power of God is usually represented — or rather covered and veiled — as a shadow or a misty cloud; for the angel contrasts this spiritual shadow of the Holy Ghost with the carnal marital embrace. As if to say: The power of God, like a most secret, most chaste shadow, shall work in thee that which usually the husband does carnally; namely it will make you fruitful and pregnant and the mother of God. For, first, it will form in thee the perfect humanity of Christ; and, secondly, it will unite the same in a certain ineffable manner to the Person of the Word.[166]

Noting the correspondence between the Greek, *episkian*, 'to overshadow', and the Hebrew word *innen*, 'to cover with a cloud' (or 'to rain upon'), Cornelius a Lapide suggests that, just as the cloud pours down rain and makes the earth fruitful by 'overshadowing' it, so the power of the Most High 'overshadowed' Mary and made her fruitful. In this respect, the image has both Judaic and pagan overtones: on the one hand, one thinks of Psalm 71 (72): 'He shall come down like upon the fleece: and as showers falling gently upon the earth' (Psalm 71 (72): 6), with its allusion to the fleece of Gideon (Judges 6: 36–40); on the other, one thinks of how, according to Greek legends, Jupiter turns into a golden shower and glides into Danae, who gives birth to Perseus.[167]

In turn, the manner of Christ's conception gave rise in the Patristic tradition to a similarly intense interest in a whole host of related issues. How was Christ born? Remembering how Mary conceived him 'without concupiscence', many concluded that she gave birth to Christ while remaining a virgin: she gave birth without pain, without blood, and (needless to say) without a midwife. (According to St Basil of Caesarea, as the rays of the sun penetrate glass, so Christ was born from the closed womb of the Virgin.[168] 'Like light through clear glass', Basil said in a homily on the solemnity of the Epiphany, 'the power of the Godhead shone through that human body for those whose inner eye was pure'.[169] Indeed, the Virgin Mary herself is said to have told St Bridget of Sweden that when Christ was born of her, 'he came forth' from her 'untouched virginal womb' with 'an indescribable feeling of exultation and a wonderful swiftness'[170].) From the pseudepigraphical *Ascension of Isaiah* (late first to third century), one learns that Mary gave birth before reaching the full term of her pregnancy — miraculously, after only two months. Even more miraculously, while alone she suddenly finds a small child beside her, and her womb returns to its state prior to conception.[171]

Such considerations then naturally led, in theological circles, to other questions. Was there an afterbirth? Saints Augustine, Epiphanius, Cyprian, and (in a *Synodical Letter* read out at the Sixth Ecumenical Council, held in Constantinople in 680–681), Saint Sophronius of Jerusalem — all concur that Mary's parturition was perfectly 'pure' (*virginitas in partu*), and there was no blood or afterbirth. (Nevertheless, after forty days Mary went to the Temple for her ritual purification, or so St Luke records: the significance of this gesture naturally gave rise to much debate.) Francisco de Toledo went so far as to wonder: if the Virgin Mary remained a virgin before, during, and after birth, did she ever have a menstrual period? (Because she was free from all concupiscence and all sin, Toletus concluded, she did not[172].)

The term 'overshadow' — *obumbratio* — ἐπισκιάζω — is thus rich in associations of all kinds. Today they might strike us as bizarre, perverse, even obscene: but they reflect an immense struggle to come to terms with the doctrine of the Incarnation, and an attempt to think through its theological implications in a systematic way. Here, however, I want to concentrate on an important biblical tradition associating the divine, not just with a cloud, albeit with a bright cloud of glory, but with darkness — indeed, 'gross darkness', as Isaiah puts it (Isaias 60: 2). This darkness is not simply, as in the passage from Isaiah, something external that 'covers the earth, and [...] the people', but a darkness *out of which* God speaks, as in the accounts in Exodus and Deuteronomy of the theophany on Sinai (Exodus 20: 19–21; Deut. 4: 11–12; Deut. 5: 22), in the epiphanies as described in the Psalms (Psalm 17[18]: 9–14; Psalm 96 [97]: 2–4), or in the apocalyptic visions of Joel and Zephaniah (Joel 2: 2–11; Sophonias 1: 14–16).

In Exodus, God promises Moses, 'Lo now will I come to thee in the darkness of a cloud' (Exodus 19: 9), while in Deuteronomy Moses recalls how, as he looked up from the foot of Mount Horeb, 'there was darkness, and a cloud, and obscurity' (Deut. 4: 11). In his psalm of thanksgiving to God for deliverance from his enemies, David describes how the Lord 'bowed the heavens, and came down, and darkness was under his feet', and how 'he made darkness his covert, his pavilion around him: dark waters in the clouds of the air' (Psalm 17[18]: 10, 12); in a psalm meditating on Israel's past, it is recalled how, after the crossing of the Red Sea, 'great was the noise of the waters: the clouds sent out a sound' (Psalm 76[77]: 18); in a psalm for the Feast of Tabernacles, Yahweh himself reminds the people of Israel of how, at the theophany on Mount Horeb, 'I heard thee in the secret place of tempest' (Psalm 80[81]: 8); while in another psalm praising the triumph of Yahweh, David says that 'clouds and darkness are round about him' (Psalm 96[97]: 2). In the masterpiece of biblical wisdom literature, the Book of Job, we are told of God that 'the clouds are his covert, and he doth not consider our things, and he walketh about the poles of heaven' (Job 22: 14).

(We find a similar set of motifs in pagan literature, where the classical poets represent Jupiter as surrounded by clouds and darkness. In his *Works and Days*, Hesiod relates how the 'guardians of mortal men' roam 'everywhere over the earth, clothed in mist', later associating with Zeus these 'thrice ten thousand spirits, watchers of mortal men', who 'keep watch on judgements and deeds of wrong as they roam, clothed in mist, all over the earth'.[173] And in the *Iliad*, Homer uses the metaphors, 'as when from the towering heights of a great mountain Zeus / who gathers the thunderflash stirs the cloud dense upon it'; 'as when a cloud goes deep into the sky from Olympos / through the bright upper air when Zeus brings on the hurricane'; and 'as underneath the hurricane all the black earth us burdened / on an autumn day, when Zeus sends down the most violent waters / in deep rage against mortals when they stir him to anger', to describe how Patroklos falls upon the Trojans.[174] Similarly, in the *Æneid* Virgil tells of how Æneas and his companions are led away, protected by a shadow, by his mother, the goddess Venus: 'They march, obscure; for Venus kindly shrouds / With mists their persons, and involves in clouds, / That, thus unseen, their passage none might stay, / Or force to tell the causes of their way'.[175])

In the Third Book of Kings the wise king Solomon is prompted to recall that God himself says that he will 'dwell in thick darkness' (3 Kings 8: 12; cf. 2 Paralipomenon 6: 1), echoing God's earlier promise to Moses and to Aaron regarding ceremonial in the sanctuary (Leviticus 16: 2). Indeed, it is because God dwells in darkness that, in the eighth century BCE (or later, according to modern biblical scholarship), the prophet Isaiah famously describes God as a *deus absconditus*, as a 'hidden god' (Isaias 45: 15) — a striking phrase that caught the attention of numerous theological thinkers, from Clement of Alexandria[176] to Nicolas of Cusa (in his *Dialogue on the Hidden God*), Luther (in his *Heidelberg Disputation* and in *The Bondage of the Will*), and Pascal.[177] And in the book of Jeremiah, Yahweh uses the image of darkness to convey a vision of exile: 'Give ye glory to the Lord your God, before it be dark, and before your feet stumble upon the dark mountains: you shall look for light, and he will turn it into the shadow of death, and into darkness' (Jeremias 13: 16); in the book of Amos, the Day of the Lord is described as 'darkness, and not light', as 'obscurity, and no brightness in it' (Amos 5: 18, 20).

(Similarly, in the Hermetic or alchemical tradition, the *lapis* or the Philosophers' Stone is conceived as light *and* dark, as Jung was swift to point out [*CW* 12 §140]. In the *Tractatus aureus* in the *Ars chemica*, Venus says: 'I beget the light, and the darkness is not of my nature [...] therefore nothing is better or more worthy of veneration than the conjunction of myself and my brother' [*Iam Venus ait. Ego genero lumen, nec tenebrae meae naturae sunt* [...] *Me igitur & fratri meo iunctis nihil melius ac venerabilius*], and in the *Rosarium philosophorum*, almost those very words are attributed by Hermes to the *lapis*:

> Understand, you sons of wisdom, that this precious Stone crieth out saying, defend me and I will defend thee, give me my right that I may help thee, for Sol is mine and the beams thereof are my inward parts; but Luna is proper to me, and my light excelleth all light, and my goods are higher than all goods. I give much riches and delights to men desiring them, and when I seek after anything they acknowledge it, I make them understand and I cause them to possess divine strength. *I engender light, but my nature is darkness.* [...] Therefore I and my son being joined together, there can be nothing made more better nor more honourable in the whole world.[178]

Correspondingly, Jung observes, in the Gnostic tradition the Monogenes (or 'only-begotten child') mentioned in a Coptic Gnostic treatise (and identifiable as the Son of God) is referred to as a 'dark light': 'This is the Only-Begotten [*monogenis*] who is hidden in the Sētheus [*setheus*]: "The Dark Light" have they called him, because through the excess of his Light they themselves were darkened'.[179] For Jung, this Gnostic figure is an analogous figure to the 'black sun' or *sol niger* of the alchemical tradition[180].)

And this notion of the dark, obscure, or hidden God continues and persists into the present day. In an address given in his weekly General Audience on 19 December 2012, only a few months before his retirement, the Pope Emeritus Benedict XVI spoke of the Virgin Mary in terms that recapitulate what is at stake in this ancient theological tradition.[181] Here Benedict observed that 'the opening of the soul to God and to his action in faith' includes an element of 'darkness' or 'obscurity' (*oscurità*). His immediate context for this remark is precisely the mystery of the Annunciation and Gabriel's greeting to Mary, 'an invitation to joy, deep joy', but not just joy. For Benedict recalls that, prior to Mary, Abraham's journey of faith had included a moment of great joy in the gift of his son, Isaac, but also a time or period of 'darkness', when he was told to climb Mount Moriah and asked to execute his son. Correspondingly, Mary's faith experienced the joy of the Annunciation, but also passed through the 'darkness' or 'gloom' of the Crucifixion of her son in order to reach the 'light' of the Resurrection. In turn, Benedict argued, the individual believer will not only encounter 'moments of light', but 'passages where God seems absent, when His silence weighs on our hearts and His will does not correspond to ours' — in other words, moments of darkness.

True, Benedict's response to this situation will be different from — will be diametrically opposed to — Nietzsche's, but significantly, Benedict highlights Mary's 'interior attitude' to God's action after the Nativity and the adoration of the shepherds. For when the Gospel tells us that Mary 'kept all these things, pondering them in her heart' (Luke 2: 19), the Greek term used is *symballon*. So she 'kept together' or she 'pieced together' in her heart, one might even say: she 'symbolized' everything that was happening to her. Theology put to one side, this approach to a response to 'darkness' is essentially a *symbolical* one …

Meister Eckhart and Pseudo-Dionysius the Areopagite

Why, one might well ask, does God dwell in darkness? After all, in Psalm 35 (36) David tells Yahweh, 'For with thee is the fountain of life; and in thy light we shall see light' (35 [36]: 10), a line that is interpreted by such Patristic writers as St Ambrose and Theodoret to apply respectively to Christ and to the Holy Spirit. Indeed, in the Psalms, 'the light of the face of God' is a constant theme: 'The Lord is my light and my salvation', says David, 'whom shall I fear?' (26 [27]: 1); in an earlier psalm, he declares: 'The light of thy countenance, O Lord, is signed upon us: thou hast given gladness in my heart' (4: 7); and 'blessed is the people that knoweth jubilation', he says elsewhere, for 'they shall walk, O Lord, in the light of thy countenance' (88 [89]: 16); while Job, reflecting in the midst of his discourses with his comforters, recalls his former happiness, 'when [God's] lamp shined over my head, and I walked by his light in the darkness' (Job 29: 4).

Likewise, in the New Testament the light of God becomes an important theme. In the ecstatic canticle that bursts forth from John the Baptist's father on the occasion of the Precursor's circumcision, Zachariah praises God because, 'through the bowels of [His] mercy', a shining light — 'the Orient, from on high' — 'hath visited us', to 'enlighten them that sit in darkness, and in the shadow of death' (Luke 1: 78–79). Then again, St John tells us that 'God is light, and in him there is no darkness' (1 John 1: 5); the famous prologue to his gospel tells us that 'the light shineth in the darkness, and the darkness did not comprehend it' (John 1: 5), while Christ himself tells the scribes and the pharisees, 'I am the light of the world' (John 8: 12), and St Paul tells Timothy that Christ 'hath immortality, and inhabiteth light inaccessible' (1 Timothy 6: 16). (This passage from Paul to Timothy inspired St Anselm of Canterbury [c. 1033–1109] to explore the dialectic of light and dark.[182]) And in the Epistle to the Hebrews, its author contrasts the theophany on Sinai — 'a mountain that might be touched, and a burning fire, and a whirlwind, *and darkness*, and tempest' (Hebrews 12: 18; my emphasis) — with Mount Sion, 'the city of the living God, the heavenly Jerusalem, and [...] the company of many thousands of angels' (Hebrews 12: 22).

Then again, in his 'catholic' epistle St James argues that God is 'the Father of lights', i.e., both as the maker of the stars and as the source of spiritual light', adding in terms that allude to astronomy — and in a way that, significantly, associates the shadow with change — that in him 'there is no change, nor shadow of vicissitude' (James 1: 17; cf. NJB, NT 1997). (Subsequently this image appealed to such later commentators as Cyril of Alexandria [c. 376–444] and Hildegard of Bingen [1098–1779].[183]) Elsewhere St Peter, in his First Epistle, describes believers as 'a chosen generation, a royal priesthood, a holy nation, a purchased people, that you may declare [God's] virtues, who hath called you out of darkness into his admirable light' (1 Peter 2: 9). Here Peter is recollecting the promise made by Yahweh in the Book of Isaiah: 'And I will lead the blind into the way which they know not: [...] I will make darkness light before them' (Isaias 42: 16). Subsequently, in the Neoplatonic tradition to which Christianity was also to lay claim, God is presented in luminous terms as pure light, as a divine radiance. As Pierre Grimes has pointed out, Platonic philosophy sought the realization and vision of what Socrates calls 'the most brilliant light of being'; while Plotinus maintained, for instance, that the soul could experience the One as pure light or divine radiance.[184]

So what lies behind the association, found in Isaiah and elsewhere, between God and darkness, between God and being 'hidden', between divinity and obscurity? For an answer to the question as to why God might be (in) darkness, we can turn to that extraordinary German theologian, philosopher, and mystic, Eckhart of Hochheim (c. 1260–c. 1327), for whom the *intellectus inquantum intellectus* (absolute intellectuality) of God is, indeed, light.[185] Yet Meister Eckhart also relates this metaphor of light to the theme of the *deus absconditus*, the hidden god and the unnameable god. According to Eckhart, God is inaccessible light, entirely contained within itself, and because it does not emerge from itself, it is therefore *dark*.[186] At numerous points in his sermons and treatises, Eckhart insists on this point, and it is worth considering some of the cases where he does.

In his sixth sermon (*Intravit Jesus in templum dei …*), for instance, Eckhart adopts the simplistic position that 'light and darkness cannot exist together', and because 'God is the truth, He is the light in himself'. So, with reference to the episode of the expulsion of the dealers, Eckhart says that 'when God enters the Temple He drives out ignorance, which is darkness, and reveals Himself in light and in truth'.[187] Here Eckhart operates with a simple opposition of darkness and light; elsewhere, however, his argumentation is far more complex.

In sermon 53 (*Ave, gratia plena …*), for instance, he talks about 'the hidden darkness of the eternal Godhead', which is 'unknown and never has been known and never shall be known', where 'God abides […] unknown in Himself'.[188] (In another sermon, number 83 [*Haec dicit dominus …*], and with specific reference to Moses' entrance into the cloud after his ascent of Mount Horeb, Eckhart repeats this position.[189]) Then again, in sermon 51 (*Homo quidam nobilis …*), Eckhart describes 'the final end of being' as 'the darkness or the nescience' — i.e., ignorance or lack of knowledge — 'of the hidden Godhead whose light illumines it',[190] referring to the namelessness of God in the episode of Moses and the burning bush (Exodus 3: 14)[191] and the hiddenness of God in Isaiah (45: 15).

In other sermons, however, Eckhart talks about God precisely in terms of light. In sermon 94 (*Homo quidam erat dives …*), for instance, he takes as his starting-point the parable of the rich man and Lazarus, an observation by St Gregory the Great, and the *Liber de causis* (The Book of Causes), also known as *De lumine luminum* (The Light of Lights),[192] a summary of the *Elements of Theology*, the great systematic work of Proclus. (In turn, Proclus' conception of light draws on the myth of Er, narrated by Socrates in book 10 of the *Republic*, in which it is related how Er journeys to the world beyond, and witnesses, 'extended from above throughout the heaven and the earth, a straight light like a pillar, most nearly resembling the rainbow, but brighter and purer', in the middle of which the spindle of Necessity can be seen.[193]) Eckhart emphasizes the 'unknowable nature' of God and His 'hidden stillness', supporting this position with Proclus' understanding of God as 'superessential and beyond extolling, superrational and beyond comprehension'.[194]

In sermon 30 (*Beatus es, Simon bar Jona …*), Eckhart remarks that 'blessed is that man who diligently listens to what God is saying to him, and he will be directly exposed to the ray of divine light', because 'the divine light shines directly above him'. Of this divine light, Eckhart says that it is 'so pure and transcendent and lofty that all lights are darkness and nothing compared with this light'. Indeed, 'all creatures, as such, are as nothing; but when they are illumined from above with the light from which they receive their being, they are something'.[195] Yet he also draws on Albert Magnus, the great Dominican friar and bishop of Cologne in the thirteenth century, who is said to have described God as 'flowing forth', in a way entirely consistent with Neoplatonic thinking, and flowing into things in general in three ways: with 'being', with 'life', and with 'light'.[196]

Is, then, there a problem here? God dwells in darkness, and yet he is light: surely this is a contradiction? The answer to this question must be 'no', as becomes clear from sermon 19 (*Surrexit autem Saulus de terra …*), a long exposition of the moment, narrated in the Acts of the Apostles, when Saul (soon to become Paul), during his conversion on the road to Damascus, 'arose from the ground, and his eyes being open, *he saw nothing*' (Acts 9: 8; my emphasis). It means, to take in reverse order Eckhart's analysis, first, that when Paul saw God, he saw all things as nothing; second, that in all things he saw nothing but God; third, that when he got up, what he saw was nothing but God; and fourth, and formulated in a typically Eckhartian paradox, that 'when he rose up from the ground with open eyes he saw Nothing, and the Nothing was God', for when Paul saw God, St Luke (the author of the Acts of Apostles) calls that Nothing.[197]

In his development of this thought, Eckhart explains that 'the light that is God flows out and darkens every light'.[198] And because 'the light that is God is unmingled, no admixture comes in', it brings about a special kind of sight, or more precisely a special kind of blindness: 'In seeing nothing, [Paul] saw the divine Nothing […] He who sees nothing else and is blind, sees God'.[199] This seeing, or this blindness, brings about an effect in the believer. Hence, St Paul tells the Ephesians in his letter to them: 'For you were heretofore darkness, but now light in the Lord' (Ephesians 5: 8), a text that was another occasion for a sermon by Meister Eckhart (sermon 93; *Eratis enim alaquando tenebrae, nunc autem lux in Domino*).[200]

Correspondingly, in sermon 95 (*Videns Jesus turbas, ascendit in montem*), in which Meister Eckhart recapitulates St Augustine's doctrine about three kinds of knowing — i.e., 'bodily', 'mental', and 'in the interior mind, which knows without image or likeness'[201] — we find further commentary on the prologue to the Gospel of John, 'God is a true light that shines in darkness' (cf. John 1: 9 and 5), and the idea that God is LIGHT and the creature is NIGHT: 'What I know of God, that is light: what touches creatures is night'.[202] Here Eckhart, in a sense, leads us into darkness, inasmuch as he urges us to know nothing of creatures, for we must become blind: 'A man should cling to nothing and hang on to nothing, be blind and know nothing of creatures'.[203] (This argument is entirely in line with his position in sermon 19, where he maintained that 'he who would see God must be blind').[204] This blinding is an inevitable consequence of the nature of the light of God: 'He is a light that blinds us', which means 'a light of such nature that it is uncomprehended'.[205] In turn, 'the blinding of the soul means that she knows nothing and is aware of nothing', and this 'third "darkness" is best of all'.[206]

In so arguing, Meister Eckhart is restating a position maintained by the unknown mystical theologian and philosopher, called Pseudo-Dionysius the Areopagite (late fifth century to early sixth century), an authority whom Eckhart cites on numerous occasions. In *On the Celestial Hierarchy* (Chapter 3, §2), Pseudo-Dionysius explains that God is a light *beyond light*: 'The Divine blessedness […] is full of invisible light — perfect, and needing no perfection: cleansing, illuminating, and perfecting, yea, rather a holy purification, and illumination, and perfection — above purification, above light, preeminently perfect, self-perfect source and cause of every

Hierarchy, and elevated pre-eminently above every holy thing'.[207] To ordinary eyes, this light beyond light appears as darkness, just as the effect on the eye of the most intense light is — literally — blinding.

(In turn, Pseudo-Dionysius is drawing on a central idea in the Platonic and Neoplatonic tradition, reflected in a remark made by Damascius (c. 480–c. 550), known as 'the last of the Neoplatonists'. In his treatise *On First Principles*, Damascius noted, with reference to Plato's explanation of the transcendent nature of the Good using the analogy of the sun in book 6 of the *Republic* (507b–509c), that 'this highest god is seen afar off as it were obscurely; and, if you approach nearer, he is beheld still more obscurely; and lastly, he takes away the ability of perceiving other objects', and so: 'He is, therefore, truly an incomprehensible and inaccessible light, and is profoundly compared, by Plato, to the sun: upon which the more attentively you look, the more you will be darkened and blinded; and will only bring back with you eyes stupefied with excess of light'.[208] According to this view, precisely the transcendence of the One explains why the Pythagoreans applied such terms as 'obscurity', 'without illumination', and 'darkness' to its unity. After all, a phrase used by Damascius, the 'thrice-unknown darkness', had been employed by the Egyptians to describe the First Principle, as a way of signifying how — to the limited human intelligence — the dazzling radiance of the super-essential light produces an effect so blinding that nothing can be seen.[209])

Equally, in the context of the passage under discussion from *Thus Spoke Zarathustra*, it is significant that Pseudo-Dionysius the Areopagite elsewhere emphasizes the connection between darkness and divinity. In the opening exclamatory paragraph of his *Mystical Theology*, Pseudo-Dionysius prays to the Trinity: 'Lead us up beyond unknowing and light, up to the farthest, highest peak of mystic scripture, where the mysteries of God's Word lie simply, absolute and unchangeable in the brilliant darkness of a hidden silence', for 'amid the deepest shadow they pour overwhelming light on what is most manifest'.[210] Pseudo-Dionysius expresses the hope that his correspondent, Timothy, will be 'uplifted to the ray of the divine shadow which is above everything that is', thus setting up a parallel between Timothy and Moses's ascent of Mount Horeb that informs the rest of this chapter in his *Mystical Theology*.

Drawing on Exodus, which tells us: 'And the people stood afar off, but Moses went to the dark cloud where God was' (Exodus 20: 21), and appealing to the authority of the apostle St Bartholomew, Pseudo-Dionysius praises those all those 'who pass beyond the summit of ever holy ascent [...] and who plunge into the darkness where, as scripture proclaims, there dwells the One who is beyond all things'.[211] The model proposed here is, of course, Moses, who at Mount Horeb 'hears the many-voiced trumpets', 'sees the many lights, pure and with rays streaming abundantly', but 'breaks free of them, away from what sees and is seen', and 'plunges into the truly mysterious darkness of unknowing'.[212] Pseudo-Dionysius goes on to pray that he and Timothy might, too, 'come to this darkness so far above light', in order to 'know, unseeing and unknowing, that which lies beyond all vision and knowledge'.[213] He goes on to speak of such knowing as leading to *agnosia*, to 'know[ing] that unknowing which itself is hidden from all those possessed of knowing amid all beings, so that we may see above being that darkness concealed from all the light among beings', or what other translators call 'the super-bright gloom' that leads to the 'superessential gloom'.[214]

(Inspired by Pseudo-Dionysius, other mystical writers describe the experience of ecstasy as being 'clouded', or 'veiled', or 'in darkness'. The twelfth-century theologian Richard of St-Victor [d. 1173], for instance, is working entirely within a Dionysian framework when he relates that the 'ecstasy of mind' that occurs during the 'contemplation of divine things' takes place behind 'a dense veil of forgetting' and 'as though in the middle of a cloud'; indeed, mystical ecstasy 'means the same thing as to enter the cloud and to penetrate within the veil'.[215] And an English mystical treatise of the fourteenth century, whose authorship remains unknown, is itself entitled *The Cloud of Unknowing*.[216])

In his discussion of Exodus, Pseudo-Dionysius (and the writers who subsequently follow him) can be seen to be drawing on a tradition centred on the notion of divine darkness that goes back to the Hellenistic Jewish philosopher, Philo (c. 20 BCE–c. 50 CE), to the early Christian theologian, Clement of Alexandria (c. 150–c. 215), and to St Gregory of Nyssa. In his writings, Philo interpreted the Hebrew scriptures in an essentially allegorical way, and accordingly he read the biblical account of how Moses 'entered into the darkness where God was' to mean he entered 'into the invisible, and shapeless, and incorporeal world, the essence, which is the model of all existing things, where he beheld things invisible to mortal nature'; in so doing, Philo added, Moses 'established himself as a *most beautiful* and God-like work, to be *a model* for all those who were inclined to imitate him'.[217] In his *Stromata* (or *Miscellanies*), Clement interpreted the darkness Moses entered as representing the paradox of the inaccessibility, yet omnipresence, of God. He argued that 'the power of God is always present, in contact with us, in the exercise of inspection, of beneficence, of instruction', and so Moses, 'persuaded that God is not to be known by human wisdom, said, "Show me thy glory" [Exodus 33: 18], and into the thick darkness where God's voice was, pressed to enter' — in other words, 'into the inaccessible and invisible ideas respecting Existence'.[218] Thus 'when the Scripture says, "Moses entered into the thick darkness where God was" [Exodus 20: 21], this means to those capable of understanding, that God is invisible and beyond expression by words', for 'the "darkness" — which is, in truth, the unbelief and ignorance of the multitude, obstructs the gleam of truth'.[219] (In this link between darkness and ignorance, Clement is in line with the argument presented by such Neoplatonists as Proclus, for whom darkness is 'a privation of light', just as ignorance is 'the absence of knowledge.[220])

In the fourth century, Gregory of Nyssa drew on biblical, philosophical, and Rabbinic sources to offer an account of the life of the great prophet, and its 'contemplative' significance. In book 1, §46 of *The Life of Moses*, Gregory offers an account of Moses's encounter with Yahweh on Horeb that is essentially mystical:

> Since [Moses] was alone, by having been stripped as it were of the people's fear, he boldly approached the very darkness itself and entered the invisible

things where he was no longer seen by those watching. After he entered the inner sanctuary of the divine mystical doctrine, there, while not being seen, he was in company with the Invisible. He teaches, I think, by the things he did that the one who is going to associate intimately with God must go beyond all that is visible and — lifting up his own mind, as to a mountaintop, to the invisible and incomprehensible — believe that the divine is *there* where the understanding does not reach.[221]

In book 2, Gregory analysed the 'literal history' of Moses in further detail, in order to 'gain some benefit for the virtuous life' (and to develop his own thesis that perfection is to be found in progress itself).[222] Here Gregory tries to solve the apparent contradiction that whereas, in the first theophany — that is, when Yahweh appears to Moses in the burning bush (Exodus 3: 1–6) — 'the Divine was beheld in light', in the theophany on Horeb God is 'seen in darkness'. He does so by pointing out that 'scripture teaches [...] that religious knowledge comes at first to those who receive it as light', but that 'as the mind progresses and, through an ever greater and more perfect diligence, comes to apprehend reality, as it approaches more nearly to contemplation, it sees more clearly what of the divine nature is uncontemplated'.[223] Consequently, to attain perfection one has to go beyond both the senses *and* ordinary, everyday reason: in contemplation one has to 'go out of oneself' at the same time as 'interiorizing' or 'going into' oneself:

> For leaving behind everything that is observed, not only what sense comprehends but also what the intelligence thinks it sees, it keeps on penetrating deeper until by the intelligence's yearning for understanding it gains access to the invisible and the incomprehensible, and there it sees God. This is the true knowledge of what is sought; this is the seeing that consists in not seeing, because that which is sought transcends all knowledge, being separated on all sides by incomprehensibility *as by a kind of darkness.*[224]

Hence, Gregory concludes, when Moses 'grew in knowledge', he declared that he 'had seen God in the darkness', that is, that he 'had come to know that what is divine is beyond all knowledge and comprehension'.[225]

In another work, his commentary on the Lord's Prayer, Gregory of Nyssa returned to this theme. In his second sermon, Gregory develops the contrast, expounded by the New Testament and by other Patristic writers, between Moses and Christ. On the one hand, 'when the great Moses undertook to initiate the Israelites into the Divine mysteries which has been inaugurated on the Mount', they were not brave enough and were 'struck down by all the apparitions, the fire and *the darkness*, the smoke and the trumpets'.[226] On the other, when Jesus Christ 'is bringing us to the Divine Grace', he does not present Mount Sinai 'covered with darkness and smoking with fire', nor 'leave all the assembly behind at the foot of the mountain, granting only to one the ascent to its summit, which [...] is hidden by a darkness completely concealing the glory of God.' On this account, we are led, not to a mountain, but to Heaven itself; we are given, not simply a vision of, but a share in, divine power; and Christ 'does not hide the supernal glory in darkness, making it difficult for those who want to contemplate it', but he 'first illumines *the darkness* by the brilliant light of his teaching' and then 'grants the pure of heart the vision of the ineffable glory of his shining splendour'.[227] What here is only implicit — that the light illuminating this darkness might be just as blinding as the darkness to those whose vision is not equal to this shining splendour and to its ineffable glory — was what Eckhart was determined to work out more explicitly, if remarkably subtly.

So there is a profound theological context to the manner of the conception of Christ through the 'overshadowing' of Mary by the Holy Spirit, and many other early Christian theologians contributed to the development of this tradition. Let us consider two further examples: Origen, some of whose propositions were condemned at the Second Ecumenical Council in Constantinople (and who is not considered a saint), and Proclus of Constantinople (died c. 446/447) — not to be confused with Proclus, the Platonic successor — who *is* a saint in the Orthodox Church. What Origen and Proclus have to say underlines the richness of the theological tradition that links, on the one hand, the shadow, and, on the other, the divine.

In his second homily on *The Song of Songs*, for instance, Origen drew a link between a passage in the Old Testament text and the birth of Jesus in order to argue that, just as the conception of Christ took place through the overshadowing (or indwelling) of the Holy Spirit in Mary, so the birth of Christ took place in every believer. Origen's argument ran as follows. In the first poem in *The Song of Songs*, which consists of a dialogue between two lovers, the beloved says of her lover: 'I sat down under his shadow, whom I desired' (2: 3). Origen constellates this passage with two other texts, from the Lamentations of Jeremiah and from the Book of Isaiah: 'The breath of our mouth, Christ the Lord, is taken in our sins: to whom we said: Under thy shadow we shall live among the Gentiles' (Lamentations 4: 20), and 'The people that walked in darkness, have seen a great light: to them that dwelt in the region of the shadow of death, light is risen' (Isaias 9: 2).

Origen fuses the sense of these two passages: 'at the beginning', he comments, 'we enjoy [...] what may be called a sort of shadow of His majesty', 'so that our passing over is from the shadow of death to the shadow of life'.[228] He went on to argue that 'the birth of Jesus also originated *from* — not *in* — the shadow', and he took Gabriel's announcement to the Mary as the basis for his parallel between the Song of Songs and the prophetic books: 'The birth of Christ took its inception from the shadow; yet not in Mary only did His nativity begin with overshadowing; in you too, if you are worthy, the Word of God is born', concluding with this exhortation: 'See, then, that you may be able to receive His shadow; and, when you have been made worthy of the shadow, His body, from the shadow is born, will in a manner of speaking come to you [...]'.[229]

(Following a similar line of thought, Meister Eckhart opened a sermon given on Christmas Day with the remark, 'Here, in time, we are celebrating the eternal birth which God the Father bore and bears unceasingly in eternity, because this birth is now born in time, in human nature'.[230] Thus Eckhart implies the existence of four different kinds of birth of Christ: eternally, born of God the Father; in historical time, in the form of the Incarnation; in the liturgical time of the celebration of the Feast of the Nativity; and in the historical now, in the soul of the believer; which, in turn, would bring about a fifth birth — our own spiritual rebirth in God.[231])

In the third book of his commentary on the *Song of Songs*, written only a few years before his homilies, Origen's take on this biblical verse had been slightly different. Here he had contrasted two biblical images of the shadow, one negative, one positive: 'the shadow of death', in the famous passage from Isaiah (9:2), echoed in the gospel of Matthew (4: 16),[232] as opposed to the shadow as an anticipation, so that the Jewish Law represents 'a shadow of the good things to come' (instead of 'the very image of the things') (Hebrews 10: 1); the Jewish festivals (the feast of the new moon, the sabbath, etc.) function as 'a shadow of things to come' (Colossians 2: 17), and the Jewish priesthood 'serve[s] unto the example and shadow of heavenly things' (Hebrews 8: 5).[233] Pursuing this thought, originally found in the Apostle Paul and later highlighted by Procopius of Caesarea (c. 500–c. 565) in *his* commentary on the *Song of Songs*, Origen detected 'a certain progress' from 'the shadow of the Law' to 'the shadow of Christ' in a way that emphasized the *necessity* of the shadow:

> Since Christ is the Life and the Truth and the Way, we must first be fashioned in the shadow of the Way and in the shadow of the Life and in the shadow of the Truth, and apprehend in part and in a glass and in a riddle, in order that later on, if we persevere in this Way that is Christ, we may be able to achieve the face-to-face apprehension of those things which formerly we had beheld in the shadow and in a riddle.[234]

Even though their assumptions in regard to theology are diametrically opposed (or are they?),[235] both Origen and Nietzsche find in the shadow a powerful image for something radically new, and have recourse in their use of the shadow and of the idea of the riddle[236] to a motif, dear to St Paul, of seeing through a glass 'in an obscure manner' (1 Corinthians 13: 12).

A couple of centuries or so after Origen, Proclus of Constantinople engaged with the heretical view of Arius (c. 250/256–336) in a famous sermon on the Incarnation given on the Feast of the *Theotokos* (the Greek term for the Virgin Mary as the 'Bearer' or 'Birth-Giver of God'). Arius, of course, had denied that Christ was truly God (or, in theological terms, that the Son was 'consubstantial' with the Father), because he had been 'made' by God, not 'begotten'.[237] For Proclus, this view had to be resisted; and the definition of the Virgin Mary as *theotokos* was a strategic way to do this.

In his sermon, which deserves to be read in full, Proclus placed a text from the New Testament — in this case, a line from the Benedictus and its reference to 'the shadow of death' (Luke 1: 79) — in the context of numerous biblical passages from the epistles of St Paul to the Psalmist and Isaiah. Taking issue with Arius, Proclus declared that '[God] was both with the virgin and of the virgin; by his overshadow-ing, he was with her; by becoming incarnate, he was of her. [...] Do not rend the tunic of the incarnation which is woven from above'.[238] For Proclus, this imagery of weaving could be intermingled — seamlessly, as it were — with the notion of auricular conception. In this same sermon for the Feast of Mary as *theotokos*, Proclus hailed the Virgin as 'the awesome loom of salvation on which the robe of union was mysteriously woven', explaining that:

> [the] weaver was the Holy Spirit, the workman the power that overshad-owed from on high [cf. Luke 1: 35], the wool the ancient fleece of Adam, the fabric the unsullied flesh of a virgin, the shuttle the immeasurable grace of him who wove it, and the craftsman the Word who entered through the ear.[239]

(In the conclusion to this sermon, Proclus found in the manner of Christ's concep-tion further evidence for the perpetual virginity of Mary.[240])

Jung on the *obumbratio* ('Overshadowing') of Mary

So the notion of auricular conception — the conception of Christ through the ear of the Virgin Mary, thus ensuring she remained pure and immaculate — explains how Mary could become pregnant and remain a virgin; while, at the same time, being an idea with enormous symbolic potency, as we shall see. Drawing on cur-rents of Greco-Judaic religious philosophy found in Alexandria and on Gnostic speculation alike, this theological model of explanation argued that, just as God had spoken the world into existence, so the voice of the Most High, in the salutation uttered through the mouth of an angel, caused Mary to conceive — and the Word, the *Logos*, was made flesh; that just as spoken words, addressed to the ear, lodge in the mind and bear fruit, so the Incarnation of Christ, the Divine *Logos*, was similarly accomplished.[241]

According to Augustine in a sermon attributed to him, 'God spoke through the angel and the Virgin conceived by her ear' (*Deus per angelum loquebatur et Virgo per aurem impregnabatur*), and numerous other ecclesiastical writers — from St Ephrem the Syrian (c. 306–373) to Agobard of Lyons (c. 779–840) — support this view.[242] In a verse attributed to St Thomas à Becket, their view is reflected in the lines, 'Rejoice, virgin mother of Christ, / Thou who has conceived by the ear' (*Gaude Virgo, mater Christi, / Quæ per aurem concepisti*), while this miracle is elsewhere recorded in a verse attributed to Walther von der Vogelweide, 'Through her ear she conceived the sweetest one, / Who had entered her and is without end' (*dur ir ôre enpfienc si den viel süezen, / der ie ân anegenge was und muoz ân ende sîn*).[243]

The motif of the ear as simultaneously an aural and genital orifice has, not surprisingly, caught the attention of psychoanalysts and art historians alike. For example, Ernest Jones (1879–1958) devoted a lengthy paper to the motif of the Madonna's conception through the ear.[244] For Jones, a card-carrying Freudian, 'the idea of gaseous fertilization constitutes a reaction to an unusually intense castration-phantasy' and 'one of the most remarkable of the various modes of dealing with the primordial Œdipus situation' (p. 350). Although Jones confesses to being 'impressed by the ingenuity and fine feeling with which an idea so repellent to the adult mind has been transformed into a conception not merely tolerable, but lofty in its grandeur' (p. 355), he comes to the conclusion, however, that 'the Christian myth is perhaps the most gigantic and revolutionary phantasy in history, and its striking characteristic is the completely veiled way in which this phantasy is carried through to success under the guise of sacrificial submission to the Father's will' (p. 356).

In a more recent study, the art historian Barbara Baert has examined several Annunciation scenes in the light of this motif,[245] and (drawing on Jones) she notes various parallels in other cultural traditions, both Islamic and pagan. In the Qu'ran, the account of the conception of Jesus insists on the fact that she retained her chastity (see Surah 21: 91, and Surah 66: 12), while Arabic scholarly commentaries variously interpret this as meaning that Allah sent Jibreel (or Gabriel) to breathe into her — into the opening of her garment, or even actually into her vagina — as a result of which she conceived.[246] A similar link between the breath of the wind and sexual union — but of a rather more violent kind — can be found in the pagan tradition. According to Ovid,[247] for instance, Chloris was abducted by Zephyrus, the god of the west wind, and was raped by him; his brother, Boreas or the north wind, similarly abducted and raped Orithyia, a princess of Athens.

(In *The Greeks and Their Gods*, the Scottish classicist W.K.C. Guthrie [1906–1981] had noted the ancient belief connecting the soul with air or wind. This belief in the kinship of the vital principle with wind or air gave rise to the notion that a female could be impregnated by the wind. Guthrie cites a number of sources, from Homer [who, in the *Iliad*, says that the horses of Achilles were born by their mother Podarge to the wind, Zephyros] to Virgil [who, in his *Georgics*, describes the impregnation of mares by the wind in detail].[248] And in Lucian of Samosata, the god Hephaistos is described as a 'wind-child', because he was conceived parthenogetically by Hera, because she was angry at her Zeus.[249] In addition, Guthrie observes that 'the doctrine that our souls are air, or of a material substance closely akin to air and entering wind-borne into our souls', was 'not the property of any single philosophical school, but antedated all philosophical schools whatsoever': strikingly, it is common to the atomist school of Democritus and the mystical teachings of the Orphic cult alike.[250])

This is just the sort of material that interested Jung, and that he was familiar with the notion of auricular conception is clear from his *Zarathustra* seminar of 4 December 1935, when he cited the line, *Quae per aurem concepisti*, 'Thou who hast conceived by the ear', from the hymn, *Gaude virgo, Mater Christi*, 'Rejoice, virgin mother of Christ' (cf. *SNZ* 1, 732). (Jung raised the intriguing possibility of a link with the unusual conception of Buddha, whose mother became pregnant when she was dreaming of a sacred white elephant.) We find Jung discussing this doctrine on two other occasions: first, in *Transformations and Symbols of the Libido* (1911–1912), when he cited the example of a work called 'The Overshadowing of Mary', a

FIGURE 1.5 *Marienkapelle, Würzburg.* In public domain via Wikimedia Commons.

tempera painting on wood by an early German artist displayed in Erfurt Cathedral, in which 'the conception is represented by a tube or pipe coming down from heaven and passing beneath the skirt of Mary', into which 'flies the Holy Ghost in the form of a dove for the impregnation of the Mother of God'.[251] A similar example can be found in the Annunciation scene on the tympanon of the north portal of the Marienkapelle am Markt in Würzburg, reproduced here as Figure 1.5. Jung compared such depictions of 'the fructification of Mary' with the delusions entertained by one of his patients, Emile Schwyzer, who has been given the sobriquet 'Solar Phallus Man' (*PU* §173; cf. *CW* 5 §151; cf. *SNZ* 2, 853).[252]

In addition, in his paper entitled 'The Spirit Mercurius' (1943/1948), Jung explained how:

> the alchemists related their concept of *anima mundi* on the one hand to the world soul in Plato's *Timaeus* and on the other to the Holy Spirit, who was present at the Creation and played the role of procreator (*phutos*), impregnating the waters with the seed of life just as, later, he played a similar role in the *obumbratio* (overshadowing) of Mary.[253]

(In this context, Jung referred his reader to a work by the seventeenth-century alchemical writer, Johann Christoph Steeb's *Coelum Sephiroticum* of 1679.[254]) In his seminar on *Zarathustra*, the question arose in the context of the chapter entitled 'Of Old and Young Women', and of the presence in Nietzsche's text of the anima. For Jung, when Mary conceives through the ear — 'she heard the Word, the Word came to her' — it shows that, in psychological terms, 'the anima has heard something' (*SNZ* 1, 732). Expressed 'in Christian symbolism', Jung added (misapplying a theological term), the biblical story shows 'the *conceptio immaculata* through the Word, and she is pregnant with a saviour'; expressed in Jungian terms, 'the anima has heard something, she had an audition, she conceived the Word' (*SNZ* 1, 732). But to what, in the case of *Thus Spoke Zarathustra*, is the anima trying to give birth?

A Text Pregnant with Meaning?

The motif of pregnancy is an eminently philosophical one, and it plays an important role in Plato. In the *Symposium*, Socrates tells his fellow-guests (or so Apollodorus relates to his unnamed friend) of how his philosophical tutor, Diotima of Mantinea, in turn had taught him that 'all of us are pregnant'.[255] We are pregnant both 'in body and in soul', and 'when we reach a certain age we naturally desire to give birth'.[256] There is, says Diotima, 'a divinity in human propagation, an immortal something in the midst of man's mortality'.[257] Those who are 'pregnant in body [...] turn to woman as the object of their love, and raise a family, proving themselves with immortality and remembrance and happiness', while those who are 'pregnant in soul' are 'pregnant with what is fitting for a soul to bear and bring to birth' — i.e., 'wisdom and all her sister virtues'.[258]

Because, as Diotima puts it, to love is 'to bring forth upon the beautiful, both in body and soul',[259] this means that the role of the philosopher is to act as a kind of midwife, and in another dialogue, the *Theaetetus*, it is precisely in these terms that Socrates is presented. If Sophroniscus, Socrates's father was a sculptor (see Chapter 2), his mother was a midwife (indeed, 'a fine buxom woman'), Phaenarete — a name that means 'she who brings virtue into light'.[260] Correspondingly, Socrates describes himself as a kind of spiritual or philosophical midwife.[261]

This motif in the Platonic dialogues has given rise — or given birth, one might say — to a variety of philosophical practices known as Socratic Midwifery or Philosophical Midwifery, essentially a kind of philosophical counselling.[262] Yet it is also an image that we find Nietzsche repeatedly using in his early writing, as well as in *Thus Spoke Zarathustra*.[263] In his preface to the first volume of *Human, All Too Human*, Nietzsche talks about the 'great liberation' experienced by the 'free spirit', and about how the free spirit comes to believe that what has happened to him must happen to everyone in whom a task wants to come into the world. 'The secret force and destiny of this task', Nietzsche explains, 'will rule among and in the individual facets of [the free spirit's] destiny like an unconscious pregnancy'.[264] (And, in an astonishing link between this image and another key Nietzschean motif, i.e., the image of the great noontide, he adds that 'only now, at the midday of [one's] life', can one understand 'what preparations, bypaths, experiments, temptations, disguises' the problem needed 'before it was *allowed* to rise up'...)

In the second volume of *Human, All Too Human*, the image recurs on a number of occasions: in 'Assorted Opinions and Maxims', in an aphorism entitled 'Pregnancy after birth' (§63), in another aphorism (§216) where Nietzsche suggests that some 'highly gifted spirits' are 'always unfruitful' because they are 'too impatient to wait out the term of their pregnancy', and in yet another (§285) where, a propos of the 'condition' of 'young talents', he says that it 'resembles the sicknesses of pregnancy and is attended by strange appetites'.[265] And Nietzsche subjects Schopenhauer's famously misogynist thoughts on the pregnancy of women to a devastating critique.[266]

In striking contrast to Schopenhauer, Nietzsche asked in *Daybreak*: 'Is there a more holy condition than that of pregancy?',[267] describing pregnancy as a state of '*ideal selfishness*', as '[a] *state of consecration* [in which] one should live!' — and '[in which] one can live'. For 'continually to watch over and care for and keep our soul still, so that our fruitfulness shall *come to a happy fulfilment*', means that, 'as intermediaries, we watch over and care for to the *benefit of all*; and the mood in which we live, this mood of pride and gentleness, is a balm which spreads far around us and on to restless souls too'.[268]

In passages such as these it becomes evident that, when he talks about pregnancy, Nietzsche does not mean it in a literal, biological sense. And this is confirmed by his distinction in *The Gay Science* (§72) about the sociological consequences of biological pregnancy, on the one hand, and 'spiritual pregnancy' on the other.[269] In his preface, Nietzsche rejects a populist dualism that would separate soul from body (or even soul from spirit), for philosophers have to 'give birth to our thoughts out of our pain and, like mothers, endow them with all we have of blood, heart, fire, pleasure, passion, agony, conscience, fate, and catastrophe'.[270] Ultimately, Nietzsche comes to associate pregnancy with his master category, the Dionysian; as he does later in *The Gay Science*, when he writes that 'the desire for *destruction*, change, and becoming can be an expression of an overflowing energy that is pregnant with the future (my term for this is, as is known, "Dionysian")'.[271]

The Dionysian implications of this kind of 'spiritual' pregnancy come to the fore in *Thus Spoke Zarathustra*. The theme of pregnancy is first adduced in a playful, if problematic passage. In Part One, Zarathustra recounts to a disciple a conversation that had taken place earlier between a little old woman and his soul. She tells him that 'everything about woman is a riddle', and that 'everything about woman has one solution: it is called pregnancy'.[272] Yet it becomes clear in Part Two — and, in fact, in Zarathustra's discourse on the blissful islands — that 'pregnancy' is not just a solution for women, but a solution for all. In an impassioned outburst, Zarathustra declares:

> Creation — that is the great redemption from suffering, and life's easement. But that the creator may exist, that itself requires suffering and much transformation.
>
> Yes, there must be much bitter dying in your life, you creators! Thus you are advocates and justifiers of all transitoriness.

For the creator himself to be the child new-born he must also be willing to the mother and endure the mother's pain.

Truly, I have gone my way through a hundred souls and through a hundred cradles and birth-pangs. I have taken many departures, I know the heart-breaking last hours.[273]

In this way Zarathustra identifies himself *both* with the (pregnant) mother *and* with his offspring, with the 'new-born' child. Later, in Part Three, he returns to this theme of spiritual pregnancy and spiritual (re)birth:

Once the creator sought companions and children of *his* hope: and behold, it turned out that he could not find them, except he first create them himself.

Thus I am in the midst of my work, going to my children and turning from them: for the sake of his children must Zarathustra perfect himself.

For one loves from the very heart only one's child and one's work; and where there is great love of oneself, then it is a sign of pregnancy: thus have I found.[274]

Subsequently, the use of the motif of pregnancy becomes increasingly dithyrambic. In 'The Seven Seals', Zarathustra speaks of himself as full — as 'full of that prophetic spirit that wanders on high ridges between two seas', and he describes that spirit as being 'like a heavy cloud', a cloud that is:

ready for lightning in its dark bosom and for redeeming beams of light, pregnant with lightnings which affirm Yes! laugh Yes! ready for prophetic lightning-flashes:

but blessed is he who is thus pregnant![275]

Furthermore, in Part Four, in 'Of the Higher Man', he recapitulates his teaching on 'spiritual pregnancy' and even envisages a sort of rite of purification after the soul has given birth:

You creators, you Higher Men! One is pregnant only with one's own child.
[...]
You creators, you Higher Men! Whoever has to give birth is sick; but who-ever has given birth is unclean.

Ask the women: one does not give birth for pleasure. The pain makes hens and poets cackle.

You creators, there is much in you that is unclean. That is because you have to be mothers.

A new child: oh how much new filth has also entered the world! Go aside! And whoever has given birth should wash his soul clean![276]

Given their textual proximity — especially in the chapter 'On the Blissful Islands' — and their conceptual compatability, one might see the relationship between the motifs of pregnancy-leading-to-birth and sculpting-the-form-of-a-statue as one of complementarity. In pregnancy, the individual *brings* a new form out of the self, while in *sculpture*, the individual *gives form* to something already existing: in both cases, the process is creative and it leads to *something new*.

And in *Zarathustra*, these two motifs or metaphors fuse: for the Zarathustra who is giving birth is identical with the Zarathustra who is wresting the image from the stone.

Conclusion

As we have seen in this chapter, Nietzsche's imagery in 'On the Blissful Islands' is extraordinarily rich in its intertextual and iconographic references, and there are enormous associations in play when we read that the superman came to Zarathustra *as a shadow*. In the place of the Judeo-Christian God, Zarathustra wishes to set up the superman: and the arrival of this figure, which is to replace and supersede the divine, is announced as being analogous to that of the Old Testament God, Yahweh, in his various manifestations in the desert, on the mountain, and before the Tabernacle and in the Temple, as well as to the Incarnation of God in the very act of His conception subsequent to the moment of Annunciation when, in the New Testament, Gabriel visits Mary. The Judeo-Christian God dwells in thick darkness and manifests Himself in the cloud; the superman, by extension and by contrast, is the lightning from the dark cloud: as Zarathustra says, 'I love all those who are like heavy drops falling singly from the dark cloud that hangs over mankind: they prophesy the coming of the lightning and as prophets they perish', and: 'Behold, I am a prophet of the lightning and a heavy drop from the cloud: but this lightning is called *Superman*'.[277]

(In his notes from the summer and autumn of 1883, where Nietzsche sketched out possibilities for the second and third parts of *Zarathustra*, the image of the lightning bolt acquires increasing importance — 'I want to vanish into the dark storm: and for my last moment I want to be a human being and at the same time a bolt of lightning'[278] — and increasing intensity: 'If only a bolt of lightning would strike your food, and your mouths would have to eat fire!'.[279] Thus the image of lightning combines two important themes or motifs: the image of intense light emerging from darkness and the ecstatic culmination of the *Augenblick* or 'moment', so that the bolt of lightning represents 'the sudden release of spiritual potential, for its conversion into rapturous and all-consuming activity'.[280])

The overshadowing of Mary is theological and spiritual, thanks to the indwelling of the Holy Spirit which leaves her full of spirit; the superman, who is a shadow, is non-theological, non-metaphysical, and entirely immanent; he announces a new priority for the senses and a new understanding of the spirit. Because he represents a totality, the superman is beautiful, hence it is *the beauty of the superman that came to Zarathustra as a shadow*. Beauty is totality; it is both light and dark, both illumination and shadow, both good and evil: as Hans-Georg Gadamer (1900–2002) put it, 'the experience of the beautiful, and particularly the beautiful in art, is the invocation of a potentially whole and holy order of things, wherever it may be found'.[281] Correspondingly, we are invited to embrace the totality of life and to respond, in the words of Lynceus the Watchman at the end of *Faust*, Part Two: 'Let it be as it may, / It was lovely to me' (*Es sei, wie es wolle, / Es war doch so schön*).[282]

Whereas the Incarnation of the Christ as the indwelling of the Holy Spirit proceeds as something that happens *from outside* and *moves in to* Mary, the new conception of spirit that will be incarnated in the superman is something that happens in a way that is entirely internal to the individual. Hence, to articulate this beautiful totality in the lines that precede the advent of the superman (or his beauty) *as a shadow*, Zarathustra has recourse to a different, but equally significant, image: the image of *sculpting*.

Notes

1 'The Prophet', in F. Nietzsche, *Thus Spoke Zarathustra*, tr. R.J. Hollingdale, Harmondsworth: Penguin, 1969, p. 155.

2 'The Cry of Distress', in *Thus Spoke Zarathustra*, p. 255.

3 'The Cry of Distress', in *Thus Spoke Zarathustra*, p. 255.

4 'The Cry of Distress', in *Thus Spoke Zarathustra*, p. 256.

5 'The Prophet', in *Thus Spoke Zarathustra*, pp. 157–158.

6 'The Cry of Distress', in *Thus Spoke Zarathustra*, p. 256.

7 See Hesiod, *Works and Days*, ll. 166–173; in *The Homeric Hymns and Homerica*, tr. H.G. Evelyn-White, Cambridge, MA; London: Harvard University Press; Heinemann, 1982, p. 15.

8 See Homer, *Odyssey*, book 4, ll. 560–565; in Homer, *The Odyssey*, ed. and tr. A. Cook, 2nd edn, New York and London: Norton, 1993, p. 46.

9 See Pindar, *Olympian Odes*, no. 2, ll. 59–75; Pindar, *The Odes of Pindar*, tr. R. Lattimore, Chicago: The University of Chicago Press, 1947, p. 7. For the distinctive difference, under the influence of the cult of Orpheus, of Pindar's conception of the blissful islands from Hesiod's and Homer's, see F.E. Manuel and F.P. Manuel, *Utopian Thought in the Western World*, Oxford: Blackwell, 1979, p. 76.

10 See Plato, *Gorgias*, 523 b and 526 c; in Plato, *Collected Dialogues*, ed. E. Hamilton and H. Cairns, Princeton, NJ: Princeton University Press, 1989, pp. 304 and 306; cf. *Menexenus*, 235 c; *Symposium*, 179 c and 180 b; in *CD*, pp. 187 and p. 534.

11 See Plato, *Republic*, 519 c and 540 b; in *CD*, pp. 751 and 771.

12 Virgil, *The Aeneid*, book 6, translated J. Dryden, ll. 867–872.

13 Virgil, *The Aeneid*, book 6, translated J. Dryden, ll. 873–876 and 890–894.

14 According to Taylor, these lines 'must not be understood as if the soul in the regions of felicity retained any affection for material concerns, or was engaged in the trifling pursuits of a corporeal life; but that when separated from generation, she is constantly engaged in intellectual employments; either in exercising the divine contests of the most exalted wisdom; in forming the responsive dance of refined imaginations; in tuning the sacred lyre of mystic piety to strains of deific fury and ineffable delight; in giving free scope to the splendid and winged powers of the soul; or in nourishing the intellect with the substantial banquets of intelligible food' (in *A Dissertation on the Eleusinian and Bacchic Mysteries* [1790], 'On the Eleusinian Mysteries', in *Oracles and Mysteries* [Thomas Taylor Series = TTS, vol. 7], Frome: Prometheus Trust, 2001, p. 80).

15 Olympiodorus, *Commentary on Plato's "Gorgias"*, tr. R. Jackson, K. Lycos, and H. Tarrant, Leiden: Brill, 1998, p. 302.

16 Flavius Philostratus, *Life of Apollonius of Tyana*, book 5, §3; Philostratus, *The Life of Apollonius of Tyana*, vol. 1, tr. F.C. Conybeare, London: Heinemann; New York: Macmillan, 1912, p. 471.

17 Plutarch, *Life of Sertorius*, chapter 8; in Plutarch, *Lives*, vol. 8, tr. B. Perrin, London; New York: Heinemann; Putnam, 1919, pp. 21–23.

18 Pliny the Elder, *Natural History*, book 6, §37; in Pliny the Elder, *Natural History*, vol. 2, *Libri III-VII*, tr. H. Rackham, Cambridge, MA; London: Harvard University Press; Heinemann, 1941, p. 491.

19 Whether there are links to the Buddhist tradition must remain for now an open question; see the section entitled 'Friedrich Nietzsche: Europas Buddha?', in V. Zotz, *Auf den glückseligen Inseln: Buddhismus in der deutschen Kultur*, Berlin: Theseus Verlag, pp. 125–132.

20 'Human, All Too Human', §2; in *Ecce Homo*, tr. R.J. Hollingdale, Harmondsworth: Penguin, 1992, p. 60.

21 Nietzsche, *KSB* 6, 429; for the context, see R.J. Benders and S. Oettermann, *Friedrich Nietzsche: Chronik in Bildern und Texten*, Munich and Vienna: Hanser, 2000, p. 563.

22 'The human fetus too is an island, and in their island utopias men have often expressed a longing for the protective fluid than once surrounded them. The maternal symbols of most Elysian, golden-age, and paradisiacal utopias are compelling and the point need not be labored' (Manuel and Manuel, *Utopian Thought in the Western World*, p. 76).

23 See 'The Dance Song', in *Thus Spoke Zarathustra*, pp. 130–133.

24 'The Child with the Mirror', in *Thus Spoke Zarathustra*, p. 108.

25 Cf. Zarathustra's remark at the beginning of this discourse that 'it is fine to gaze out upon distant seas from the midst of superfluity' ('On the Blissful Islands', in *Thus Spoke Zarathustra*, p. 109), suggesting that Zarathustra is looking out to sea or is already on board a ship.

26 'On the Blissful Islands', in *Thus Spoke Zarathustra*, p. 109.

27 *TSZ*, 'Prologue', §2; cf. *The Gay Science*, §125, in Nietzsche, *The Gay Science*, tr. W. Kaufmann, New York: Vintage, 1974, pp. 181–182.

28 M. Onfray, *Le crépuscule d'un idole: L'affabulation freudienne*, Paris: Grasset, 2010, p. 542.

29 S. Hough, *Nietzsche's Noontide Friend: The Self as Metaphoric Double*, University Park, PA: Pennsylvania State University Press, 1997, pp. 100 and 89–90.

30 H. Theierl, *Nietzsche — Mystik als Selbstversuch*, Würzburg: Königshausen & Neumann, 2000, S. 13–14; cf. pp. 47–48 and 90.

31 'On the Blissful Islands', in *Thus Spoke Zarathustra*, pp. 111–112.

32 See P. Bishop, 'The Superman as Salamander: Symbols of Transformation or Transformational Symbols?', in *International Journal of Jungian Studies*, March 2011, vol. 3, no. 1, 4–20.

33 For further discussion, see the entry on 'amplification' in A. Samuels, B. Shorter and F. Plaut, *A Critical Dictionary of Jungian Analysis*, London and New York: Routledge, 1986. For an example of Jung's method in practice, see his *Psychology of the Unconscious* (or *Transformations and Symbols of the Libido*) (1911–1912).

34 Jung, *SNZ* 2, 951–952; cf. *Psychology and Religion*, in *CW* 11, §32, fn. 12 (citing St Athanasius, *The Life of St Anthony*, in E.A. Wallis Budge (ed.), *The Book of Paradise, being the Histories and Sayings of the Monks and Ascetics of the Desert*, 2 vols, London: Drugulin, 1904, vol. 1, pp. 3–108, esp. pp. 33–37 and 47). According to St Athanasius, 'there is a time when we see no man and yet the sound of the working of the devils is heard by us, and it is like the singing of a song in a loud voice' (p. 33), while he cites St Anthony as saying: 'On another occasion [...] [the devils] came unto me with whistlings and they were beating their hands together and dancing with joy; but when they saw that notwithstanding all their clamour I did not cease to pray [...], they turned their songs of joy into lamentations' (p. 47).

35 Is Jung touching here on the fact that the 'shadow of the Superman' stands in a relationship of correspondence to the 'shadow of God'? For, just as Zarathustra teaches in 'On the Blissful Islands' that 'once you said "God" when you gazed upon distant seas; but now

I have taught you to say "Superman"' (*Thus Spoke Zarathustra*, p. 109), so the shadow of the superman is a reaction and a response to the shadow of God — to 'these shadows of God', of which Nietzsche asks: when will they 'cease to darken our mind?' (*The Gay Science*, §109; in *The Gay Science*, p. 169).

36 For this second image, see Psalm 117 (118): 22, 'The stone which the builders rejected; the same is become the head of the corner'; cited by Christ in Matthew 21: 42, Mark 12: 10, Luke 20: 17, and applied to Christ by St Peter in Acts 4: 11 and 1 Peter 2: 7. In Ephesians 2: 19–22, St Paul uses the metaphor of the Church as a 'holy temple', built 'on the foundation of the apostles and prophets, Jesus Christ himself being the chief corner-stone'. The messianic theme of the 'keystone' that becomes the 'stone of stumbling' (JB commentary), see Isaiah 8: 14 and 28: 16 — 'Therefore, thus saith the Lord God: Behold, I will lay a stone in the foundations of Sion, a tried stone, a corner-stone, a precious stone, founded in the foundation' — Zechariah 3: 9 and 4:7, cf. St Paul to the Romans 9: 33, and 1 Peter 2: 8.

37 In his letter to the Ephesians, §9, St Ignatius of Antioch appears to allude to this Petrine and Pauline motif when he writes: 'You are stones of the Father's temple, prepared for the building of God the Father' (B.D. Ehrman [ed.], *The Apostolic Fathers*, vol. 1, *I Clement; II Clement; Ignatius; Polycarp; Didache*, Cambridge, MA, and London: Harvard University Press, 2003, p. 229). And in the tenth of his *Catechetical Lectures*, St Cyril of Jerusalem drew a link between Christ's status as the Son of God and the description of him as a stone: 'We say One Lord Jesus Christ, to signify that God's Son is Only-begotten; we say, One, lest thou shouldest suppose another [...] He is called a Stone; not a lifeless one, quarried by men's hands: but the chief corner-stone, on whom whosoever believeth shall not be ashamed' (*The Catechetical Lectures of S. Cyril, Archbishop of Jerusalem* [Library of Fathers of the Holy Catholic Church, vol. 2], Oxford: Parker, 1839, p. 99). In his sermons on the occasion of church dedications (cf. Sermons §336, §337, and §338), Augustine made extensive use of the Petrine (1 Peter 2: 5) and Pauline (1 Cor. 3: 10–11) imagery of ecclesiastical construction out of stones (see F.G. Clancy, 'Augustine's Sermons for the Dedication of a Church', in M.F. Wiles, E.J. Yarnold, and P.M. Parvis, *St Augustine and His Opponents* [Studia Patristica, vol. 38], Louvain: Peeters, pp. 48–55; and J.E. Merdinger, 'Building God's House: Augustine's Homilies at Episcopal Consecrations, Church Dedications, and Funerals', in F. Young, M. Edwards, and P. Parvis (eds.), *Augustine* [Studia Patristica, vol. 42], Louvain: Peeters, 2006, pp. 195–200 [pp. 197–198]). In a sermon for the Sunday after Ascension, Johannes Tauler refers to the Gospel allusions and Paul's letter to the Ephesians, adding that 'if you are not sharpened thoroughly by this stone, all Solomon's wisdom and all Solomon's strength will be of no avail' (*Sermons*, tr. M. Shrady, New York and Mahwah: Paulist Press, 1985, p. 83).

38 *Republic*, 534e; in *CD*, p. 766.

39 See Dorn's *Speculativa philosophia*, in *Theatrum chemicum* [1602], vol. 1, p. 267; cited by Jung in his Eranos lecture on 'Religious Ideas in Alchemy' (1937), in *CW* 12, §378.

40 Cf. in 'On the Virtuous', we are told that 'the voice of beauty speaks softly: it steals into only the most awakened souls' (*Thus Spoke Zarathustra*, p. 117); and in 'The Stillest Hour', the paradoxically voiceless voice tells Zarathustra: 'It is the stillest words which bring the storm. Thoughts that come on doves' feet guide the world' (*Thus Spoke Zarathustra*, p. 168).

41 W. Santaniello, 'Socrates as the Ugliest Murderer of God', in W. Santaniello (ed.), *Nietzsche and the Gods*, Albany, NY: State University of New York Press, 2001, pp. 73–83 (esp. pp. 75–80); and W. Santaniello, *Zarathustra's Last Supper: Nietzsche's Eight Higher Men*, Aldershot and Burlington, VT: Ashgate, 2005, pp. 43–50.

42 R.J. Hollingdale, 'Introduction', in *Thus Spoke Zarathustra*, p. 35.

43 J. Young, 'Review of Zarathustra's Last Supper: Nietzsche's Eight Higher Men', *Ars Disputandi*, 2007, vol. 7. Available online at www.ArsDisputandi.org (accessed 16 February 2013).

44 Nietzsche, *The Will to Power*, §809; in *The Will to Power*, ed. W. Kaufmann, tr. R.J. Hollingdale and W. Kaufmann, New York: Vintage, 1968, p. 427.

45 *The Will to Power*, §809; in *The Will to Power*, p. 427.

46 *Ecce Homo*, 'Thus Spoke Zarathustra', §6; in *Ecce Homo*, tr. Hollingdale, p. 77. For further discussion of the motif of dance in Nietzsche, see C. Crawford, 'Nietzsche's Dionysian Arts: Dance, Song, and Silence', in S. Kemal, I. Gaskell, and D.W. Conway (eds), *Nietzsche, Philosophy and the Arts*, Cambridge: Cambridge University Press, 1998, pp. 310–341; K. King, 'The Dancing Philosopher', *Topoi*, January 2005, vol. 24, no. 1, 103–111; and K.L. Lamothe, *Nietzsche's Dancers: Isadora Duncan, Martha Graham, and the Revaluation of Christian Values*, New York and Houndmills: Palgrave Macmillan, 2006.

47 *Symposium*, §206d; in *CD*, p. 558.

48 'The Ugliest Man', in *Thus Spoke Zarathustra*, p. 276.

49 Nietzsche, *Thus Spoke Zarathustra*, p. 276. Cf. L. Lampert, *Nietzsche's Teaching: An Interpretation of "Thus Spoke Zarathustra"*, New Haven and London: Yale University Press, 1986, p. 297.

50 'Preface', §4; in Nietzsche, *The Gay Science*, p. 38.

51 Nietzsche, *Thus Spoke Zarathustra*, p. 276.

52 Nietzsche, *Thus Spoke Zarathustra*, p. 279.

53 'The Intoxicated Song', §1; Nietzsche, *Thus Spoke Zarathustra*, p. 326.

54 *The Gay Science*, §278; Nietzsche, *The Gay Science*, p. 225.

55 *The Gay Science*, §299; in *The Gay Science*, p. 239.

56 *The Gay Science*, §276; in *The Gay Science*, p. 223.

57 Hough, *Nietzsche's Noontide Friend*, p. 97.

58 'Of Great Events', in *Thus Spoke Zarathustra*, p. 152.

59 On this 'obscure symbol', compare the remark of Gilles Deleuze: 'The fire-dog is the image of species activity, it expresses man's relation to the earth' (in *Nietzsche and Philosophy* [1962], tr. H. Tomlinson, London and New York: Continuum, 2006, p. 139).

60 For Jung, this part of *Zarathustra* constituted a case of cryptomnesia, or so he argued in his dissertation for his medical degree, 'On the Psychology and Pathology of So-Called Occult Phenomena' (1902), in *CW* 1 §140–§142.

61 'Of Great Events', in Nietzsche, *Thus Spoke Zarathustra*, p. 155.

62 For further discussion of this motif in Nietzsche, see P. Bishop, 'Remain True to the Earth: Home and Wandering in Nietzsche', *Spring: A Journal of Archetype and Culture*, Spring 2011, vol. 85, 125–163.

63 For the text and discussion, see P. Grundlehner, *The Poetry of Friedrich Nietzsche*, New York and Oxford: Oxford University Press, 1986, pp. 64–70. For further discussion of Nietzsche's relationship to Rohde, see A. Cardew, 'The Dioscuri: Nietzsche and Rohde', in P. Bishop (ed.), *Nietzsche and Antiquity: His Reaction and Response to the Classical Tradition*, Rochester, NY: Camden House, 2004, pp. 458–478.

64 Hollingdale, 'Introduction', in Nietzsche, *Thus Spoke Zarathustra*, p. 35.

65 Lampert, *Nietzsche's Teaching*, p. 298.

66 S. Rosen, *The Mask of Enlightenment: Nietzsche's "Zarathustra"*, Cambridge: Cambridge University Press, 1995, p. 223.

67 *Der Geist als Widersacher der Seele*, chapter 72; in L. Klages, *Sämtliche Werke*, ed. E. Frauchiger et al., 9 vols, Bonn: Bouvier, 1964–1999, vol. 2, p. 1282.

68 Klages, *Der Geist als Widersacher der Seele*, in *Sämtliche Werke*, vol. 2, p. 1282.

69 J.J. Bachofen, *Das Mutterecht: Eine Untersuchung über die Gynaikokratie der alten Welt nach ihrer religiösen und rechtlichen Natur*, Stuttgart: Krais & Hoffmann, 1861, p. 163.

70 Klages, *Der Geist als Widersacher der Seele*, in *Sämtliche Werke*, vol. 2, p. 1283.

71 Klages, *Der Geist als Widersacher der Seele*, in *Sämtliche Werke*, vol. 2, pp. 1283–1284.

72 Aeschylus, *Agamenon – Libation-Bearers – Eumenides – Fragments*, tr. H. Weir Smyth, London; New York: Heinemann; Putnam, 1926, p. 281.

73 For further discussion of this text, see R. Reitzenstein, *Poimandres: Studien zur griechisch-ägyptischen und frühchristlichen Literatur* [1904], Leipzig: Teubner, 1966; and R.A. Segal,

The Poimandres as Myth: Scholarly Theory and Gnostic Meaning, Berlin and New York: de Gruyter, 1986.

74 *Corpus hermeticum I*, 'Discourse of Hermes Trismegistus: Poimandres', §13–§14, in B.P. Copenhaver (ed.), *Hermetica: The Greek Corpus Hermeticum and the Latin Asclepius in a New English Translation, with Notes and Introduction*, Cambridge: Cambridge University Press, 1992, p. 3; my emphasis. For further discussion, see M.P. Hall, *The Secret Teachings of All Ages*, New York: Tarcher/Penguin, 2003, p. 191.

75 *Corpus hermeticum I*, 'Discourse of Hermes Trismegistus: Poimandres', §14–§15, in Copenhaver, *Hermetica*, p. 3; cf. Hall, *Secret Teachings of All Ages*, p. 191.

76 *Alcibiades I*, 133c; in Plato, *Complete Works*, ed. J.M. Cooper, Indianapolis and Cambridge: Hackett, 1997, p. 592.

77 Proclus, *On the Theology of Plato*, book 1, chapter 3; in Proclus, *The Theology of Plato*, tr. T. Taylor [TTS, vol. 8], Westbury: Prometheus Trust, 1995, pp. 57–58.

78 Proclus, *On the Theology of Plato*, book 1, chapter 3; in *The Theology of Plato*, p. 58; my emphasis.

79 Proclus, *On the Theology of Plato*, book 1, chapter 3; in *The Theology of Plato*, p. 58.

80 A.D. Thomson, *On Mankind: Their Origin and Destiny*, London: Longmans, Green, 1872, p. 79.

81 Thomson, *On Mankind*, p. 80.

82 For further discussion, see E.G. d'Alviella, *The Migration of Symbols* [1891], New York: Franklin, 1972, chapter 6, 'The Winged Globe, the Caduceus, and the Trisula', esp. pp. 204–226.

83 Thomson, *On Mankind*, p. 80.

84 Thomson, *On Mankind*, p. 80.

85 Hall, *Secret Teachings of All Ages*, p. 404. According to Hall, 'herein is the key to the allegorical creation of Eve out of the side of Adam; for Adam, representative of the *idea* or pattern, is reflected into the material universe as a multitude of ensouled images which are collectively designated *Eve*' (p. 404).

86 Pliny, *Natural History*, book 35, chapter 5; in Pliny, *Natural History*, vol. 9, *Books 33–35*, tr. H. Rackham, Cambridge, MA; London: Harvard University Press; Macmillan, 1961, p. 271.

87 Thomson, *On Mankind*, p. 81.

88 Pliny, *Natural History*, book 35, chapter 43, in Pliny, *Natural History*, vol. 9, *Books 33–35*, pp. 371–373.

89 Jung's interpretative schema in these opening seminars in 1934 becomes complex to the point of appearing fraught (see *SNZ* 1, 130). Compare with his later comments in 1938: 'In his solitude [Nietzsche] tapped the unconscious and was instantly filled with the inflation of Zarathustra: he became Zarathustra. […] Zarathustra is a figure of speech perhaps, or a more or less aesthetic metaphor. […] Throughout the whole book we have had the greatest trouble on account of the constant intermingling with an archetypal figure. One is never sure whether Zarathustra is speaking, or Nietzsche — or is it his anima? […] Nietzsche is Zarathustra, he is the anima, he is the shadow; and so on' (*SNZ* 2, 1357–1358). This hermeneutic problem only arises because Jung shies away from the implications of reading *Zarathustra* as an aesthetic text (although he gestures towards this when he calls the figure of Zarathustra an 'aesthetic metaphor'), and insists on reading it as a transparent (or not so transparent) document of psychological development. One thinks, for instance, of Jung's criticism of Nietzsche's 'love of the play of words' (*SNZ* 2, 1367), which is a highly backhanded way of recognizing Nietzsche's rhetorical sophistication.

90 Compare with Jung's remark that 'the really good life is half happiness and half suffering' (*SNZ* 1, 502).

91 Nietzsche, *Thus Spoke Zarathustra*, p. 89.

92 On the tragic dimension of *Zarathustra*, see Jung's remark elsewhere: 'The end of the tragic *peripetie*, the drama of Zarathustra, is really that he cannot accept the shadow, cannot accept the ugliest man, and so loses the connection with the body altogether' (*SNZ* 2, p. 960).

93 Nietzsche, *Thus Spoke Zarathustra*, p. 90.

94 Compare with Jung's dictum that 'the conscious [...] is identified [...] with the figure of Zarathustra, the wise old man, with an all-embracing, benevolent truth, very beautiful, very meaningful and all that' (*SNZ* 1, 125).

95 Compare with Zarathustra's cry: 'You solitary one, you go the way of the creator: you will create a god for yourself out of your seven devils!' ('On the Way of the Creator', in Nietzsche, *Thus Spoke Zarathustra*, p. 89).

96 Nietzsche, *Thus Spoke Zarathustra*, p. 192.

97 According to Jung, 'this saying of Nietzsche is really the key to the cure of that split between the superior and the inferior man, the upper and the lower, the bright and the dark'. He added that 'this passage is one of those which Nietzsche really felt, for Nietzsche was a great genius, and it is in the deepest sense in keeping with his whole style and tendency' (*SNZ* 2, 1367).

98 Elsewhere, Jung assimilates as 'a very active shadow, identical with the inferior man', the figure of the buffoon who jumps over the tightrope-walker with/to the figure of 'the frothing fool' in 'Of Passing By' whom the people call 'Zarathustra's ape' (Nietzsche, *Thus Spoke Zarathustra*, p. 195; cf. Jung, *SNZ* 2, 1392).

99 Nietzsche, *Thus Spoke Zarathustra*, p. 211.

100 'The truth of this sentence is valid under certain conditions; if you understand properly what it means to love oneself with a wholesome and healthy love, that one may endure to be with oneself and not go roving about, then it is a very excellent truth [...] and one of the most modern, most moral tasks you can imagine' (*SNZ* 2, 1471; cf. 1475 and 1477–1478)

101 Nietzsche, *Thus Spoke Zarathustra*, p. 211.

102 Here, too, Jung shies away from describing this task as an *aesthetic* one: 'It needs more than art: it needs a great deal of philosophy, even of religion, in order to make that bond between yourself and your shadow a lasting one. When Nietzsche assumes that it is an art and even the highest art, he doesn't put it strongly enough, because he doesn't realize what it is' (*SNZ* 2, 1478–1479). Yet one might equally conclude that it is Jung who does not realize what the ambition of aesthetics is.

103 Jung knew, for example, Elisabeth Förster-Nietzsche's *Das werdende Nietzsche: Autobiographische Aufzeichnungen*, Munich: Musarion, 1924; and Carl Albrecht Bernoulli's *Franz Overbeck und Friedrich Nietzsche: Eine Freundschaft*, 2 vols, Jena: Diederichs, 1908.

104 Bernoulli, *Franz Overbeck und Friedrich Nietzsche: Eine Freundschaft*, vol. 1, p. 72. Compare with Nietzsche's *Nachlass* for 1876–1877 and 1878 (*KSA* 8, 21[21], 370 and *KSA* 8, 28[42], 509). The proximity of this dream to such passages in *Thus Spoke Zarathustra* as 'Of the Vision and the Riddle' and especially 'The Convalescent' — 'Ah! Come here! Give me your hand – ha! don't! Ha, ha! – Disgust, disgust, disgust – woe is me!' (*Thus Spoke Zarathustra*, p. 233) — has been noted by Roger Hollinrake in *Nietzsche, Wagner, and the Philosophy of Pessimism*, London: Allen & Unwin, 1982, p. 275.

105 Nietzsche, *Thus Spoke Zarathustra*, p. 54.

106 For a reproduction of this alchemical image of the eagle and the toad from the *Viridarium Chymicum* (1624), see also *SNZ* 2, 1412–1413.

107 H. Tilton, *The Quest for the Phoenix: Spiritual Alchemy and Rosicrucianism in the Work of Count Michael Maier (1569–1622)*, Berlin and New York: de Gruyter, 2003, p. 78.

108 G. Bruno, *The Heroic Frenzies*, tr. P.E. Memmo, Jr., Chapel Hill, NC: University of North Carolina Press, 1965, p. 201.

109 B. Vergely, *Deviens qui tu es: Quand les sages grecs nous aident à vivre*, Paris: Albin Michel, 2014, p. 122.

110 Vergely, *Deviens qui tu es*, pp. 124 and 122.

111 See Samuels, Shorter, and Plaut, *A Critical Dictionary of Jungian Analysis*, p. 138.

112 For further discussion of the problem of the shadow from a Jungian perspective, see C. Zweig and J. Abrams (eds), *Meeting the Shadow: The Hidden Power of the Dark Side of Human Nature*, New York: Tarcher/Putnam, 1991.

113 In *Aion*, Jung is deeply concerned with the problem of the veil and veiling. See his comments in the next chapter, 'The Syzygy: Anima and Animus', on the anima as Maya, the 'spinning woman' (*CW* 9/ii §20), and his references to the fallacy (or the paradox) of the veiled one (or *enkekalymmenos*), attributed to Eubulides of Miletus, a philosopher of the Megarian school (*CW* 9/ii §37, n. 4) (see Diogenes Laërtius, book 2, §108, in *The Lives and Opinions of Eminent Philosophers*, tr. C.D. Yonge, London: Bell, 1895, pp. 97–98).

114 For a general discussion of the religious background formed by ancient Greek mystery cults, see M.B. Cosmopoulos (ed.), *Greek Mysteries: The Archaeology and Ritual of Ancient Greek Secret Cults*, London and New York: Routledge, 2003; J. Larson, *Ancient Greek Cults: A Guide*, New York and London: Routledge, 2007; and H. Bowden, *Mystery Cults in the Ancient World*, London: Thames & Hudson, 2010. In one of his lectures on ancient philosophy given in 1928, Manly P. Hall offered an imaginative reconstruction of the initiatory rites in the ancient Mysteries (see *Lectures on Ancient Philosophy*, New York: Tarcher/Penguin, 2005, pp. 371–374).

115 In his introduction to *The Red Book*, Sonu Shamdasani places Jung's work in the tradition of the inner dialogue that goes back to the *Soliloquies* of St Augustine (*RB*, 199). Equally, does the *Red Book* illustrate the 'visionary' (as opposed to the 'psychological') mode of artistic creation, as discussed by Jung in his paper, 'Psychology and Literature' (1930; 1950) (*CW* 5 §141–§152)? I am grateful to Peter Kingsley for pointing out to me this possibility.

116 S. Reinach, *Cultes, mythes et religions* 5 vols, Paris: Laroux, 1905–1923. See also S. Reinach, *A Short History of Christianity*, tr. F. Simmonds, New York: Putnam's Sons, 1922.

117 Freud, 'Totem and Taboo', in *Standard Edition of the Complete Works of Sigmund Freud*, ed. J. Strachey and A. Freud, London: Hogarth Press, 1965–1974, vol. 13, pp. 1–61.

118 For further discussion of Freud's reception of Nietzsche, see R. Lehrer, *Nietzsche's Presence in Freud's Life and Thought: On the Origins of a Psychology of Dynamic Unconscious Mental Functioning*, Albany, NY: State University of New York Press, 1995; and R. Gasser, *Nietzsche und Freud*, Berlin and New York: Walter de Gruyter, 1997; É. Vartzbed, *La troisième oreille: Essai sur un précurseur de Freud*, Paris: Éditions L'Harmattan, 2003; and P.-L. Assoun, *Freud et Nietzsche* [1980; 1982], Paris: Quadrige/PUF, 1998.

119 Behind this complementarism lies a 'philosophical relativism', which Jung relates to Eastern thought and modern, post-Einstein physics alike, and whose 'ultimate effects' are at present unforeseen (*CW* 16 §146).

120 For further discussion of the Delphic Oracle, see C.G. Carus, *Die Lebenskunst nach den Inschriften des Tempels zu Delphi*, Dresden: Woldemar Türk, 1863; and M. Scott, *Delphi: A History of the Center of the Ancient World*, Princeton, NJ: Princeton University Press, 2014.

121 For a discussion of this suggestive phrase, see S. Shamdasani, '"The Boundless Expanse": Jung's Reflections on Life and Death', *Quadrant: Journal of the C. G. Jung Foundation for Analytical Psychology*, 2008, vol. 38, 9–32.

122 For further discussion of Jung's interest in Neoplatonism in general and in Plotinus in particular, see H.E. Barnes, 'Neo-Platonism and Analytical Psychology', *The Philosophical Review*, November 1945, vol. 54, no. 6, 558–577; and H.-R. Schwyzer, 'Archetyp und absoluter Geist: C.G. Jung und Plotin', in *Neue Zürcher Zeitung*, 25–26 July 1975, 'Literatur und Kunst', p. 38. For further discussion, see R. Robertson, 'Stairway to Heaven: Jung and Neoplatonism', *Psychological Perspectives: A Quarterly Journal of Jungian Thought*, 2002, vol. 44, no. 1, 80–95; and B.J. MacLennan, 'Individual Soul and World Soul: The Process of Individuation in Neoplatonism and C.G. Jung', in T. Arzt and A. Holm (eds), *Wegmarken der Individuation* [Studienreihe zur Analytischen Psychologie, vol. 1], Würzburg: Königshausen & Neumann, 2006, pp. 83–116. In *Revisioning Psychology*, James Hillman drew links between Renaissance Neoplatonism and archetypal psychology (New York: Harper & Row, 1975, pp. 193–211). See also H.-R. Schwyzer, 'The Intellect in Plotinus and the Archetypes of C.G. Jung', in J. Mansfeld and L.M. de Rijk (eds), *Kephalaion: Studies in Greek Philosophy and its Continuation offered to Professor C.J.*

de Vogel, Assen: Van Gorcum, 1975, pp. 214–222; and G. Shaw, 'Archetypal Psychology, Dreamwork, and Neoplatonism', in H.T. Hakl (ed.), *Octagon: The Quest for Wholeness: Mirrored in a library dedicated to religious studies, philosophy and esotericism in particular*, vol. 2, Gaggenau: scientia nova, 2016, pp. 327–358.

123 The problem of good and evil, and the doctrine of *privatio boni* (or privation of good), usually attributed to St Augustine, informed Jung's correspondence in the late 1940s and 1950s with the Dominican monk, Father Victor White; see *The Jung-White Letters*, ed. A.C. Lammers and A. Cunningham, London and New York: Routledge, 2007.

124 The principle of *enantiodromia* — 'the emergence of the unconscious opposite in the course of time' — is attributed by Jung to the pre-Socratic philosopher Heraclitus (*CW* 6 §709). Although the actual source in Heraclitus is unclear, the idea of *Enantiodromie* and *Enantiotropie* as things always having a mutual effect on one another is attributed to him in *Meyers Konversations-Lexikon*, 4th edn, Leipzig and Vienna: Verlag des Bibliographischen Instituts, 1885–1892, vol. 5, p. 611.

125 For further discussion, see S. Marlan, *Black Sun: The Alchemy and Art of Darkness*, College Station: Texas A & M University Press, 2005.

126 *Aurora consurgens*, I, chapter 6, 'The First Parable: Of the Black Earth, wherein the Seven Planets Took Root', in *Aurora consurgens: A Document attributed to Thomas Aquinas on the Problem of Opposites in Alchemy*, ed. M.-L. von Franz, tr. R.F.C. Hull and A.S.B. Glover, Toronto: Inner City Books, 2000, pp. 56–57. The Latin text of this work, also known as *De alchimia* and *Liber Trinitatis*, was included in J. Rhenanus (ed.), *Harmoniae inperscurtabilis chymico-philosophicae sive Philosophorum antiquorum consentiu Decades duae* (Frankfurt, 1625); another text, called its second part, was included in *Artis auriferae, quam chemiam vocant* (Basel, 1593), volume 1.

127 Psalm 37 (38): 3 (NJB).

128 According to the axiom of Maria Prophetissa, 'one becomes two, two becomes three, and out of the third comes the One as the fourth' (cf. 'Practica Mariae Prophetissae in Artem Alchimicam', in *Artis auriferae*, vol. 1, Basel: Waldkirch, 1593, pp. 319–324; and M. Berthelot, *Collection des Anciens Alchimistes grecs*, vol. 3, Paris: Steinheil, 1888, VI.v.[6], p. 389; cited in *CW* 12 §26 and *CW* 12 §209. In his comments in *The Psychology of the Transference* on the tetrameria (i.e., fourfold nature) of the transforming process, Jung states the axiom as the inverse of this precept: 'It begins with the four separate elements, the state of chaos, and ascends by degrees to the three manifestations of Mercurius in the inorganic, organic, and spiritual worlds; and, after attaining the form of Sol and Luna (i.e., the precious metals gold and silver, but also the radiance of the gods who can overcome the strife of the elements by love), it culminates in the one and indivisible (incorruptible, ethereal, eternal) nature of the *anima*, the *quinta essentia*, *aqua permanens*, tincture, or *lapis philosophorum*. This progression from the number 4 to 3 to 2 to 1 is the "axiom of Maria", which runs in various forms through the whole of alchemy like a *leitmotiv*' (*CW* 16 §404).

129 In this work, Jung claims, we find 'fundamentally [...] the same theme, the same "Axioma Mariae"', which tells of how Rosencreutz 'is transformed out of his former unenlightened condition and comes to realize that he is related to "royalty"'. In keeping with its seventeenth-century assumptions, however, the process is 'projected' and 'the withdrawal of the projection into the hero' is something at which the work can only hint (*CW* 16 §407).

130 For further discussion of *Selige Sehnsucht*, see F.O. Schrader, 'Selige Sehnsucht', *Euphorion*, 1952, vol. 46, 48–58; and M. Böhler and G. Schwieder, 'Schöpferischer Augenblick', in B. Witte (ed.), *Interpretationen: Gedichte von Johann Wolfgang Goethe*, Stuttgart: Reclam, 1998, pp. 202–216. Of the poem as a whole, Eduard Spranger has explained: 'It is the old, Platonic way out of existence in the cave into the light. For human beings do does not only follow the spiral tendency of organic growth, they enter, through an apparent process of ethical self-destruction, into new, purer forms of life. Even for this there exist eloquent symbols in the visible world; for the ladder of existence does not end with the organic realm. In such hours of self-rediscovery it is as if masses of cloud disperse into

light wisps of cirrhus: dispersal becomes redemption' ('Goethes Weltanschauung' [1932], in *Goethe: Seine geistige Welt*, Tübingen: Rainer Wunderlich Verlag Hermann Leins, 1967, pp. 275–317 [pp. 307–308]).

131 J.W. von Goethe, *Poems of the West and East: West-Eastern Divan — West-Östlicher Divan: Bi-Lingual Edition of the Complete Poems*, tr. J. Whaley, Bern, Berlin, and Frankfurt am Main: Lang, 1998, p. 47.

132 Goethe, *Poems of the West and East*, p. 47.

133 *Enneads*, V.9.10, in E. O'Brien (ed. and tr.), *The Essential Plotinus: Representative Treatises from the Enneads*, Indianapolis, ID: Hackett, 1964, p. 86.

134 *Enneads*, VI.9.4, in *The Essential Plotinus*, p. 78.

135 For further discussion of Goethe and Giordano Bruno, see: L. Kuhlenbeck, *Giordano Brunos Einfluss auf Goethe und Schiller*, Leipzig: Thomas, 1907; and W. Saenger, *Goethe und Giordano Bruno: Ein Beitrag zur Geschichte der Goethischen Weltanschauung*, Berlin: Ebering, 1930. See also Rudolf Steiner's lecture given in Berlin on 26 January 1911, 'Galilei, Giordano Bruno und Goethe', in *Antworten der Geisteswissenschaft auf die großen Fragen des Daseins* [*Gesamtausgabe*, vol. 60], Dornach/Schweiz: Rudolf Steiner Verlag, 1983, pp. 284–314.

136 Bruno, *The Heroic Frenzies*, Part 1, Dialogue 3, p. 38.

137 Nietzsche, 'Ecce homo', in *The Gay Science*, p. 67.

138 'Preface', §3; in *The Gay Science*, p. 38.

139 V. Jankélévitch, *Quelque part dans l'inachevé*, Paris: Gallimard, 1978, p. 161; cf. R.M. Rilke, *Schriften: Kommentierte Ausgabe*, ed. M. Engel et al., 4 vols, Frankfurt am Main and Leipzig: Insel, 1996, vol. 4, *Schriften*, ed. H. Nalewski, p. 384.

140 Bergson, *La Pensée et le Mouvement: Essais et conférences* [1934], in H. Bergson, *Œuvres*, Paris: Presses universitaires de France, 1970, p. 1347.

141 Jankélévitch, *Quelque part dans l'inachevé*, p. 22.

142 Jankélévitch, *Quelque part dans l'inachevé*, p. 23.

143 'Entretien avec Raphaël Enthoven', 29 September 2007. Available online at: http://temporel.fr/Entretien-avec-Raphael-Enthoven (accessed 22 August 2013).

144 Jankélévitch, *Quelque part dans l'inachevé*, pp. 23–24.

145 S. Meitinger, '«Mehr Licht!»: Quelle lumière?', in S. Meitinger, *Bornoyages du champ poétique*, Mazères: Le chasseur abstrait éditeur, 2008, pp. 111–122 (esp. pp. 113–115). See also 'Pour Goethe: Quelques réflexions sur le classicisme'. Available online at: www.oeuvresouvertes.net/autres_espaces/meitinger5.html (accessed 21 August 2013).

146 See 'Of the Great Longing', in Nietzsche, *Thus Spoke Zarathustra*, pp. 238–240.

147 Prologue, §4 and §5; Nietzsche, *Thus Spoke Zarathustra*, pp. 44 and 46.

148 Nietzsche, *Thus Spoke Zarathustra*, p. 144.

149 Nietzsche, *Thus Spoke Zarathustra*, p. 180.

150 Nietzsche, *Thus Spoke Zarathustra*, pp. 215 and 230–231.

151 'Of the Three Evil Things', §2; Nietzsche, *Thus Spoke Zarathustra*, p. 209. Cf. S. Corngold, *The Fate of the Self: German Writers and French Theory*, New York: Columbia University Press, 1986, p. 113; cited in E.L. Jurist, *Beyond Hegel and Nietzsche: Philosophy, Culture, and Agency*, Boston: MIT Press, 2000, p. 321, fn. 11.

152 See the extremely helpful notes by Davitt Moroney in the booklet accompanying the recording to Biber's cycle by John Holloway (violin), Davitt Moroney (chamber organ, harpsichord), and Tragicomedia; Virgin Classics, 1990. VCD 7 90838-2.

153 For an overview of this literature, see the commentary of the Flemish Jesuit and biblical exegete, Cornelius a Lapide (1567–1637), in *The Great Commentary: The Holy Gospel According to Saint Mark; The Holy Gospel According to Saint Luke*, tr. T.W. Mossman, revised M.J. Miller, Fitzwilliam, NH: Loreto, 2008, pp. 162–163.

154 S. Gregory the Great, *Morals on the Book of Job* [*Library of Fathers of the Holy Catholic Church*, vols. 35–38], Oxford; London: Parker; Rivington, 1844–1850, vol. 2, part 4, book 18, §33, p. 340; and vol. 3, part 6, book 33, §5, p. 558.

155 The reference here to Christ the Lord, or 'Yahweh's anointed' (NJB), pertains in the immediate context to King Zedekiah, to the sack of Jerusalem by the Chaldeans and the second deportation (see 4 Kings 25: 1–21); and, in an extended sense, to Christ.

156 Origen, homily 8, in Origen, *Homilies on Joshua*, ed. C. White and tr. B.J. Bruce, Washington, DC: Catholic University of America Press, 2002, p. 88.

157 See Cornelius a Lapide, *Commentary*, p. 162; see Sermon Five, §3: 'That beautiful pillar of cloud that moved before the Israelites,' — in the story of the Exodus — 'mysteriously signifies the Lord Jesus coming in a pure cloud, as Isaiah says [cf. Isaiah 19: 1]. The cloud is the Virgin Mary, because of her descent from Eve. She is pure because of her virginal integrity. Pure too, because she sought not to please the world, but to please God. Pure because she did not conceive in sin, but became fruitful by the overshadowing of the Spirit'; and Sermon Five, §4: 'Another interpretation is that Christ came into Egypt in a light cloud, that is, he came into this world by taking on himself a body. In a cloud he came, for the cloud of the body overshadowed him; but his flesh was pure, for no sin weighed it down' (*Homilies of Saint Ambrose on Psalm 118 (119)*, tr. Í. Ni Riain, Dublin: Halcyon Press, 1998, p. 55). But commenting, as so many of the early Church Fathers do, on the Song of Songs, specifically verse 2: 3, 'I sat down under his shadow, whom I desired', Ambrose also remarks: '[The Bride] has accepted the Law. This is the path she pursued, this the race she ran. Reposing in the Law, she rested in the shadow of Christ. His shade is good and it alone protects us from sin's burning heat. Undoubtedly God's Law is Christ's Shadow. What can the festal day of new moon or sabbath mean unless it were a prelude of things to come? […] The seventh year in which all debts are pardoned prefigures Christ. In his shade the faith of our fathers rested and the love of the holy prophets found repose' (*Homilies*, p. 57).

158 Ambrose, *On the Mysteries*, chapter 3, §12–§13, in St Ambrose, *On the Mysteries and the Treatise "On the Sacraments" by an Unknown Author*, ed. J.H. Shrawley, tr. T. Thompson, London; New York: SPCK; Macmillan, 1919, p. 50.

159 Gregory the Great, *Morals on the Book Job*, vol. 2, part 4, book 18, §33, p. 340; and vol. 3, part 6, book 33, §5, p. 557.

160 Augustine, Letter 187, to Dardanus, chapter 31, in Saint Augustine, *Letters*, vol. 4, *165–203*, tr. W. Parsons, Washington, DC: Catholic University of America Press, 1955, p. 246.

161 *Quaestiones Veteris et Novi Testamenti*, chapter 51, in Augustine, *Opera Omnia*, vol. 3, part 2 [*Patrologiae cursus completus, Series Latina*, ed. J.-P. Migne, vol. 35], Paris: Migne, 1864, cols. 2250–2251.

162 *On the Trinity*, book 2, §26; in *Hilary of Poitiers, John of Damascene* [*Nicene and Post-Nicene Fathers*, second series, vol. 9], ed. P. Schaff and H. Wallace [1893], New York: Cosimo, 2007, p. 59.

163 *On the Trinity*, book 2, §27; in *Hilary of Poitiers, John of Damascene*, p. 59.

164 St Gregory of Nyssa, *Oration of the Nativity of Christ*, in St Gregory of Nyssa, *Opera quæ reperiri potuerunt omnia*, vol. 3 [*Patrologia Graeca*, ed. J.-P. Migne, vol. 46], Paris: Migne, 1863, cols 1128a–1149c. Translation from online source. Available online at: www.synodinresistance.org/pdfs/2011/01/11/ (accessed 7 May 2013).

165 Cornelius a Lapide, *Commentary*, p. 163.

166 Cornelius a Lapide, *Commentary*, p. 163.

167 Cornelius a Lapide, *Commentary*, p. 163.

168 Compare with the mode of Christ's exit from the tomb after the resurrection. Although the Gospels themselves do not describe the moment of resurrection on Easter Day, the scene within the tomb has been imaginatively reconstructed by Prosper Guéranger (1805–1875): 'The day of light, Sunday, has begun, and its early dawn is struggling with the gloom. The Soul of Jesus immediately darts from the prison of limbo […]. In a twinkling of an eye, it reaches and enters the sepulchre, and reunites itself with that Body which, three days before, it had quitted amidst an agony of suffering. The sacred Body returns to life, raises itself up, and throws aside the winding-sheet, the spices, and the bands. The bruises have disappeared, the Blood has been brought back to the veins;

and from these limbs that had been torn by the scourging, from this head that had been mangled by the thorns, from these hands and feet that had pierced with nails, there darts forth a dazzling light that fills the cave. […] But Jesus is not to tarry in the gloomy sepulchre. Quicker than a ray of light through a crystal, he passes through the stone that closes the entrance of the cave' (*The Liturgical Year*, vol. 7, *Paschal Time: Book 1*, tr. L. Shepherd [1949], Great Falls, MT, 2000, pp. 102–103).

169 St Basil the Great, 'Homily 2 on the Holy Birth of the Lord', in *Opera omnia quæ exstant*, vol. 3 [*Patrologia Graeca*, ed. J.-P. Migne, vol. 31], Paris: Migne, 1885, cols 1472–1476; translated in S.M. Holmes (ed.), *The Fathers on the Sunday Gospels*, Collegeville, MN: Liturgical Press, 2012, p. 40.

170 See St Bridget's *Revelations*, book 6, chapter 88; in *The Revelations of St. Birgitta of Sweden*, vol. 3, *Liber Caelestis: Books VI-VII*, tr. D. Searby, New York: Oxford University Press, 2012, p. 155.

171 See J.H. Charlesworth (ed.), *The Old Testament Pseudepigrapha*, 2 vols, Garden City, NY: Doubleday, 1985, vol. 2, pp. 163–176.

172 In his *Commentary*, Cornelius a Lapide shows himself to be worried by some of the implications of this debate, writing that 'the difficulty concerning the afterbirth is greater, namely, the question as to whether Christ in the womb was enclosed within His own *secundinae* or membrane, as other infants are', and discussing the question in great detail (*Commentary*, p. 265). The entire discussion surrounding the virginity of Mary *ante partum, in partu, et post partum* (before, during, and after birth) reminds one of the strictures Nietzsche places in Zarathustra's mouth in 'Of Immaculate Perception': 'For he is lustful and jealous, the monk in the moon, lustful for the earth and for all the joys of lovers. […] Your spirit has been persuaded to contempt of the earthly, but your entrails have not: these, however, are the strongest part of you!' (*Thus Spoke Zarathustra*, pp. 144–145).

173 Hesiod, *Works and Days*, in *'The Homeric Hymns' and 'Homerica'*, ll. 125 and 255 (pp. 11 and 21).

174 Homer, *Iliad*, book 16, ll. 296–297, 364–365, 384–386; Homer, *The Iliad*, tr. R. Lattimore, Chicago and London: University of Chicago Press, 1951, pp. 338 and 340.

175 Virgil, *The Æneid*, book 1; translated John Dryden.

176 *Stromata*, book 2, chapter 2, in St Clement of Alexandria, *Opera quæ exstant omnia*, vol. 1 [*Patrologia Graeca*, ed. J.-P. Migne, vol. 8], Paris: Migne, 1891, cols 936b–937a.

177 Dismissing attempts to develop a proof of the existence of God, such as those offered by Stoics, rationalist theologians, or Deist thinkers, Pascal responded in his *Pensées*: 'To tell [unbelievers] that they have only to look at the least thing around them and they will see in it God plainly revealed […] is giving them cause to think that the proofs of our religion are indeed feeble, and reason and experience tell me that nothing is more likely to bring it into contempt in their eyes. This is not how Scripture speaks, with its better knowledge of the things of God. On the contrary it says that God is a hidden God, and that since nature was corrupted he has left men to their blindness. […] It tells us elsewhere: *Vere tu es Deus absconditus* [i.e., *Verily thou art a God that hidest thyself*, KJV]' (*Pensées*, #781–242; in Pascal, *Pensées*, tr. A.J. Krailsheimer, Harmondsworth: Penguin, 1966, pp. 263–264; *Œuvres complètes*, ed. L. Lafuma, Paris: Seuil, 1963, p. 599).

178 *Rosarium philosophorum*, in *Artis auriferae*, vol. 2, Basel: 1593, pp. 239–240; my emphasis. Translated by Adam Mclean on The Alchemy Website. Available online at: www.levity.com/alchemy/rosary1.html (accessed 28 August 2013).

179 Jung, *CW* 12 §138–§139 and §140; see C.A. Baines, *A Coptic Gnostic Treatise Contained in the Codex Brucianus — Bruce MS. 96, Bodleian Library, Oxford*, Cambridge: Cambridge University Press, 1933, p. 87.

180 See Jung, 'Individual Dream Symbolism in Relation to Alchemy', in *CW* 12 §140; and *Mysterium coniunctionis*, *CW* 14 §21 fn.

181 For the text and translations of Benedict XVI's General Audience on 19 December 2012, see the Vatican website. Available online at: www.vatican.va/holy_father/benedict_xvi/audiences/2012/documents/hf_ben_xvi_aud_20121219_en.html (accessed 28 March 2013).

182 See *Proslogion*, §1, §9, and §16, in Anselm of Canterbury, *The Major Works*, ed. B. Davies and G.R. Evans, Oxford and New York: Oxford University Press, 2008, pp. 85, 91, 96. Cf. 'My understanding is not able [to attain] to that [light]. It shines too much and [my understanding] does not grasp it nor does the eye of my soul allow itself to be turned towards it for too long' (§16; p. 96).

183 'I also consider them wholly to rave who think a shadow of change could occur concerning the nature of the Word of God' (letter of Cyril to John of Antioch, in H.P. Percival [ed.], *The Seven Ecumenical Councils* [Nicene and Post-Nicene Fathers, Series II, vol. 14], Edinburgh: T. & T. Clark, 1899, p. 253); 'And the sun continued to shine as it had done from the beginning, and continued so that absolutely no shadow of change fell upon it, as had happened to the first angel and to Adam through the instigation of the devil' (Hildegard to Adam, Abbot, before 1166, in *The Letters of Hildegard of Bingen*, vol. 1, tr. J.L. Baird and R.K. Ehrman, Oxford and New York: Oxford University Press, 1994, p. 197).

184 P. Grimes and R.L. Uliana, *Philosophical Midwifery: A New Paradigm for Understanding Human Problems With Its Validation*, Costa Mesa, CA: Hyparxis, 1998, p. 11; cf. *Republic* 518c; translated by W.H.D. Rouse as 'the sight of being and the most brilliant light of being', in *Great Dialogues of Plato*, ed. E.H. Warmington and P.G. Rouse, tr. W.H.D. Rouse, New York: Mentor, 1956, p. 317 (alternatively translated by Paul Shorey as 'the contemplation of essence and the brightest region of being', in *CD*, p. 751); and Plotinus, 'On the Good, or the One', i.e., *Enneads*, VI.9.9, in *The Essential Plotinus*, p. 86.

185 For the Jungian tradition, Eckhart is an important figure; see J.M. Clark, 'C.G. Jung and Meister Eckhart', *Modern Language Review*, April 1959, vol. 54, no. 2, 239–244; and J. Dourley, *Jung and His Mystics: In the End it All Comes to Nothing*, New York and Hove: Routledge, 2014.

186 See the commentary in Meister Eckhart, *Werke I*, ed. N. Largier, Frankfurt am Main: Deutscher Klassiker Verlag, 2008, p. 750. For further discussion in relation to Meister Eckhart as well as Pseudo-Dionysius and other thinkers, see D. Turner, *The Darkness of God: Negativity in Christian Mysticism*, Cambridge: Cambridge University Press, 1995.

187 Meister Eckhart, *Sermons & Treatises*, ed. and tr. M. O'C. Walshe, 3 vols, Longmead: Element Books, 1987, vol. 1, p. 56. Because the system of numbering Eckhart's sermons is inconsistent across different editions of his works, the beginning of the biblical text on which each sermon is based is provided in parentheses to assist the reader in tracing the particular sermon in question.

188 Eckhart, *Sermons & Treatises*, vol. 2, p. 67.

189 Eckhart, *Sermons & Treatises*, vol. 2, p. 254.

190 Eckhart, *Sermons & Treatises*, vol. 2, p. 53.

191 For further discussion, see Eckhart's commentary on the Book of Exodus, excerpted in Meister Eckhart, *Selected Treatises and Sermons*, tr. J.M. Clark and J.V. Skinner, London: Faber and Faber, 1958, pp. 225–230.

192 See Meister Eckhart, *Deutsche Predigten und Traktate*, ed. and tr. J. Quint, Munich: Hanser, 1963, p. 523.

193 Plato, *Republic*, 616b, in *CD*, p. 840.

194 Eckhart, *Sermons & Treatises*, vol. 2, p. 322.

195 Eckhart, *Sermons & Treatises*, vol. 1, p. 225.

196 Eckhart, *Sermons & Treatises*, vol. 2, p. 323.

197 Eckhart, *Sermons & Treatises*, vol. 1, p. 153.

198 Eckhart, *Sermons & Treatises*, vol. 1, p. 159.

199 Eckhart, *Sermons & Treatises*, vol. 1, p. 159.

200 Eckhart, *Sermons & Treatises*, vol. 2, pp. 317–320.

201 Eckhart, *Sermons & Treatises*, vol. 2, p. 326; cf. Eckhart, sermon 68 (*Impletum est tempus Elizabeth*), in *Sermons & Treatises*, vol. 2, pp. 159–160.

202 Eckhart, *Sermons & Treatises*, vol. 2, p. 328.

203 Eckhart, *Sermons & Treatises*, vol. 2, p. 328.

204 Eckhart, *Sermons & Treatises*, vol. 2, p. 328; cf. sermon 19 (*Surrexit autem Saulus de terra …*), in *Sermons & Treatises*, vol. 2, p. 159.

205 Eckhart, *Sermons & Treatises*, vol. 2, p. 328.

206 Eckhart, *Sermons & Treatises*, vol. 2, p. 328.

207 Dionysius the Areopagite, *Works*, tr. J. Parker, 2 vols, London: Parker, 1897, vol. 2, p. 15; cf. Pseudo-Dionysius, *The Complete Works*, tr. C. Luibheid, New York and Mahwah, NJ: Paulist Press, 1987, p. 155. For further discussion of Dionysius in relation to Jung, see D. Henderson, *Apophatic Elements in the Theory and Practice of Psychoanalysis: Pseudo-Dionysius and C.G. Jung*, London and New York: Routledge, 2014.

208 See Damascius, *Concerning Principles*, cited in Aristotle, *The Metaphysics of Aristotle*, tr. T. Taylor, London: Davis, Wilks, and Taylor, 1801, 'Additional Notes', p. 431.

209 See 'Damascius on First Principles', in *Shrine of Wisdom Magazine*, 37, 1928. Available online at: http://shrineofwisdom.weebly.com/damascius-on-first-principles.html (accessed 2 June 2014). For further discussion and the full text of Damascius's treatise, see S. Ahbel-Rappe (ed. and tr.), *Damascius' Problems & Solutions Concerning First Principles*, Oxford and New York: Oxford University Press, 2010.

210 *Mystical Theology*, 997a–b; in Pseudo-Dionysius, *Complete Works*, p. 135.

211 *Mystical Theology*, 1000c; *Complete Works*, p. 136.

212 *Mystical Theology*, 1000d and 1001a; *Complete Works*, p. 137.

213 *Mystical Theology*, 1025a; *Complete Works*, p. 138.

214 *Mystical Theology*, 1025b; *Complete Works*, p. 138; cf. *The Works of Dionysius the Areopagite*, trans. Parker, vol. 1, p. 133.

215 *The Mystical Ark*, book 4, chapter 23; in Richard of St-Victor, *The Twelve Patriarchs; The Mystical Ark; Book Three of the Trinity*, tr. G.A. Zinn, New York and Mahwah: Paulist Press, 1979, p. 306.

216 C. Wolters (tr.), *The Cloud of Unknowing and Other Works*, Harmondsworth: Penguin, 1978.

217 Philo, *On the Life of Moses, I*, XXVIII (158), in *The Works of Philo: Complete and Unabridged: New Updated Edition*, tr. C.D. Yonge, Peabody, MA: Hendrickson, 1993, p. 474; my emphases.

218 Clement of Alexandria, *The Stromata, or Miscellanies*, book 2, chapter 2, in *Ante-Nicene Fathers*, vol. 2, *Fathers of the Second Century: Hermas, Tatian, Athenagoras, Theophilus, and Clement of Alexandria*, ed. P. Schaff, New York: Christian Literature Publishing, 1885, p. 348.

219 Clement of Alexandria, *Stromata*, book 5, chapter 12, in *Fathers of the Second Century*, p. 463.

220 Proclus, *Commentary on "Parmenides"*, book 3, 832; in Proclus, *Commentary on Plato's "Parmenides"*, tr. G.R. Morrow and J.M. Dillon, Princeton, NJ: Princeton University Press, 1987, p. 191.

221 Gregory of Nyssa, *The Life of Moses*, tr. A.J. Malherbe and E. Ferguson, Mahwah, NJ: Paulist Press, 1978, p. 43. For further discussion, see M. Laird, 'Darkness', in L.F. Mateo-Seco and G. Maspero (eds), *The Brill Dictionary of Gregory of Nyssa*, Leiden: Brill, 2010, pp. 203–205.

222 Gregory of Nyssa, *The Life of Moses*, book 1, §77, pp. 50–51; cf. p. 150.

223 Gregory of Nyssa, *The Life of Moses*, book 2, §162, pp. 94–95.

224 Gregory of Nyssa, *The Life of Moses*, book 2, §163, p. 95; my emphasis. For further discussion, see H. Koch, 'Das mystische Schauen beim hl. Gregor von Nyssa', *Theologische Quartalschrift*, 1898, vol. 80, 404–427; and P. Kariatlis, '"Dazzling Darkness": The Mystical or Theophanic Theology of St Gregory of Nyssa', *Phronema*, 2012, vol. 27, no. 2, 99–123.

225 Gregory of Nyssa, *The Life of Moses*, book 2, §164, p. 95.

226 St Gregory of Nyssa, *The Lord's Prayer; The Beatitudes*, tr. H.C. Graef, Westminster, ML; London: Newman Press; Longmans, Green, 1954, p. 35; my emphasis.

227 Gregory of Nyssa, *The Lord's Prayer; The Beatitudes*, pp. 35–36; my emphasis.

228 Origen, *The Song of Songs: Commentary and Homilies*, tr. and annotated R.P. Lawson, Westminster, MD; London: Newman Press; Longmans, Green and Co., 1957, p. 293. In this respect Origen discerned a general law, remarking that 'advances are always on this pattern: a person desires at the outset to be at least in the shadow of the virtues' (p. 293).

229 Origen, *The Song of Songs: Commentary and Homilies*, p. 294.

230 Meister Eckhart, *Sermons & Treatises*, vol. 1, p. 1.

231 Eckhart, *Sermons & Treatises*, vol. 1, p. 12: 'May the God who has been born again as man assist us to this birth, eternally helping us, weak men, to be born in him again as God'.

232 Compare with another famous line, 'though I should walk in the midst of the shadow of death, I will fear no evils' in Psalm 22 (23) (here, verse 4).

233 Origen, *The Song of Songs: Commentary and Homilies*, pp. 182–183.

234 Origen, *The Song of Songs: Commentary and Homilies*, p. 183.

235 For a theological approach to Nietzsche, see G. Fraser, *Redeeming Nietzsche: On the Piety of Unbelief*, London and New York: Routledge, 2002; and P. Köster, *Kontroversen um Nietzsche: Untersuchungen zur theologischen Rezeption*, Zurich: Theologischer Verlag Zürich, 2003. For further discussion of Nietzsche's Pietist upbringing, see M. Pernet, 'Friedrich Nietzsche and Pietism', *German Life and Letters*, October 1995, vol. 48, no. 4, 474–486.

236 See the discourse entitled 'Of the Vision and the Riddle', in Nietzsche, *Thus Spoke Zarathustra*, pp. 176–180.

237 For an account of the intricacies of Arianism, including its influence and its misrepresentation, see M. Wiles, *Archetypal Heresy: Arianism Through the Centuries*, New York: Oxford University Press, 1996.

238 Proclus, Sermon 1, in M. Wiles and M. Santer (eds), *Documents in Early Christian Thought*, Cambridge: Cambridge University Press, 1975, pp. 61–65 (p. 65).

239 Proclus, Sermon 1, in Wiles and Santer (eds), *Documents in Early Christian Thought*, p. 62.

240 'What a mystery! Beholding the miracles, I extol the deity; seeing the sufferings, I cannot deny the humanity. As man, Emmanuel opened the gates of human nature; as God, he left the bars of virginity unbroken. As he entered through the ear, so too did he come out from the womb; as he was conceived, so was he born. His entering in was altogether without passion, and his coming out was altogether beyond understanding — as the prophet Ezekiel said: […] "And the gate shall be shut"' (Proclus, Sermon 1, in Wiles and Santer (eds), *Documents in Early Christian Thought*, p. 66; cf. Ezekiel 44: 1–2).

241 E.P. Evans, *Animal Symbolism in Ecclesiastical Architecture*, London: Heinemann, 1896, p. 99. See also J. Kayser, *Zur Geschichte der Kirchenhymnen* [1881], Bremen: DOGMA in Europäischer Hochschulverlag, 2012, p. 358, esp. fn. 4.

242 See St Augustine, *Sermo de Tempore*, no. 22; Agobard of Lyons, *Liber de Correctione Antiphonarii*, chapter 8; and Ephrem of Syria, in *De divers. Serm.*, no. 1, *De Nativ. Dom.*, cited in M. Bettini, *Women and Weasels: Mythologies of Birth in Ancient Greece and Rome*, tr. E. Eisenach, Chicago and London: University of Chicago Press, 2013, pp. 113–122.

243 Walther von der Vogelweide, *Die Gedichte*, ed. K. Lachmann, Berlin: Reimer, 1827, p. 36.

244 E. Jones, 'The Madonna's Conception through the Ear: A Contribution to the Relation between Aesthetics and Religion' [1914], in *Essays in Applied Psycho-Analysis*, vol. 2, *Essays in Folklore, Anthropology and Religion*, London: Hogarth Press, 1951, pp. 266–357.

245 B. Baert, 'The Annunciation Revisited: Essay on the Concept of Wind and the Senses in Late Medieval and Early Modern Visual Culture', in *Critica d'Arte*, 2013, vols 47–48, 57–68. For further discussion, see B. Kottwitz, 'Im Anfang war das Ohr: Eine nicht nur kunsthistorische Betrachtung: Empfängnis und Geburt durch das Ohr', *Die Waage*, 1990, vol. 29, no. 4, 134–143; reprinted in R. Kahn and B. Kreutz (eds), *Das Buch vom Hören*, Freiburg: Herder, 1991, pp. 29–37.

246 For the Qu'ran's account of the story of Mary, see Surah 3: 42–51, Surah 19: 16–21, and Surah 66: 12. For the relevant tafsir, see Tafsir 'Ibn Kathir, Qu'ran 21: 91, and Tafsir 'Ibn Kathir, Qu'ran 66: 12. In the *Qu'ran*, however, Mary cries out in pain during the pangs of birth (Surah 19: 23), in contrast to the tradition discussed above.

247 Ovid, *Festivals*, book 5, ll. 195–202, in: Ovid, *Fasti*, tr. J.G. Frazer, London; New York: Heinemann; Putnam, 1931, p. 275.

248 W.K.C. Guthrie, *The Greeks and their Gods*, London: Methuen, 1950, p. 139; see Homer, *Iliad*, book 16, l. 150; and Virgil, *Georgics*, book 3, ll. 271–275.

249 Lucian, *Of Sacrifice* (*De Sacrificiis*), §6: 'Without intercourse with her husband [Hera] became the mother of a wind-child, Hephaestus' (Lucian, *Works*, vol. 3, tr. A.H. Harmon, Cambridge, MA, and London: Harvard University Press, 1921, p. 161).

250 Guthrie, *The Greeks and their Gods*, pp. 139 and 141.

251 Jung, *PU* §172; cf. *Symbols of Transformation*, *CW* 5 §150 and plate VIII. The source of Jung's illustration is Karl von Spieß, *Marksteine der Volkskunst*, 2 vols, Berlin: Stubenrauch, 1937–1942, vol. 2, fig. 112. In his study of animal symbolism, Evans cites examples at Oppenheim, on the portal of the cathedral at Würzburg, while in the parish (and former abbey) church at Eltenberg on the Rhine a relief of the Annunciation shows the infant Jesus descending from heaven on the breath of God, attended by the Holy Spirit, and entering the ear of the Virgin (*Animal Symbolism in Ecclesiastical Architecture*, p. 99).

252 For an overview of the discussion surrounding Solar Phallus Man, see R. Wolin, *The Seduction of Unreason: The Intellectual Romance with Fascism from Nietzsche to Postmodernism*, Princeton and Oxford: Princeton University Press, 2004, pp. 85–87.

253 For further discussion of this passage, see E. Monick, *Phallos: Sacred Image of the Masculine*, Toronto, Canada: Inner City Books, 1987, pp. 72–76.

254 J.C. Steebus, *Coelum Sephiroticum, Hebræorum*, Mainz: Bourgeat, 1679, p. 39. After a career as a doctor in Mainz, Steeb died in 1698.

255 *Symposium*, 206c; in *CD*, p. 558 (translation modified).

256 *Symposium*, 206c; in *CD*, p. 558 (translation modified).

257 *Symposium*, 206d; in *CD*, p. 558.

258 *Symposium*, 208e–209a; in *CD*, p. 560 (translation modified).

259 *Symposium*, 206b; in *CD*, p. 558.

260 *Theaetetus*, 149a; in *CD*, p. 853.

261 *Theaetetus*, 150b–151b; in *CD*, p. 865. For further discussion, see M.F. Burnyeat, 'Socratic Midwifery, Platonic Inspiration', *Bulletin of the Institute of Classical Studies*, 1977, vol. 24, 7–16; J. Tomlin, 'Socratic Midwifery', *The Classical Quarterly*, 1987, [NS] vol. 37, no. 1, 97–102; R.G. Edmonds III, 'Socrates the Beautiful: Role Reversal and Midwifery in Plato's *Symposium*', *Transactions of the American Philological Association*, 2000, vol. 130, 261–285; and P. Stern, *Knowledge and Politics in Plato's "Theaetetus"*, Cambridge: Cambridge University Press, 2007, chapter 3, 'Socratic Midwifery', pp. 32–81.

262 See Grimes and Uliana, *Philosophical Midwifery*, esp. Part 1, pp. 1–22.

263 For further discussion, see Hough, *Nietzsche's Noontide Friend*, pp. 119–148.

264 Nietzsche, *Human, All Too Human*, vol. 1, 'Preface', §7; in *Human, All Too Human*, tr. R.J. Hollingdale, Cambridge: Cambridge University Press, 1986, p. 10.

265 *Human, All Too Human*, vol. 2, 'Assorted Opinions and Maxims', §64, §216 and §285; in *Human, All Too Human*, pp. 228, 264, and 279.

266 *Human, All Too Human*, vol. 2, 'The Wanderer and His Shadow', §17; in *Human, All Too Human*, pp. 309–310. See Schopenhauer, *Parerga and Paralipomena*, vol. 2, 'On Affirmation and Denial of the Will to Live', in *Essays and Aphorisms*, tr. R.J. Hollingdale, Harmondsworth: Penguin, 1970, pp. 61–65 (esp. p. 64).

267 *Daybreak*, §552; in Nietzsche, *Daybreak*, tr. R.J. Hollingdale, Cambridge: Cambridge University Press, 1982, p. 223.

268 *Daybreak*, §552; in *Daybreak*, p. 223.

269 *The Gay Science*, §72; in *The Gay Science*, p. 129.

270 *The Gay Science*, 'Preface', §3; in *The Gay Science*, pp. 35–36.
271 *The Gay Science*, §370; in *The Gay Science*, p. 329.
272 'Of Old and Young Women', in *Thus Spoke Zarathustra*, p. 91.
273 'On the Blissful Islands', in *Thus Spoke Zarathustra*, p. 111.
274 'Of Involuntary Bliss', in *Thus Spoke Zarathustra*, p. 181.
275 'The Seven Seals', §1; in *Thus Spoke Zarathustra*, p. 244.
276 'Of the Higher Man', §11 and §12; in *Thus Spoke Zarathustra*, pp. 301–302.
277 'Zarathustra's Prologue', §4; in *Thus Spoke Zarathustra*, p. 45.
278 *KSA* 10, 13[1], 427 and *KSA* 10, 16[7], 498.
279 *KSA*, 13[1], 424 and *KSA*, 16[7], 497.
280 Theierl, *Nietzsche — Mystik als Selbstversuch*, p. 34.
281 H.-G. Gadamer, 'The Relevance of the Beautiful: Art as Play, Symbol, and Festival', in *The Relevance of Beauty and Other Essays*, Cambridge: Cambridge University Press, 1986, pp. 3–53 (p. 32).
282 Goethe, *Faust*, Part Two, ll. 11302–11303; in J.W. Goethe, *Faust*, ed. E. Trunz, Munich: Beck, 1972, p. 341.

2

'NEVER CEASE CHISELLING'

Statues and Self-Sculpting

> Sculpture deserves our high esteem because it can and must achieve ultimate perfection in the representation of its subject, since it divests man of all inessential elements.
>
> (Goethe, 'On the Laocoön Group', 1798)

'Ah, you men', cries Zarathustra, 'I see an image sleeping in the stone, the image of my visions! Ah, that it must sleep in the hardest, ugliest stone!' The superman is thus something to do with Zarathustra's VISION. But then Zarathustra says: 'Now my hammer rages fiercely against its prison. Fragments fly from the stone'; in other words, the vision is followed by ACTION. 'What is that to me?' asks Zarathustra, and following his QUESTION, he makes a RESOLUTION: 'I will complete it' — and so we move into the image of the superman as 'the most silent, the lightest of all things'.[1]

To understand this sequence, from VISION to ACTION via QUESTIONING and RESOLUTION, we need to examine the central idea that informs this passage and its argumentational dynamic — the image of sculpting a statue. After all, Nietzsche enjoys the reputation of being the philosopher with a hammer; a reputation derived from the subtitle he gave to *Twilight of the Idols* (1888), namely 'how to philosophize with a hammer'.[2] In his foreword to that work, Nietzsche implicitly acknowledged the violence of a hammer, speaking of his book as 'a grand declaration of war', as well as explicitly outlining a different use for the hammer — as an instrument for 'the sounding-out of idols', for investigating '*eternal* idols which are here touched with the hammer as with a tuning fork'.[3] In the very last section of the *Twilight*, this hammer itself is allowed to have a voice: in 'The Hammer Speaks', we find an extract from 'Of Old and New Law-Tables' in Part Three of *Thus Spoke Zarathustra*, which opens with a small parable of the charcoal (as a symbol of softness) and the diamond (as a symbol of hardness). Zarathustra tells his brothers, 'For creators are hard. And it must seem bliss to you to press your hand upon millennia as upon wax, / bliss to write upon the will of millennia as upon metal'.[4]

In a series of fragments from his unpublished *Nachlass*, Nietzsche noted that 'the heaviest thought' — that is, 'the doctrine of eternal recurrence' — could function as a 'hammer',[5] while implicitly suggesting that the task of sounding out idols is essentially a psychological one.[6] As Walter Kaufmann has argued, Nietzsche's philosophy invites both an esoteric and an exoteric reading, and 'one may well wonder whether he deliberately chose terms whose exoteric meaning would put off uncongenial souls even when he expressly disowned it'.[7] In presenting himself as the philosopher with a hammer, Nietzsche is moreover inserting himself into a long philosophical tradition that uses metaphors of sculpting and creating statues.

Statues in Antiquity

The cultural heritage of the Western world is twofold: on the one hand, it is pagan or classical, drawing on Greek, Latin, and other sources alike; on the other, it is Judeo-Christian, drawing on the two sacred books of the Hebrew Bible and the New Testament. Conventionally, this dual source is presented in terms of two cities: Athens and Jerusalem. On the question of statues, however, Athens and Jerusalem tend to adopt entirely different — indeed, diametrically opposed — positions.

In numerous places in the Hebrew Bible (or, as it is regarded by Christians, the Old Testament), the prohibition against idols — i.e., statues — is stated time and again. The most obvious example is in the Decalogue, the Ten Commandments promulgated by Yahweh on Mount Horeb as narrated in the Book of Exodus and recapitulated by Moses in his long discourse that constitutes the Book of Deuteronomy. Here Yahweh condemns both the manufacture of images, idols, and statues — 'Thou shalt not make to thyself a graven image, nor the likeness of any thing that is in heaven above, or in the earth beneath, nor of those things that are in the waters under the earth' — and especially worship or adoration of them: 'Thou shalt not adore them, nor serve them' (Exodus 20: 4–5; cf. Deut. 8–9). The logic behind this prohibition is expounded in a homiletic passage found in Deuteronomy, which explains that — with the exception of Moses and the elders ('the ancients of Israel') —Yahweh did not allow himself to be seen during the theophany on Mount Horeb, only heard, and that He did so for strategic reasons:

> You saw not any similitude, in the day that the Lord God spoke to you in Horeb, from the midst of the fire: lest perhaps being deceived you might make you a graven similitude, or image of male or female, the similitude of any beasts, that are upon the earth, or of birds, that fly under heaven, or of creeping things, that move on the earth, or of fishes, that abide in the waters under the earth.
>
> (Deut. 4: 15–18)

So the prohibition of images had a dual function: first, it prevented the Israelites from the pagan representation of the gods in the form of human, animal, bird, or reptile form (in this respect the Egyptians were particularly inventive); second, it prevented the Israelites from the worship of the heavenly bodies, of the sun, moon, and the stars (as was the case in the worship of, say, Baal or Astarte or Moloc or Chamos). (In practical terms, this prohibition served to separate Israel from the other peoples and cultures surrounding it.)

This prohibition was disregarded by the Israelites in various ways, some disapproved of — such as the manufacture of the golden calf at the instigation of Aaron (provoking the wrath of Yahweh) — and some not — from the two cherubim placed on either side of the propitiatory or 'mercy-seat' in the Tabernacle, later imitated in the Temple (Exodus 25: 17–20; cf. 1 Paralipomenon 28: 18; 2 Paralipomenon 3: 10–13) to the bronze serpent set up by Moses in the desert of Edom (Numbers 21: 4–9) but later destroyed by Hezekiah (4 Kings 18: 4).[8] Despite this fact (or perhaps because of it), it is a constant theme for the Psalmist and for the Prophets.

One thinks, for example, of Psalm 113b (115) or Psalm 134 (135): 15–18, which contrast the vanity of idols with the praise of the true God. In the Book of Isaiah, the prophet speaks out no fewer than four times against the fatuity of idols (Isaias 40: 19–20; cf. 41: 21–29; cf. 44: 9–20; cf. 45: 15–26). In his turn, the prophet Jeremiah, ostensibly writing about a century later, in the time before and after the capture of Jerusalem and the deportation of its population to Babylon by Nebuchadnezzar, lambasted the idols and contrasted them to the true God in no uncertain terms (Jeremias 2: 26–28, cf. 10: 1–16). Modern biblical criticism has suggested that some of these passages in Isaiah and Jeremiah are later additions, and it is true that in some of the latest Jewish writings included in the Septuagint, such as the Book of Wisdom, the indictment on the cult of the idols continued (Wisdom, chapters 13–15). In Isaiah, Yahweh proclaims to Zion that her name is 'graven [...] in my hands' to indicate that He will not forget her (Isaias 49: 16), and the prophet himself uses the image of a potter to describe the supreme power of Yahweh (Isaias 29: 16, cf. 45: 9) — an image that is the occasion for a striking prophetic gesture and enacted parable on the part of Jeremiah (18: 1–12, cf. 19: 1–11).

Jeremiah's image is taken up by St Paul in his Epistle to the Romans (9: 20–21), and Paul continued the campaign against the idols. When Paul visited Athens, we are told that 'his spirit was excited within him, seeing the city given up to idolatry' (Acts 17: 16). In his speech before the council of the Areopagus, he took the altar dedicated to THE UNKNOWN GOD as the starting-point of his discourse. Mixing his theological sources, and indeed drawing directly on such pagan writers as Epimenides of Knossos and on the *Phainomena* of Aratus, Paul argued explicitly against the representation of divinity in the form of status. 'Being the offspring of God', he asserted, 'we must not suppose the Divinity to be like unto gold or silver, or stone, the graving of art, and the device of man' (Acts 19: 29). (One of Paul's listeners in Athens was Dionysius — a figure as whom that later Christian writer, Pseudo-Dionysius the Areopagite, was to identify himself.)

Subsequently, in Ephesus, this sort of teaching is said to have led to a riot of the silversmiths there; Demetrius, one of the craftsmen employed in making miniature silver shrines of the goddess Diana, complained that Paul's teaching, that 'they are no gods which are made with hands', was going to rob them of their living (Acts 19: 26), but it is also possible to read a genuine sense of religious indignation in his words and in the reaction of his colleagues. According to St Luke, a mob took to the street, crying 'Great is Diana of the Ephesians!', and it took the intervention of a local Roman official to calm the crowd. (This episode caught the attention of Goethe, who wrote a short poem about it,[9] and Freud, who dedicated a short, if enigmatic, paper to it.[10])

In this respect there is a strict line of continuity between the Judaic prohibition of images and the Christian argument — whatever the later practice concerning icons — against idols and statues. Indeed, St Paul (or at any rate the author of the Epistle to the Hebrews) would subsequently develop the idea that 'the world was framed by the word of God', or in other words that 'from invisible things visible things might be made' (Hebrews 11: 3), clearly establishing the priority of the invisible Word over the visible world. And it is here that we find the real point of contrast between paganism and Christianity. Compare, for example, the stance of the Latin novelist and philosopher, Lucius Apuleius (c. 125–c. 180), in his treatise, *On the God of Socrates*, in which it is maintained that, 'of these celestial Gods', 'some we apprehend by the sight, but others we investigate by intellect; and by the sight, indeed, we perceive "Ye, the world most refulgent lights, / Who through the heavens conduct the gliding year" [Virgil, *Georgics*, i]'.[11] Concomitantly, the pagan tradition entertained a positive attitude towards the sheer visibility of sculpture in general and statues in particular.

Statues in Platonism and Neoplatonism

In the ancient world, the question of the statues was tied up with the larger question of representation — representation in general, and the representation of divinity in particular.[12] Already the Presocratics had subjected the representation of gods in material form to harsh criticism — echoing in this respect their contemporaries, the prophets of the Hebrew bible. Xenophanes of Colophon, for instance, had drawn attention to the anthropomorphic assumptions implicit in representing the gods in human form. In one surviving fragment, he observed that 'mortals think that the gods are born, and have clothes and speech and shape like their own', and remarked caustically that if cows, or horses, or lions could draw, then 'horses would draw the forms of gods like horses, cows like cows', and 'they would make their bodies similar in shape to those which each had themselves'.[13] And in one of the fragments that has been preserved of his thought, Heraclitus of Ephesus declared that worshippers of idols had misunderstood the nature of the gods: 'They pray to these statues as though one were to gossip to the houses, not knowing who the gods and who the heroes are'.[14] (Nor was Heraclitus an admirer of the Dionysian rites, which featured the procession of a giant, statuesque phallus.[15])

In Plato's dialogues, the status of an image as a material object is a problem that is interrogated on a number of occasions. In the *Cratylus*, for instance, Socrates argues that a perfect image of something or someone (say, Cratylus) is not *just* an image, but a duplicate, which raises a question about the criterion according to which we can judge images: 'The image, if expressing in every point the entire reality, would no longer be an image', and he considers the following example: 'Suppose [...] that some god makes not only a representation such as a painter would make of your outward form and colour, but also creates an inward organization like yours, having the same warmth and softness, and into this infuses motion, and soul, and mind, such as you have, and in a word copies all your qualities, and places them by you in another form' — then, he concludes, we would have not one Cratylus, but two Cratyluses, and so 'we must find some other principle of truth in images, and also in names, and not insist that an image is no longer an image when something is added or subtracted'.[16]

In the course of this dialogue with Cratylus, the question of how to judge images turns into the question of how to judge truth itself. As Socrates poses the question, 'Which is likely to be the nobler and clearer way — to learn of the image, whether the image and the truth of which the image is the expression have been rightly conceived, or to learn of the truth itself whether the truth and the image of it have been duly executed?'.[17] (Cratylus, rightly, chooses the latter.)

In a later dialogue, the *Sophist*, the Eleatic Stranger sets up a distinction between two kinds of imitation, one of which involves making copies or likenesses, the other of which involves making appearances or semblances. In the case of the former, we are dealing with someone 'creating a copy that conforms to the proportions of the original in all three dimensions and giving moreover the proper colour to every part'; in the case of the latter, it is a question of a kind of likeness 'which only appears to be a likeness of a well-made figure because it is not seen from a satisfactory point of view, but to a spectator with eyes that could fully take in so large an object would not even be like the original it professes to resemble'.[18] (In this second case, Plato is thinking of the practice, found in sculptors and architects of the time, of making the head of a tall statue too large, so that to the observer it did not appear too small, or making the horizontal edges of a temple curve slightly upward, so that to the observer they appear straight.[19]) In this second case of what is produced by 'those sculptors or painters whose works are of colossal size', the artist 'leaves the truth to take care of itself': unlike the production of an *eikon*, in the case of *eikastike techne* or the production of *phantasmata*, it is argued in this dialogue, the artist is leaving behind the truth is some way.[20]

But what does this mean? In the course of their discussion in the *Sophist*, Theaetetus and the Eleatic Stranger examine the position that, because 'falsity has never any sort of existence anywhere', 'the very existence of any copy or image or semblance' can be disputed.[21] Nevertheless, they subsequently conclude that, in fact, because of 'the existence of false statement and of false judgement', 'it is possible that there should be imitations of real things' — and 'that this condition of mind' (i.e., false judgement) should account for the existence of an art of deception'.[22] (Such an art, in Socrates's view, constitutes the hallmark of the philosophical Sophist.)

In another late dialogue, the *Timaeus*, Socrate's eponymous interlocutor sets up a different (but, in its way, analogous) distinction — here between, on the one hand, 'that which always is and has no becoming', and, on the other, 'that which is always becoming and never is'.[23] Whereas the former is 'apprehended by intelligence and reason', the latter is 'conceived by opinion with the help of sensation and without reason'.[24] Within these terms, Timaeus argues, the world itself, as 'visible and tangible' and 'having a body', is an object of sense perception — hence, it is a copy. But of *what* is it a copy? Or, to put it another way, *which of these two models did the maker use when he fashioned it — the model of what does not change and stays the same, or the model of what has come to be?*

> Everyone will see that [the father and maker of all this universe] must have looked to the eternal, for the world is the fairest of creations, and he is the best of causes. And having been created in this way, the world has been framed in the likeness of that which is apprehended by reason and mind and is unchangeable, and must therefore of necessity, if this is admitted, be a copy of something. […] As being is to becoming, so is truth to belief.[25]

In other words, the entire world is a kind of giant statue, and thus the beauty of this world comes to play a significant role in Platonic philosophy. So it should come as no surprise that there are several significant references to a particular kind of copy — that is, to statues — in other parts of the corpus of the Platonic dialogues.

In the *Phaedrus*, Phaedrus undertakes, like the nine archons (or rulers) of Athens had done, to set up in a Delphi a golden life-sized statue, only this time of himself and of Socrates; 'How kind you are', is Socrates's response.[26] And in the *Symposium*, Alcibiades praises Socrates, by saying (in a passage that would attract Jung's interest) that 'what he reminds me of more than anything is one of those little silent sileni that you see on the statuaries' stalls; you know the ones I mean', he says to Agathon, Eryximachus, and the others — 'they're modelled with pipes or flutes in their hands, and when you open them down the middle there are little figures of the gods inside'.[27] Externally, says Alcibiades, Socrates looks like Silenus, the drunken satyr; but internally, there are 'little images inside', ones that are 'so godlike, so golden, so beautiful, and so utterly amazing'.[28] (For the later commentator and expositor of Plato, Plotinus, these 'images' within 'the soul of the wise' serve to illustrate that the forms in the intellect are something very much alive, not merely something abstract.[29])

In the *Republic*, Socrates complements Glaucon on his descriptions of the just man and the unjust man, before asking his interlocutors to decide which of the two is the happier, by exclaiming: 'Heavens! my dear Glaucon, […], how energetically you polish them up for the decision, first one and then the other, as if they were two statues'.[30] In his turn, Socrates is later hailed by Glaucon as being, so to speak, a sculptor: 'You are a sculptor, Socrates, and have made statues of our governors faultless in beauty' (540c).[31] Indeed, Socrates is said to have followed the profession of his father, Sophroniscus, and exercised the craft of being a sculptor or stonemason, before turning to philosophy.[32] (According to Pausanias, Socrates made a statue of Hermes [called Hermes of the Gateway] at the entrance to the Acropolis, as well as the statues of the Graces at the entrance.[33])

In the *Euthyphro*, Socrates twice claims that Daedalus, a maker of moving statues, is one of his ancestors,[34] while in the *Meno* he refers to Daedalus's moving statues again.[35] (The technical accomplishment of Daedalus is recognised by Diodorus of Sicily in his *Bibliotheca historica*, book 4, §76, and by Pseudo-Apollodorus in his *Bibliotheca*, who tells us that Daedalus's portrait statue at Pisa of Hercules was so lifelike, Hercules himself mistook it at night for living and threw a stone at it [book 2, chapter 6].) As Babette Babich has argued, the idea that Daedalus's statues could move is essentially allegorical, a figure of speech to express their lifelike qualities;[36] as we shall see, however, later writers attribute telestic (or mystical) properties to certain statues.

According to Diogenes Laertius, Socrates used to say that 'he wondered at those who made stone statues, when he saw how careful they were that the stone should be like the man it was intended to represent, but how careless they were of themselves, as to guarding against being like the stone'.[37] Here we find the essential idea: that a statue is not simply an exemplar of the work of art, which is how it features elsewhere in Plato's dialogues — for instance, in the words of the Eleatic Stranger to Theaetetus in the *Sophist* —[38] but can serve as a model for something more existential — for the creating or, one might say, sculpting of the self.

While the occasional references to statues in Plato's dialogues give one little sense of the importance with which such representations were regarded in the ancient world; and while, for reasons of space, we cannot go into this question in detail here (nor, for the purposes of our comparative argument, do we need to), one should nevertheless note a number of passages by later writers that testify to the immense significance of statues in the world of antiquity.[39]

In book 34 of his *Natural History* (a vast, 37-volume compendium of Roman knowledge), Pliny the Elder discusses in some detail techniques of metallurgy, in particular the use of bronze in the ancient world to manufacture statues. He tells us that the first image of a god made of bronze in Rome was dedicated to Ceres; that it was customary in Olympia to make statues of all who had won a competition in the games; that whereas it was Greek practice to depict figures in the nude, in Roman statuary it was usual to add a breastplate; that it became popular in Rome to erect equestrian statues; and he expresses surprise that when, during one of the Samnite Wars, Pythian Apollo commanded the erection of an effigy of the bravest Greek man and the wisest Greek man, the senators decided to set up in the corners of the Place of Assembly a statue to Pythagoras and one to Alcibiades (rather than Socrates, 'whom the same deity has put above all the rest of mankind in respect of wisdom', or Themistocles, who combined 'wisdom and manly virtue').[40]

According to Pliny, at the beginning of the first millennium there were around three thousand bronze statues in Rhodes, and an equal number in Athens, Olympia, and Delphi: 'What mortal man could recapitulate them all', he wondered, 'or what value can be felt in such information?'.[41] Pliny goes on to tell us about some of the Colossi of the ancient world: the colossos of Apollo on the Capitol, the Jupiter in the Campus Martius, and the giant statue of Helios on the island of Rhodes;[42] and he lists some of the most famous sculptors: including Phidias (the sculptor of the statue of Zeus at Olympia, and the statues of Athena on the Acropolis), Polyclitus of Sicyon (the sculptor of the Diadumenos, a youth binding his hair; the Doryphoros, a youth carrying a spear; the Apoxyomenos, a man using a body-scraper; and the Astragalizontes, two boys playing dice); and Myron of Eleutherae (the sculptor of a statue of a heifer, celebrated in verse; a Discobolos, a man throwing a discus; and a statue of a satyr marvelling at the flute and Athene); Pythagoras of Rhegium and Pythagoras of Samos (now considered to be the same artist); Lysippos of Sicyon, and his three sons, Laippus, Boëdas, and Euthycrates; and, famous for his works in marble and bronze alike, Praxiteles of Athens.

Understandably, Babette Babich asks: what would it have been like to live in a world full of so many statues, what must have been the effect of walking amid such a number of them?[43] And one could also ask: what was the *point* of so many statues? Here, later writers can be helpful in understanding the immense importance attached to statues in the ancient world. In the opening pages of his 'Oration to the Mother of the Gods' (362), for instance, Emperor Julian (known as 'the Apostate' or 'the Philosopher') (331/332–363) tells of an event that happened during the translation of a statue of Cybele from Asia Minor to Rome. (The story is developed elsewhere by Ovid in his *Festivals*, and by Livy in his *History of Rome*.[44]) During the Second Punic War (218–201 BCE), the Roman Senate consulted the oracle of Apollo and decided to introduce the cult of the Great Mother and to import the statue of Cybele from Phrygia (now modern-day Turkey), specifically from Pergamon. When the ship carrying the statue got stuck in the Tiber, a vestal virgin called Claudia Quinta saw an opportunity to clear her name of accusations of being unchaste. Tying her girdle to the ship, she prayed to the goddess that her chastity be confirmed and was given strength to pull the ship along the river. And so the goddess herself had intervened, 'as if willing to convince the Roman people that they had not led from Phrygia an inimate image, but something endued with a greater and more divine power than ordinary', as Julian remarks.[45] (Subsequently the goddess also demonstrated her power by helping the Romans military success against the Carthaginians.)

Commenting on this episode, the translator and Neoplatonic revivalist Thomas Taylor (1758–1835) noted that the ancient belief in the power of statues of the gods to exercise a divine influence was by no means ridiculous, since their close resemblance to divine natures turned them into 'participants of divine illumination'.[46] Taylor cites a number of authorities — including Sallust, Iamblichus, and Proclus — that bear out this observation and bear witness to the sheer vitality of representation through sculpture, or to what Zarathustra calls 'the image of my visions' in the stone.

For instance, the second-century rhetorician and philosopher, Maximus of Tyre, devoted one of his dissertations or discourses to the question of whether statues should be dedicated to the gods. Looking askance at the Persian (i.e., Zoroastrian) worship of fire and the honour paid by the Egyptians to animals, Maximus argued that, while a few individuals have 'no need of statues', for the majority they serve as 'tokens of honour which should be paid to divinity, and a certain manuduction as it were and path to reminiscence'.[47] Maximus highlighted the diversity of statues — 'O many and all-various statues! of which some are fashioned by art, and others are embraced through indigence; some are honoured through utility, and others are venerated through the astonishment which they excite; some are considered as divine through their magnitude, and others are celebrated for their beauty!' — and he highlighted the spiritual function of their aesthetic appeal:

> For divinity [*theos*], indeed, the father and fabricator of all things, is more ancient than the sun and the heavens, more excellent than time and eternity, and every flowing nature, and is a legislator without law, ineffable by voice, and invisible by the eyes. Not being able, however, to comprehend his essence, we apply for assistance to words and names, to animals and figures of gold, and ivory and silver, to plants and rivers, to the summits of mountains, and to streams of water; desiring, indeed, to understand his nature, but through imbecility calling him by the names of such things as appear to us to be beautiful.[48]

Maximus compares this approach to statues with the behaviour of lovers, who are 'delighted with surveying the images of the objects of their love, and with recollecting [...] every thing, in short, which excites the memory of the beloved object'.[49] In conclusion, his investigation into the question of respect for statues leads him to affirm 'the subsistence of deity'.

Julian the Apostate himself, in the fragment that survives of his oration or epistle 'On the Duties of a Priest' (c. 362), explains that 'statues and altars, and the preservation of the unextinguished fire' had been established 'as symbols of the presence of the gods', emphasizing 'not that we should believe that these symbols are gods, but that through these we should worship the gods'.[50] He went on to distinguish different categories or 'kinds' of statues, including the stars, 'circularly revolv[ing] round the whole of heaven', and another kind of statues, 'by the worship of which we render the gods propitious to us'.[51] In response to the accusation (clearly coming from the Christians) of idolatry — 'O! you who have admitted into your soul every multitude of dæmons, who though, according to you, they are formless and unfigured, you have fashioned into a corporeal resemblance, it is not fit that honour should be paid to divinity through such works' —, Julian replied with a vigorous defence, concluding that 'he who is a lover of divinity gladly surveys the statues and images of the gods', while 'venerating and fearing with a holy dread the gods who invisibly behold him'.[52] (Similar arguments would, of course, be exchanged between Christians in the iconoclast controversies of the eighth and ninth centuries, and during the Reformation and Counter-Reformation.)

Then again, in his treatise *On the Gods and the World*, the fourth-century writer Sallust wrote in its fifteenth chapter: 'Since the providence of the gods is every where extended, a certain habitude, or fitness, is all that is requisite in order to receive their beneficent communication'.[53] For Sallust, this principle of likeness or analogy enabled him to make the following assertion about architecture, sculpture, and even plants and animals: 'All habitude is produced through imitation and similitude; and hence temples imitate the heavens, but altars the earth; *statues resemble life, and on this account they are similar to animals*; [...] herbs and stones resemble matter; and animals which are sacrificed, the irrational life of our souls'.[54]

Sallust's catechetical treatise is indebted to the Syrian Neoplatonist Iamblichus (c. 245–c. 325), to whom the following view is attributed by Photius in his *Bibliotheca* (or *Myriobiblon*) in the codex discussing a work by John Philoponus (c. 490–570) written in response to a lost treatise by Iamblichus, *On Statues*. On this account, Iamblichus argued that 'statues are divine, and full of divine participation', a judgment that applied to all works, both those produced for commercial reasons and those 'fashioned by the hands of men, by an occult art, and which are denominated *diopetes* [i.e., descended from Jupiter, or from heaven], through the immanifestness of the art by which they were made'.[55] Although this text by Iamblichus has not survived, there are significant references to statues in his treatise *On the Mysteries of the Egyptians, Chaldeans, and Assyrians*, in which the notion of theurgy (see below) plays an important part.[56] In a passage that uses the usual Platonic solar analogy ('in the same manner as the sun externally irradiates all things with his rays'), we are told that 'sacred statues' — like 'certain parts of the universe', such as 'heaven or earth', 'sacred cities and regions', or 'certain groves' — are 'externally illuminate[d]' by 'a divine nature'.[57] More precisely, the relation between the gods and their statues is explained as follows, implying (as Julian the Apostate had done) that they form part of an imagistic chain that includes the stars:

> [T]he visible statues of the gods originate from divine intelligible paradigms, and are generated by them. But being thus generated, they are entirely established in them, and being also extended to, they possess an image which derives its completion from them. These images likewise fabricate another order; sublunary natures are in continuity with them, according to one union; and the divine intellectual forms, which are present with the visible bodies of the gods, exist prior to them in a separate manner.[58]

Moreover, there exists a correspondence between the status of the image depicted by a statue, and the extent to which a statue is not just seen in light but itself radiates a kind of spiritual light. At the upper end of the Neoplatonic spectrum of gods and souls, 'in the forms of the gods which are seen by the eyes, the most clear spectacles of truth itself are perceived', which are themselves 'splendid, and shine forth with an evolved light', while 'the images of souls appear to be of a shadowy form'.[59]

Iamblichus's *On the Mysteries* is presented as a response from an Egyptian priest, Anebo, to an enquiry about the gods from the philosopher Porphyry (c. 234–c. 305), who himself wrote a treatise *On Images*, fragments of which have survived.[60] In the first fragment of this treatise, Porphyry undertook to show, to 'those who have learned to read from the statues as from books the things there written concerning the gods', 'the thoughts of a wise theology, wherein men indicated God and God's powers by images akin to sense, and sketched invisible things in visible forms'.[61] For Porphyry, it is *because* the deity is 'of the nature of light' and hence 'invisible to sense', that both the white marble from Paros and black marble can be used 'to show his invisibility', while artists 'moulded their gods in human form because the deity is rational, and made these beautiful, because in those is pure and perfect beauty; and in varieties of shape and age [...] to represent their diversity'.[62]

Subsequently Proclus, known as 'the Successor' (412–485), discussed the function of forms, images, and statues in numerous places in his extensive œuvre. For instance, in his *Commentary* on the First Book of Euclid's *Elements of Geometry*, Proclus defines 'figure' as 'something that results from change, arising from an effect produced in things that are struck, or divided, or decreased, or added to, or altered in form, or affected in any one of various other ways', ranging from 'figures produced by art (for example, by modelling or sculpturing), in accordance with the idea preexisting in the artist's mind, the art providing the form and the matter receiving therefrom its shape, beauty, and seemliness', to 'the works of nature's craftsmanship', including 'the heavenly bodies'.[63] Of particular significance for Proclus are those works produced by *theurgy*, or a kind of ritual magic:[64]

> [The] properties [of the gods] have been represented for us by the theurgic art in its statues of the gods, whom it clothes in the most varied figures. Some of them it portrays by means of mystic signs that express the unknowable divine potencies; others it represents through forms and shapes, making some standing, others sitting; some heart-shaped, some spherical, and some fashioned still otherwise; some simple, others composed of several shapes; some stern, others mild and expressing the benignity of the gods; and still others fearful in shape. To these figures, it adjoins various symbols for different gods, as they are appropriate to the divinities themselves.[65]

Thus for Proclus it would seem that FORM itself is divine, and this is the principle behind the efficacy of such 'divine images' that served in the initiatory temples of the Great Mysteries as 'breathing semblances'.[66] These breathing semblances or statues of the gods, Taylor notes, were fabricated by *telestae* or 'mystic operators', 'initiators into the mysteries' and 'capable of performing divine operations', and were fashioned 'so as to become animated, illuminated by divinity, and capable of delivering oracles'.[67] (How were these statues animated? According to the Byzantine monk, historian, and philosopher, Michael Psellos [c. 1017/18–1078], such *telestikhé* involved placing stones, herbs, or even small animals within the cavity of a statue, thereby establishing a 'sympathetic' relation with the god. By consecrating the 'material image' of the god and placing it in the god's statue, the theurgist aimed to persuade the god to appear and to answer questions.[68])

There are allusions to such statues in writings by Proclus on Plato's dialogues, the *Timaeus* and the *Cratylus*, by Iamblichus (see above), and by the author of the so-called *Asclepian Dialogue*, a text attributed to Hermes Trismegistus and translated into Latin by Apuleius. Thus in his *Commentary* on the *Timaeus* Proclus uses, in the course of explicating the next passage in the *Timaeus* after the one mentioned above (29b), the creation of a statue as an example of the relation between the model and the copy (and as an analogy for the creation of the world by the demiurge):

> Hence Phidias also, who made the celebrated statue of Jupiter [i.e., Zeus], would not have arrived at the conception of the Jupiter in Homer, if he had looked at a generated resemblance of the god. And if he had been able to extend himself to the intellectual Jupiter, it is evident that he would have rendered his work still more beautiful. For from the paradigm indeed, beauty or the want of beauty accedes to the image; but from the maker, similitude or dissimilitude to the archetype is derived. With reference to both[,] however, the image is said to be the image of the paradigm, but the work an effect of the maker.[69]

Thus the statue, especially the living, telestic statue, reveals for Proclus something about the nature of the very cosmos itself:

> [A]s of statues established by the telestic art, some things pertaining to them are manifest, but others are inwardly concealed, being symbolical of the presence of the gods, and which are only known to the mystic artists themselves; after the same manner, the world being a statue of the intelligible, and perfected by the father, has indeed some things which are visible indications of its divinity; but others, which are the invisible impressions of the participation of being received by it from the father who gave it perfection, in order that through these it may be eternally rooted in real being.[70]

And later, in book 4 of his *Timaeus Commentary*, Proclus returns to this theme, saying of this creator of the world, the demiurge: 'Plato establishes the Demiurgus conformably to the most consummate of the initiators into the mysteries', for 'he exhibits him as the statuary of the world, just as before he represented him the maker of divine names, and the enunciator of divine characters, through which he gave perfection to the soul', and Proclus underscores the parallel with 'these things [...] effected by those that are telestae in reality, who give completion to statues, through characters and vital names, and render them living and moving'.[71] Is Zarathustra in the conclusion to the chapter called 'On the Blissful Islands' acting as a *telestos*, a divine operator? Or is he really a kind of *demiurge*, fashioning an entirely new world?

Commenting on Timaeus's assertion in the Platonic dialogue bearing his name that 'when the father and creator saw the creature which he had made moving and living, the created image of the eternal gods, he rejoiced, and in his joy determined to make the copy still more like the original, and as this was an eternal living being, he sought to make the universe eternal, so far as might be',[72] Proclus declares that 'the world is the statue of the intelligible gods', and he continues:

> It is a statue in motion, and full of life, and deity; fashioned from all things within itself; preserving all things, and filled with an at-once-collected abundance of all good from the father. It likewise peculiarly receives from nature motion, more than any thing else; but from soul, motion and life; and from intellect, intelligence and life, and the receptacle of the mundane gods. From the mundane gods[,] however, it receives that which remains, *viz.* the being fashion in perfection, the most true statue, or resemblance, of the intelligible gods.[73]

Thus the entire point about a statue is that, in a special yet almost indefinable sense, it is very much alive, it is something vital, and it is so because it participates in the divine. In his commentary on Plato's *Parmenides*, Proclus discusses three different modes of participation — by impression, by reflection, and by likeness — pointing out how these different modes often intersect, as in the case of the beautiful man or the animated statue, of the kind we have been describing:

> The body of a good and wise man, for example, appears itself handsome and attractive because it participates directly in the beauty of nature and has its bodily shape moulded by it, and by receiving reflections from the beauty of the soul it carries a trace of ideal beauty, the soul serving as a connecting term between his own lowest beauty and Beauty Itself. So that the reflection reveals this species of soul as being wise, or courageous, or noble or a likeness of some other virtue. And the animated statue, for example, participates by way of impression in the art which turns it on a lathe and shapes it in such and such a fashion; while from the universe it has received reflections of vitality which even cause us to say that it is alive; and as a whole it has been made like the god whose image it is. For a theurgist who sets up a statue as a likeness of a certain divine order fabricates the tokens of its identity with reference to that order, acting as does the craftsman when he makes a likeness by looking to its proper model.[74]

The principle of likeness, then, serves as the source of vitality, and so the statue is not a dead copy of something living, but rather it itself, by virtue of being an imitation of something living, becomes alive.

Similarly, in his Scholia on Plato's *Cratylus*, Proclus remarks that:

> as the telestic art, through certain symbols, and arcane signatures, assimilates statues of the gods, and makes them adapted to the reception of divine illuminations, so the legislative art, according to the same assimilative power, gives subsistence to names, the statues of things; through such and such sounds shadowing forth the nature of things, and having given subsistence to them, delivers them to the use of mankind.[75]

Thus the statue, as well as being alive in some sense, can help us to become more alive as well.

For a confirmation of this understanding of the telestic art, we can turn to the Neoplatonist philosopher Hermias (born c. 410). In his *Scholia* on Plato's *Phaedrus*, Hermias here answers a question about how such statues can be said to have an 'enthusiastic energy' (*legetai enthousian*):

> May we not say that a statue[,] being inanimate, does not itself energize about divinity, but the telestic art purifying the matter of which the statue consists, and placing round it certain characters and symbols, in the first place renders it, through these means, animated and causes it to receive a certain life from the world; and in the next place, after this, it prepares the statue to be illuminated by a divine nature, through which it always delivers oracles, as long as it is properly adapted. For the statue, when it has been rendered perfect by the telestic art, remains afterwards [endued with pro- phetic power], till it becomes entirely unadapted to divine illumination; but he who receives the inspiring influence of the gods, receives it only at cer- tain times, and not always. But the cause of this is that the soul, when filled with deity, energizes about it. Hence, in consequence of energizing above its own power, it becomes weary. For it would be a god, and similar to the souls of the stars, if it did not become weary. But the statue, conformably to its participations, remains illuminated. Hence the inaptitude of it entirely proceeds into privation, unless it is again *de novo* perfected and animated by the mystic operator.[76]

Finally, aside from the role of statues in these theurgic techniques of the Neoplatonists, the moral dimension of the metaphor of sculpting is important to one of the last philosophers in the Neoplatonist tradition, Simplicius of Cilicia (c. 490–c. 560). In his *Commentary* on the *Enchiridion* (or *Handbook*) of Epictetus, the Greek slave turned sage and Stoic philosopher, Simplicius, answers the question, 'what place or esteem is due to a philosopher, or what regard should the state have to him?', with reference to the formative or sculptural (*anthropoios*, 'sculptor of men') role he plays:

> The philosopher may claim precedence, as a former [or 'sculptor'] and maker of men; one that frames and moulds them into vertuous persons, and useful honest subjects. For the matter he hath to work upon, is himself and oth- ers; and the pains he is at about them, is to refine and purifie their nature, and exalt them to a life of reason and vertue. He is indeed, and ought to be respected, as a common father, and master, a corrector of errors, and a counsellor and assistant in goodness; one that is liberal of his care, makes every other man's benefit and improvement his endeavour and concern, and hath a hand in all the good that is done. One that adds to the enjoyments of the prosperous, by congratulating and rejoycing with them; and lightens the

burden of the wretched, by ministring seasonable comforts; and himself bearing a part in their afflictions.[77]

And this moral dimension — albeit in support of a different set of values — of the sculptural motif is, even more than the theurgic implications, clearly implied in Zarathustra's work on the marble block as he envisions the superman. Moreover, what the Neoplatonists say about the telestic art should be read against the relativizingly (and perhaps reassuringly) sceptical tones, from the first and second century, of the poet Juvenal.

In the thirteenth of his sixteen *Satires*, Juvenal proposes 'some words of comfort that even a layman may offer — / one who has never read the Cynics, or the rules of the Stoics / [...] or admired Epicurus', after indulging in sarcastic mockery at the expense of a statue of Jupiter which — faced with a man who, despite believing in the gods, is nevertheless prepared to commit perjury — can only maintain silence:

> How *can* you,
> Jupiter, hear such lies without a murmur? Now really,
> you ought to give utterance, whether you be of bronze or marble.
> Otherwise, why should people unwrap the holy incense
> and place it upon your glowing coals with slices of calves'
> liver and white pork sausages? As far as I can discover,
> there's nothing to choose between statues of you and Vagellius' image![78]

Vagellius was a rhetorically minded advocate singled out elsewhere by Juvenal for his 'mulish brain'.[79] Satirical tone aside, Juvenal's mockery of the statue or idol of Jupiter is not all that far removed from the biblical scorn for 'the idols of the Gentiles' — 'silver and gold, the works of the hands of men': 'They have mouths, and speak not: they have eyes, and see not. They have ears, and hear not: they have noses, and smell not. They have hands, and feel not: they have feet, and walk not: neither shall they cry out through their throat' (Psalm 113b [115]: 4–7). Just as fervently as the psalmist and the prophets condemned them, so the statues and the idols persisted in their presence in the cultural scene. But over time their significance shifts: and the statue becomes an exemplar, not so much of idolatry, as of autonomous creativity.

Five Case Studies: Seneca, Plotinus, Gregory of Nyssa, Pseudo-Dionysius the Areopagite, and Meister Eckhart

The significance of the statue can be seen across a number of philosophical traditions in antiquity, including the Neoplatonic (as we have seen) as well as the Stoic and the early Christian. As five 'case studies', let us briefly consider one of the most celebrated of the Roman philosophers in the Stoic tradition, Seneca (4 BCE–65 CE); one of the most eminent of the commentators on Plato, Plotinus (c. 204/205–270); one of the most venerable figures in the early Christian tradition, Gregory of

Nyssa (c. 335–c. 395), the youngest of the three Cappadocian Fathers, a bishop of Nyssa, and now regarded as a saint; the mysterious figure of Pseudo-Dionysius the Areopagite from the late fifth and early sixth centuries; and the German medieval theologian, Meister Eckhart (c. 1260–c. 1327).

In one of his letters to the young procurator of Sicily, Lucilius, Seneca asks his correspondent to adjudicate in a philosophical dispute: which system can better explain the universe, the Platonic, the Aristotelian, or the Stoic? To illustrate the differences between these three approaches, Seneca uses a telling example: 'Take a statue: it had the matter to be worked on by the sculptor and it had the sculptor to give configuration to the matter — bronze, in other words, in the case of the statue, being the matter and the craftsman the cause', and 'it is the same with all things'.[80] Thus Stoicism admits two elements in the universe, matter and cause (the cause which brings things into being, i.e., the efficient cause or acting force, in other words 'creative reason' or 'God'). In contrast, Aristotle recognizes four 'causes': matter, force (*to kinoun*), form (*eidos*), and the end (*to telos*), as Seneca explains with reference to statues in general (and two works by Polyclitus in particular):

> The "first cause" of the statue is the bronze, as it would never have been made unless there had been something out of which it could be cast or moulded. The "second cause" is the sculptor, as the bronze could not have been shaped into the state in which it is without those skilled hands having come to it. The "third cause" is the form, as our statue could not have been called "The Man with the Spear" or "The Boy tying up his Hair" had this not been the guise impressed on it. The "fourth cause" is the end in view in its making, [...] what attracted the sculptor, [...] money [...] or fame [...] or religion.[81]

To these four 'causes', Plato adds (as Seneca notes) a fifth — the idea (*idea*), or 'what the sculptor had constantly before his eyes as he executed the intended work', and hence the sculpting of a statue represents in miniature the creation of the universe:

> God has within himself models like this of everything in the universe, his mind embracing the designs and calculations for his projects; he is full of these images which Plato calls *ideas*, eternal immutable, ever dynamic. [...] As Plato has it, then, there are five causes: the material, the agent, the form, the model and the end; and finally we get the result of all these. In the case of the statue [...] the material is the bronze, the agent is the sculptor, the form is the guise it is given, the model is what the sculptor making it copies, the end is what the maker has in view, and the final result is the statue itself.[82]

For Seneca, the assortment of Aristotelian and Platonic causes 'embraces either too much or too little', and some of the questions that gives him cause for concern are technical ones: 'All those things [...] are not an array of individual causes, but dependent on a single one, the cause that actually creates', for instance, and 'you may say that form is a cause, but form is something which the artist imposes on his work — a part of the cause, yes, but not a cause' and 'the model, too, is an indispensable instrument of the cause, but not a cause'.[83] But some of them are more existential: what should be the relation between the soul and body? How much can one find out about the universe? And how should one face one's death? From the philosophical 'causes' at work in a statue as in the universe, Seneca's epistle to Lucilius moves towards the question of how to fashion the self — or how to sculpt it.

Self-sculpting: this is the sense in which the image of making a statue is used a couple of centuries after Seneca by another of the great commentators on Plato, Plotinus. In one of his earliest treatises, 'On Beauty' in his *Enneads* (*Ennead* 1, Tractate 6, §9), Plotinus focuses on the role of beauty in the construction of the self. In one of his most famous passages, Plotinus urges us:

> Withdraw into yourself and look. And if you do not find yourself beautiful yet, act as does the creator of a statue that is to be made beautiful: he cuts away here, he smoothes there, he makes this line lighter, this other purer, until a lovely face has grown upon his work. So do you also: cut away all that is excessive, straighten all that is crooked, bring light to all that is overcast, labour to make all one glow of beauty and never cease chiselling your statue,[84] until there shall shine out on you from it the godlike splendour of virtue.[85][86]

In another tractate on the different, but related, theme, 'On Intellectual Beauty' (*Ennead* 5, Tractate 8, §1), Plotinus asks us to consider two blocks of stone, lying side by side. One is entirely untouched, the other has been turned into a sculpture — a statue of a god or a man, a Grace or Muse, or anything in which 'the sculptor's art has concentrated all loveliness'. What, Plotinus asks, is it that makes the work of art beautiful? The answer is: the same thing as makes the inner statue of the soul beautiful — FORM:

> Now it must be seen that the stone thus brought under the artist's hand to the beauty of form is beautiful not as stone — for so the crude block would be as pleasant — but in virtue of the Form or Idea introduced by the art. This form is not in the material; it is in the designer before it ever enters the stone; and the artificer holds it not by his equipment of eyes and hands but by his participation in his art. The beauty, therefore, exists in a far higher state in the art; for it does not come over integrally into the work; that original beauty is not transferred; what comes over is a derivative and a minor; and even that shows itself upon the statue not integrally and with entire realization of intention but only in so far as it has subdued the resistance of the material.[87]

As we shall see, the notion of *form*, or *idea*, is essential to this tradition: yet we should also note that, on this account, the material realm and the 'spiritual' (or 'formal', or 'ideal') realms are interdependent, even if the 'spiritual' is prior to the material in terms of logic and efficacy; indeed, both are different aspects of the One. We shall return to this question in Chapter 3, but for the moment (and until Chapter 4), let us note Tim Addey's observation that, contrary to popular belief, Plato — and, by extension, the Platonic tradition — does not despise the material world.[88] Indeed, Pierre Hadot has argued that Plotinus's strictures against the body were not grounded in fear of or disgust at it, but were motivated rather by a concern to promote the practice of 'spiritual exercises' that an excessive concern for the body or an obsessively materialistic concern could undermine.[89]

Nor should we be surprised by Hadot's argument, since Plotinus indexes artistic beauty to existential vitality. In his tractate on 'How the Multiplicity of the Ideal-Forms came into Being; and on the Good', Plotinus describes the effect on the individual soul of the light of the Good: it causes the soul to become 'stirred', so that, moving and dancing wildly — 'seized with a Bacchic passion' — it is 'goaded by these goads' and 'becomes love'.[90] In support of his argument that 'beauty is that which irradiates symmetry rather than symmetry itself' and is 'that which truly calls out our love', Plotinus points out that there is more light of beauty on a living face, but only a trace on a dead one; that something 'ugly', but 'living', is more attractive than something 'handsome', but 'sculptured'; and that the more lifelike statues are the more beautiful ones.[91]

In another of the early treatises, 'On the Immortality of the Soul' (*Ennead* 4, Tractate 7), Plotinus uses the original and dynamic image of 'living gold' that hammers away at its own dross, to convey how the soul can uncover the moral forms, not as transcendent realities (as which they are described in Plato; see *Phaedrus*, 247 c–e), but as realities within the soul, from which the 'rust of time' is cleansed in the process of the soul returning to a true vision of itself:

> For it is certainly not by running around outside that the soul "sees self-control and justice", but itself by itself in its understanding of itself and what it formerly was, seeing them standing in itself like splended statues all rusted with time which it has cleaned: as if gold had a soul, and knocked off all that was earthy in it; it was before in ignorance of itself, because it did not see the gold, but then, seeing itself isolated, it wondered at its worth […].[92]

This image restates and develops what Plotinus had earlier argued in his earlier treatise on beauty, where he had written (§5): 'Gold is degraded when it is mixed with earthy particles; if these be worked out, the gold is left and is beautiful, isolated from all that is foreign, gold with gold alone', and so it is with the soul, for it is 'cleared of the desires […], emancipated from all the passions, purged of all that embodiment has thrust upon it […] — in that moment the ugliness that came only from the alien is stripped away'.[93]

As well as being prominent in the pagan tradition, this motif of sculpting can be found in Patristic writing as well. In his *Life of Moses* by St Gregory of Nyssa we find that the Old Testament prophet is explicitly compared to a sculptor. In §313 of

Life, Gregory tells us that 'after all these things' — following the pillar of cloud or fire, the miraculous crossing the Red Sea, his song of victory, the journey through the desert, the manna and the quails, the water from the rock, the battle against the Amalekites, his ascension of Mount Sinai and receiving the Covenant — Moses 'went to the mountain of rest', i.e., Mount Nebo: 'He did not set foot on the land below for which the people were longing by reason of the promise', and 'he who preferred to live by what flowed from above no longer tasted earthly food'. Rather than a symbol of his failure to enter the Promised Land, the death of Moses on Mount Nebo is seen here as a great culminating act: 'Having come to the very top of the mountain, he, like a good sculptor who has fashioned well the whole statue of his own life, did not simply bring his creation to an end but he placed the finishing touch on his work'.[94] Was Gregory of Nyssa influenced in his choice of this image by the tractate on beauty (*Ennead* 1, Tractate 6) by Plotinus?[95] Elsewhere, Gregory expands on the use of this image: in his *Treatise on the Inscriptions of the Psalms*, for instance, he says in his discussion of Psalm 2:

> Anything undertaken with a purpose has a certain natural, necessary order which brings about the end one strives after. Similarly, a sculptor's goal is to make stone conform to some kind of image. He does not immediately begin from a completed form, but his art of fashioning stone must proceed with order and care, otherwise he could accomplish nothing. The grosser parts of useless stone must first be stripped away to bring out the intended form, and so the sculptor laborously prunes away those parts of stone. Once they are removed, the remaining stone begins to take on the form of a living subject on which the artisan has exerted his talent. The sculptor next removes the rough parts of the stone with more subtle, precise instruments and then imposes upon the stone the likeness of the model's form. He polishes and smoothes the stone's surface, actions which will enhance his work.[96]

But Gregory is not just simply giving us a free lesson in sculptural technique; his point is to establish an analogy, arguing that 'similarly, when earthly inclinations have turned our human nature to stone, God's chiseling us to his divine likeness proceeds according to a certain method and order to complete his goal':

> Then [the divine sculptor] cuts away superficial material and begins to form his subject matter to the likeness of his final goal by removing anything which hinders the representation. Thus by more subtle teachings of his intentions the divine sculptor scrapes and polishes our minds and forms Christ in us according to the pattern of virtue. We had Christ's image from the very beginning and are now restored.[97]

Similarly, in his *Commentary on the Song of Songs*, Gregory observes that 'in the case of chiseling a certain form in marble, sculptors chisel and remove material to represent the model's form', from which he derives (using again a Plotinian image, this time gold) the following message: 'Thus the many hands of the Church's body must be fashioned into something beautiful by the chiseling effected through much reflection so that their hands may be pure gold', which means that:

> what pleases men, love of glory, greed, looking to externals, notoriety, concern about one's glory, and satisfaction with luxury and pleasure from giving orders [...] must be removed by the instruments of reflection so that the pure, unadulterated gold of free will might alone remain which has been compared to a pure head of gold.[98]

In writing as he does, Gregory of Nyssa is mindful of a long tradition in Judeo-Christian thinking, whatever the prohibition against statues or idols. In Deuteronomy, Moses commands Israel: 'Circumcise therefore the foreskin of your heart' (10: 16), and the idea of interior circumcision is taken up later by St Paul (Romans 2: 28–29; and 2 Corinthians 3: 3). In turn, another New Testament document, the Epistle to the Hebrews, twice reminds its readers of Yahweh's promise to Jeremiah, 'I will give my law in their bowels, and I will write it in their heart' (Jeremiah 31: 33; cf. Hebrews 8: 10 and 10: 16). So it comes as no surprise when, towards the end of his *Life of Moses* (§316), Gregory of Nyssa turns directly to his readers and addresses them in the following terms: 'And when you, as a sculptor, carve in your own heart the divine oracles which you receive from God; and when you destroy the golden idol [...] then you will draw near to the goal'.[99]

While there is a difference between the Judeo-Christian and the pagan tradition as far as the creation and function of statues is concerned, the image of self-sculpting forms a common link between these two traditions — between the Christian and the pagan, or between the biblical and the Stoic-Neoplatonic. Indeed, Neoplatonic thought in general, and the work of Plotinus in particular, exercised a profound influence on the thought of the anonymous Christian theologian (active in the late fifth and early sixth centuries) known as Pseudo-Dionysius the Areopagite. In his *Mystical Theology*, which fused Neoplatonic thinking with Christian beliefs, Dionysius spoke of the possibility of a richer, deeper kind of *knowledge*, through a particular kind of *knowing*: 'For this would be really to see and to know: to praise the Transcendent One in a transcending way, namely through the denial of all beings'.[100] And in order to describe this kind of knowledge, Dionysius used a highly Plotinian image when he writes that 'we would be like sculptors who set out to carve a statue', explaining his choice of image by adding that 'they remove every obstacle to the pure view of the hidden image, and simply by this act of clearing aside' — or *aphairesis* — 'they show up the beauty which is hidden'.[101]

(Here the sense of the term 'clearing aside', which translates the Greek word, *aphairesis*, could be understood in relation to what Nietzsche says in *Ecce Homo* about the need to 'leave aside' those tasks which distract us from the 'real task', while nevertheless recognizing that 'even the *blunders* of life — the temporary sidepaths and wrong turnings, the delays, the "modesties", the seriousness squandered on tasks which lie outside *the* task — have their own meaning and value' as 'an expression of a great sagacity, even the supreme sagacity'.[102])

From Pseudo-Dionysius the Areopagite this image becomes mediated to the Christian mystical tradition, featuring for instance in the *Commentary on the Gospel of John* by Meister Eckhart. In the course of his extensive discussion of the famous opening of this gospel, 'In the beginning was the Word' (*In principio erat verbum*), Eckhart refers to the sixty-fifth letter of Seneca to Lucilius (see above), Averroes's commentary on Aristotle's *Metaphysics*, and on Aristotle's *Metaphysics* itself. Eckhart interprets the biblical text in an essentially aesthetic sense, in a way that applies to 'every work of nature and of art'.[103] He argues that 'a painter possesses an inherent form of the figure and its image that he paints externally on the wall', that 'it is necessary that the image be with him as an exemplar toward which he looks and according to which he works', and that 'the image depicted in the painter's mind is the art itself by which the painter is the principle' — or, in a sense, *the beginning* — of the painted image'.[104] In this passage, Eckhart directly cites Averroes (*Commentary on the Metaphysics*, 12. 36 on 1072a) and Aristotle (*Metaphysics*, 1013b–1014a), using aesthetics to interpret the biblical text:

> [W]e have the text, "God was the Word", that is, the principle or cause of the effect, just as the bath in the mind is the principle of the material bath, [...] and the figure in the mind is the principle of the figure on the wall. [...] [I]t is evident that Polycletus is not the principle of the statue before he acquires the art to make it, nor would he be able to be its principle if he lost the art. So it is clear from the beginning that the art itself remains with the artist as soon as he is an artist and as long as he is an artist who is able to be the principle of a work of art. This is what the text means [...].[105]

Further on in his *Commentary*, Eckhart uses the image of statue to help explicate the words spoken by Philip to Jesus after he has washed the disciples' feet: 'Lord, shew us the Father, and it is enough for us' (John 14: 8). Eckhart interprets this text in no fewer than eighteen ways, and he finds yet further 'moral meanings', writing that 'we can see an example when an image is sculpted from wood or stone by changing nothing, but only clearing away, cutting off and drawing out', so that 'when these things have been taken away by the artist's hand, the image appears and shines forth'.[106] The way Eckhart understands the analogy of sculpting is very close to the way Gregory of Nyssa uses it, and elsewhere, in a sermon on a text from the Gospel of Matthew, Eckhart expands on the relation between *image* and *transformation*.[107] (This transformative element can also be found in the use of the sculpting image in the thought of one of Eckhart's disciples, Johannes Tauler [c. 1300–1361].[108])

Similarly, in his famous treatise, 'On the Noble Man', part of the *Liber benedictus*, Eckhart takes as his text the opening line of the parable of the pounds as found in the Gospel of Luke. He reads this text in the light of the dual nature of the human being — part body, part spirit — which he turns into the duality of the outer man and the inner man. Drawing on St Jerome, Origen, and St Augustine, as well as on Cicero and Seneca, Eckhart discerns six stages in the development of the transformation of the individual into a life of eternal bliss. And he draws on the image which he had used earlier in his *Commentary on the Gospel of John* to exemplify the transformation involved:

> If an artist wants to make an image from wood or stone, he does not put the image into the wood, but he cuts away the chips that had hidden and concealed the image: he *gives* nothing to the wood but *takes* from it, cutting away the overlay and removing the dross, and then that which was hidden under it shines forth.[109]

Thus Eckhart sets up and describes what emerges in this transformative process of sculpting using the image of treasure hidden in a field (Matthew 13: 44), which in turn recalls Jung's emphasis in his writings on alchemy on the image of the 'treasure hard to attain'.[110] All of which prompts us to ask: in philosophical terms, is the transformation of which Eckhart is speaking essentially a *mystical* one, a *psychological* one, or an *aesthetic* one?

True, the notions of purification (in Gregory of Nyssa), of *aphairesis* (Dionysius), of 'turning-away' (*abekêren*), and 'abstraction' (*entbildung*) (Meister Eckhart) look as if they belong to that ascetic tradition about which, in *On the Genealogy of Morals* and elsewhere, Nietzsche is apparently so scathing (and about which Jung, in *Transformations and Symbols of the Libido*, later revised as *Symbols of Transformation*, is so insightful) (*CW* 5 §119, fn. 5 and §339). But Nietzsche's critique is surely directed at the goal of Christian asceticism as he saw it, that is, the abnegation of the individual, not at its techniques as such; one might recall (and we shall do so again in Chapter 4) that Nietzsche's own choice of lifestyle was highly Epicurean in its simplicity, even austerity.

Michelangelo and the Renaissance

In Zarathustra's concluding words in his discourse about the blissful islands one can also hear an echo of Renaissance aesthetics, as stated — and embodied in his art — by the great Italian sculptor, Michelangelo (1475–1564).[111] When Zarathustra says, 'I see an image sleeping in the stone, the image of my visions! Ah, that it must sleep in the hardest, ugliest stone!', one hears an echo of the principle attributed to Michelangelo that 'every block of stone has a statue inside it and it is the task of the sculptor to discover it'.[112] And when Zarathustra announces, 'Now my hammer rages fiercely against its prison. Fragments fly from the stone: what is that to me?', one recalls a further statement attributed to Michelangelo:

In every block of marble I see a statue as plain as though it stood before me, shaped and perfect in attitude and action. I have only to hew away the rough walls that imprison the lovely apparition to reveal it to the other eyes as mine see it.[113]

(These or similar passages from Michelangelo were cited by the English mathematician and theologian, Isaac Barrow [1630–1677], one of the developers of infinitesimal calculus, when he argued in his *Lectures* that 'all imaginable geometrical figures are really inherent in every particle of matter, [...] though not apparent to the sense':

Just as the effigies of Caesar lies hid under the unhewn marble, and is no new thing made by the statuary, but only is discovered and brought to sight by his workmanship, i.e., by removing the parts of the matter which involve and overshadow it. Which made Michael Angelus, the most famous carver, say, *That Sculpture was nothing else but a purgation from things superfluous. For take all that is superfluous* (says he) *from the wood or stone, and the rest will be the figure you intend.* So if the hand of an angel (at least the power of God) should think fit to polish any particle of matter without vacuity, a spherical superfice would appear to the eyes of a figure exactly round; not as created anew, but as unveiled and laid open from the disguises and covers of his circumjacent matter.[114]

Whereas Barrows locates such 'ideas' or 'types' in external matter, Thomas Taylor foregrounds, in his analysis of the *Commentary* by Proclus on Euclid's *Elements*, the argument that the 'figures of geometric speculation' subsist in what Taylor calls 'the receptacle of imagination' — or '*the matter of phantasy*'.[115])

These statements attributed to Michelangelo are based on ideas to be found in his poetry and correspondence. For instance, in one of his sonnets written around 1528 Michelangelo writes:

If my rough hammer in hard stones can form
A human semblance, one and then another,
Set moving by the agent who is holder,
Watcher and guide, its course is not its own.

But that divine One, staying in Heaven at home,
Gives others beauty, more to itself, self-mover;
If hammers can't be made without a hammer,
From that one living all the others come.

And since a blow will have the greatest force
As at the forge it's lifted up the highest,
This above mine to Heaven has run and flown.

Wherefore with me, unfinished, all is lost,
Unless the divine workshop will assist
In making it; on earth it was alone.[116]

Then again, in another sonnet, written some time between 1538 and 1544, and dedicated to Vittoria Colonna (*Non ha l'ottimo artista alcun concetto*), Michelangelo sets out his aesthetics in the first stanza as follows:

> No block of marble but it does not hide
> The concept living in the artist's mind —
> Pursuing it inside that form, he'll guide
> His hand to shape what reason has defined.[117]

These lines acquired particular significance in the Renaissance, when this poem (and three other sonnets) provided the basis for two lectures on painting and sculpture given by the Italian humanist and intellectual, Benedetto Varchi (1502/1503–1565) to the Florentine Academy in March 1547.[118] In a letter written to Varchi in March 1547, Michelangelo emphasized the reciprocity of sculpture and painting, defining sculpture in relation to painting as follows: 'Every painter should do as much sculpture as painting and every sculptor as much painting as sculpture. I mean by sculpture work which is fashioned by dint of taking away; what is done by way of adding is similar to painting'.[119]

There was an important Renaissance context within which Varchi and Michelangelo were thinking and working. In his dialogue *Della poetica* (1536), the Paduan scholar Bernardino Daniello (c. 1500–1565) used sculpture as a model of poetical procedure:

> Each perfect and excellent sculptor ought first of all to find that marble or stone that he judges should be the most ready and proper material, [suitable] to having to take that form that the sculptor intends subsequently to give it; and after he has found it, he contrives to give [...] some part of it to the head, some to the arms, some to the feet and so by order through the other parts of the body until the whole is suitably disposed [...]. One may not yet say that it is perfect form, nor, on the other hand, simple material, until he, with more subtle chisels and other instruments, has given it such perfection that, although it be without any spirit or feeling, it seems nevertheless, to all who see it, that it lives and breathes.[120]

And in his treatise *Da pintura antiga* (1548), the Portuguese humanist and artist Francisco de Holanda (1517–1585) wrote — albeit about painting, rather than sculpture — in terms very similar to those of Michelangelo's sonnet to Colonna:

> In painting, the *idea* is an image that the intellect of the painter has of the truth, seen with the interior eyes in the greatest silence and secrecy. This he must imagine and select from the most excellent and rare things that his imagination and prudence may attain, as an exemplar sounded or seen in heaven, or in some other place, which he continues to follow and desire, then

to imitate and to show outside with the work of his hand, as is proper, and as he conceives it and sees it in his intellect.

[…]

So that the *idea* is the highest thing in painting that may be imagined in the intellect; because, as it is the work of the intellect and of the spirit, it is right that it conform greatly to itself; and being thus, it must rise each time higher and make itself spirit, and mix with the font and pattern of the first ideas, which is God.[121]

The thinkers and artists of the Renaissance, including Michelangelo, drew deeply on the philosophy of Neoplatonism[122] — after all, this is also the era of Marsilio Ficino (1433–1499) and his great commentaries on Plato — but they drew also on the philosophy of Aristotle, an important influence on the Scholastic tradition to which they were heirs.[123] Thus, as well as the influence of Neoplatonism, there is an important Aristotelian strand in Michelangelo's aesthetics. For in his discussion of the difference between material, formal, efficient, and final causes (see above), Aristotle had used the example of a bronze or marble statue.[124] Central to Aristotle's thinking here is the idea of *potency* or *potentiality*:[125] the statue exists in the block of marble in a potential state. (In his commentary on Aristotle's *Physics*, St Thomas Aquinas pursued further the implications of Aristotle's example of the sculpture.[126])

Consequently, one might think that, back on the blissful islands, the image in the stone — 'the image sleeping in the stone, the image of my visions' — can be read as potentiality in this Aristotelian sense, but arguably this 'image' is, in fact, closer to the Neoplatonic conception of 'living form' (Plotinus).[127] For the statue is 'in' the stone, just as the Superman is 'in' Man, yet the Superman is not just a potentiality of Man but an expression of the will-to-power, even of 'the most spiritual will-to-power' (*der geistigste Wille zur Macht*), to borrow a phrase from *Beyond Good and Evil*.[128]

As David Summers has argued, in the sonnet *No ha l'ottimo artista alcun concetto* Michelangelo distinguishes between three aspects of artistic inspiration: first, matter; second, *arte* or *ingegno* ('skill' or 'ingenuity'); and third, love or beauty. The relation between these three terms is important, for 'it is not simply the sculptor and his stone, but the sculptor, the stone, and most vitally […] the love, received as grace, that completes the lover's sense of beauty', so that 'his *arte* and *ingegno* are at once healed and given direction', then 'his hand obeys his intellect', and the sculptor becomes 'the excellent artist' — but 'he is first of all a lover'.[129] Nevertheless, there is one Platonic term that Michelangelo never actually uses: *idea*.

Now we *do* find the *idea* in de Hollanda (who talks about the 'ideas' of the soul and the 'ideas' of the Intellect), we *do* find it in Ficino (who talks about 'ideas innate in the soul'), and we *do* find it in Varchi (who talks about *concetto* as a Platonic idea and as a kind of internal image).[130] And because in Renaissance aesthetics the idea of *idea* becomes increasingly wide, covering 'invention', *fantasia* ('imagination') and *giudizio* ('judgment'), and many other terms (including *disegno*, *igegno*, and *bella maniera*), one is inclined to agree with Summers that the idea becomes 'the broadest faculty of the artist, his sense of beauty and rightness which, in the works he made, linked them to one another and at the same time distinguished them from the works of others',[131] and as such it entirely underpins Michelangelo's aesthetic theory and praxis alike. Nor do we find the term *idea* (used in a commensurate sense), either in *Thus Spoke Zarathustra* or in Nietzsche's writings in general. But in the 'drive' of his 'creative will' — that is, both in his perception of the 'image sleeping in the stone' *and* in his use of the hammer: 'I will complete it' — Zarathustra proves himself to be just as much an artist as Michelangelo was.

Moreover, although the intellectual background to Michelangelo's aesthetics is Neoplatonism; although his theory of sculpture as 'abstraction' — the removal of material to reveal the pre-existent form within — draws heavily on the Neoplatonic assumptions of Cinquecento art theory; and although it is true that, on the face of it, Nietzsche's philosophical starting-point stands in complete opposition to the assumptions of Neoplatonism, nevertheless Michelangelo's theories can also be understood in an almost entirely non-philosophical, very direct and almost visceral way. Surprisingly, perhaps, it is precisely this visceral aspect that we find emphasized by the founder of anthroposophy, Rudolf Steiner (1861–1925), in a lecture on Michelangelo, the sixth in a series of twelve on the subject of *Spiritual Science as "Lebensgut"* in the Architektenhaus in Berlin on 8 January 1914.[132] Whatever Steiner's subsequent reputation, he argues here in a way that draws on the major sources of German classicism — notably, Lessing and Goethe — to develop an approach to history as a science, or a 'spiritual' science, or as a science of the development of *Geist*.

Greek art and, above all, Greek sculpture must have spoken to the Greeks, Steiner suggests, 'like a message from another world' (p. 188). Yet the creation of such forms was only possible, he continues, because something lived in the souls of the Greeks that had not come from their senses, an 'inner feeling-knowledge' of how the human organism is formed, an 'immediately-felt knowledge' that gave them an understanding of muscular structure and anatomy. To support this claim, Steiner invited his listeners to consider a statue of Zeus. 'Even what survives to us of Greek sculpture', Steiner explained, 'reveals that when the sculptor set his hand to a statue of Zeus, for instance, his soul was permeated with a sort of Zeus feeling', so that he knew 'what inner tensions this feeling could resolve' and thus, 'from within outwards', he could 'give to matter its appropriate form' (p. 189). We should not concern ourselves, he continued, with whether Zeus, or Hera, or any of the others are really gods: because that would reduce art to a question of mere story-telling. Rather, what matters is *how* the sculptor made his Zeus or his Hera, how they stand 'enclosed in themselves', just as 'the life of our soul is enclosed within us and we feel ourselves enclosed within it, when we experience, in the organic reflex of the muscular tension, what happens to the soul in the organism when it is experiencing itself in this mood' (pp. 189–190). This quality of something enclosed in the soul, but nevertheless emerging into space (*dieses mehr oder weniger in der Seele Abgeschlossene, das hinausdringt in den Raum, das sich offenbart in den Raum hinaus*), is what, for Steiner, defines the essence of Greek sculpture.

As evidence for his argument, Steiner cited that most iconic of ancient Greek sculptures, the Laocoön, but he moved on to consider the work of Michelangelo as demonstrating a 'significant change' between the 'old' and the 'new' (p. 192). Whereas the Greeks had created art-works 'which deny the outer world and produce an effect on our souls as if from another world', Michelangelo's figures inhabit 'the same world in which we live' and 'share our life' within that world; whereas the statues of the Greek gods 'breathe the air of the gods', Michelangelo's statues 'breathe the same air as ourselves' (p. 192). In his lecture, Steiner referred to specific sculptures by Michelangelo — his Moses (c. 1513–1515), commissioned by Pope Julius II for his tomb and housed in San Pietro in Vincoli in Rome, the same statue that fascinated Freud; his David (1501–1504), placed outside the Palazzo della Signoria in Florence; and his Pietà (1498–1499), housed in St Peter's Basilica in the Vatican — as well as to his frescoes on the ceiling of the Sistine Chapel, especially the scene of the Creation of Adam and the pictures of the Prophets and Sibyls.

For Steiner, we can see how, in Michelangelo, 'two currents' flowed together: on the one hand, an 'energetic and intensive study of anatomy', and, on the other, the 'inner life sense' of the 'soul' (p. 194). Herein lies the greatness of Michelangelo: that, in an epoch dependent on sense observation, he could carry over from earlier epochs what Goethe called the 'spirit of bodies' (*Geist der Körper*), or 'the spirit of outer nature' (*Geist der äußeren Natur*) (p. 199).[133] In a wonderfully expressive passage, Steiner develops his account of Michelangelo's creative intuition and activity:

> And on a soul like Michelangelo's, a block in front of him has the effect of making him set to work on it by making a model for his thoughts [*indem er sich nur für seine Gedanken ein Modell macht*]. The model, however, has no other significance than as an expression of its own idea. What he creates, is what essentially the stone wants to be. He stands in front of the stone — let me put this in a radical way — and as the stone is, so he sees it: *this* is how the hand must be, *this* is how the leg must be positioned, *this* is how everything must be and no other way. [...] Only now can the actual work begin with the auger — the barrel drill did not exist in Michelangelo's day — and only now can he begin to knock out larger pieces. Then begins the continuous work with a pick hammer and chisel, and finally we have the impression that the block itself has given, after everything has been removed that did not belong to it, what the block had to give. (p. 200)

Steiner thus comes to a controversial conclusion that an artist like Michelangelo would never be able to create in bronze or in another material what he was able to create in marble. Less controversial, yet more surprising, is Steiner's definition of anthroposophy as an essentially aesthetic enterprise: 'If through spiritual science [*Geisteswissenschaft*] we acquire a certain view of the imagination [*die Phantasie*], and we go, not even though a field of marble, but through any masses of rock, then we shall feel when we see all the different shapes of stone: each one must become this or that. We can see from each stone as we find it, what it must become' (p. 199).

Without any reference to Neoplatonism or to anthroposophy, what Steiner is trying to get at here is made clear in Irving Stone's classic novel, *The Agony and the Ecstasy* (1961), subsequently turned into a film in 1965.[134] What emerges from the novel (and the film) is how Michelangelo emphasizes the reciprocal interaction of intellect and body, much as we find in the later tradition of German classical aesthetics of, say, Herder or Goethe or Schiller. For these thinkers and writers, in the aesthetic mode both the intellectual and the sensuous faculties of the body are coordinated, permitting not just *erkennen* (intellectual awareness) but *begreifen* (experiential knowledge), a coordination symbolically presented — by Herder, as we shall see, in his *Sculpture* (1778) and by Goethe in the seventh of his *Roman Elegies* (1795) — as a connection between the eye and the hand.[135]

What Zarathustra's cry at the end of his discourse on the blissful islands certainly captures is the passionate intensity — the 'ecstasy' and, by the same token, the 'agony' — of Michelangelo's statements and sonnets on the task of the sculptor. Whereas Michelangelo is reputed to have declared, 'I saw the *angel* in the marble and carved until I set him free', in the marble — and in humankind — Zarathustra sees the *superman*; and, with equal single-mindedness and determination, he sets to work …

Enlightenment Thinkers

Subsequent to Neoplatonism, Patristic writing, Christian mysticism, and Renaissance Neoplatonism, one finds in modern philosophy, from the early Enlightenment (exemplified by Leibniz, Condillac, and Herder) to such twentieth-century figures as Ernst Cassirer and Ludwig Klages (as well as Manly P. Hall and Heidegger, not to mention Jung) a persistence of interest in the motif of the statue and of an insistence on the need to sculpt and to shape one's self. It is within this tradition that Jung, too, finds a place, thanks to his belief, expressed in *The Relations between the Ego and the Unconscious* (1929), that 'the living form needs deep shadow if it is to appear plastic' (*CW* 7 §400).

For instance, in his *New Essays on Human Understanding* (completed in 1704, but not published until 1765), Gottfried Wilhelm Leibniz (1646–1716) took issue with the position adopted by John Locke (1632–1704) in *An Essay on Human Understanding* (1689). There Locke had argued against the existence of innate ideas, claiming that *nihil in intellectu quod prius non fuerit in sensu* (i.e., 'there's nothing in the mind that wasn't previously in the senses'). On the contrary, Leibniz maintained, it might be that nothing is in the mind without being first in the senses — but what about the mind itself? To pursue this case against what he saw as Locke's simplistic view of the mind, Leibniz focused on Locke's admission in book 2 of his *Essay* that some ideas do not originate in sensation, but rather in reflection. But, or so Leibniz argued, 'reflection is nothing but attention to what is within us, and the senses do not give us what we carry with us already'.[136] In order to illustrate his argument, Leibniz imagined a sculptor creating a statue of Hercules out of a block of marble:

> I have also used the analogy of a veined block of marble, as opposed to an entirely homogeneous block of marble, or to a blank tablet — what the philosophers call a *tabula rasa*. For if the soul were like such a blank tablet then truths would be in us as the shape of Hercules is in a piece of marble when the marble is entirely neutral as to whether it assumes this shape or some other. However, if there were veins in the block which marked out the shape of Hercules rather than other shapes, then that block would be more determined to that shape and Hercules would be innate in it, in a way, even though labour would be required to expose the veins and to polish them into clarity, removing everything that prevents their being seen.[137]

In Leibniz's example, the marble is veined: it has a predisposition, so to speak, to yield up Hercules to the sculptor: similarly, in Nietzsche's text, the superman lies within the human being, it is, so to speak, an innate idea — but it requires, like the figure of Hercules for the sculptor, an immense effort to 'release' from the stone what might well be 'innate' within it yet cannot, without the application of energy (physical and conceptual), be realized.

The image or analogy of a statue became central to the entire question of the relation between sensations and ideas in the work of Étienne Bonnot de Condillac (1715–1780). Condillac radicalized Locke's position, and argued for a view that could be called 'sensationism': there are no innate ideas, and no innate abilities or faculties of any kind. But there are sensations — sense impressions, sensory stimuli, so that we are (in)formed (out) of *feeling* … In his *Treatise on Sensations* (1754), Condillac posited that the individual human being was simply a statue: inanimate, insentient, and presumably without any veins in its marble. For Condillac, the individual begins life, not as a *tabula rasa* or empty page, but as a three-dimensional blankness: in other words, a statue.[138] In his *Essay*, Condillac progressively animated this statue, just as through experience the individual acquires an increasingly sophisticated sensorial apparatus. For Condillac, the most basic form of experience is smell; different senses accrue, while touch introduces an ability to organise senses and attribute them to objects.

By contrast, for Johann Gottfried Herder (1744–1803) the most basic form of experience *is* touch: 'the beauty of a form, of a body', he argued, 'is not a visual but a tactile concept', and so 'every one of these beauties must originally be sought in the sense of touch'.[139] True, sight and sound are always 'gateways to the beautiful', with lesser importance being attached to taste and smell; but 'the beauty of bodies, *as forms*, is […] tactile', as is suggested by the fact that 'all aesthetic terms that describe such beauty' are 'derived from touch: rough, gentle, tender, full, in motion'.[140] Hence it is, in Herder's view, erroneous to assume that the 'whole essence of sculpture' is visual; rather, 'sculpture — as the fine art of bodies — is above all tangible'.[141] Although Herder wrote this text, the 'Fourth Grove' in his series of 'Critical Woods', in the late 1760s, it did not appear in print until 1846; had it been published earlier, Robert T. Clark has argued, it might 'have changed the entire course of German aesthetics'.[142] But Herder's emphasis on the tactile informs a short treatise written at around the same time, and published in 1778, entitled *Sculpture: Some Observations on Shape and Form from Pygmalion's Creative Dream*.

Inserting his argument into the classical context of Ovid's *Metamorphoses* (book 10) and the Enlightenment context of the 'Molyneux problem' alike; drawing across a wide range of references from Diodorus, Pausanias, Strabo, Pliny, Virgil, and Homer, to Norse myth, Shakespeare, and Milton; and citing at least fifteen major works of classical sculpture (including the Apollo Belvedere, the Belvedere Torso of Hercules, the Borghese Gladiator, the Laocoön, and the Barberini Suppliant or Danae), Herder advanced a powerful argument about sculpture — and about the body. Sculpture (in contrast to painting), he wrote, 'creates *in depth*', it 'creates *one* living thing, an animate work that *stands there* and endures'; it 'creates *beautiful forms*', it 'forms *shapes in depth* and *places* the object *there before us*', and in some sense the nobility of this enterprise argues for a nobility of subject matter:

> What sculpture should create, and what it has succeeded in creating, are forms in which the living soul animates the entire body, forms in which art can compete in the task of representing the *embodied soul* — that is to say, gods, human beings, and noble animals.[143]

These sculptures speak to us, by appealing to our sense of touch as well as our sense of sight or, in other words, they represent totality by appealing to the totality of our own sensory apparatus. In fact, this sort of statue does not merely represent totality, it *embodies* it, and consequently it is *beautiful*:

> The well-proportioned human being is not an abstraction derived from the clouds or composed from learned rules or arbitrary conventions. It is something that can be *grasped* and *felt* by all who are able to recognize *in themselves* or *in others* the form of life, the expression of force in the human vessel. Beauty is nothing but the *meaning of inner perfection*.[144]

Or to reformulate this final statement in another, and more Zarathustrian, way: is *the beauty (of the superman) nothing but the meaning (of the earth)?*

Although Condillac's statue is far from being an *Übermensch*, one can see his sensationist position — and *a fortiori* the tactile approach to sculpture advanced by Herder — as so many steps on the road to the position eventually articulated by Nietzsche's Zarathustra that there is only the body (and its senses), and that 'soul is only a word for something in the body'.[145] At the end of this philosophical trajectory stands Jung, whose notion of the archetype unites (imaginative) image and (physiological) instinct. Before such a radical position as Nietzsche's could be adopted, however, Enlightenment thought had to develop further, leading to the multiple strands of philosophical systematization which are collectively given the label 'Romanticism'. In the tradition of German philosophical Romanticism, one of the most prominent figures is Friedrich Wilhelm Joseph Schelling (1775–1854). Romanticism can be seen as reaction and a response to (as well as a partial acceptance and a partial rejection of) the thought of the two decades preceding its inception at the beginning of the nineteenth century, associated with Johann Wolfgang von Goethe (1749–1832) and with Friedrich von Schiller (1759–1805).

Schiller, Schelling, and Nietzsche

In a poem called 'The Favour of the Moment' (*Die Gunst des Augenblicks*), written in 1802 on the occasion of a leaving meal in honour of the Crown Prince of Weimar (Karl Friedrich von Sachsen-Weimar-Eisenach) before a journey to Paris and the start of his Grand Tour, and published in the second volume of Schiller's *Gedichte* in 1805, we once again find the motif that has become familiar to us over the course of this chapter. Despite its whimsical tone, and its allusion to the celebratory dinner at which it was recited, the poem makes a serious point, including a reflection on the nature of inspiration itself:

> Since Creation began
> All that mortals have wrought,
> All that's godlike in MAN
> Comes — the flash of a Thought!
>
> For ages the stone
> In the quarry may lurk,
> An instant alone
> Can suffice to the work;
>
> An impulse give birth
> To the child of the soul,
> A glance stamp the worth
> And the fame of the whole.[146]

Here the familiar motifs of Renaissance Platonism are taken up again — in the contrast between the mass of stone forming slowly, ever so slowly, over the ages, while the flash of thought that uncovers its potential as a work of art takes place in just a second. Two years later after this poem's publication, F.W.J. Schelling — in an essay entitled 'On the Relation Between the Plastic Arts and Nature' (1807) —[147] talked about the dynamic character of nature in a way that demonstrates striking similarities, even if the imagery of light, stone, and the flash of inspiration serve a somewhat different argument.

Schelling's language here has, with good reason, been called 'quasi-alchemical',[148] but it could also more simply be seen as purely descriptive. Illustrating his proposition that 'the entire creation is but a work of the highest manifestation', Schelling observes of nature that:

> the power of fire, the flash of light, she conceals in the hard stone [*die Kraft des Feuers, den Blitz des Lichtes verschließt sie in harten Stein*]; the pure soul of melody in severe metal; even on the threshold of life, and while meditating on organic form, she sinks, overpowered by the might of form, into petrification.[149]

As a consequence of the fact that, in his eyes, 'the entire creation is but a work of the highest manifestation', Schelling concludes that 'the artist must first deny himself, and descend into the particular, not shunning the remoteness nor the pain, nay, torment of form [*noch den Schmerz, ja die Pein der Form*]'.[150]

Is it not precisely this 'pain', this 'torment' — the pain and torment of *form* — to which Zarathustra alludes when, earlier in his discourse 'On the Blissful Islands', he declares that 'creation' is 'the great redemption from suffering, and life's easement', but ominously adds: 'That the creator may exist, that itself requires suffering and much transformation'?[151] Indeed, Zarathustra — echoing the *stirb und werde* of *Selige Sehnsucht* — says: 'Yes, there must be much bitter dying in your life, you creators! [...] For the creator himself to be the child new-born he must also be willing to be the mother and endure the mother's pain'.[152] Exploring further this call to philosophical midwifery, Zarathustra states aloud its erotic implications, not in Goethean terms of *Begattung*, it is true, but nevertheless in terms of begetting (*Zeugung*): 'In knowing-and-understanding [*Im Erkennen*], too, I feel only my will's delight in begetting and becoming [*Zeuge- und Werde-Lust*]; and if there be innocence in my knowledge it is because will-to-begetting (*Wille zur Zeugung*) is in it'.[153]

This notion of a will-to-begetting or an urge to self-formation is taken up by Nietzsche — in part an inheritor of the Romantic, in part an inheritor of the classical tradition — when, in his autobiographical work *Ecce Homo*, he discusses the concept of *Wohlgeratenheit*, of 'having-turned-out-well'. Being someone who has 'turned out well' is the exact opposite of what Nietzsche terms being a *décadent*, but it is also precisely what he means when he talks about the *Übermensch*.[154] To illustrate the idea of having 'turned out well', Nietzsche has recourse to the image of self-sculpting:[155]

> That a human being who has turned out well does our senses good: that he is carved out of wood at once hard, delicate and sweet-smelling. He has a taste only for what is beneficial to him; his pleasure, his joy ceases where the measure of what is beneficial to him is overstepped.[156]

In an unpublished note from 1880, Nietzsche underscores the essential significance of the project of self-sculpting, when he writes — against the mythology that the self is something simply to be discovered — that '*to make ourselves*, to *shape* a form from all the elements — that is the task! The task of a sculptor! Of a productive human being!' And he emphasizes the preeminently existential nature of this project, adding that 'it's *not* through knowledge but through practice and a model that we become *ourselves!*'.[157] Elsewhere in Nietzsche's writings we find him returning to the motif of sculpture and sculpting on a significant number of occasions.

At the end of the first section of *The Birth of Tragedy*, for instance, where he describes the effect of the Dionysian, Nietzsche argues that, 'under the charm of the Dionysian', the individual is 'no longer an artist, he has become a work of art', using a sculptural metaphor to emphasize this point: 'The noblest clay, the most costly marble, man, is here kneaded and cut, and to the sound of the chisel strokes of the Dionysian world-artist rings out the cry of the Eleusinian Mysteries: "Do you prostrate yourselves, millions? Do you sense your Maker, world?"'.[158] (The Eleusinian Mysteries were the most revered and celebrated of all the ancient mystery cults.[159] It might come as a surprise to learn that, in the ancient mystery cult of Eleusis, the participants recited a poem by Schiller, but the allusion to 'Ode to Joy' reveals the extent to which Nietzsche's argument, ostensibly about the origins of the Greek tragedy of Aeschylus, Sophocles, and Euripedes, is really an engagement with the aesthetics of German classicism.)

Significantly, Nietzsche's metaphor in this passage complicates his distinction at the outset of *The Birth of Tragedy* between 'the Apollonian art of sculpture' and 'the nonimagistic, Dionysian art of music': by applying a sculptural metaphor to the Dionysian, Nietzsche is underscoring the interdependence of the Apollonian and the Dionysian that he will later explicitly state at the end of section 21: 'Thus the intricate relation of the Apollonian and the Dionysian in tragedy may really be symbolized by a fraternal union of the two deities: [...] and so the highest goal of tragedy and of all art is attained'.[160]

Indeed, in a short work of 1870 that preceded and develops the fundamental theses of *The Birth of Tragedy*, 'The Dionysian Worldview', Nietzsche had located a complex dialectic of dream and reality, of Apollonian and Dionysian, in the statue itself:

> As a block of marble the statue is something very real, but the reality of the statue *as a dream figure* is the living person of the god. As long as the statue hovers as an image of fantasy before the eyes of the artist, he is still playing with the real; when he translates this image into marble, he is playing with the dream.[161]

In this approach, different levels of reality both collide and coincide, as the reality of the marble is to be distinguished from the reality of the dream figure, which in turn is to be distinguished from the reality of the god, which transforms our experience of the statue just as, in ancient Greece, all experiences were transformed inasmuch as 'a god shone through them'.[162]

A god? Or a hero? In an aphorism in the first volume of *Human, All Too Human* entitled 'The Statue of Humanity', Nietzsche offered a commentary on the famous bronze sculpture of Perseus with the head of Medusa, made by Benvenuto Cellini (1500–1571) in Florence in 1545. In this work Nietzsche found a symbol of 'the

FIGURE 2.1   *Benvenuto Cellini,* bronze sculpture of Perseus with the head of Medusa, 1545.

genius of culture', which does in general what Cellini had done in creating his statue: 'the liquefied mass seemed to be insufficient, but he was *determined* to produce enough: so he threw into it keys and plates and whatever else came to hand'. By extension, Nietzsche argued, the genius of culture throws in 'errors, vices, hopes, delusions, and other things of baser as well as nobler metal', for 'the statue of humanity must emerge and be completed'. In this respect, Nietzsche posed the question in terms of aesthetics as the one which Jung would take up and frame in psychological terms of the shadow: 'What does it matter if here and there inferior material is employed?'[163]

The theme of Cellini's statue was of especial interest to Nietzsche, for in *The Birth of Tragedy* he had alluded to precisely the moment it depicts, applying it to Doric art and to the Dionysian barbarian festival: 'The figure of Apollo, rising full of pride, held out the head of Medusa to this grotesquely uncouth Dionysian power — and really could not have countered any more dangerous force', and 'it is in Doric art that this majestically rejecting attitude of Apollo is immortalized'.[164] And in the second volume of *Human, All Too Human*, Nietzsche offered an extensive reflection on the relation between art and the sacred, arguing that the function of the sacred was to reveal *and* conceal at the same time: 'No Greek ever truly *beheld* his Apollo as a wooden obelisk, his Eros as a lump of stone; they were symbols whose purpose was precisely to excite fear *of* beholding him', and 'one thing was specifically avoided: direct statement'. Correspondingly, Nietzsche explained, 'as the cella' — i.e., the inner chamber of a temple — 'contains the holy of holies, the actual *numen* of the divinity, and conceals it in mysterious semi-darkness, *but does not wholly conceal it*; as the peripteral temple' — i.e., the front and side porticos with their columns — 'in turn contains the cella and as though with a canopy and veil shelters it from prying eyes, *but does not wholly shelter it*: so the image is the divinity and at the same time the divinity's place of concealment'.[165] (As we shall see, the configuration of a temple — and the place of the statue of the god inside it — would greatly interest Heidegger, too.)

In a sequence of aphorisms in the first volume of *Human, All Too Human*, Nietzsche discusses our complex relationship to symbolism, as encountered in music (§215 and §217), in gesture (§216), and in architecture (§218). Here Nietzsche is talking about buildings, rather than about statues, but his observation that 'stone is more stony than it used to be' can be applied to sculpture as well. 'We have grown out of the symbolism of lines and figures', he laments, 'just as we have weaned ourselves from the side-effects of rhetoric', and so we no longer understand how 'everything in a Greek or Christian building originally signified something, and indeed something of a higher order of things'.[166] For, as Nietzsche had argued at the outset of this work, 'formerly the spirit was not engaged in rigorous thinking, its serious occupation was the spinning out of forms and symbols', whereas now the locus of the symbolic has shifted and 'serious occupation with the symbolic has become a mark of a lower culture'.[167]

Nietzsche's attitude towards the symbol is, like so much else, characterized, not so much by ambivalence, as by paradox. On the one hand, the dialogue of Greek tragedy is a remarkable achievement, inasmuch as 'the great choral lyrics of the tragedy' led to 'a people who revelled in symbolism and allusions' being 'educated away' from this;[168] on the other, this path led to a culture whose drawbacks he attributed with clear-sightedness, if an uncharacteristic acerbity, to the pre-eminent participants in the classical circles of Weimar and in Romantic Germany in general, to Schiller, Wilhelm von Humboldt, Schleiermacher, Hegel, and Schelling, as reflected in their correpondence. Nietzsche criticized 'their thirst for appearing *morally* excited at all cost', 'their desire for brilliant, boneless generalities', and 'the intention of seeing everything [...] in as beautiful a light as possible', but 'beautiful' in the sense of 'a vague and bad taste which nonetheless boasted of a Greek ancestry'.[169] (By contrast, Nietzsche praised Goethe for 'observ[ing] these goings-on in his own way' and for 'standing aside, gently remonstrating, keeping silent, ever more determined to follow his own, better path' — in short, the path of the symbolic.)

Elsewhere in his 'Assorted Opinions and Maxims' in volume 2 of *Human, All Too Human*, Nietzsche uses the statue as one of a series of metaphors for his theme of self-fashioning, remarking that 'the older Greeks demanded of the poet that he should be a teacher of adults', but a modern poet would be 'embarrassed' if this were demanded of him — 'he who was no good teacher of himself and thus himself failed to become a fine poem, a fair statue, but at best as it were the modest, attractive ruins of a temple [...] a cave of desires, overgrown with flowers, thistles and poisonous weeds'.[170] In this aphorism, it becomes evident that, for Nietzsche, sculptural and architectural metaphors relate ultimately to the construction of the self.

In an aphorism in *The Gay Science*, the motif of the statue is indexed to Stoicism, when Nietzsche notes that science 'may still be better known for its power of depriving man of his joys and making him colder, more like a statue, more Stoic'; instead, he proposes, science might yet be found to be 'the *great dispenser of pain*', whose counterforce might at the same time be found, 'its immense capacity for making new galaxies of joy flare up'.[171] (Perhaps this aphorism, for all its — literally — lapidary tone, can be understood as a modified version of an earlier aphorism in *Daybreak*, in which Nietzsche tells us how one 'ought to turn to stone', namely: 'Slowly, slowly to become hard like a precious stone — and at last to lie there, silent and a joy to eternity'.[172]) And subsequently, in *Beyond Good and Evil*, Nietzsche will intensify this sculptural image from *The Birth of Tragedy* in a terrifying passage about 'the discipline of suffering, of *great* suffering':

> In man *creature* and *creator* are united: in man there is material, fragment, excess, clay, dirt, nonsense, chaos; but in man there is also creator, form-giver, hammer hardness, spectator divinity, and seventh day: do you understand this contrast? And that *your* pity is for the "creature in man", for what must be formed, broken, forged, torn, burnt, made incandescent, and purified — that which *necessarily* must and *should* suffer? And *our* pity — do you not comprehend for whom our *converse* pity is when it resists your pity as the worst of all pamperings and weaknesses? Thus it is pity *versus* pity [*Mitleid also gegen Mitleid!*].[173]

Here the 'creature-in-man' undergoes the same fate as the moth, representing Psyche, in *Selige Sehnsucht*: 'torn', 'burnt', 'made incandescent', it must learn to understand why Zarathustra says that he loves those who 'go down', because they 'go over'.[174] Moreover, the metaphor of sculpting is surely implicit in Zarathustra's exclamation, 'all praise to what makes hard!';[175] in his description of redemption in the following terms:

> I walk among men as among fragments of the future: of that future which I scan.
>
> And it is all my art and aim, to compose into one and bring together what is fragment and riddle and dreadful chance;[176]

and in his injunction to his disciples, 'become hard':

> For creators are hard. And it must seem bliss to you to press your hand upon millennia as upon wax,
>
> bliss to write upon the will of millennia as upon metal — harder than metal, nobler than metal. Only the noblest is perfectly hard.
>
> This new law-table do I put over you, O my brothers: *Become hard!*[177]

And on the final pages of *Twilight of the Idols*, Nietzsche underscored the link between this passage and his concept of Dionysos, reproducing the entirety of 'Of Old and New Law-Tables', §29, after the concluding chapter, entitled 'What I Owe to the Ancients', with its praise of the 'exalted symbolism' of 'the symbolism of the Dionysian'; its contention that 'the psychology of the orgy', as 'an overflowing feeling of life and energy within which even pain acts as a stimulus', provided the key to 'the concept of the *tragic* feeling'; and Nietzsche's salutation, as 'the teacher of the eternal recurrence', of 'the philosopher Dionysos', as whose 'last disciple' he saw himself.[178]

At the conclusion of his discussion of *Thus Spoke Zarathustra* in *Ecce Homo*, Nietzsche returned to this injunction, linking it with the motif of the hammer and the concluding lines of his discourse 'On the Blissful Islands':

> Among the decisive preconditions for a *Dionysian* task is the hardness of the hammer, *joy even in destruction*. The imperative "become hard", the deepest certainty *that all creators are hard*, is the actual mark of a Dionysian nature.[179]

Dionysos as a sculptor — as a self-sculptor — represents that fusion of the Apollonian and the Dionysian that Nietzsche had posited as the basis of all art (and, by extension, the art of life) in *The Birth of Tragedy*.

Not all of Nietzsche's remarks about sculptures and self-sculpting, however, are made in a cultural context that could be described — because of its references to Apollo, to the head of Medusa, to tragedy — as pagan. In *Daybreak*, for instance, Nietzsche has the following — for him, in some respects surprisingly positive — remarks to make about, of all people, Catholic priests:

> From [the spirit of countless people who joy in submission], and in concert with the power and very often the deepest conviction and honesty of devotion, [Christianity] has *chiselled out* perhaps the most refined figures in human society that have ever yet existed: the figures of the higher and highest Catholic priesthood, especially when they have descended from a noble race and brought with them an inborn grace of gesture, the eye of command, and beautiful hands and feet.[180]

This example illustrates the central tenet of this aphorism — that 'all spirit in the end becomes bodily visible', and in a note from his *Nachlass* from the Spring of 1884 entitled 'On the Means of Making Beautiful', Nietzsche observed that 'the Greek philosophers did not pursue "*happiness*" other than in the form of *finding* **oneself** *beautiful*, hence making a statue of oneself *whose appearance was beneficent*'.[181] Indeed, the image of sculpting as used here and in the passage from *Ecce Homo* is intimately related to the idea of 'character', which derives, etymologically, from the Greek χαρακτή [*kharaktēr*], or an instrument for marking, from χαράσσειν [*kharassein*], to engrave.[182] And so we should not be surprised that the motif of sculpting can also be found in a thinker who meditated long and hard on the entire question of character and characterology, the German vitalist philosopher Ludwig Klages (1872–1956).

Klages, Cassirer, and Manly P. Hall

When, in his *Fundamentals of Characterology* (1926), Klages wished to discuss the metaphysical principles underpinning different kinds of personality, he turned — as so many thinkers before him had done — to the topos of the statue. In this passage we see Klages, with typical intellectual and stylistic vigour, pondering what is really going on when an artist or a great sculptor creates a statue — in this case, a statue of a god — and providing the following answer:

> When a great artist carves the image of a god with chisel and hammer out of a block of marble, it is by no means his will [*sein Wille*] which has inspired him with the outline of the divine image: it is the capacity for intuition, to which life has given its blessing [*sein lebenbegnadetes Vermögen der Schauung*], and to this capacity the will-act [*die Willenshandlung*] of carving is related exactly like the chisel, which can never do anything but destroy the stone. The example shows perfectly clearly why the destructive nature of volition does not preclude the employment of volition [*des Wollens*] in the service of affirmative movements and creative impulses after formation [*im Dienste bejahender Regungen und schöpferischer Gestaltungsantriebe*], but it also shows that the event of willing itself [*die Wollung selber*] always consists in a series of acts which are simply destructive, and that will [*der Wille*] is a completely negative power.[183]

Here we see Klages using the same topos of sculpting a statue as Zarathustra, but he does so to make an argument that runs completely contrary to Nietzsche's. For whereas Zarathustra hails the will as his key driving force — 'again and again it drives me to mankind, my ardent, creative will'[184] — it is a key tenet of Klages's philosophy that the will, regarded as a tool of *der Geist* (and concomitantly as something negative), is something fundamentally problematic.[185] Rather than it being the will that creates 'the divine image', it is the artist's capacity for intuition, for vision, for *Schauung*, that drives the creative process, or so Klages argues. Hence, it will come as no surprise to learn that, in his monograph entitled *The Psychological Achievements of Nietzsche* (1926), precisely the doctrine of the will-to-power formed a major point of disagreement for Klages.[186] One could, to use a German phrase, say that the will-to-power represented for Klages *der Stein des Anstoßes* — or the 'stumbling-block'.

Similarly, albeit with a characteristically less dramatic tone, the German philosopher Ernst Cassirer (1874–1945) offers a subtle inflexion of this topos of sculpting the self. Coming from the Marburg School of Neo-Kantianism, rather than from Freudian psychoanalysis, Cassirer developed a theory of the symbol that is as rich and as profound as Jung's, if entirely independent of him. In 'On Basis Phenomena' (c. 1940), part of his draft for a fourth volume of his monumental *Philosophy of Symbolic Forms* (3 vols, 1923–1929), Cassirer examines the problem of the relation between 'intuition' (*Intuition*, not necessarily the same as Klagesian *Schauung*), 'action' (*Aktion*), and pure 'contemplation' (*Kontemplation*), between 'theory' (*Theorie*) and 'practice' (*Praxis*), between knowledge and practical action, between conceptual analysis (or the art of *diaeresis*) and willing and doing (or the practice of virtue, *arete*).

The context for Cassirer's discussion is the figure of Socrates, the great 'artist of reason' (as he appears in the early Platonic dialogues, such as the *Laches* and the *Euthyphro*), the great 'discoverer of the concept' (as Aristotle called him),[187] but also the practician, the moralist, the teacher of practical wisdom (as Xenophon saw him). For Cassirer, Socrates's originality lies in his concept of *theama* (or 'aspect', 'look', rendered by Cassirer as *eine neue "Schau" des Wirkens*, 'a new "view" of productive action'), which underpins his conception of *theoria* (or 'theory', 'seeing'). This kind of Socratic *theoria* is, Cassirer suggests, neither theoretical nor practical, neither intuitive nor active, but rather 'genuinely contemplative' (*echt-kontemplativ*).[188] And it is in this contemplation that 'the realm of form' (*das Reich der Form*), i.e., the realm of *eidos* and *idea*, is discovered. Hence, although Socrates acknowledged (as he does, for instance, in the opening pages of the *Phaedrus*) the call of the Delphic oracle, *gnothi seauton* (i.e., 'know thyself'),[189] he construed it in a different sense from the one in which it has usually been understood (thereby confirming Goethe's view of Socrates, as expressed in his *Maxims and Reflections*).[190] For what the injunction of the Delphic oracle really amounts to is a call to action:

> This call now means: know your *work* and know "yourself" *in* your work; know what you do, so you can do what you know. Give shape to what you do; give it form by starting from mere instinct, from tradition, from convention, from routine, from *empeiria* [= experience] and *tribē* [= habituation] in order to arrive at "self-conscious" action — a work in which you recognize yourself as the sole creator and actor.[191]

Hence: 'know thyself' is not a call to embark on 'some pure (monadic) looking inward (intro-spection, intuition of the I in the pure act of the *cogito*)'; no, it means one should 'submit to the imperative of the work'.[192] In so arguing, one might contend, Cassirer in fact remains true to the totality of the original injunction inscribed above the temple of the oracle at Delphi: 'Know thyself — and thou shalt know all the mysteries of the gods and of the universe.' And it means that Cassirer is interested in 'transcendence', but in a specifically non-metaphysical sense.

For when Socrates, in the *Phaedrus*, tells us that 'every human soul has, by reason of her nature, had contemplation of true being',[193] Cassirer interprets this as meaning that above, on the one hand, 'the realm of abstract thought and conceptualization', and above, on the other, 'the realm of immediate activity and performance', there exists a 'third realm', the 'realm of pure forms' (*das "Reich der reinen Formen"*). So the *idea*, the Idea, is neither a mere concept (something abstractly logical) nor merely 'doing' (empirical, technical-practical, concrete productive activity), but, while 'rooted in both', it 'goes beyond them both', and it is from this realm of *form* that truth, goodness, and beauty derive.[194] Cassirer's argument about contemplation cuts right to the heart of the kind of activity proposed in Zarathustra's discourse on the blissful islands, which is neither a call for purely speculative engagement, nor an injunction to embark on a course of sculpture-lessons.

Finally, evidence of how a powerful sense of how statues may have functioned in the ancient world persisted into the modern age is provided by a series of lectures given in 1928 by the Canadian-born occultist, Manly Palmer Hall (1901–1990). In his *Lectures on Ancient Philosophy*, designed to amplify his earlier volume,

An Encyclopaedic Outline of Masonic, Hermetic, and Rosicrucian Symbolical Philosophy (1927), later (and better) known under the title *The Secret Teachings of All Ages*, Hall turned to a consideration (amid a consideration of so much else…!) of the ancient Mystery rituals such as those of Eleusis, Sais, and so on. Before he embarked on a speculative reconstruction of those Mystery rituals, Hall paused for a moment to consider the effect on an initiate of contemplating a statue, such as the statue of Zeus mentioned above — the one fashioned by Phidias for the temple of Zeus at Olympus. Addressing his audience directly, Hall invited his listeners to imagine themselves standing within the portals of an ancient temple:

> Upon its lofty pedestal before you looms the figure of Olympian Zeus. The face, many times life-sized, is carved from ivory, as are the arms and the sandaled foot that extends beyond the folds of his golden robes. The noble brow is encircled by a wreath of gold and the gilded sandals were pounded from the ornaments of worshippers. In one hand great Zeus holds out the globe of the earth, surmounted by the figure of Athena; in the other are his thunderbolts, symbolic of his might. Though you may disbelieve, yet will you be silent; for in the presence of great beauty the soul is stilled.[195]

And this is Hall's thesis: that the power behind the ancient mystery rituals is nothing other than the power of beauty. Warming to his theme, Hall continues his description:

> Remember, it is neither the face nor the stone — it is the something that is caught upon the stone as a sound caught by the breeze, as a ray of light reflected upon the ripples of the sea, or a smile given and returned in another's eyes. So "high heaven" in its grandeur is more than an image of stone to a tired and troubled humanity which creeps away from its sorrow to gaze upon a noble brow, or contemplate the quality of a sculptor's skill.[196]

In his lecture Hall captures with unusual precision the entire paradox of the aesthetic experience: when, from 'that which is seemingly not real', there issues 'a beautiful reality'. In a series of rhetorical questions — can we blame the ancient pagan when, 'feeling the force that emanates from a harmonious figure', he declared (as, for example, Proclus did) that 'a divinity had taken up its abode' in it? and is a stone really 'dead', if it can make strong men weep, heals the sick of their maladies, and inspires man to 'cast off his natal ignorance and aspire to the beauty which he senses in a carven face'? — Hall drives towards an inevitable conclusion about the power of the aesthetic. 'Nothing', he concludes, 'that is beautiful is dead', for 'beauty is life, and wherever beauty exists life is more abundant'.[197]

Seen within this perspective, a particular symbolic significance accrues to sculpture, as Hall explained in his exposition of exoteric and esoteric knowledge. Arguing that 'proficiency in certain arts and sciences stimulates the sensitivity of the superphysical rational faculties', Hall noted that, because of 'the definite impulse toward orderliness and exactitude', the study of mathematics was elevated in the mystical-philosophical tradition to 'chief place among the stimuli to rationality'.[198] Analogously, in this aesthetic sphere, sculpture was 'highly venerated' because it is 'a medium in which beauty could be liberated from the shapeless block of marble'. Shamelessly reprising the Neoplatonic aesthetics of the Renaissance, Hall provided an eloquent restatement of those principles:

> The sculptor was not regarded as a creator of beauty but rather as one who chipped away the rough exterior and thus brought to light the concealed symmetry of an inner nature. In short, the statue existed in the stone before the artist released it and made its symmetry apprehensible to the casual observer.[199]

The biocentric metaphysican and philosopher of vitalism — Klages; the *Kulturwissenschaftler* and philosopher of symbolic forms — Cassirer; the twentieth-century mystic and esotericist, who propounded 'the secret teachings of all ages' — Manly P. Hall: each, in his own way, discovered in the statue an example of the philosophical principles he wished to propose, nor were they the only ones to do so. For the philosopher of phenomenology and existentialism — Martin Heidegger (1889–1976) — also took an interest for philosophical reasons in statues and in sculpture.

Heidegger

In a famous encounter held at Davos in 1929, Cassirer debated with a major up-and-coming philosophical figure of his age, the phenomenologist and existentialist Martin Heidegger. In 1927, Heidegger published his major philosophical work, *Being and Time (Sein und Zeit)*, and in his later writings he concerned himself with questions about art and technology, discussing in particular the poetry of Stefan George, Friedrich Hölderlin, and Rainer Maria Rilke, and the paintings of Van Gogh, Cézanne, and Paul Klee. Yet it is frequently overlooked that, in his later thought, Heidegger developed an interest in sculpture, or it was until Andrew J. Mitchell published an account of Heidegger's relation to such sculptors as Bernhard Heiliger and Eduardo Chillida.[200] Although, for reasons of space, there is no room to engage this subject in detail, it seems appropriate, given the affinities between Heidegger and Jung that have been noted, for instance, by Alan Cardew or by Gerhard Schmitt,[201] to round off this overview of the role of the statue in philosophical discourse by briefly considering Heidegger's interest in sculpture. After all, it is sculpture that Heidegger gives as an example of what he is interested in, speaking in a lecture given in 1927 and 1928 under the title 'Phenomenology and Theology':

> The statue of Apollo in the museum at Olympia we can indeed regard as an object of natural-scientific representation; we can calculate the physical weight of the marble; we can investigate its chemical composition. But this

objectifying thinking and speaking does not catch sight of [*erblickt nicht*] the Apollo who shows forth his beauty and so appears as the visage of the god [*Anblick des Gottes*].[202]

For Heidegger, it is precisely the task of phenomenology to help us 'catch sight' of Apollo, or in the technical prose of *Being and Time*, 'to let what shows itself be seen from itself, just as it shows itself from itself', and in this sense to remain true to Husserl's phenomenological slogan, 'to the things themselves!'.[203]

As Mitchell points out, Heidegger's turn to sculpture in the second half of his career began at first tangentially in the early 1950s, then more directly in express collaboration with several sculptors themselves in the mid- to late 1960s.[204] Theoretically, these reflections on sculpture arose out of a rethinking of his notion of 'limit', understood by Heidegger as marking, not so much the end of a thing, as its beginning. In a sense, the entire question of sculpture is implicit in *Being and Time*, where Heidegger offers an existential analysis of *Dasein* or 'being-in-the-world' — i.e., 'being-*there*-in-the-world'. Indeed, in a lecture given in 1927 on *The Basic Problems of Phenomenology*, Heidegger had summarized the medieval (and, ultimately, ancient Greek) view of the world as the *ens creatum*, the creature of the creation, of God the (uncreated) creator. Examining the Greek notion of *ousia* (variously translatable as 'essence' or 'being'), Heidegger wrote that God was 'regarded as a sculptor and specifically as the protypical modeller of all things who needs nothing given to him beforehand and therefore also is not determined by receptivity'.[205] But because of his concern with what Heidegger, alluding to Plato's dialogue, the *Sophist* (244a), called 'the question of being' (and its concomitant 'forgetting' in the Western metaphysical tradition), Heidegger had not been greatly interested in the spatiality of objects (at the level, for instance, of a chair 'touching' the wall) — let alone in the ritual use of statues in theurgic practices ...

Just as, however, in 'The Origin of the Work of Art' (1935; 1936) Heidegger shifted away from this view of spatiality to a more intense focus on the inscription within space of the work of art,[206] so in a series of more overt engagements and collaborative projects with exhibition curators and sculptors he took his interest in a new direction. This interest is reflected in a series of texts, beginning with 'The Abandonment of Being and Errancy' (*Seinsverlassenheit und Irrnis*), Heidegger's contribution to a catalogue accompanying a retrospective exhibition in 1951 of the work of the German Expressionist sculptor, Ernst Barlach (1870–1938).[207] Without addressing himself explictly to the work of the anti-war Barlach, Heidegger's discussion of the 'abandonment' and the 'emptiness' of being can be read as an attempt to articulate the sense of existential insufficiency embodied in the sculptor's figures. Over a decade later, in a speech entitled 'Remarks on Art—Sculpture—Space' (*Bemerkungen zu Kunst—Plastik—Raum*), delivered in 1964 at the opening of a show of work in the Erker-Galerie, St Gallen, by Bernhard Heiliger (1915–1995), Heidegger spoke in more explicit terms about the task of the sculptor.[208] For Heidegger, sculpture exemplified well what he understood by the ancient Greek concept of *poiēsis*, meaning 'production' or 'poetry': '*Poiēsis* means: bringing-here-forth, forth into unconcealment and here from out of concealment, this however so that the concealed and the concealing are not pushed aside, but instead are precisely preserved'.[209]

In 1967, Heidegger gave a lecture in Athens entitled 'The Provenance of Art and the Determination of Thinking' (*Die Herkunft der Kunst und die Bestimmung des Denkens*), in which he contrasted the ancient Greek notion of *technē* and our modern, cybernetic understanding of technology.[210] Here Heidegger took as his starting-point two ancient representations of Athena: a metope from the Temple of Zeus in Olympia showing Athena, Hercules, and Atlas with the golden apples of the Hesperides, and a marble relief from the Acropolis depicting Athena, apparently in mourning. In the first work, Athena — the goddess with shining eyes, the goddess who 'sees' — is herself, as Heidegger remarks, unseen: the Atlas metope 'lets the goddess appear: invisible yet while standing by and at the same time distant with the high distance of the divinity'.[211] In the second, the relief from the Acropolis prompts Heidegger to reflect that 'Athena's gaze rests on that which lets the things that do not first require human production emerge by themselves into the stamping [*Gepräge*] of their presence', or what the Greeks named *physis* (or 'nature').[212] 'Only here in Hellas', Heidegger continued, 'where the entirety of the world as *physis* has promised itself to the human and taken him under its charge, can and must human perception and action correspond to this claim', and this response is *technē* ('craftsmanship' or 'art'), when 'the human being is urged by this claim to bring forth into presence, by his own capacity, that which, as work, will allow a world to appear which has not hitherto appeared'.[213] So nature and art, *physis* and *technē*, 'belong in a secret way together'.[214]

In 1962, Heidegger wrote a short essay entitled *Art and Space* (*Die Kunst und der Raum*), published by the Erker-Galerie in a limited edition booklet that included seven lithocollages by the Spanish Basque sculptor Eduardo Chillida (1924–2002).[215] Heidegger's essay opened with two quotations taken from Lichtenberg and Aristotle, and concluded with an aphorism by Goethe: 'It is not always necessary that what is true embody itself; it is already enough if spiritually it hovers about and evokes harmony, if it floats through the air like the solemn and friendly sound of a bell'.[216] This is a remarkable claim, for the supposedly anti-idealist Goethe, and it enables Heidegger to conclude that while sculpture is 'the embodiment of the truth of Being in its work of instituting places', 'even a cautious insight into the special character of this art causes one to suspect that truth, as unconcealment of Being, is not necessarily dependent on embodiment'.[217] As Mitchell observes in his commentary, this quotation from Goethe thus captures for Heidegger an important insight — that truth is 'not necessarily a matter of embodiment', but while 'not always a body', it is 'always in a medium':

> Consequently, to think space apart from bodies is not to give up on embodiment but to think the body as no longer distinct or separable from space, to think the body as dissolved in space yet defined by it, as mediated, an inhabitant of the between, neither present nor absent but always arriving sensibly

and shining out beyond itself through space. To think space is to think the middle, the between. Space is the truth, the space through which [...] what is true resounds, not as raw noise but like a bell, that is, as something rippling through a medium. The truth of sculpture is the truth of being: mediation.[218]

Or, as Goethe put it in another maxim, 'the true mediatrix is art'.[219]

From Heidegger's other writings, we can place this interest in sculpture in the context of his other writings about art and, in particular, architecture. In 'The Origin of the Work of Art', Heidegger laments how the Aegina sculptures in the Glyptothek in Munich are 'torn from their own native sphere', and even when we actually go and visit the temple complex at Paestum or the cathedral in Bamberg, we discover that 'the world of the work that stands there has perished'.[220] (Is Heidegger right about this? Other thinkers would disagree with Heidegger in this respect; for example, Bertrand Vergely when he describes the effect on the viewer of the Parthenon on the Acropolis in Athens: 'In Athens, when one looks at the Parthenon, one is gripped, its stones and marble columns making sense': 'because its stone and columns make sense, things begin to exist', and 'because wisdom becomes palpable, words and ideas begin equally to exist', and in fact 'everything begins to exist' — 'what is visible with its stones, what is invisible with its meanings', so that 'the world reveals itself as presence, not simply as an object' and 'one becomes oneself a presence, not simply a subject'.[221])

Yet even if 'the works are no longer the works they were' (and they have become merely objects of conservation), Heidegger's analysis of the relationship between the temple and the statue of the god within it suggests that we can at least begin to appreciate what has been lost. And 'Building Dwelling Thinking' (1951) demonstrates how the concepts of concealment, presencing, and space can be applied to architecture[222] and to sculpture[223] alike. Could one say that the image Zarathustra sees 'sleeping in the stone', the 'image of [his] visions', his vision of the Superman — *dwells* in the stone? Or is the superman precisely the image of someone who does not merely inhabit the world, but brings *forth* the world, by the very act of living in it?

Jung on Stone Symbolism and the Statue

What does Jung have to say about the symbolism of the stone? And what does he have to say about the sculpted stone, that is to say, the statue? Given his fascination with the alchemical tradition, Jung's discussions are as numerous as they are extensive; nevertheless, with a focus on the passage from the end of 'On the Blissful Islands', some passages stand out as particularly relevant to our concerns.

In 'The Visions of Zosimos' (1938/1954), Jung offered a commentary on the writings of an Egyptian (or Greek) alchemist and Gnostic mystic active in the third century CE, known as Zosimos of Panopolis; the work consists of a sequence of texts drawn from his alchemical treatises. A section of Jung's paper, originally given as a lecture to the Eranos conference of 1937, is dedicated to the symbolism of the stone. As we shall see, in the course of his discussion Jung alludes to a passage from Nietzsche's *Zarathustra*, licensing our application of his general remarks about the alchemical stone to the conclusion of Zarathustra's discourse 'On the Blissful Islands'. Not that the stone on which Zarathustra brings his hammer to bear is, as it were, *the* Philosopher's Stone; but the process of transformation common to both, to *Zarathustra* and to the alchemical tradition, may nevertheless point to an important (and meaningful) intersection of ideas.

Drawing attention to the distinction made in the third century by Zosimos — as it would later be made by Meister Eckhart in the thirteenth and fourteenth centuries — between the bodily man and the spiritual man (*CW* 13 §126), Jung noted that the attributes of the *lapis* or stone, which signifies the *inner man* — i.e., its incorruptibility, permanence, divinity, triunity, etc. — are 'so insistently emphasized that one cannot help taking it as the *deus absconditus*' — that is, the hidden God — 'in matter' (*CW* 13 §127). (The concept of the 'inner man' is a favourite one in the thoughts of St Augustine.[224] Its source can be traced back to Plato, who speaks of 'the human being within us',[225] while this sense of the self was developed by Plotinus.[226]) This emphasis on the qualities of the *lapis*, Jung argued, provided the basis of the parallel between the alchemical stone and the figure of Christ, so that 'the lapis may therefore be understood as a symbol of the inner Christ, of God in man' (*CW* 13 §127). But why should the God within be represented by, of all things, *a stone*?

This is the perfect question for Jung to ask — and for him to answer! His meditation on the stone as 'the birthplace of the gods' takes him back beyond Greek alchemy to the cult of Mithras (who was born from a stone), and to the Australian aborigines and their *churingas* (*CW* 13 §128). In Australia, the indigenous people of the Arrente were known for the practice that involved making a *tjurunga* (or *churinga*), an item of religious significance consisting of a piece of polished stone or wood. These sacred objects were of huge interest to such anthropologists and sociologists as Emile Durkheim (1858–1917), who suggested the term *churinga* meant 'most sacred', or T.G.H. Strehlow (1908–1978), who understood the term to mean something 'secret' or 'personal'.[227] Inspired by such anthropological sources, Ludwig Klages argued that *tjurungas* allowed modern researchers to investigate 'the experiential layer where idols come into being'.[228]

In Jung's day, however, one did not have to travel to the other side of the world to find such objects. In 1910, Fritz Sartorius-Preiswerk (1862–1935) had discovered in Arlesheim, a small town in the Swiss canton of Basel, not far away from where Jung lived, a neolithic burial site in a cave at the local hermitage. (As it happens, Arlesheim lies close to Dornach and, according to Rudolf Steiner, the town was the actual site where, in the ninth century, Parzival had met his cousin Sigune and his uncle Trevrizent, both living as hermits in the Grail palace, Munsalvaesche!) In this and surrounding caves, ancient cult artefacts, thought to date back to Celtic times, have been recovered: bowls, tools, and flintstones painted with ochre — the so-called 'soul-stones', believed to have been death masks).

Today these painted stones (or *galets coloriés*) are in the Museum der Kulturen in Basel, and their discovery was of great interest to Jung, who in his autobiographical

(a)

(b)

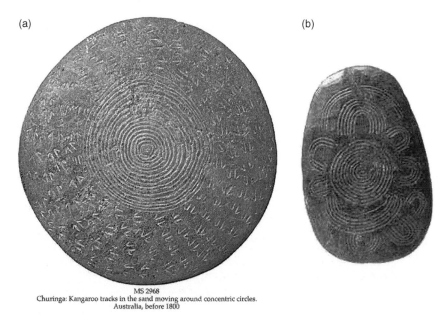

MS 2968
Churinga: Kangaroo tracks in the sand moving around concentric circles.
Australia, before 1800

FIGURE 2.2   *Tjurungas*. Collection of Georgia Sales, photo by Joe James.

(a)

(b)

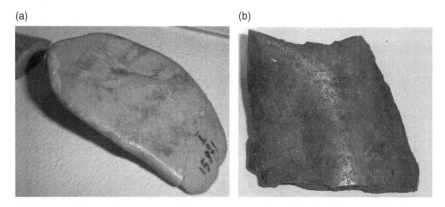

FIGURE 2.3   Painted stones (or *galets coloriés*) from Arlesheim.

work, *Memories, Dreams, Reflections* (1961), referred to them and to the Australian *churingas* as analogues of his own sculpting and carving activities as a child (*MDR*, 38).[229] (Other, more classical analogues of sculpting mentioned by Jung are the monuments carved by the Greeks to Asclepius, the god of medicine and healing, on which a tiny cloaked god, or Telesphorus, graces the work and stands reading from a scroll;[230] while in the cult of Demeter, the goddess of the harvest, the Kabeiroi, the mysterious name of an equally mysterious set of miniature deities, played a similarly protective role.[231])

In his paper entitled 'The Visions of Zosimos', Jung surveyed the idea of the magic stone in India, in Burma, and in Europe itself (*CW* 13 §129); and among the Navaho Indians of Arizona (*CW* 13 §130). Shrewdly, Jung pointed to an important feminine aspect to the stone or, to put it another way, to its anima aspect. According to Greek tradition and legend, the madness of Orestes was cured by a stone in Laconia; Zeus found respite from his amorous woes by sitting on a stone in Leukadia; Omphale held Hercules in thrall; and Circe reduced her captives to a state of bestial consciousness; while in a more recent work by the French novelist Pierre Benoît (1886–1962), his novel *L'Atlantide* (1919), Atlantida made a collection of her mummified lovers (*CW* 13 §129 and §131). Hence, in Jung's view, 'the anima contains the secret of the precious stone', and here he cited Nietzsche's *Zarathustra*: for 'all joy wants eternity' (*CW* 13 §131).[232] How can we make sense of this allusion?

To do so, we need to look more closely at Nietzsche's text, where Zarathustra's ecstatic cry occurs. In his Roundelay, Zarathustra envisages an acceptance — no: more, an affirmation — of all that is, as an expression of a Dionysian faith, of the kind Nietzsche attributed to Goethe, that 'in the totality everything is redeemed and affirmed'.[233] It is an affirmation of the insight found in the words of the ancient Iranian alchemical figure of Ostanes, speaking to Cleopatra in the *Dialogue of Cleopatra and the Philosophers* from the *Book of Komarios*: 'In thee is concealed a strange and terrible mystery. […] Tell us how the highest descends to the lowest and how the lowest rises to the highest, and how that which is in the midst approaches the highest and is united to it';[234] or an affirmation of the conception of beauty found in Schiller's *On the Aesthetic Education* (1795), according to which beauty 'restores harmony to him who is over-tensed, and energy to him who is relaxed, and thus, in accordance with its nature, brings the limited condition back to an absolute condition, and makes of the individual a whole perfect in itself [*zu einem in sich selbst vollendeten Ganzen*]';[235] an affirmation of the drive felt by the sentimental poet on Schiller's account 'to restore from within oneself every unity which has been dissolved in one by abstraction, to make humanity in itself complete again and to pass from a limited state to an infinite one', 'to make of oneself a whole, to bring humanity in oneself to a complete expression' (*ein Ganzes aus sich zu machen, die Menschheit in sich zu einem vollendeten Ausdruck zu bringen*).[236] What is 'midmost' is, Jung says, the stone, understood as 'the mediator which unites the opposites' (*CW* 13 §131): or, in the image of the *Übermensch* as whom Nietzsche conceived Goethe as being, someone who 'aspires to *totality* […]' and who 'disciplines himself to a whole', who '*creates* himself'.[237]

It is this 'joyous and trusting fatalism', 'the *faith* that only what is separate and individual may be rejected',[238] that confirms upon the stone — hence, the superman or *Übermensch* — its quality of immortality, an idea that Jung develops with reference to the practice in the civilization of the Nile valley from megalithic times of 'turn[ing] its divine kings into stone statues for the express purpose of making the king's *ka* everlasting' (*CW* 13 §132). This practice, like the importance (attested to by Mircea Eliade) attached in shamanism to crystals, informs Jung's reading of a text found in the work of another ancient authority, the Persian alchemist Ostanes, as cited in the third century by Zosimos, which begins: 'Go to the waters of the Nile and there you will find a stone that has a spirit [*pneuma*]. Take this, divide it, thrust in your hand and draw out its heart: for its soul [*psyche*] is in its heart [...]'.[239] The quality of having a spirit — like all the other qualities associated with the lapis (it is the panacea, the universal medicine, the alexipharmic, the tincture transforming base metal into gold; it brings riches, power, health) — is a sign of its power as a symbol of the saviour, of the Anthropos (in Gnosticism, the primeval Man), of immortality. Or, one might say, as a symbol of the *Übermensch*.

Jung points to two further examples of the stone as an image of sanctity: first, the tradition that the body of a saint turns to stone. This idea goes back a long way: in the third or even second-century Coptic apocryphal text, *The Apocalypse of Elijah*, for instance, the prophet foretells the fate of the saints: 'The Lord will receive to himself their spirits and their souls. Their flesh will be as permanent as rock: no wild beast shall eat them up until the last day of the great judgement'.[240] True, this is an image of petrification, rather than the release of a figure from the stone, but Jung's second choice of example is a more apt fit with Zarathustra's discourse. In a legend from an area of South Africa now known as Lesotho, recorded by the German ethnologist Leo Frobenius (1873–1938) in *The Age of the Sun God* (1904), a hero figure called Litaolane is pursued by his people. So what does the hero do? On the bank of a river, he turns himself into a stone, which his pursuers throw across to the other side.[241] Here we find, Jung remarks, the motif of the *transitus*, in which 'the other side' represents eternity. Or in Zarathustra's words, we should arm ourselves with 'arrows of longing' — longing for 'the other bank'.[242]

So much for the stone; is there an archetypal dimension to a specific configuration of stone in the image of a statue? In *Mysterium coniunctionis* (1955–1956), Jung recalls that 'the statue plays a mysterious role in ancient alchemy', citing again from the early Greek alchemical treatise, the *Book of Komarios*, a passage that is full of imagery relating to statues and to shadows. Here Komarios, reputedly the teacher of Cleopatra, reveals to the Ptolemaic queen of Egypt nothing less than 'the mystery of the philosophers' and the process of alchemical rebirth:

> After the body has been hidden in darkness, [the spirit] finds it full of light. And the soul has united with the body, since the body has become divine through its relation to the soul, and it dwells in the soul. For the body has clothed itself in the light of divinity (and they have become one), and the shadow has departed from it, and all have been united in love: the body, the soul, and the spirit. They have all become one: in this unity the mystery has been hidden. By the fact of their coming together the mystery has been fulfilled. The house has been sealed, and a statue has been erected full of light and divinity.[243]

Here the shadow departs, whereas in Zarathustra the shadow arrives; here the statue is erected, whereas in Zarathustra the statue is brought out of the stone. Yet in both cases the statue represents, as Jung observes, 'the end-product of the process, the lapis philosophorum or its equivalent' (*CW* 14 §559).

So the statue lies within the stone, but could it also be that something lies within the statue? According to 'an old tradition', says Jung, 'a precious substance [is] hidden in the "statue"' (*CW* 14 §564), especially if they are statues of Hermes or Mercurius, i.e., gods closely associated with the alchemical tradition. For instance, Pseudo-Dionysius the Areopagite is mentioned in Vigenerus's *Treatise on Fire and Salt* as describing the sun as 'the clear and manifest statue of God', a text whose translation history is pursued by Jung in considerable depth.[244] Equally, Pseudo-Dionysius is cited in a paraphrase of *The Celestrial Hierarchy* by the late thirteenth-century Byzantine Greek historian and philosopher, Georgius Pachymeres, as saying that '[the pagans] made in [their statues] both doors and hollows, in which they placed images of the gods they worshipped', and so 'statues of Mercury after this kind appeared of little worth, but contained within them ornaments of gods'.[245]

Earlier, Plato had appeared to refer to this practice when, in the *Symposium*, Alcibiades says that Socrates reminds him of 'those little sileni that you see on the statuaries' stalls; you know the ones I mean — they're modelled with pipes or flutes in their hands, and when you open them down the middle there are little figures of the gods inside'.[246] (It is to these little statues that Plotinus alludes when he talks about 'images' in 'the soul of the wise man', in his *Ennead* on intellectual beauty.[247]) On this passage, Jung remarks that 'it must have appealed very much to the imagination of the alchemists that there were statues of Mercurius with the real god hidden inside' (*CW* 14 §565), but we should note that, for Jung, the alchemical tradition uses Mercurius in a very precise sense, namely to refer to 'that being who changed himself, during the work, from the prima materia into the perfected lapis philosophorum' (*CW* 14 §565). It is this *transformational element* that underpins the conceptual link between the alchemical tradition and Nietzsche's philosophy, and in turn the project of analytical psychology.

By speaking of the *statua Dei*, rather than the *imago Dei*, Vigenerus implied a connection between the Kabbalistic interpretation of the stone of Bethel, the stone set up by Jacob after his dream of the ladder and declared by him to be 'the house of God' (Genesis 28: 22), and the statue that stands for the inert materiality of Adam, awaiting an 'animating soul' — in Jung's words, 'a symbol for one of the main preoccupations of alchemy' (*CW* 14 §569) — and, by that token, one of the main preoccupations of Jungian psychoanalysis as well.

Alchemy's reply to this problem was 'a stone that has a spirit', in the words of Ostanes;[248] and the core of this notion is explored (as well as in *Collected Works*, vol. 13, *Alchemical Studies*, and vol. 14, *Mysterium coniunctionis*) in a detailed footnote in Jung's Terry Lectures on 'Psychology and Religion' (1938/1940). Here Jung discussed the meaning of this mysterious stone with reference to the Platonic context as explored by Johann Christoph Steeb in his *Coelum sephiroticum, Hebraeorum*. The relevant text here is Plato's *Timaeus*, a dialogue that offers nothing less than an account of the formation of the entire universe. It takes as its starting-point the distinction between the physical world (or the world of becoming) and the eternal world (or the world of being), an ontological dualism for which Nietzsche was subsequently to take Plato famously to task.

At the core of this distinction, however, is the principle that the world can be apprehended by reason, and all the important elements in Timaeus's account — the creation of the world soul by the demiurge, so that the world is 'a blessed god' (34b), the geometrical shape (tetrahedron, octahedron, icosahedron, and cube) of the minute particles in each element (fire, air, water, and earth) (53c), and the golden ratio (31c–32a) — are to be understood in the light of this principle of fundamental intelligibility.[249] Now for Steeb (and, by extension, for the alchemical tradition as a whole), the 'stone' — also called *hyle*, chaos, or *massa confusa* — is the *prima materia* in exactly the sense it is defined by Timaeus, when he says that:

> the mother and receptacle of all created and visible and in any way sensible things is not to be termed earth or air or fire or water, or any of their compounds, or any of the elements from which these are derived, but is an invisible and formless being which receives all things and in some mysterious way partakes of the intelligible, and is most incomprehensible (51b).[250]

In Steeb's terms, the *prima materia* is 'the primeval chaotic earth, hyle, chaos, the abyss, the mother of things',[251] and from this 'first chaotic matter' emerges the world, when it is infused with 'the spirit of God':

> The fostering warmth of the Holy Spirit brought about, therefore, in the waters that are above the heavens, a virtue subtly penetrating and nourishing all things, which, combining with light, generated in the mineral kingdom of the lower regions the mercurial serpent [*serpentum Mercurij*], in the vegetable kingdom the blessed greenness, in the animal kingdom a formative virtue, so that the supracelestial spirit of the waters united in marriage with light may justly be called the soul of the world [*anima mundi*].[252]

As Jung explained in his lectures, the alchemical-cum-Gnostic world-view believed that 'the *anima mundi*, the demiurge or divine spirit that incubated the chaotic waters of the beginning, remained in matter in a potential state'; hence, the *prima materia* was essentially 'a part of the original chaos pregnant with spirit' (*CW* 11 §160). This 'spirit' was identified with Mercurius or with Hermes (who, as Hermes Trismegistus, was the 'arch-authority' on alchemy). Now, none of this would appear to have any kind of a connection with Nietzsche, who has nothing explicit to say about either Mercurius or Hermes. Nevertheless, we should recall that, in *Thus Spoke Zarathustra*, the notion of spirit or *Geist* plays an important role: not the *Geist* of which, in 'Of the Despisers of the Body', Zarathustra says: 'Your little intelligence, my brother, which you call "spirit", is also an instrument of the body, a little instrument and toy of your great intelligence',[253] but the *Geist* of which, in 'Of the Famous Philosophers', Zarathustra declares: 'Spirit is the life that itself strikes into life: through its own torment it increases its own knowledge — did you know that before?' (*Geist ist das Leben, das selber ins Leben schneidet; an der eignen Qual mehrt sich das eigne Wissen — wußtet ihr das schon?*).[254] (This statement is so important that it is repeated later in Part Four by one of the higher men, the conscentious man of the spirit, who relates how this saying had 'led and seduced' him to Zarathustra's teaching.[255])

In turn, it is *this* life that is personified and given a voice in 'Of Self-Overcoming', betraying in a whisper to Zarathustra the following secret: 'Behold, […] I am that *which must overcome itself again and again*' (*ich bin das, was sich immer selber überwindet*).[256] The notion of 'self-overcoming' harks back to Zarathustra's rhetoric in the 'Prologue' about 'going-across' (*Übergang*) and 'down-going' (*Untergang*), and it is linked with another major concept, the will-to-power (*der Wille zur Macht*) — explicitly so, when Life herself proclaims: 'Truly, where there is perishing and the falling of leaves, behold, there life sacrifices itself — for the sake of power!'.[257] And it is the individual who embraces this knowledge about 'self-overcoming' (*Selbst-Überwindung*) who is the individual who 'overcomes' himself and hence becomes an 'overman' (*Übermensch*).

Thus we can begin to discern, as surprising as it might seem, the outline or the contours of a common link between the Platonic tradition, alchemy, and Nietzsche — a link that lies in the close attention all of them paid to the ideas of transformation and self-transformation. Whether they called it embarking on the path of ascent (Plato), or transforming the *prima materia* into the Philosopher's Stone (alchemy), or embracing the will-to-power, overcoming one's self, and becoming the superman (Nietzsche), the transformative urge informs all of them at every single level of their thought.

Taken together, these ideas constitute a persistent appeal to their reader to embark on the path of self-transformation as well. To undertake this journey implies a dissatisfaction with the *status quo*, or the current state of affairs; that much is plain. But does wanting something else — or wanting something *better* — imply one believes there can be actually be something better? Or that there is something one could call the best? Does it imply one believes in something that might be called — the *ideal* …?

Notes

1   Compare with Zarathustra's opening statement in 'Of the Virtuous': 'One has to speak with thunder and heavenly fireworks to feeble and dormant senses. / But the voice of beauty speaks softly: it steals into only the most awakened souls' (in F. Nietzsche, *Thus Spoke Zarathustra*, tr. R.J. Hollingdale, Harmondsworth: Penguin, 1969, p. 117); and with the voiceless words heard by Zarathustra in 'The Stillest Hour': 'It is the stillest words which bring the storm. Thoughts that come on doves' feet guide the world' (*Thus Spoke Zarathustra*, p. 168).

2   For further discussion, see Babette Babich, 'Nietzsche and the Sculptural Sublime: On Becoming the One You Are'. Available online at: www.nietzschecircle.com/AGONIST/ Agonist-Spring2012/Sculptural_Sublime.pdf (accessed 28 February 2013).

3   *Twilight of the Idols*, 'Foreword'; in Nietzsche, *Twilight of the Idols; The Anti-Christ*, tr. R.J. Hollingdale, Harmondsworth: Penguin, 1968, p. 22.

4 *Twilight*, 'The Hammer Speaks', in *Twilight of the Idols; The Anti-Christ*, p. 231; cf. 'Of Old and New Law-Tables', §29, in *Thus Spoke Zarathustra*, p. 231.

5 Nietzsche, *KSA* 11, 26[298], 229; *KSA* 12, 5[70], 210; and *KSA* 12, 7[45], 309.

6 Nietzsche, *KSA*, 13, 22[6], 586.

7 W. Kaufmann, *Discovering the Mind*, vol. 2, *Nietzsche, Heidegger, and Buber*, New Brunswick and London: Transaction, 1992, p. 153.

8 In *Der Geist als Widersacher der Seele* (1929–1932), Ludwig Klages pointed out how 'a subterranean layer of previous idolatry can be made out, even in the case of the Jews, in their numerous customs and through the most pious of their accepted legends', citing the blood sacrifice; the figure of Asherah, the sacred tree of the local altars; the water of the sacred source, by which one swore; Mount Sinai or Mount Horeb as the mountain of God; the 'burning bush', surely the site of a desert daimon; and the frequent references to the storms and thunder-and-lightning that accompanied the anger of Yahweh (*Der Geist als Widersacher der Seele*, chapter 72, in L. Klages, *Sämtliche Werke*, ed. E. Frauchiger et al., 9 vols, Bonn: Bouvier, 1964–1999, vol. 2, p. 1268). Klages's argument is borne out by a curious incident surrounding the capture of the Ark of the Covenant by the Philistines, when Yahweh smites the Philistines with a painful affliction, causing the men to suffer from tumours on their genitals. After seven months, the Philistines want to send back the Ark, and are told by the Jewish priests to make a guilt offering through fashioning five golden models of their tumours — and five golden models of the rats that may, as carriers of bubonic plague, have been the source of the infection (1 Kings 5: 9 to 6: 5).

9 See Goethe, 'Groß ist die Diana der Epheser' (1812), in *Gedichte*, ed. E. Trunz, Munich: Beck, 1974, pp. 285–286.

10 See S. Freud, 'Great is Diana of the Ephesians' (1911), in *The Standard Edition of the Complete Works of Sigmund Freud*, ed. J. Strachey and A. Freud, 24 vols, London: Hogarth Press, 1953–1974, vol. 12, pp. 342–344.

11 Apuleius, *"Golden Ass" or "The Metamorphosis"*, *and other Philosophical Writings*, tr. T. Taylor [Thomas Taylor Series = TTS, vol. 14], Frome: Prometheus Trust, 1997, p. 233.

12 For further discussion, see C. Ando, *The Matter of the Gods: Religion and the Roman Empire*, Berkeley and Los Angeles: University of California Press, 2008, pp. 27–34.

13 Xenophanes, DK B14 and B15, in J. Barnes, *Early Greek Philosophy*, Harmondsworth: Penguin, 1987, p. 95.

14 Heraclitus, DK B5, in Barnes, *Early Greek Philosophy*, p. 118.

15 Heraclitus, DK B15, in Barnes, *Early Greek Philosophy*, p. 118.

16 *Cratylus*, 432 b–d; in Plato, *Collected Dialogues*, ed. E. Hamilton and H. Cairns, Princeton, NJ: Princeton University Press, 1989, p. 466.

17 *Cratylus* 439a–b; in *CD*, p. 473.

18 *Sophist*, 235d–236c; in *CD*, pp. 978–979.

19 See C. Lamb and L. Curtius, *Die Tempel von Paestum*, Leipzig: Insel, 1944, p. 17. See G. Böhme, 'The Art of the Stage set as a Paradigm for an Aesthetics of Atmospheres', *Ambiances: International Journal of Sensory Environment, Architecture and Urban Space*, 2013. Available online at: http://ambiances.revues.org/315 (accessed 24 July 2013).

20 *Sophist*, 235d–236c; in *CD*, pp. 978–979.

21 *Sophist*, 264c–d; in *CD*, p. 1012.

22 *Sophist*, 264d; in *CD*, p. 1012.

23 *Timaeus*, 27d; in *CD*, p. 1161.

24 *Timaeus*, 27d–28a; in *CD*, p. 1161.

25 *Timaeus*, 29a; in *CD*, p. 1162.

26 *Phaedrus*, 235d–e; in *CD*, p. 483.

27 *Symposium*, 215b; in *CD*, p. 566.

28 *Symposium*, 216e–217a; in *CD*, p. 568.

29 Plotinus, *Enneads*, V.8.5, in Plotinus, *The Enneads*, tr. S. MacKenna, abridged J. Dillon, Harmondsworth: Penguin, 1991, p. 416. As another translator of Plotinus has commented on this passage, 'the Forms in the Intellect are concrete living realities, not mental

abstractions like propositions' (A.H. Armstrong, in Plotinus, *Ennead V*, tr. A.H. Armstrong, Cambridge, MA, and London: Harvard University Press, 1984, p. 255).

30 *Republic*, 361d; in *The Dialogues of Plato*, tr. B. Jowett, 5 vols, vol. 3, Oxford; London: Oxford University Press; Humphrey Milford, 1931, p. 41.

31 *Republic*, 540c; in *Dialogues of Plato*, tr. Jowett, vol. 3, p. 245.

32 Diogenes Laërtius, *Lives and Opinions*, book 2, §18; in *Lives and Opinions of Eminent Philosophers*, tr. C.D. Yonge, London: Bell, 1895, p. 63.

33 Pausanias, *Description of Greece*, book 1, chapter 22, §8; and book 9, chapter 35, §7; see J.J. Pollitt, *The Art of Ancient Greece: Sources and Documents*, Cambridge: Cambridge University Press, 1990, pp. 74–75.

34 *Euthyphro*, 11d and 15b; in *CD*, pp. 180 and 184.

35 *Meno*, 97d–98a; in *CD*, pp. 381–382.

36 B. Babich, 'Greek Bronze: On Sculptures, Mirrors, and Life', *Yearbook of the Irish Philosophical Society*, 2006, 1–30 (p. 2).

37 Diogenes Laërtius, *Lives and Opinions*, book 2, §33; in *Lives and Opinions of Eminent Philosophers*, p. 69.

38 *Sophist*, 235e–236a. As we saw above, what is at stake here is the Eleatic Stranger's distinction between 'the making of likenesses' and 'the making of semblances' [*phantastiki*]: 'One art that I see contained in [the art of imitation]', says the Stranger, 'is the making of likenesses [*eikastiki*]. The perfect example of this consists in creating a copy that confirms to the proportions of the original in all three dimensions and giving moreover the proper colour to every part'. In response to Theaetetus's protestation that all imitators try to do this, the Stranger responds: 'Not those sculptors or painters whose works are of colossal size. If they were to reproduce the true proportions of a well-made figure, as you know, the upper parts would look too small, and the lower too large, because we see one at a distance, the other close at hand' (in *CD*, p. 978).

39 For further discussion, see N. Spivey, *Understanding Greek Sculpture: Ancient Meanings, Modern Readings*, London: Thames and Hudson, 1996; and D.T. Steiner, *Images in Mind: Statues in Archaic and Classical Greek Literature and Thought*, Princeton, NJ: Princeton University Press, 2001.

40 Pliny the Elder, *Natural History*, book 34, chapters 9, 10, and 12; in Pliny, *Natural History*, vol. 9, *Books 33–35*, tr. H. Rackham, Cambridge, MA; London: Harvard University Press; Heinemann, 1961, pp. 139, 141 and 147.

41 Pliny the Elder, *Natural History*, book 34, chapter 16; in Pliny, *Natural History*, vol. 9, *Books 33–35*, p. 155.

42 Pliny, *Natural History*, book 34, chapter 18; in Pliny, *Natural History*, vol. 9, *Books 33–35*, pp. 157–159.

43 Babich, 'Greek Bronze', p. 7.

44 Ovid, *Festivals*, book 4, ll. 291–348, in *Fasti*, tr. J.G. Frazer, London; New York: Heinemann; Putnam, 1931, pp. 211–215; and Livy, book 29, chapter 10, in *Books XXVIII-XXX*, tr. F.G. Moore, London; New York: Heinemann; Harvard University Press, 1949, p. 245.

45 Julian, 'Oration to the Mother of the Gods', in T. Taylor (ed.), *Collected Writings on the Gods and the World*, tr. T. Taylor [TTS, vol. 4], Sturminster Newton: Prometheus Trust, 1994, p. 78.

46 Taylor, 'Endnote', in *Collected Writings on the Gods and the World*, p. 97.

47 *The Dissertations of Maximus Tyrius*, tr. T. Taylor [TTS, vol. 6], Sturminster Newton: Prometheus Trust, 1994, p. 310.

48 *The Dissertations of Maximus Tyrius*, pp. 313–314.

49 *The Dissertations of Maximus Tyrius*, p. 314.

50 'Extracts from the Fragment of an Oration or Epistle: On the Duties of a Priest', in T. Taylor (ed.), *"Against the Christians" and other Writings*, tr. T. Taylor [TTS, vol. 33], Sturminster Newton: Prometheus Trust, 2006, p. 37.

51 'On the Duties of a Priest', in *"Against the Christians" and other Writings*, p. 37.

52 'On the Duties of a Priest', in *"Against the Christians" and other Writings*, p. 38.

53 Sallust, *On the Gods and the World*, chapter 15; in *Collected Writings on the Gods and the World*, trans. Taylor, p. 19.

54 Sallust, *On the Gods and the World*, chapter 15; in *Collected Writings on the Gods and the World*, trans. Taylor, p. 19. On this statement, Taylor comments: 'Statues therefore, through their habitude or fitness, conjoin the souls of those who pray to them with the gods themselves: and when we view the ancient mode of worshipping images in this light, we shall find it equally as rational as any other mode of conduct in which a certain end is proposed to be obtained by legitimate means' ('Endnote', p. 98).

55 Photius, *Bibliotheca*, codex 215: John Philoponus, *Against the Treatise on the Statues of Iamblichus*; cited in Apuleius, *"Golden Ass" or "The Metamorphosis" and other Philosophical Writings*, p. 232; cf. Taylor, 'Endnote', in *Collected Writings on the Gods and the World*, p. 98.

56 For further discussion, see G. Shaw, *Theurgy and the Soul: The Neoplatonism of Iamblichus*, University Park, PA: Pennsylvania State University Press, 2010.

57 Iamblichus, *On the Mysteries of the Egyptians, Chaldeans and Assyrians*, book 1, chapter 9, in *"On the Mysteries of the Egyptians, Chaldeans, and Assyrians" and "Life of Pythagoras"*, tr. T. Taylor [TTS, vol. 17], Sturminster Newton: Prometheus Trust, 1999, p. 33.

58 Iamblichus, *On the Mysteries*, book 1, chapter 19; in *"On the Mysteries of the Egyptians, Chaldeans, and Assyrians" and "Life of Pythagoras"*, p. 45.

59 Iamblichus, *On the Mysteries*, book 2, chapter 4; in *"On the Mysteries of the Egyptians, Chaldeans, and Assyrians" and "Life of Pythagoras"*, Taylor, p. 54.

60 For the text, see Porphyry, *On Images*, tr. E.H. Gifford. Available online at: http://classics.mit.edu/Porphyry/images.html (accessed 29 July 2013). For further discussion, see A.P. Johnson, *Religion and Identity in Porphyry of Tyre: The Limits of Hellenism in Late Antiquity*, Cambridge: Cambridge University Press, 2013, esp. pp. 30–31; and A. Smith, *Porphyry's Place in the Neoplatonic Tradition: A Study in Post-Plotinian Neoplatonism*, The Hague: Nijoff, 1974.

61 Porphyry, *On Images*, fragment 1, tr. Gifford.

62 Porphyry, *On Images*, fragment 2, tr. Gifford.

63 Proclus, *Commentary on the First Book of Euclid's "Elements"*, 136–137 ('Definitions', XIV), in *A Commentary on the First Book of Euclid's Elements*, tr. G.R. Morrow, Princeton, NJ: Princeton University Press, 1970, p. 110.

64 See Proclus's definition of *theurgy* as a power 'more excellent than all human wisdom' and as comprehending 'prophetic good, the purifying powers of perfective good, and […] all such things as are the effects of divine possession' (*Platonic Theology*, book 1, chapter 25, 113), in Proclus, *The Theology of Plato*, tr. T. Taylor [TTS, vol. 8], Westbury: Prometheus Trust, 1995, p. 118.

65 Proclus, *Commentary on the First Book of Euclid's "Elements"*, 138 ('Definitions', XIV), in Proclus, *A Commentary on the First Book of Euclid's Elements*, p. 111.

66 Apuleius, *Metamorphoses* (or *The Golden Ass*), 11.17, in *"Golden Ass" or "The Metamorphosis" and other Philosophical Writings*, p. 211.

67 See Apuleius, *"Golden Ass" or "The Metamorphosis" and other Philosophical Writings*, trans. Taylor, p. 230. Cf. the explanation given elsewhere: 'The telestae were initiators into the mysteries, and were theurgists, or capable of performing divine operations', and 'this *theurgy*, in which these initiators were deeply skilled, formed the last part of the sacerdotal science' (see Proclus, *Commentary on the "Timæus" of Plato: Volume II*, tr. T. Taylor [TTS, vol. 16], Sturminster Newton: Prometheus Trust, 1998, p. 729). For further discussion, see A. Sheppard, 'Proclus' Attitude to Theurgy', *The Classical Quarterly*, 1982, [NS] vol. 32, no. 1, 212–224.

68 R. Majercik (ed.), *The Chaldean Oracles*, Westbury: Prometheus Trust, 2013, 'Introduction', p. 26. For further discussion, see N. Janowitz, *Icons of Power: Ritual Practices in Late Antiquity*, Pennsylvania, PA: Pennsylvania State University Press, 2002, pp. 1–18; the chapter 'Animation of Statues in Ancient Civilizations and Neoplatonism', in A. Uždavinys, *Philosophy as a Rite of Rebirth: From Ancient Egypt to Neoplatonism*, Westbury: Prometheus Trust, 2008, pp. 219–236; S.I. Johnston, 'Animating Statues: A Case Study in Ritual', *Arethusa*, 2008, vol. 41, 445–477; and, most recently,

I. Tanaseanu-Döbler, *Theurgy in Late Antiquity: The Invention of a Ritual Tradition*, Göttingen: Vandenhoeck & Ruprecht, 2013.

69 Proclus, *Commentary on the "Timaeus" of Plato*, book 2, 1,265, in *Proclus' Commentary on the "Timæus" of Plato: Volume I* [TTS, vol. 15], Sturminster Newton: Prometheus Trust, 1998, p. 246.

70 Proclus, *Commentary on the "Timaeus" of Plato*, book 2, 1,273, in *Proclus' Commentary on the "Timæus" of Plato: Volume I*, p. 253.

71 Proclus, *Commentary on the "Timaeus"*, book 4, 3, 6, in *Proclus' Commentary on the "Timæus" of Plato: Volume II*, pp. 729–730.

72 *Timaeus* 37 c–d; in *CD*, p. 1167.

73 Proclus, *Commentary on the "Timaeus"*, book 4, 3, 6, in *Proclus' Commentary on the "Timæus" of Plato: Volume II*, p. 729.

74 Proclus, *Commentary* on the *Parmenides*, 847, in Proclus, *Commentary on Plato's "Parmenides"*, tr. G.R. Morrow and J.M. Dillon, Princeton, NJ: Princeton University Press, 1987, pp. 217–218.

75 Proclus, *Scholia on the "Cratylus"*, 51, in T. Taylor (ed.), *The Works of Plato in Five Volumes: Volume V*, tr. T. Taylor and F. Sydenham [TTS, vol. 13], Westbury: Prometheus Trust, 1996, p. 552. In 'The Home-Coming', when he returns to his solitude, Zarathustra offers an extensive reflection on language when he realizes that, through him, both being and becoming are articulated: 'Here, the words and word-chests of all existence spring open to me: all existence here wants to become words, all becoming here wants to learn speech from me' (*Thus Spoke Zarathustra*, p. 203). Talking to the animals in his cave during his convalescence, Zarathustra praises the power of language — the power to link what is otherwise separate — in a way that exemplifies Proclus's thoughts on language:

> How lovely it is, that there are words and sounds: are not words and sounds rainbows and bridges of semblance between things eternally apart?
>
> To every soul belongs another world; for each soul, every other soul is an afterworld.
>
> Between what is most similar, precisely there semblance tells lies most beautifully; for the smallest gap is the hardest to bridge.
>
> For me — how could there be an outside-me? There is no outside! But we forget this because of sounds; how lovely it is that we forget!
>
> Are not names and sounds given to things, so that humankind might refresh itself with things? Speech is a beautiful folly: with it humankind dances over all things.
>
> How lovely is all speech, and all the lies of sounds! With sounds our love dances on many-hued rainbows

('The Convalescent', §2; in *Thus Spoke Zarathustra*, p. 234; translation modified).

76 Cited in *Proclus' Commentary on the "Timæus" of Plato: Volume I*, 'Additional Notes to the first volume of Proclus on the Timæus of Plato', p. 520; cf. Apuleius, *"Golden Ass" or "The Metamorphosis", and Other Philosophical Writings*, p. 231.

77 Simplicius, *Epictetus his Enchiridion, with Simplicius his Commentary*, in *Epictetus His Morals, with Simplicius His Comment*, tr. G. Stanhope [2nd edn], London: Sare, 1700, Chapter 31, p. 191.

78 Juvenal, Satire 13, ll. 113–119; *The Satires*, tr. N. Rudd, Oxford and New York: Oxford University Press, 1992, p. 115.

79 Juvenal, Satire 16, l. 24; *Satires*, pp. 136–137.

80 Seneca, *Epistulae Morales ad Lucilium*, Letter 65, in Seneca, *Letters from a Stoic*, tr. R. Campbell, Harmondsworth: Penguin, 1969, pp. 118–119.

81 Seneca, *Letters from a Stoic*, p. 119.

82 Seneca, *Letters from a Stoic*, p. 120.

83 Seneca, *Letters from a Stoic*, p. 121.

84 Compare with Socrates's words in the *Phaedrus*: '[S]o each selects a fair one for his love after his disposition, and even as if the beloved himself were a god he fashions for himself as it were an image' (*Phaedrus*, 252d; in *CD*, p. 499).

85 Compare with the *Phaedrus*: 'At that sight [of the spectacle of the beloved] the driver's memory goes back to that form of beauty, and he sees her once again enthroned by the side of temperance upon her holy seat; then in awe and reverence he falls upon his back [...]' (*Phaedrus*, 254b; in *CD*, p. 500).

86 Plotinus, *Enneads*, I.6.9, in *The Enneads*, p. 54. For further discussion of this passage in relation to the topos of self-sculpting, see M. Onfray, *La sculpture de soi: La morale esthétique*, Paris: Grasset, 1993, pp. 77–90.

87 Plotinus, *Enneads*, V.8.1, in *The Enneads*, pp. 410–411.

88 T. Addey, *The Seven Myths of the Soul*, Frome: Prometheus Trust, 2000, p. 19.

89 P. Hadot, *Plotinus or the Simplicity of Vision* [1963], tr. M. Chase, Chicago: Chicago University Press, 1998.

90 Plotinus, *Enneads*, VI.7.22, in *The Enneads*, p. 492.

91 Plotinus, *Enneads*, VI.7.22, in *The Enneads*, p. 492.

92 Plotinus, *Ennead IV*, tr. A.H. Armstrong, Cambridge, MA and London: Harvard University Press, 1984, p. 385.

93 Plotinus, *Enneads*, I.6.5, in *The Enneads*, p. 51.

94 Gregory of Nyssa, *The Life of Moses*, tr. A.J. Malherbe and E. Ferguson, Mahwah, NJ: Paulist Press, 1978, p. 134.

95 J. Daniélou, 'Grégoire de Nysse et Plotin', in Association Guillaume Budé, *Congrès de Tours et de Poitiers 3–9 Septembre 1953: Actes du congrés*, Paris: Les Belles Lettres, 1954, pp. 259–262.

96 St Gregory of Nyssa, *Commentary on the Inscriptions of the Psalms*, tr. C. McCambley, Brookline, MA: Hellenic College Press, 1990, p. 99.

97 Gregory of Nyssa, *Commentary on the Inscriptions of the Psalms*, p. 100.

98 St Gregory of Nyssa, *Commentary on the Song of Songs*, tr. C. MacCambley, Brookline, MA: Hellenic College Press, 1987, p. 408.

99 Gregory of Nyssa, *The Life of Moses*, pp. 135–136.

100 *Mystical Theology*, 1025b; in Pseudo-Dionysius, *The Complete Works*, tr. C. Luibheid, New York and Mahwah, NJ: Paulist Press, 1987, p. 138.

101 *Mystical Theology*, 1025b; *Complete Works*, p. 138.

102 'Why I am So Clever', §9, in *Ecce Homo: How One Becomes What One Is*, tr. R.J. Hollingdale, Harmondsworth: Penguin, 1992, p. 34.

103 Meister Eckhart, *The Essential Sermons, Commentaries, Treatises, and Defense*, tr. E. Colledge and B. McGinn, New York, Ramsey, NJ, Toronto: Paulist Press, 1981, p. 134.

104 Meister Eckhart, *Essential Sermons*, p. 134.

105 Meister Eckhart, *Essential Sermons*, pp. 134–135.

106 Meister Eckhart, *Teacher and Preacher*, ed. B. McGinn, New York, Mahwah, Toronto: Paulist Press, 1986, pp. 192–193.

107 See his sermon for the Twenty-Third Sunday after Trinity, in Meister Eckhart, *Teacher and Preacher*, pp. 234–238.

108 In one of his sermons for the Fifth Sunday after Trinity, Tauler announces that 'all the riches of Heaven and earth, of the Angels and the saints, must really and truly flow into me' — 'if only I am formed according to God's will [...] and so sculptured into His likeness as to be lifted out of my own self' (*Sermons*, tr. M. Shrady, New York and Mahwah: Paulist Press, 1985, p. 141).

109 Meister Eckhart, *Sermons & Treatises*, vol. 3, p. 109.

110 See Jung, *CW* 12 §155, §205, §222, §438, §442–§446 and §448; cf. *Symbols of Transformation*, *CW* 5 §393, §450, §510, §569 and §659.

111 Nietzsche discussed Michelangelo at various points in his writings. In *Human, All Too Human* he reflected on Michelangelo as a religious artist, one of those who depicts

'the Beyond in art' (vol. 1, §220; in *Human, All Too Human*, tr. R.J. Hollingdale, Cambridge: Cambridge University Press, 1986, p. 102) and as 'the father or grandfather of the artists of the Italian baroque' (vol. 2, 'Assorted Opinions and Maxims', §144; in *Human, All Too Human*, p. 246). In *Daybreak*, he discussed Michelangelo's differentiation between himself and Raphael in terms of nature (or talent) and study (or learning), a distinction Nietzsche regarded as 'pedantic' (§540; in *Daybreak*, tr. R.J. Hollingdale, Cambridge: Cambridge University Press, 1982, pp. 212–214). And in his *Nachlass* from April–June 1885, Nietzsche remarked on the distance as well as the excitement he felt in relation to Dante and Plato, dwelling as each did in his 'carefully fashioned and firmly believed house of knowledge', the latter in his own, the former in a Christian-Patristic house; a thought which prompted him further to reflect that it required a different sort of power and flexibility to live in an incomplete system with open perspectives, so that Leonardo da Vinci stood above Michelangelo, and Michelangelo above Raphael (*KSA* 11, 34[25], 429).

112 Cited in J. Russon, 'The Project of Hegel's *Phenomenology of Spirit*', in S. Houlgate and M. Baur (eds), *A Companion to Hegel*, Malden, MA and Oxford: Blackwell, 2011, pp. 47–67 (p. 48).

113 Cited in Russon, 'The Project of Hegel's *Phenomenology of Spirit*', p. 63.

114 I. Barrows, *The Usefulness of Mathematical Learning Explained and Demonstrated: Being Mathematical Lectures*, London: Austen, 1734, Lecture 5, pp. 76–77; first emphasis mine, second emphasis by Barrows.

115 Proclus, *Proclus' Commentary on the First Book of Euclid's "Elements"* [1788], tr. T. Taylor [TTS, vol. 29], Sturminster Newton: Prometheus Trust, 2006, 'Additional Notes to Proclus on Euclid', note 8, p. 388. For the distinction with reference to sculpting a statue (in this case, of a nymph) between 'participated' and 'unparticipated' beauty, see T. Addey, 'The Universe of Being', in G. Wyndham-Jones and T. Addey, *Beyond the Shadows: The Metaphysics of the Platonic Tradition*, Dilton Marsh, Westbury: Prometheus Trust, 2011, pp. 93–151 (pp. 110–113).

116 Michelangelo, *Complete Poems and Selected Letters*, ed. R.N. Linscott, tr. C. Gilbert, Princeton, NJ: Princeton University Press, 1980, p. 28.

117 Michelangelo, *Life, Letters, and Poetry*, ed. G. Bull, tr. G. Bull and P. Porter, Oxford: Oxford University Press, 1987, p. 153.

118 See Varchi, *Due lezioni sopra la pittura a scultura*, 1547. For further discussion, see D. Summers, *Michelangelo and the Language of Art*, Princeton, NJ: Princeton University Press, 1981, pp. 203–233; and J. Hall, 'Michelangelo Buonarroti (1475–1564)', in C. Murray (ed.), *Key Writers on Art: From Antiquity to the Nineteenth Century*, London and New York: Routledge, 2003, pp. 55–59.

119 Michelangelo, *Life, Letters, and Poetry*, p. 120.

120 Bernardino Daniello, *Della Poetica*; cited in translation in Summers, *Michelangelo and the Language of Art*, p. 208.

121 Francisco de Hollanda, *Da pintura antigua*; cited in translation in Summers, *Michelangelo and the Language of Art*, p. 223.

122 For further discussion, see E. Panofsky, 'The Neoplatonic Movement and Michelangelo', in *Studies in Iconology: Humanistic Themes in the Art of the Renaissance*, New York: Oxford University Press, 1939, pp. 172–230.

123 See 'Michelangelo as an Aristotelian', in E. Panofsky, *Idea: A Concept in Art Theory* [1923], tr. J.J.S. Peake, Columbia: University of South Carolina Press, 1968, pp. 118–121.

124 See Aristotle *Metaphysics*, book 5, chapter 2 (1013a–1101a), and *Physics*, book 2, chapter 3 (194b–195b), in Aristotle, *Basic Works*, ed. R. McKeon, New York: Random House, 1941, pp. 752–754 and 240–242.

125 See Aristotle, *Metaphysics*, book 7, chapters 7–8 (1033a–1034a), in *Basic Works*, pp. 793–795.

126 See Thomas Aquinas, *Commentary on Aristotle's "Physics"*, tr. R.J. Blackwell, R.J. Spath, W.E. Thirkell, London: Routledge and Kegan Paul, 1963, pp. 93–96 and 185–187.

127 According to Panofsky, at a certain point the Aristotelian intention in the mind of the artist fuses with the Platonic idea (see Panofsky, *Idea*, chapter 2). Similarly, in his discussion Summers points to the *concetto* of the artist as Aristotle's intentional form in the artist's imagination and as a Platonic idea (Summers, *Michelangelo and the Language of Art*, p. 228).

128 Nietzsche, *Beyond Good and Evil*, §9; in F. Nietzsche, *Basic Writings*, ed. and tr. W. Kaufmann, New York: Modern Library, 1968, p. 206.

129 Summers, *Michelangelo and the Language of Art*, p. 219.

130 See Summers, *Michelangelo and the Language of Art*, pp. 222 and 227.

131 Summers, *Michelangelo and the Language of Art*, p. 232.

132 R. Steiner, 'Michelangelo and his Time from the Viewpoint of Spiritual Science' [Schmidt Number: S-2867], in *Geisteswissenschaft als Lebensgut: Zwölf öffentliche Vorträge gehalten zwischem dem 30. Oktober 1913 und 23. April 1914 im Architektenhaus zu Berlin* [Gesamtausgabe, vol. 63], Dornach/Schweiz: Rudolf Steiner Verlag, 1986, pp. 183–223. I have drawn here on the translation made by E. Goddard.

133 For the expression 'spirit of bodies', see Goethe's poem, 'Artist's Apotheosis' (*Künstlers Apotheose*) (for discussion of this poem see Rudolf Steiner's first lecture, given to the Goethe Society in Vienna in November 1888, entitled 'Goethe as the Founder of a New Science of Aesthetics' [S-0001], reprinted in *Art: An Introductory Reader*, ed. A. Stockton, Forest Row: Rudolf Steiner Press, 2003, pp. 36–64 (p. 63); and N. Boyle, *Goethe: The Poet and the Age*, vol. 1, *The Poetry of Desire*, Oxford and New York: Oxford University Press, 1991, pp. 547–548). In *Goethe's World View* and 'Goethe's Spiritual Nature and its Revelation in his *Faust* and through "The Fairytale of the Snake and the Lily"', Steiner identifies the 'spirit of nature' with the Earth Spirit (or *Erdgeist*) in *Faust*, Part 1, while in 'From Paracelsus to Goethe' (a lecture given in Berlin in 1911) Steiner identifies it with the 'sublime spirit' (*erhabener Geist*) of the scene *Wald und Höhle* (Wood and Cave) in *Faust I*. The precise expression *Geist der Natur* can be found in Caroline von Wolzogen's notes of lectures given by Goethe in 1806 (see E. and R. Grumach (eds), *Goethe: Begegnungen und Gespräche*, vol. 6, *1806–1808*, Berlin and New York: de Gruyter, 1999, p. 3).

134 For further discussion, see S.A. Punchuk, 'Ethical and Aesthetical Issues in the Novel *The Agony and the Ecstasy* by I. Stone', in M. Jurak (ed.), *Cross-cultural Studies: American, Canadian and European Literatures: 1945–1985*, Ljubljana: Filozofska Fakulteta, 1988, pp. 177–181.

135 'The eye is only the initial guide, the reason of the hand; the hand alone reveals the forms of things, their concepts, what they mean, what dwells therein. [...] Through the painter's magical deception, what is seen can now be touched, just as the painter transforms what is touched into something seen' (Herder, *Sculpture*, §4 and §1.2; in J.G. Herder, *Sculpture: Some Observations on Shape and Form from Pygmalion's Creative Dream*, tr. J. Gaiger, Chicago and London: University of Chicago Press, 2002, pp. 64 and 38); and compare with the coordination of eye and hand celebrated in Goethe's seventh poem in the *Roman Elegies* cycle: 'Only thus I appreciate marble; reflecting, comparing, / See with an eye that can feel, feel with a hand that can see' (*Dann versteh' ich den Marmor erst recht: ich denk' und vergleiche, / Sehe mit fühlendem Aug', fühle mit sehender Hand*) (translated by Michael Hamburger in J.W. von Goethe, *Selected Poems*, ed. C. Middleton, Boston, MA: Suhrkamp/Insel Publishers, 1983, p. 107).

136 *New Essays on Human Understanding*, 'Preface', in Leibniz, *New Essays on Human Understanding*, ed. P. Remnant and J. Bennett, Cambridge: Cambridge University Press, 1996, p. 52.

137 Leibniz, *New Essays on Human Understanding*, p. 52.

138 For further discussion, see H. Aarsleff, 'Condillac's Speechless Statue', in *Akten des II. Internationalen Leibniz-Kongresses, 17.-22. Juli 1972*, 4 vols, Wiesbaden: Franz Steiner, 1973–1975, vol. 4, pp. 287–302; and B. Baertschi, 'La statue de Condillac, image du réel ou fiction logique?', *Revue philosophique de Louvain*, 1984, vol. 82, 335–364.

139 J.G. Herder, 'Critical Forests: Fourth Grove', §1, in *Selected Writings on Aesthetics*, ed. and tr. G. Moore, Princeton and Oxford: Princeton University Press, 2006, p. 210. For further discussion, see R. Zuckert, 'Sculpture and Touch: Herder's Aesthetics of Sculpture', *Journal of Aesthetics and Art Criticism*, 2009, vol. 67, no. 3, 285–299; and R. Bailey, 'Herder's Sculptural Thinking', *Parallax*, 2011, vol. 17, no. 2, 71–83.

140 Herder, *Selected Writings*, p. 210; my emphasis.

141 Herder, *Selected Writings*, p. 210.

142 R.T. Clark, *Herder: His Life and Thought*, Berkeley: University of California Press, 1955, p. 88.

143 Herder, *Plastik*, part 1, §4, in Herder, *Sculpture*, p. 45.

144 Herder, *Plastik*, part 4, in Herder, *Sculpture*, p. 77.

145 'Of the Despisers of the Body', in Nietzsche, *Thus Spoke Zarathustra*, p. 61.

146 Schiller, *Poems and Ballads*, tr. E.B. Lytton, New York: Harper, 1887, p. 175; Schiller, *Sämtliche Gedichte und Balladen*, ed. G. Kurscheidt, Frankfurt am Main: Insel, 2004, pp. 152–153. (As a note in the English translation observes, 'the idea diffused by the translator through this and the preceding stanza, is more forcibly condensed by Schiller in four lines' — but the density of Schiller's thought here requires expansion to be understood.)

147 Schelling, 'On the Relation between the Plastic Arts and Nature', in *The Philosophy of Art: An Oration on the Relation between the Plastic Arts and Nature*, tr. A. Johnson, London: Chapman, 1845, p. 12.

148 M. ffytche, *The Foundation of the Unconscious: Schelling, Freud and the Birth of the Modern Psyche*, Cambridge: Cambridge University Press, 2012, p. 162.

149 Schelling, *The Philosophy of Art: An Oration on the Relation between the Plastic Arts and Nature*, pp. 12–13; cf. Schelling, *Sämmtliche Werke*, 14 vols, Stuttgart and Augsburg: Cotta, 1856–1861, vol. I.7, p. 304.

150 Schelling, *The Philosophy of Art*, p. 12; cf. *Sämmtliche Werke*, vol. I.7, p. 304.

151 Nietzsche, *Thus Spoke Zarathustra*, p. 111.

152 Nietzsche, *Thus Spoke Zarathustra*, p. 111.

153 Nietzsche, *Thus Spoke Zarathustra*, p. 111.

154 *Ecce Homo*, 'Why I am so Wise', §2; in Nietzsche, *Ecce Homo*, tr. R.J. Hollingale, Harmondsworth: Penguin, 1992, p. 10. Elsewhere Nietzsche explains: 'The word "superman" to designate a type that has turned out supremely well, in antithesis to "modern" men, to "good" men, to Christians and other nihilists' (*Ecce Homo*, 'Why I Write Such Good Books', §1; in *Ecce Homo*, p. 41).

155 Compare, not just with Nietzsche's use of this image in the immediate context of his discourse entitled 'On the Blissful Islands', but also in *Beyond Good and Evil*, §231: 'At the bottom of us, really "deep down", there is, of course, something unteachable, some granite of spiritual *fatum*, of predetermined decision and answer to predetermined selected questions' (in *BW*, p. 352).

156 *Ecce Homo*, 'Why I am so Wise', §2; in *Ecce Homo*, pp. 10–11.

157 Nietzsche, *KSA* 9, 7[213], 361. Translated in G. Parkes, 'Nietzsche on Rock and Stone: The Dead World, Dance and Flight', *International Journal of Philosophical Studies*, 2013, vol. 21, 20–40 (p. 26).

158 *The Birth of Tragedy*, §3; in *BW*, pp. 37–38.

159 For further discussion, see H. Bowden, *Mystery Cults in the Ancient World*, London: Thames & Hudson, 2010, chapter 1, 'The Eleusinian Mysteries', pp. 26–48; and Manly P. Hall, *Lectures on Ancient Philosophy*, New York: Penguin/Tarcher, 2005, chapter 16, 'Ancient Mystery Rituals', pp. 361–383.

160 *The Birth of Tragedy*, §21; in *BW*, p. 130.

161 Nietzsche, 'The Dionysiac World View', in F. Nietzsche, *The Birth of Tragedy and Other Writings*, ed. R. Geuss and R. Speirs, tr. R. Speirs, Cambridge: Cambridge University Press, 1999, pp. 118–119 (translation modified).

162 *The Gay Science*, §152; in Nietzsche, *The Gay Science*, tr. W. Kaufmann, New York: Vintage, 1974, p. 196.

163 *Human, All Too Human*, vol. 1, §258; in *Human, All Too Human*, p. 121.

164 *The Birth of Tragedy*, §2; in *BW*, p. 39 (translation modified).

165 *Human, All Too Human*, vol. 2, 'Assorted Opinions and Maxims', §222; in *Human, All Too Human*, p. 267.

166 *Human, All Too Human*, vol. 1, §218; in *Human, All Too Human*, p. 101.

167 *Human, All Too Human*, vol. 1, §3; in *Human, All Too Human*, pp. 13–14.

168 *Human, All Too Human*, vol. 2, 'Assorted Opinions and Maxims', §219; in *Human, All Too Human*, pp. 264–265.

169 *Daybreak*, §190, in *Daybreak*, p. 111–112.

170 *Human, All Too Human*, 'Assorted Opinions and Maxims', §172; in *Human, All Too Human*, p. 254.

171 *The Gay Science*, §12; in *The Gay Science*, p. 86.

172 *Daybreak*, §541; in *Daybreak*, p. 215. Even in as characteristically Nietzschean an aphorism as this, one can hear a biblical allusion, cf. 'Therefore have I set my face as a most hard rock' (Isaias 50: 7), alluded to when St Luke says of Christ, 'he steadfastly set his face [or 'fixed his countenance'] to go to Jerusalem' (Luke 9: 51). In a famous *logion* in the apocryphal Gospel of Thomas (§77), known to Jung, Jesus says: 'lift up the stone and you will find me there' (*The Apocryphal New Testament*, ed. J.K. Elliott, Oxford: Clarendon Press, 1993, p. 144). On the function of the image of the stone in Nietzsche, see Parkes, 'Nietzsche on Rock and Stone'.

173 *Beyond Good and Evil*, §225; in *BW*, p. 344.

174 Cf. 'Zarathustra's Prologue', §4; in *Thus Spoke Zarathustra*, p. 44.

175 'The Wanderer', *Thus Spoke Zarathustra*, p. 174.

176 'Of Redemption', *Thus Spoke Zarathustra*, p. 161.

177 'Of Old and New Law-Tables', §29; in *Thus Spoke Zarathustra*, p. 231.

178 *Twilight of the Idols*, 'What I Owe to the Ancients', §4 and §5; in *Twilight of the Idols; The Anti-Christ*, pp. 110 and 111.

179 *Ecce Homo*, 'Thus Spoke Zarathustra', §8; in *Ecce Homo*, p. 81.

180 *Daybreak*, §60; in *Daybreak*, p. 36. Was Heidegger thinking of this passage when he made his notorious remark about Hitler having 'beautiful hands'? (In a conversation with Jaspers on 30 June 1933, Heidegger is reported as replying to Jasper's objection about how such a man could govern Germany: *Bildung ist ganz gleichgültig* […] *Sehen Sie nur seine wunderbaren Hände an!* (V. Farias, *Heidegger und der Nationalsozialismus*, Frankfurt am Main: Fischer, 1989, p. 175). Curiously, after meeting the Führer in 1936, the British historian Arnold Toynbee remarked: 'He has beautiful hands' (O. Pöggeler, 'Den Führer führen? Heidegger und kein Ende' [1985], in *Neue Wege mit Heidegger*, Freiburg im Breisgau and Munich: Alber, 1991, pp. 203–254 [p. 248]).

181 Nietzsche, *KSA* 11, 25[101], 36.

182 C. Seidel, 'Charakter, §I', in J. Ritter et al. (eds), *Historisches Wörterbuch der Philosophie*, 13 vols, Basel and Stuttgart: Schwabe, 1971–2007, vol. 1, cols 984–991 (here: col. 984).

183 L. Klages, *The Science of Character*, tr. W.H. Johnston, London: Allen & Unwin, 1929, p. 201; cf. Klages, *Sämtliche Werke*, vol. 4, *Charakterkunde I*, 1983, p. 350.

184 'All *feeling* suffers in me and is in prison: but my *willing* always comes to me as my liberator and bringer of joy. / Willing liberates: that is the true doctrine of will and freedom — thus Zarathustra teaches you' ('On the Blissful Islands', in *Thus Spoke Zarathustra*, p. 111).

185 For an outline of Klages's philosophical position, see M. Ninck, 'Zur Philosophie von Ludwig Klages', *Kant-Studien*, 1931, vol. 36, 148–157; L. Baer, 'The Literary Criticism of Ludwig Klages and the Klages School: An Introduction to Biocentric Thought', *Journal of English and Germanic Philology*, January 1941, vol. 40, no. 1, 91–138; H.E. Schröder, 'Einführung in das Lebenswerk von Ludwig Klages', in H.E. Schröder (ed.), *Schiller–Nietzsche–Klages: Abhandlungen und Essays zur Geistesgeschichte der Gegenwart*,

Bonn: Bouvier, 1974, pp. 269–318; and P. Bishop, 'The Battle between Spirit and Soul: Messianism, Redemption, and Apocalypse in Klages', in W. Cristaudo and W. Baker (eds), *Messianism, Apocalypse and Redemption in 20th Century German Thought*, Adelaide: ATF Press, 2006, pp.181–194.

186 See L. Klages, *Die psychologischen Errungenschaften Nietzsches*, in Klages, *Sämtliche Werke*, vol. 5, *Charakterkunde II*, Bonn: Bouvier, 1989, pp. 1–216. For further discussion of Klages's reception of Nietzsche, see P. Bishop, 'Ludwig Klages's Early Reception of Friedrich Nietzsche', *Oxford German Studies*, 2002, vol. 31, 129–160; and P. Bishop, 'Ein Kind Zarathustras und eine nicht-metaphysische Auslegung der ewigen Wiederkehr', *Hestia: Jahrbuch des Klages-Gesellschaft*, 2002/2003, vol. 21, 15–37.

187 See Aristotle, *Metaphysics*, book 1, chapter 6 (987b) and book 13, chapter 4 (1078b); in *BW*, pp. 700–701 and 894.

188 E. Cassirer, *The Philosophy of Symbolic Forms*, vol. 4, *The Metaphysics of Symbolic Forms*, ed. J.M. Krois and D. Phillip Verene, tr. J.M. Krois, New Haven and London: Yale University Press, 1996, pp. 182–185.

189 *Phaedrus*, 230a; in *CD*, p. 478.

190 See Goethe, *Maxims and Reflections*, ed. Hecker, §657 and §663: 'If we take the significant dictum "know thyself" and consider it, we mustn't interpret it from an ascetical standpoint. It does not by any means signify the kind of self-knowledge advocated by our modern hypochondriacs, humorists and "Heautontimorumeus" ["self-torturers": an allusion to the title of a comedy by Terence], but quite simply means: pay some attention to yourself, watch what you are doing so that you come to realize how you stand vis-à-vis your fellows and the world in general. This needs no psychological self-torture; any capable person knows and appreciates this. It is good advice and of the greatest practical advantage to everyone' (§657); 'As Socrates made an appeal to moral man so that he might quite simply become somewhat clearer about himself, so too Plato and Aristotle looked on nature as competent individuals: the former seeking to adapt himself by spirit and temperament, the latter to win it by analytical insight and method. And so every approach we can make to these three philosophers, as a whole or in detail, is an event that fills us with the greatest joy and always furthers our education in the most positive way' (§663). Available online at: http://wolfenmann.com/goethe-maxims-and-reflections-full-text.html (accessed 20 March 2014).

191 Cassirer, *The Metaphysics of Symbolic Forms*, p. 186.

192 Cassirer, *The Metaphysics of Symbolic Forms*, p. 186.

193 *Phaedrus*, 249e; in *CD*, p. 496.

194 Cassirer, *The Metaphysics of Symbolic Forms*, p. 187.

195 M.P. Hall, *Lectures on Ancient Philosophy*, New York: Tarcher/Penguin, 2005, p. 365.

196 Hall, *Lectures on Ancient Philosophy*, p. 365.

197 Hall, *Lectures on Ancient Philosophy*, p. 366.

198 Hall, *Lectures on Ancient Philosophy*, p. 322.

199 Hall, *Lectures on Ancient Philosophy*, p. 322.

200 A.J. Mitchell, *Heidegger Among the Sculptors: Body, Space, and the Art of Dwelling*, Stanford, CA: Stanford University Press, 2010.

201 See A. Cardew, 'Heidegger and Jung: The Greatest Danger and the Saving Power', *Harvest: International Journal for Jungian Studies*, 2004, vol. 50, no. 1, 136–161; and G. Schmitt, '*Wahrheit* und *Individuation*: Zum Verlauf von Denklinien bei Heidegger und Jung', in C. Maillard and V. Liard (eds), *Recherches germaniques*, hors série No. 9 (2014), *Carl Gustav Jung (1875–1961): Pour une réévaluation de l'œuvre/C.G. Jung (1875–1961): Ein neuer Zugang zum Gesamtwerk*, pp. 239–256.

202 M. Heidegger, 'Phenomenology and Theology' [1927; 1928], tr. J.G. Hart and J.C. Maraldo, in Heidegger, *Pathmarks*, ed. W. McNeil, Cambridge: Cambridge University Press, 1998, pp. 39–62 (p. 58).

203 M. Heidegger, *Being and Time: A Translation of "Sein und Zeit"*, tr. J. Stambaugh, Albany, NY: State University of New York Press, 1996, p. 30; cf. Babich, 'Greek Bronze', p. 3.

204 Mitchell, *Heidegger Among the Sculptors*, p. 1.

205 M. Heidegger, *The Basic Problems of Phenomenology*, tr. A. Hofstadter, Bloomington and Indianapolis: Indiana University Press, 1982, p. 151.

206 Cf. Mitchell, *Heidegger Among the Sculptors*, pp. 8–9.

207 See M. Heidegger, *The End of Philosophy*, ed. and tr. J. Stambaugh, New York: Harper & Row, 1973, 'Overcoming Metaphysics', §26, pp. 103–109.

208 See M. Heidegger, *Bemerkungen zu Kunst—Plastik—Raum*, ed. H. Heidegger, St Gallen: Erker-Verlag, 1996.

209 Heidegger, *Bemerkungen zu Kunst—Plastik—Raum*, pp. 15–16; cited in Mitchell, *Heidegger Among the Sculptors*, p. 39.

210 See M. Heidegger, 'Die Herkunft der Kunst und die Bestimmung des Denkens', in P. Jaeger and R. Lüthe (eds), *Distanz und Nähe: Reflexionen und Analysen zur Kunst der Gegenwart*, Würzburg: Königshausen & Neumann, 1983, pp. 11–22.

211 Heidegger, 'Die Herkunft der Kunst und die Bestimmung des Denkens', p. 12; cited in Mitchell, *Heidegger Among the Sculptors*, p. 61.

212 Heidegger, 'Die Herkunft der Kunst und die Bestimmung des Denkens', pp. 13–14; cited in Mitchell, *Heidegger Among the Sculptors*, p. 62.

213 Heidegger, 'Die Herkunft der Kunst und die Bestimmung des Denkens', p. 14; cited in Mitchell, *Heidegger Among the Sculptors*, p. 64.

214 Heidegger, 'Die Herkunft der Kunst und die Bestimmung des Denkens', p. 14; cited in Mitchell, *Heidegger Among the Sculptors*, p. 65.

215 M. Heidegger, 'Art and Space', tr. C.H. Seibert, *Man and World*, February 1973, vol. 6, no. 1, 3–8.

216 Heidegger, 'Art and Space', p. 8; cf. Goethe, *Maxims and Reflections*, ed. Hecker, §466.

217 Heidegger, 'Art and Space', p. 8.

218 Mitchell, *Heidegger Among the Sculptors*, p. 91.

219 Goethe, *Maxims and Reflections*, ed. Hecker, §413.

220 M. Heidegger, 'The Origin of the Work of Art', in *Basic Writings*, ed. D.F. Krell, London: Routledge, 1993, pp. 139–212 (p. 166).

221 B. Vergely, *Deviens qui tu es: Quand des sages grecs nous aident à vivre*, Paris: Albin Michel, 2014, pp. 18–19. For further discussion of the temple, see pp. 89–92.

222 Heidegger, 'Building Dwelling Thinking', in *Basic Writings*, pp. 343–363. For further discussion of this aspect of Heidegger in relation to Jung, see L. Huskinson, 'Housing Complexes: Redesigning the House of Psyche in Light of a Serious Mistranslation of C.G. Jung Appropriated by Gaston Bachelard', *International Journal of Jungian Studies*, 2013, vol. 5, no. 1, 64–80.

223 Cf. 'Sculpture: An embodying bringing-into-the-work of places, and with them an opening of regions of possible human dwelling, regions of the possible tarrying of things surrounding and approaching the human' (Heidegger, 'Art and Space', p. 86).

224 For further discussion of the notion of the 'inner man', found frequently in the thought of St Augustine, see G.B. Matthews, 'The Inner Man', *American Philosophical Quarterly*, April 1967, vol. 4, no. 2, 166–172; C. Markschies, 'Die Platonische Metapher vom "inneren Menschen": Eine Brücke zwischen antiker Philosophie und altchristlicher Theologie', Winter 1995, vol. 1, no. 3, 3–18; and P. Cary, *Augustine's Invention of the Inner Self: The Legacy of the Christian Platonist*, Oxford: Oxford University Press, 2000.

225 *Republic*, 589a; cf. *Charmides*, 160d ('look within you'); *Theaetetus*, 189e ('a discourse that the mind carries on with itself'); *Philebus*, 40c ('in men's souls'); *Sophist*, 263e ('the inward dialogue carried on by the mind with itself without spoken sound'); and *First Alcibiades*, 132d–133c (an analysis of the Oracle's injunction, 'know thyself'); in *CD*, p. 817, cf. pp. 106, 895, 1121, 1011; and Plato, *Complete Works*, ed. J.M. Cooper, Indianapolis and Cambridge: Hackett, 1997, pp. 591–592.

226 See G. O'Daly, *Plotinus' Philosophy of the Self*, Shannon: Irish University Press, 1973; and L.P. Gearson, 'Introspection, Self-Reflexivity, and the Essence of Thinking', in J.J. Cleary (ed.), *The Perennial Tradition of Neoplatonism*, Leuven: Leuven University Press, 1997, pp. 153–173. For further discussion, see C. Taylor, *The Sources of the Self: The Making of Modern Identity*, Cambridge, MA: Harvard University Press, 1989; and P. Remes and J. Sihvola (eds), *Ancient Philosophy of the Self*, New York: Springer, 2008.

227 T.G.H. Strehlow, *Aranda Traditions*, Melbourne: Melbourne University Press, 1947, pp. 85–86. See Jung's comments in passing in *CW* 6 §325 and §496, and his *Visions* Seminar: 'The *churinga* is a slab of wood or stone, analogous to the soul-stones which are excavated from caves in Europe, hidden away in rocks and hollows since prehistoric times' (Jung, *Visions: Notes of the Seminar Given in 1930–1934*, ed. C. Douglas, 2 vols, London: Routledge, 1998, vol. 1, p. 66).

228 Klages, *Der Geist als Widersacher der Seele*, pp. 1274–1275.

229 For further discussion, see F. Sarasin, *Die steinzeitlichen Stationen des Birstales zwischen Basel und Delsberg* [*Neue Denkschriften der Schweizerischen Naturforschenden Gesellschaft*, vol. 54/2], Basel, Geneva and Lyon: Georg & Co., 1918, plates 3–4; J. Sedlmeier, 'Von der Steinzeit bis zum Frühmittelalter', in *Heimatkunde Arlesheim*, 1993, 68–84; and U. Niffeler, E. Gross-Klee, and W.E. Stöckl (eds), *Die Schweiz vom Paläolithikum bis zum frühen Mittelalter*, vol. 2, *Neolithikum – Néolithique – Neolitico*, Basel: Schweizerische Gesellschaft für Ur- und Frühgeschichte, 1995.

230 Telesphorus was, in fact, the son of Asclepius, and is typically depicted as a dwarf wearing a hooded cape or cloak, sometimes accompanied by his sister, the goddess Hygieia.

231 The Kabeiroi were deities were worshipped at various mystery sanctuaries, including Thebes in Boeotia, Lemnos, and Samothrace (where, according to Schelling, their cult was 'the most ancient in all Greece' (*Schelling's Treatise on "The Deities of Samothrace"*, ed. and tr. R.F. Brown, Missoula, MT: Scholars Press, 1977, p. 15). Prior to Schelling, Friedrich Creuzer (1771–1858) had discussed these divinities in some detail in his *Symbols and Mythology of the Ancient Peoples* (*Symbolik und Mythologie der alten Völker*) (1810–1812), vol. 2, pp. 313 et seq. In the twentieth century, moreover, the mysteries of the Kabeiroi attracted the attention of such scholars as Karl Kerényi and Walter Burkert (see Kerényi, 'The Mysteries of the Kabeiroi' [1944], in *The Mysteries: Papers from the Eranos Yearbooks*, tr. R. Manheim, Princeton, NJ: Princeton University Press, 1955, pp. 32–63; and W. Burkert, *Greek Religion*, tr. J. Raffan, Cambridge, MA: Harvard University Press, 1985, chapter 6, §1.3, pp. 281–285; see also his *Ancient Mystery Cults*, Cambridge, MA: Harvard University Press, 1987), as well as Jung. As Alan Cardew has recently pointed out, the Kabeiroi are mentioned by Jung at a significant point in his groundbreaking work, *Transformations and Symbols of the Libido* (1911–1912) (see A. Cardew, 'The Archaic and the Sublimity of Origins', in P. Bishop (ed.), *The Archaic: The Past in the Present*, New York and London: Routledge, 2012, pp. 93–146, esp. pp. 120–122). For further discussion, see A. Schachter, 'Cabiri', in S. Hornblower and A. Spawforth (eds), *The Oxford Classical Dictionary*, Oxford and New York: Oxford University Press, 1996), p. 267; and B. Hemberg, *Die Kabiren*, Uppsala: Almquist & Wiksells, 1950. The most up-to-date discussion can be found in H. Bowden, *Mystery Cults in the Ancient World*, London: Thames & Hudson, 2010, pp. 49–67.

232 Here Jung cites the penultimate line from Zarathustra's Roundelay (*Thus Spoke Zarathustra*, pp. 243–244 and 333).

233 *Twilight of the Idols*, 'Expeditions of an Untimely Man', §49; in *Twilight of the Idols; The Anti-Christ*, p. 103.

234 Jung, *CW* 13 §131; cited here from S.J. Linden, *The Alchemy Reader: From Hermes Trismegistus to Isaac Newton*, Cambridge: Cambridge University Press, 2003, p. 45.

235 F. Schiller, *On the Aesthetic Education of Man*, ed. and tr. E.M. Wilkinson and L.A. Willoughby, Oxford: Clarendon Press, 1982, Letter 17, §2, pp. 117–119.

236 Schiller, *On the Naïve and Sentimental in Literature*, tr. H. Watanabe-O'Kelly, Manchester: Carcanet, 1981, pp. 66–67 (trans. modified).

237 *Twilight of the Idols*, 'Expeditions of an Untimely Man', §49; in Nietzsche, *Twilight of the Idols; The Anti-Christ*, p. 102.

238 *Twilight of the Idols*, 'Expeditions of an Untimely Man', §49; in Nietzsche, *Twilight of the Idols; The Anti-Christ*, p. 102.

239 Cited from M. Berthelot, *Collection des anciens alchimistes grecs*, vol. 2, *Les œuvres de Zosime*, Paris: Steinheil, 1888, section III.vi, §5, pp. 121 and 129); cf. Jung, *CW* 12 §405; cf. *SNZ* 2, p. 949; cf. 'Psychology and Religion' (1938/1940), *CW* 11 §151; and 'Transformation Symbolism in the Mass' (1942/1954), *CW* 11 §355.

240 *The Apocryphal Old Testament*, ed. H.F.D. Sparks, Oxford: Clarendon Press, 1984, p. 770.

241 L. Frobenius, *Das Zeitalter des Sonnengottes*, vol. 1, Berlin: Reimer, 1904.

242 'Zarathustra's Prologue', §4; *Thus Spoke Zarathustra*, p. 44; cf. *CW* 14, §559.

243 Berthelot, *Collection des anciens alchimistes grecs*, vol. 3, Paris: Steinheil, 1888, IV.xx, p. 283.

244 See *Theatrum chemicum*, vol. 6, Blasius Vigenerus, *Tractatus De Igne et Sale* [Treatise on Fire and Salt] [1618], chapter 56, p. 51. Here Vigenerus speaks of the sun as the 'eye and heart of the sensible world and the image of the invisible God', referring to Pseudo-Dionysius's description of the sun as the 'clear and manifest statue of God' (cf. *CW* 14 §568). In one of his typically learned and scholarly footnotes, Jung sources this reference to Pseudo-Dionysius's *The Divine Names*, chapter 4: 'The great, shining, ever-lighting sun is the apparent image of the divine goodness, a distant echo of the Good' (697c; *Complete Works*, p. 74). Jung notes that Vigenerus translates *eikon* not by 'imago' but by 'statua', and he suggests that Vigenerus may have been influenced in this choice of translation by another alchemical treatise, *De Chemia* (1566) by Senior, a tenth-century alchemist also known as Ibn Umail, who speaks in that work of 'the water extracted from the hearts of statues' (*De Chemia*, p. 64). Was Vigenerus reminded, Jung wondered, by the word *cor* ('heart') in Senior's phrase, 'the hearts of statues' (*CW* 14 §568)? Or was he influenced by a line from the *Zohar* on Genesis 28: 22 where Malchuth (the lower) is called the 'statue' when united with Tifereth (the higher)? For Jung, the conceptual link between the Kabbalah and the alchemy lies in the union of higher and lower, of male and female, which in turn provides the link to the conception of totality found in Goethe, Nietzsche, and Jung.

245 *CW* 14 §564, fn. 61, citing Pachymeres's paraphrase of Pseudo-Dionysius the Areopagite's *De coelesti hierarchia* (*The Celestial Hierarchy*), chapter 2, in *Patrologiæ Cursus Completus: Series Græca*, ed. J.-P. Migne, vol. 3, Paris: Garnier, 1889, col. 162.

246 *Symposium*, 215a; in *CD*, p. 566.

247 Plotinus, *Enneads*, V.8.5, in *The Enneads*, p. 416.

248 Berthelot, *Collection des anciens alchimistes grecs*, vol. 2, section III.vi, §5, pp. 121 and 129; translation, pp. 130 and 133; cf. Jung, *CW* 13 §265.

249 Plato, *CD*, pp. 1165, 1179–1180, and 1163–1164.

250 Plato, *CD*, p. 1178; cf. Steeb, *Coelum sephiroticum*, p. 26.

251 Steeb, *Coelum sephiroticum*, p. 26; cf. Jung, *CW* 11 §160, fn. 65.

252 Steeb, *Coelum sephiroticum*, p. 26; cf. Jung, *CW* 11 §160, fn. 65.

253 'Of the Despisers of the Body', in *Thus Spoke Zarathustra*, pp. 61–62.

254 'Of the Famous Philosophers', in *Thus Spoke Zarathustra*, p. 127.

255 'The Leech', in *Thus Spoke Zarathustra*, p. 264.

256 'Of Self-Overcoming', in *Thus Spoke Zarathustra*, p. 138.

257 'Of Self-Overcoming', in *Thus Spoke Zarathustra*, p. 138.

3

SHADOWS OR FORMS

Life and the Ideal

> The most perfect production still proceeds from the most perfect thought, and [...] it is MIND alone which we admire, while we bestow our applause on the graces of a well-proportioned statue [...] The statuary [...] makes us reflect on the beauty of his art and contrivance, which, from a heap of unformed matter, could extract such expressions and proportions.
>
> (David Hume, 'The Platonist')

Does any or all of our discussion in Chapters 1 and 2 lead one to conclude that Nietzsche was an alchemist? Or that he was an idealist? No. Nevertheless, it is instructive to compare the concluding lines of Zarathustra's discourse 'On the Blissfuls Islands' in terms of imagery and import with an avowedly 'idealist' text by the famous German poet, Friedrich Schiller (1788–1805), and another of Nietzsche's favourite authors.[1] For in one of Schiller's great didactic poems, entitled 'The Ideal and Life', we find a fusion of the imagery of shadow and of sculpting a statue that anticipates, explicates, and (to the extent that Nietzsche was a close reader of Schiller) may even inform the concluding words of Zarathustra's discourse on the blissful islands.

Schiller's 'The Ideal and Life'

Originally, when it was written in 1795, Schiller had called this poem 'The Kingdom of the Shadows' (*Das Reich der Schatten*), but in 1800 he had changed this potentially misleading title (with its echoes of the shades of the dead) to 'The Kingdom of the Forms' (*Das Reich der Formen*), and then again in 1804 to its present title, 'The Ideal and Life' (*Das Ideal und das Leben*).[2] For this poem is emphatically *not* about, so to speak, the 'boundless expanse' in the sense of the afterlife, but it is about the 'boundless expanse' of freedom that can be achieved in the here-and-now. (We might recall from Chapter 2 that, similarly, Cassirer's notion of the 'realm of form' — *das Reich der Form* — turned out to be very much about activity in the present.)

Schiller's poem develops ideas found in his earlier poems and aesthetic treatises. In 'The Gods of Greece' (*Die Götter Griechenlands*), a controversial work written in 1787, published in 1788, and revised in response to criticism in 1800, Schiller had looked back at ancient Greece and lamented the loss of beauty in the modern world. And in 'The Artists' (*Die Künstler*), a philosophical poem written in 1788–1789, expanded as a result of discussions with Christoph Martin Wieland (1733–1813), and published in March 1789, he had hailed art as the mediatrix of truth and morality, arguing for their future union in beauty. In 'The Kingdom of the Shadows', finally retitled 'The Ideal and Life', Schiller took his thought one step further and envisaged this aesthetic state as achievable in the present moment, in the here-and-now.

Subsequently, Schiller imagined using his poem as the starting-point for another, using his 'didactic poem' (*Lehrgedicht*) as the basis for a poetic idyll (in the sense that he had used this term in his aesthetic treatise, *On Naïve and Sentimental Poetry*, of 1796). As he told Wilhelm von Humboldt (1767–1835) in a letter of 30 November 1795, he wanted 'to individualize objectively the ideal of beauty, thus creating an idyll in *my* sense' (*NA* 28, 118). What is this specific, Schillerian sense of the idyll? In *On the Naïve and Sentimental in Literature*, Schiller sets up a number of literary classifications or categories: he contrasts the 'naïve' (where the poet is one with nature) with the 'sentimental' (where the poet is conscious of separation from nature), and he subdivides 'sentimental' poetry into satirical and elegaic, subdividing in turn the elegaic into the elegy proper and the idyll. If nature is represented as lost and the ideal as unattainable, hence both are an object of sadness, we are dealing with an elegy; if both nature and the ideal are presented as actual and hence an object of joy, we are dealing with an idyll.[3]

Accordingly, the concept of the idyll is 'the concept of a conflict completely resolved in the individual man and in society, of a free union of the inclinations with the law, of a nature purified to the highest moral dignity', and its character consists in '*all conflict between reality and the ideal*' being 'completely resolved'.[4] Or to put it another way, the idyll is 'no other than the ideal of beauty applied to real life'. Hence, 'the dominant impression' of the idyll is *peace* — 'the peace of consummation, not of laziness; a peace which flows from equilibrium, not from the cessation of the powers, which flows from richness, not from emptiness, and is accompanied by the feeling of an endless capacity [*eines unendlichen Vermögens*]'.[5] (This notion of the idyll — of 'the ideal of beauty applied to real life' — matches closely with Nietzsche's notion of the Dionysian, and finds eloquent expression in the chapter of *Thus Spoke Zarathustra* called 'At Noontide'.)

Schiller wanted, he told Humboldt, to carry on from where 'The Kingdom of the Shadows' had left off: he wanted to *represent* (*darstellen*), not to *instruct* (*lehren*) (*NA* 28, 119). So where 'The Kingdom of the Shadows' had provided the rules, his proposed idyll would actually use them in a specific instance (*NA* 28, 119). For his choice of subject for this task, Schiller was considering the legend of Heracles, the divine hero of Greek mythology whom the Romans knew as Hercules. According to the Greek tradition, on his death Heracles rose up to Mount Olympus, on whose mountain-top the twelve deities of the Greek pantheon dwelt, and it is this moment to which Schiller refers right at the end of 'The Kingdom of the Shadows' (or 'The Ideal and Life').[6]

We should pause for a moment to consider the remarkable career of Heracles — the son of a god (Zeus) and a mortal woman (Alcmene). Among his most famous feats are his Twelve Labours, a punishment inflicted on him by Zeus's wife, Hera, via King Eurystheus, after Heracles had, in a fit of madness, murdered his family: in achieving these feats, Heracles becomes the 'glory' (*kleos*) of 'Hera'. Various aspects of his life are told by Ovid (in his *Metamorphoses*) and Pseudo-Apollodorus (in his *Bibliotheca*), as well as by tragedians (Euripides, Sophocles) and lyric poets (Pindar, Theocritus). Synthesizing accounts of Heracles's life have been provided, for instance, by Edith Hamilton or by Robert Graves.[7] In some respects, his life story marks him out as a fit candidate for psychoanalysis: as a child, he strangled two snakes sent by Hera to strangle him and his brother (a symbol of his triumph over the primordial ego?), but after marrying Megara, the daughter of King Creon, he murdered her and their three children, after a fit of insanity induced by Hera (a symbol that his primordial drives are not yet under control?).

A Sophist philosopher, Prodicus of Ceos, told an allegorical parable (retold by Xenophon in his *Memorabilia*, II.1.21–34), in which Heracles was visited by two female figures, Virtue (or Duty) and Vice (or Pleasure), between whom he has to choose: and whether through choice or through fate, his life consists of one long series of tasks, combats, and challenges. The *dodekathlon* or 'twelve labours', once the subject of an epic (now lost) by Peisander called the *Heracleia*, and depicted on the metopes of the Temple of Zeus at Olympia, exemplify a life dedicated to struggle — struggle against himself and against the world. (The order of these labours varies from one source to another, but here we follow the order in Pseudo-Apollodorus's *Bibliotheca*). In his *Emblematum liber* or *Book of Emblems* (published in various editions from 1531 onwards), the Italian humanist, Andrea Alciati (1492–1550), interpreted the twelve labours as symbolic of a quest for social and individual perfection, and they clearly invite a psychoanalytic reading as well.

First, Heracles slays the Nemean lion, a symbol of the spirit of domination. Second, he slays the nine-headed Lernaean hydra, freeing himself from vanity and its numerous ruses. Third, he captures the golden hind of Artemis, displaying infinite patience and effort to combine delicacy of soul (the hind is dedicated to Artemis, chaste goddess of the hunt) with her strength (its hooves of bronze or brass). Fourth, he captures the Erymanthian boar (a symbol of unbridled debauchey). Fifth, by diverting the rivers Alpheus and Peneus, he cleans out the stables of King Augeas, purifying the subconscious of banality (mud) and releasing the capacity for sublimation (the twelve outstanding silvery-white bulls, as opposed to the three hundred white-legged black bulls and the two hundred red stud-bulls). Sixth, he slays the Stymphalian birds, frightening them with a rattle and shooting them with arrows (and so purifying the subconscious of images that prevent us from seeing the spirit).

Seventh, Hercules captures the Cretan bull, a symbol of brutality; eighth, he steals the mares of Diomendes, killing the giant with an axe, and feeding the body to the carnivorous horses, symbolizing the slaying of impetuosity that consumes the spirit.

Ninth, he obtains the girdle of Hippolyta, the queen of the Amazons, confronting these (feminine) symbols of the soul that kill the (masculine) spirit. Tenth, he obtains the cattle of Geryon, killing this monstrous giant with three bodies (representing three forms of perversity: banal vanity, debauchery, and domination). Eleventh, he has to steal the apples of the Hesperides, the nymphs who tend a blissful garden in a far-off corner of the world. In the course of this adventure, he kills Antaeus, the seemingly invincible wrestler, thus overcoming the temptation to return to terrestrial pleasures. To collect the golden apples from the garden of the Hesperides, Heracles uses trickery, cunning, and patience to deceive Atlas, kill Ladon the dragon, and sublimate (or turn into gold) terrestrial pleasures (the apples).

Finally, Hercules is tasked with capturing alive Cerberus, the three-headed hound with a serpent's tail that guards Tartarus, the underworld. (In order to perform this task, and to discover how to enter and exit the underworld, Heracles was initiated into the Eleusinian Mysteries, or at least the Lesser ones.) In the underworld, Heracles encounters Theseus and Pirithous, rescuing the former but not the latter; and he manages to overpower Cerberus and drag him out of the underworld — thus purifying the subconscious (the Styx and the Acheron, those subterranean rivers) from imaginative excess and repression of desire.

Like all Greek mythology, the story of Heracles cries out for a psychoanalytic reading, whether of the kind proposed by Paul Diel (1893–1972) and given above, or following the intuitive insights developed by Jung. In *Symbols of Transformation*, for instance, Jung interprets the statement of the Delphic Oracle that Heracles was so named because he owed his immortal fame to Hera, whose persecutions had driven him to his great deeds, to mean that 'the great deed really means overcoming the mother and thus winning immortality' (*CW* 5 §450, fn. 60). Hence, his characteristic weapon, the club, had been cut from 'the maternal olive-tree'; like the sun, he possessed the arrows of Apollo; he slew the Nemean lion in its cave, whose meaning is 'the grave in the mother's womb'; while the fight with the hydra, along with the other deeds wished on him by Hera, all symbolize 'the fight with the unconscious'.

In some respects, however, Jung sees Heracles as a figure of defeat, as when he became, as the Oracle had prophesied, the slave of the dominatrix-like Omphale (cf. *omphalos*, i.e., 'navel'), suggesting that 'he had to submit after all to the unconscious' (*CW* 5 §450, fn. 60). Elsewhere, Jung regarded how Heracles received immortality through being unwittingly adopted by Hera as an example of 'the motif of the *dual descent*' (that is, from human and divine parents); while later he assimilated Heracles's twelve labours to such other heroic journeys as the descent of Osiris to the underworld, the travels of Enoch, and the symbolic *peregrinatio* of Michael Maier to the four corners of the world in search of Mercurius and the phoenix. (In the case of Heracles, the Cretan bull takes him south; the mares of Diomedes, to Thrace, i.e., north; Hippolyta to Scythia, i.e., east; and the cattle of Geryon to Spain, i.e., west. From the garden of the Hesperides, the western land of the dead, Heracles sets off to his twelfth and final labour, the journey to Hades to capture Cerberus.[8]

As well as being treated by Ovid and Pseudo-Apollodorus, Euripides and Sophocles, and Pindar and Theocritus, the figure of Heracles is addressed in some of the most ancient and venerable texts known in the West, such as the 'Homeric' Hymns, so called because they use the same dactyllic hexameters as the *Iliad* and the *Odyssey*, a collection of hymns (dating back to the sixth or even the seventh centuries BCE) in praise of various individual gods; or the 'Orphic' Hymns, religious poems attributed to Orpheus (and dating back to the second or third centuries BCE) which unfold what the English Neoplatonist Thomas Taylor (1758–1835) called a 'sublime theology'.

The story of Heracles furnished ample material for depiction by numerous artists, but in the eighteenth century two classical depictions of Heracles acquired a particularly iconic status, and will certainly have been known to Schiller.[9] (Indeed, we know that he saw them in the Antikensaal in Mannheim during his visit of 1784 [see *NA* 20, 101–106].) One of them was the Belvedere Torso, a fragment of a male nude statue conventionally identified as Heracles in a seated position. In his *History of Ancient Art* (1764), the German art historian and archaeologist Johann Joachim Winckelmann (1717–1768) described how 'abused and mutilated to the utmost, and without head, arms, or legs, as this statue is, it shows itself even now to those who have the power to look deeply into the secrets of art with all the splendour of its former beauty', for Heracles appears here 'purified from the dross of humanity, and after having attained immortality and a seat among the gods'.[10] In an earlier short essay of 1759, Winckelmann noted Michelangelo's admiration for this work, which he proceeded to describe — or rather to describe 'the ideal represented by the statue, especially because it is ideal in its conception'.[11] In words that echo the famous words of Michelangelo and anticipate Zarathustra's cry at the conclusion of 'On the Blissful Islands', Winckelmann — acknowledging that the statue has been 'robbed of the most attractive and significant parts of its nature', nevertheless promises the alert and sensitive spectator:

> At first glance you will probably only see a shapeless stone. But if you are able to penetrate the secrets of art, then you will perceive a miracle, if you observe this work with a calm eye. Then Hercules will appear to you as if in the midst of all his tasks, and both hero and god will be visible in this work at the same time.[12]

The second depiction is the Farnese Hercules, a marble copy made in the third century BCE by a sculptor called Glykon of a bronze original made in the fourth century BCE by Lysippos of Sicyon. Winckelmann praised the representation of Heracles 'in repose', but 'repose in the midst of his labors, and with distended veins and strained muscles', so that we see him 'resting, apparently in a heated and breathless state', after obtaining the golden apples from the garden of the Hesperides.[13] From these works (and from their analysis by Winckelmann), as well as from the account of Heracles in the *Götterlehre* (1791) of Karl Philipp Moritz (1756–1793),[14] Schiller will have developed a specific view of this divine figure before he began work on his version of the Heracles myth.

In the poem he was planning, Schiller wanted to treat the marriage of Heracles with Hebe, the goddess of youth who served the gods and goddesses on Olympus with nectar and ambrosia. In Hesiod's *Theogony*, this event is described as follows:

> And mighty Heracles, the valiant son of neat-ankled Alcmena, when he had finished his grievous toils, made Hebe the child of great Zeus and gold-shod Hera his shy wife in snowy Olympus. Happy he! For he has finished his great work and lives amongst the undying gods, untroubled and unaging all his days.[15]

In other words, Heracles finishes his days, if not on a blissful island, then on a blissful mountain … 'Beyond this material', Schiller told Humboldt, 'there is nothing left for the poet, because he cannot leave behind human nature, and this idyll would deal with precisely this transition from the human being to God [*diesem Uebertritt des Menschen in den Gott*]' (*NA* 28, 119). Schiller's ambition for this planned work was immense: 'Imagine the pleasure, my friend', he enthused to Humboldt, 'of a poetic representation in which everything mortal is extinguished, pure light, pure freedom, pure potential [*lauter Licht, lauter Freyheit, lauter Vermögen*] — no shadow, no limit, no more of anything like that to be seen' (*NA* 28, 120). Likewise, within the Platonic tradition the experience of beholding the Good is described as experiencing 'the most brilliant light of being';[16] an experience so blissful that in the *Republic* it is compared by Socrates to having been transported to the blissful islands![17]

In the end, and perhaps not surprisingly, Schiller never wrote this poem; but we find a foretaste of what it might have looked like in the concluding stanzas of 'The Kingdom of the Shadows' (or 'The Ideal and Life'), and this poem as we have it in all its various forms — original, revised, and final — always speaks of something truly heroic: the belief in the ideal.[18] (We might regret the poem we never had; we cannot but help rejoice in the excellence of Schiller's work, insofar as he managed to complete this text.)

Yet initially Schiller's message was misunderstood because of his choice of the word *Schatten*, which was widely (and incorrectly) taken to refer to the shades of the dead. But this was not at all Schiller's intention. Rather, the term recalls the sense in which it is employed when, in the allegory of the cave in the *Republic*, Socrates says that the prisoners bound in the cave can only see 'the shadows cast from the fire on the wall of the cave' (those shadows being, in part, the images of the visible world and, in part, the images of the gods found in Homer and other poets).[19] And correspondingly, the term *Schatten* was being used by Schiller in an aesthetic sense, much as it had been by Friedrich Gottlieb Klopstock (1724–1803) in his 'Alcaic Ode' of 1747, entitled 'To My Friends' (*An meine Freunde*), later called 'Wingolf' (1798). In this fifth part of this ode, Klopstock writes:

> There I see sacred shadows slowly walking!
> Not those, that sadly from the dying
>   Break free, no, those, that in poetry's
>   Hour — and in friendship — float around the poet![20]

So Schiller retitled the poem in order to make his intentions clearer: at first, by using the Platonic language of *form*,[21] and then again by using the language of *the ideal*. As he had told Christan Gottfried Körner (1756–1831) on 21 September 1795, the message of his poem concerned 'the concept of the disinterested interest in pure appearance [*am reinen Schein*], without any reference to physical or moral results, the concept of a complete absence of limiting determinations and of the *infinite potential* in the subject of the beautiful [*des **unendlichen Vermögens** im Subjecte des Schönen*]'; so by 'the realm of the shadows in an ideal sense', Schiller meant 'the aesthetic world' (*die aesthetische Welt*), as he told Goethe on 3 July 1796.

Thus the conception of Schiller's poem is entirely in line with the argument he was to develop at (considerably) greater length in his treatise *On the Aesthetic Education of Humankind* (1795), where he expounded his doctrine of the union of the two human drives, the material drive (*der Stofftrieb*) and the formal drive (*der Formtrieb*), in a third drive he called the ludic drive (*der Spieltrieb*) (see Letter 15).[22] What, in his poem, is presented as a synthesis of the sensuous and intellectual aspects of the human being, is described in this treatise (Letter 27, §8) in the following terms: 'In the midst of the fearful kingdom of forces, and in the midst of the sacred kingdom of laws, the aesthetic impulse to form is at work, unnoticed, on the building of a third joyous kingdom of play and of semblance', and in this ludic kingdom 'man is relieved of the shackles of circumstance, and released from all that might be called constraint, alike in the physical and in the moral sphere'.[23]

On its appearance, 'The Kingdom of the Shadows' was greeted with enthusiasm by those who read it closely. In a letter of 21 August 1795, Humboldt told Schiller: 'Since the day I received it, it has in the most real sense quite possessed me, I have read nothing else, have hardly thought of anything else, I have been able in a way to make it my own, which I have never succeeded in doing with any other poem [...] It contains such an extent and such a depth of ideas'. On 22 August 1795, Johann Gottfried Herder (1744–1803) praised Schiller's two poems, 'Ideals' and '[The Kingdom of the] Shadows', as 'movingly beautiful, sublimely sad' (*rührend-schön, erhaben-traurig*). Karl Theodor von Dalberg (1744–1817), a leading ecclesiastical figure whose administrative skills were advancing him to being consecrated an archbishop, told Schiller on 5 September 1795: 'In your *Kingdom of the Shadows* good people live in the best moments of their lives', but Schiller's poetic genius had been the first to have 'painted this kingdom with aetherial colours'.

As Frank Fowler has pointed out, 'it is absolutely vital to realise that in this poem — as elsewhere — Schiller does not advocate an ivory-tower escapism or a permanent withdrawal from the unpleasant realities of life'; rather, 'in order that we may make full use of our human potential Schiller reminds us that, although we are seldom if ever capable of achieving absolute perfection, we should not underestimate the value of our ability to entertain in our minds the notion of perfection' and Schiller shows 'how in the midst of our struggles and conflicts this thought may strengthen and sustain us'.[24] So the concept of the ideal functions on a number of levels all at once: on the cognitive, the moral, and the aesthetic, unifying the True, the Good, and the Beautiful into one.

Seen in this light, the Platonic echo of its second title, *Das Reich der Formen*, acquires fresh significance, and the poem itself can be read as a kind of *exercice spirituel*, or as a contribution to the field of *Philosophische Praxis*. For the contemplation of perfect beauty proposed by this text is not intended to offer moral instruction or improvement, but instead — in line with the central thesis of *On the Aesthetic Education of Humankind* — to 'restore the balance of the integrated personality', so that if 'the stresses and frustrations of everyday life' serve to 'dislocate, to disintegrate the personality', nevertheless 'the contemplation of the ideal can weld it together into a new unity':[25] into 'a unity' that will, in the words of Goethe's letter to Humboldt on 17 March 1832, 'astonish the world'.[26]

The Platonic underpinning of Schiller's poem 'The Ideal and the Life' becomes clear in the third (originally, the fourth) stanza that begins:

> Flesh alone is subject to those powers
> Weaving this dark fate of ours;
> While above the reach of time or storm,
> Playmate of the blessed ones up yonder,
> She amid the flowers of light doth wander,
> Godlike 'mid the Gods, undying FORM.[27]

And it is echoed in the thirteenth (originally, the sixteenth) stanza, with its reference to the realm of the pure forms:

> But within th' Ideal's starry portal,
> Dwelling of pure forms immortal,
> Sorrow's heavy storm is heard no more.
>
> *Aber in den heitern Regionen*
> *Wo die reinen Formen wohnen,*
> *Rauscht des Jammers trüber Sturm nicht mehr.*
>
> [original version:
> *Aber in den heitern Regionen*
> *Wo die Schatten selig wohnen*][28]

And in the fourth (originally, the seventh) stanza, in the lines

> As life's filmy phantoms, noiseless ever,
> Glancing, wander by the Stygian river, —
> As of old within its heavenly sphere
> Stood th' immortal Soul, before descending
> Into this dark tomb, Mortality[29]

Schiller recapitulates Plato's doctrine, as expressed in the *Meno*, the *Phaedo*, and the *Republic*, of the pre-existence of the soul; one thinks, for instance, of Socrates's remarks in the *Cratylus* about the body as 'the grave of the soul' (400b–400c).[30] But how truly Platonic is Schiller's conception of form?

In his treatise *On the Aesthetic Education of Humankind*, Schiller had offered a clear definition of form: whereas 'life' is the object of the *Stofftrieb*, and 'form' is the object of the *Formtrieb*, 'living form' (*lebende Gestalt*) — i.e., beauty — is the object of the ludic drive:

> The object of the play-drive, represented in a general schema, may therefore be called *living form* [*lebende Gestalt*]: a concept serving to designate all the aesthetic qualities of phenomena and, in a word, what in the widest sense of the term we call *beauty*. [...] The beautiful is to be neither mere life [*blosses Leben*], nor mere form [*blosse Gestalt*], but living form, i.e., beauty [*lebende Gestalt, das ist, Schönheit*]. (Letter 15, §2 and §8)[31]

In 'The Ideal and Life', Schiller explicitly associates beauty with shadow: in the original version, in his fourth stanza — 'Into th' shadows' pure dominion / Fly from this dull, narrow life!' (*Fliehet aus dem engen dumpfen Leben / In der Schönheit Schattenreich!*) — and in his seventh (originally, his tenth) stanza:

> But, although 'twas foaming like a torrent,
> Pent with rocks, behold life's current,
> How, with smooth and softly-spreading stream,
> Here through beauty's shadow-land it wendeth [...][32]

In both these stanzas, beauty and the shadow are posited as synonymous terms, and in turn both beauty and the shadow are synonymous with form. To put this argument in the form of a simple formula: BEAUTY = SHADOW = FORM.

In *On the Aesthetic Education*, Schiller explained his precise conception of beauty as 'living form' with reference to an example with which, in the course of our discussion in Chapters 1 and 2, we have become familiar — he uses the example of sculpture:

> A block of marble, though it is and remains lifeless, can nevertheless, thanks to the architect or the sculptor, become living form; and a human being, though he may live and have form [*wiewohl er lebt und Gestalt hat*], is far from being on that account a living form. In order to be so, his form would have to be life, and his life form [*Dazu gehört, dass seine Gestalt Leben und sein Leben Gestalt sei*]. As long as we merely think about his form, it is lifeless, a mere abstraction; as long we merely feel his life, it is formless, a mere impression. Only when his form lives in our feeling and his life takes on form in our understanding, does he become living form [*Nur indem seine Form in unsrer Empfindung lebt und sein Leben in unserm Verstande sich formt, ist er lebende Gestalt*]; and this will always be the case whenever we adjudge him beautiful.[33]

(Letter 15, §2)

Fig. 2. Kopf der Hera Ludovifi (Rom,
Villa Ludovifi).

Meyers Lexikon 1888

FIGURE 3.1   The head of Juno (or Hera) in the Villa Ludovisi, Rome. *Meyers Lexikon*,
1888.

In this paragraph, Schiller carefully explores the PARADOX OF FORM: on the one
hand, FORM is opposed to LIFE, in a sense it can even be something deadly; yet, on
the other, it can also be a vehicle to a richer and more sophisticated expression and
experience of LIFE. The sculpted statue in the block of marble — such as, for instance,
the Juno Ludovisi, the massive marble head of the goddess, Juno (or Hera), that survives from an acrolithic statue dating back to first-century CE Rome (or the torso of
Hercules in the Belvedere in Rome, which so fascinated Winckelmann) — illustrates
this paradox. On the one hand, this sculpture is simply a block of stone; on the other,
it is something amazing, something beautiful — something alive!

A similar paradox is explored by Schiller at the conclusion of Letter 15, §9, of his
Aesthetic Education. Here Schiller uses the statue of the Juno Ludovisi as an illustration of how, for the Greeks, 'both the material constraint of natural laws and the
spiritual constraint of moral laws were resolved in their higher concept of Necessity,
which embraced both worlds at once', arguing that 'it was only out of the perfect
union of those two necessities that for them true Freedom could proceed' and adding that 'it is not Grace, nor is it yet Dignity, which speaks to us from the superb
countenance of a Juno Ludovisi; it is neither the one nor the other because it is
both at once'.[34]

Although a statue (in this case, the Juno Ludovisi) is, in the strictest sense, lifeless,
nevertheless it can, through its form, seem to be alive; by contrast, a human being

FIGURE 3.2   Torso of Hercules of the Belvedere, Museo Pio-Clementino, Vatican Museums, Rome. In public domain via Wikimedia Commons.

(and we can think of plenty of examples …) can be alive in a biological sense, yet at the same time dead in every other. What is required, Schiller argues, to enhance life is to fuse form and life; more precisely, the form must be infused with life (in the case of the work of art) and life must be infused with form (in the case of the human being), so as to produce works of art that seem alive — and human beings that are works of art. (In this way, Schiller posits a relation between 'the whole edifice of the art of the beautiful', *das ganze Gebäude der ästhetischen Kunst*, and that 'of the still more difficult art of living' or *Lebenskunst*.[35])

(A similar argument has recently been made by the French philosopher and theologian, Bertrand Vergely, in his *Deviens qui tu es* [2014], a work that sets itself the task of demonstrating the relevance of Pindar's injunction, 'become who you are' — an inspiration to Ovid, St Augustine, and Nietzsche alike — to us today. Here Vergely considers the function of the statue for the ancient Greeks — and for us. To begin with, he considers how a statue can reveal the dual source of reality: as material and as formal [intellectual, abstract, spiritual]. For the sculptor, he argues, requires a block of marble, but he also requires a form [or something that produces a form — an idea or, in Greek, *eidos*]. In this way, Vergely believes, the Greeks made an important conceptual breakthrough, understanding that reality is composed of matter *and* FORM.[36])

In his poem 'The Ideal and Life' Schiller uses, in a far more extended way than he does in *On the Aesthetic Education*, the metaphor of beauty-as-shadow and the metaphor of beauty-through-sculpture. This metaphor constitutes the entirety of stanza 8 (originally, stanza 11):

> If to breathe a soul through soulless nature,
> Touch with life each marble feature,
> Genius, full of active impulse, yearns,
> Then, then every nerve of toil exert thou,
> Then the stubborn element convert thou
> To the Ideal that within thee burns.
> Only to a will, by nought defeated,
> Sparkle up the springs of Truth, unsealed;
> Only to strong chisel strokes repeated
> Will the brittle marble yield.[37]

So Schiller's sculptor, like Zarathustra in 'On the Blissful Islands', must — in order to give reality to 'the image of [his] visions' — 'drive his hammer to the stone', he must make his hammer 'rage fiercely against its prison', so that 'fragments fly from the stone'.

Schiller's poem suggests that, as we drive into the material realm, as we penetrate the physical block of marble, so we also 'rise up' into the aesthetic realm: as we chip away with the hammer — energetically, but precisely — so the statue also 'emerges' from the marble block:

> But press on; the sphere of Beauty gaining!
> There find all thy toils remaining
> With the matter, they o'er came, behind.
> [*Aber dringt bis in der Schönheit Sphäre,*
> *Und im Staube bleibt die Schwere{*[38]*}*
> *Mit dem Stoff, den sie beherrscht, zurück.*]
> Not from hard stone forced with painful wringing,
> Light and slender, as from nothing springing,
> Stands the form before the ravished mind.[39]

Thus Schiller's conception of form stands in a peculiar relation to Plato's notion of form: on Schiller's account, form can be apprehended intellectually, but also made sensible; the ideal exists in another realm, it is true, but it can also be realized in the here-and-now; beauty is absolute, but it can also be made apparent. Yet what Schiller presents as an argument in the aesthetic sphere reflects Plato's moral teaching: that by embodying form (through giving body to it), and by bringing forth the idea (and the ideal), we make our lives beautiful and thereby we attain the 'good life'. (Or as we find this idea in Michelangelo's sonnet, 'Nay, prithee tell me, Love' (*Dimmi di grazia, amor*), it is in the power of the soul not to become lost in the world of sense, but to make the sensory world like itself, *Quibi si fa divina, onesta e bella, / com' a sè simil vuol cosa immortale*, '[Beauty is] transfigured; for the soul confers / on what she holds, her own divinity'.[40])

Hence, it is entirely in line with Schiller's argument in *On the Aesthetic Education* that, in 'The Ideal and Life', the complement to the production of the work of art (here, the marble statue) is the transformation of the individual life (represented here through the fate of Heracles — a figure who already from birth, as the offspring of Zeus and Alcmene, is half-god, half-man). In his letter to Schiller, Humboldt wondered whether it was sufficiently clear that stanzas 13 and 14 (in the work's final form, stanzas 10 and 11) referred to 'the territory of beauty, the aesthetic kingdom' (*das Gebiet der Schönheit, das ästhetische Reich*), and he worried that the phrase 'in thought's free realm' (*in die Freiheit der Gedanken*) was not precise enough. Humboldt was proved right to be concerned: in fact, these lines can easily be misread in a lazily (if conventionally) Platonic way as advocating an escape from the body:

> But the senses' limit leave behind you,
> Till in Thoughts' free realm ye find you, —
> And the frightful apparition's gone,
> And th' eternal chasm ist fast filling;[41]

However, Humboldt's careful analysis of the argument in these lines accurately captures what Schiller is really saying: 'The human being who is *merely* morally developed gets caught in an anxiously difficult situation when he compares the infinite demand of the law with the limitations of his finite powers', but 'if at the same time he develops himself aesthetically', then 'this conflict in him will cease'. And here Humboldt tells us exactly what he understands by this aesthetic development when he writes: 'if he refashions his inner being, by means of the idea of beauty, into a higher nature, so that harmony enters into his drives and what previously for him was duty becomes freely-willed inclination'. Hence, in the following lines of this stanza in his poem, Schiller makes the following dramatic declaration:

> Be the God in all thine own pure willing,
> And He rises from His dreaded throne.
> [*Nehmt die Gottheit auf in euren Willen,*
> *Und sie steigt von ihrem Weltenthron.*]

Or to put it another way (and using the words of Schiller's own letter to Humboldt of 30 November 1795), the aesthetic enables the individual to make 'the transition from the human being to God' (*diesem Uebertritt des Menschen in den Gott*),[42] a transition that Schiller's poem *states in a propositional form*, but which, in his future (and never executed) poem, he wanted *artistically to represent*. Yet the references in the concluding stanzas to Heracles's ascent to Mount Olympus[43] and his nuptials with Hebe nevertheless convey a sense of the momentousness of Schiller's thinking here, as Heracles is received in the Hall of Cronion (i.e., Zeus) and welcomed by the gods, while his wife-to-be, Hebe, 'the goddess with the blushing cheeks', smiles and hands him the nectar-filled cup …

In the meantime, we are left with — with what? Not so much looking forward, as in 'The Artists' (*Die Künstler*), to a future synthesis of truth and morality, or looking forward (on the basis of Schiller's remarks in his letter to Humboldt) to a poem that, in the end, Schiller would never write, as left with something eminently present in the here-and-now, whether the here-and-now be something good or something bad. And what could be more terrible than having to struggle, as the Trojan priest Laocoön did, with the giant sea serpents sent (according to Quintus Smyrnaeus, by Athena, or, according to Apollodorus, by Apollo) to strangle and to kill him and his two sons? In this stanza Schiller invokes the idea of something 'immortal', that is nevertheless not a part of the 'beyond', but rather something effective in this world, in this time, at this very moment:

> If ye must bear mortal pains and pining,
> If, with snakes around him twining,
> Priam's son must writhe with nameless smart,
> Then speak out the Man! Let wild cries, rending
> Heaven's cold, azure vault, be heard, and sending
> Pangs of pity through your feeling heart!
> Let the voice of suffering nature win you,
> And the crimson cheek of joy grow pale,
> And, for once, above th' Immortal in you
> Holy sympathy prevail!
> [*Und der heil'gen Sympathie erliege*
> *Das Unsterbliche in euch!*].[44]

Now, by speaking here about 'the immortal in you', or *das Unsterbliche in euch*, Schiller echoes an idea found elsewhere in his reference to being 'above the reach of time' (*frei von jeder Zeitgewalt*) and in his remarks in his *Aesthetic Letters* (Letter 22, §1) about the aesthetic condition: 'The aesthetic alone is a whole in itself' — like Plotinus's conception of the One? — 'since it comprises within itself all the conditions of both its origin and its continuance. Here alone do we feel reft out of time [*Hier allein fühlen wir uns wie aus der Zeit gerissen*], and our human nature expresses itself with a purity and *integrity*, as though it had yet suffered no impairment through the intervention of external forces'.[45] In these lines from *On the Aesthetic Education* and in this stanza from 'The Ideal and Life', Schiller touches on an extremely important theme in the philosophical tradition in terms of which, as a poet and as a thinker, it may be helpful to see him.

The Eternal Within

In the crucial passage in a dialogue attributed to Plato, the *First Alcibiades*, Socrates discusses with his eponymous interlocutor the question of how the soul can know itself. As always, the argument is structured around the format of question-and-answer:

SOCRATES: Can we say that there is anything about the soul which is more divine than that where knowing and understanding take place?

ALCIBIADES: No, we can't.

SOCRATES: Then that region in it resembles the divine [*theiôi*], and someone who looked at that and grasped everything — vision [*thean*, emended from *theon* = 'god'] and understanding — would have the best grasp of himself as well.[46]

In the immediately following passage, subsequently added by a later Neoplatonist, this argument is linked to a preceding discussion about the injunction of the Delphic Oracle, 'know thyself', and the role of vision as a model of knowledge:

SOCRATES: Just as mirrors are clearer, purer, and brighter than the reflecting surface of the eye, isn't God both purer and brighter than the best part of our soul?

ALCIBIADES: I would certainly think so, Socrates.

SOCRATES: So the way that we can best see and know ourselves is to use the finest mirror available and look at God and, on the human level, at the virtue of the soul.

ALCIBIADES: Yes.[47]

I describe this passage as crucial, because of the importance attached to it in the Neoplatonic tradition. In his *Theology of Plato*, Proclus observes that Socrates here promises that 'the soul entering into herself will behold all other things, and deity itself', and he compares this experience to an inititiation into the ancient Mysteries: 'As in the most holy of the mysteries' —, i.e., the Eleusinian — 'the mystics [...] genuinely receive in their bosom a divine illumination, and divested of their garments [...] participate of a divine nature', Proclus remarks, 'the same mode [...] takes place in the speculation of wholes'.[48] By turning within, Proclus argues, the soul also turns out to the universe:

> For the soul, when looking at things posterior to herself, beholds the shadows and images of beings; but when she turns to herself, she evolves her own essence, and the reasons which she contains. And at first indeed, she only, as it were, beholds herself; but, when she penetrates more profoundly into the knowledge of herself, she finds in herself both intellect, and the orders of beings. But when she proceeds into her interior recesses, and into the adytum [...] of the soul, she perceives with her eye closed, the genus of the Gods, and the unities of beings.[49]

What this means, Proclus concludes, is that 'all things reside in us according to the peculiarity of the soul, and through this we are naturally capable of knowing all things, by exciting the powers and the images of wholes which we contain'.[50] In so arguing, Proclus was developing the position found in Plato, and in the Neoplatonic tradition founded by Plotinus, for whom the very task of philosophy was (in the words recorded by Porphyry) 'to raise the divine in himself to the divine in the All'.[51]

Similarly, in the section of the second speech of Socrates in the *Phaedrus* devoted to the soul, Socrates offers an account of 'that place beyond the heavens [of which] none of our earthly poets has yet sung, and [of which] none shall sing worthily'.[52] On this mythical account, the moral forms are to be found in this 'place beyond the heavens', and it is here that the soul may behold them:

> It is there that true being dwells, without color or shape, that cannot be touched; reason alone, the soul's pilot, can behold it, and all true knowledge is knowledge thereof. [...] And while [the soul] is borne round she discerns justice, its very self, and likewise temperance, and knowledge [...], the veritable knowledge of being that veritably is. And when she has contemplated likewise and feasted upon all else that has true being, she descends again within the heavens and comes back home.[53]

But in the thought of Plotinus, however, this account undergoes a remarkable transformation. For here, the moral forms are to be found, not in 'that place above the heavens', but within the soul itself, and what, in Plato, the soul sees as transcendent realities are, in Plotinus, introjected within and made part of the soul's self-vision:[54]

> For it is not by running hither and thither outside of itself that the Soul understands morality and right conduct: it learns them of its own nature, in its contact with itself, in its intellectual grasp of itself, seeing deeply impressed upon it the images of its primal state.[55]

This notion that the divine can be found within the individual is also expressed in a topos already touched upon in Chapter 2, the 'inner man', but it is also, through the form of what Schiller calls 'the immortal within me', a significant motif in Enlightenment and post-Enlightenment thought as well.

For instance, in a remarkable passage in the fifth and final part of his *Ethics* (pub. 1677), Baruch Spinoza (1632–1677) tells us that we know — indeed, that we *experience* — that we are 'eternal':

> We feel and know by experience that we are eternal. [...] Although, therefore, we do not recollect that we existed before the body, we feel that our mind, insofar as it involves the essence of the body under the form of eternity, is eternal, and that this existence of the mind cannot be limited by time nor manifested through duration.[56]

It would take an entire volume to 'unpack' the reasoning behind and the implications of this passage, which stands against the backdrop of two different meanings of the term 'eternity': for Plato, the antithesis of time and the exclusion of any kind of temporal relations; for Aristotle, simply endless time.[57] As Harry Austryn Wolfson explains in his commentary on Spinoza's philosophy, 'this experience of immortality during our lifetime is personal and individual, as is everything else we experience during our lifetime', and Wolfson relates this experience to what Spinoza calls the 'third kind' of knowledge, the direct and intuitive knowledge of God or *scientia intuitiva* (part 5, propositions 25–33).[58]

From this 'third kind' of knowledge there arises, Spinoza claims, 'the highest possible peace of mind' (*summa, quaae dari potest, Mentis acquiescentia*) (part 5, proposition 27), a peace of mind which is, as Wolfson emphasizes, not just 'a foretaste of the eternal blessedness which awaits us after death' but is available to us 'during our lifetime'.[59] When in Jung's *Memories, Dreams, Reflections*, we read the following question, 'Are you related to something infinite or not?' (*MDR*, 356), we might well hear in it not just an echo, but a reformulation of Spinoza's invitation in the fifth part of his *Ethics* to regard the world (as he repeatedly puts it) *sub specie aeternitatis*, 'under the form of eternity'.[60]

Spinoza's argument about the experience of our eternity recurs in a work by F.W.J. Schelling. In his *System of Transcendental Idealism* (1800), we find Schelling, in the context of a discussion of the categorical imperative (or the moral law), writing about what he calls 'the eternal in me' as follows:

> [In transcendental philosophy] even the moral law is merely deduced as a condition of self-consciousness. This law originally applies to me, not insofar as I am this particular intelligence, for indeed it strikes down everything that belongs to individuality and completely destroys; it applies to me, rather, as an intelligence in general, to that which has as its immediate object the purely objective, the eternal in me [*das Ewige … in mir*].[61]

In other words the moral law applies to the individual not *qua* individual, but rather to the individual as a vehicle for, or as a bearer of, immortality; and thereby it makes us aware of what is 'eternal' within us. In so writing, however, Schelling was reformulating a point he had expressed five years earlier, in his *Philosophical Letters on Dogmatism and Criticism*:

> We all have a secret and wondrous capacity of withdrawing from temporal change into our innermost self, which we divest of every exterior accretion. There, in the form of immutability, we intuit the eternal in us [*das Ewige in uns*]. This intuition is the innermost and in the strictest sense our own experience, upon which depends everything we know and believe of a supersensuous world.[62]

For Schelling, there was a name for this wonderful faculty' — he called it 'intellectual intuition', but it seems akin to a kind of contemplation:

> We awaken from intellectual intuition as from a state of death. We awaken through reflection, that is, through a forced return to ourselves. But no return is thinkable without resistance, no reflection without an object. We designate as alive an activity intent upon objects alone and as dead an activity losing

itself in itself. [...] The I, on finding resistance, is *obliged* to take a stand against it, that is, to return into self. However, where sensuous intuition ceases, where everything objective vanishes, there is nothing but infinite expansion without a return into self. Should I maintain intellectual intuition I would cease to live; I would go "from time into eternity".[63]

What is here presented, with specific reference back to Spinoza, as 'intellectual intuition', is taken up and broadened to apply to aesthetic apprehension more generally by Arthur Schopenhauer (1788–1860).

In a chapter in the second volume of *The World as Will and Representation* (1818; [2]1844) entitled 'On Death and its Relation to the Indestructibility of Our Inner Nature', Schopenhauer turns to a discussion of the immortality of the will: how can such a thing be? In answer to this question, Schopenhauer expounds 'nature's great doctrine of immortality', illustrated by the falling leaf — 'Fading in the autumn and about to fall, this leaf grieves over its own extinction [...] Oh, foolish leaf! Whither do you want to go? And whence are the others supposed to come? Where is the nothing, the abyss of which you fear?' — and by the insect — 'Whether the fly now buzzing round me goes to sleep in the evening and buzzes again the following morning, or whether it dies in the evening and in spring another fly buzzes which has emerged from its egg, this in itself is the same thing'. Taking these examples as models, Schopenhauer explains his (curiously secular) notion of 'temporal immortality' as follows: 'In spite of thousands of years of death and decay, there is still nothing lost, no atom of matter, still less anything of the inner being exhibiting itself as nature', so that 'accordingly we can at any moment cheerfully exclaim: "In spite of time, death, and decay, we are still all together!"'[64]

Shortly after the First World War, in 1921 the German phenomenologist and philosophical anthropologist, Max Scheler (1874–1928) published a collection of papers under the title, *On the Eternal in Man* (*Vom Ewigen im Menschen*).[65] In his preface to the first edition, Scheler explained that these essays were intended to develop ideas in his major philosophical work, *Formalism in Ethics and Non-Formal Values of Ethics* (*Der Formalismus in der Ethik und die materiale Wertethik*) (1913–1916).[66] His choice of title was intended to highlight 'that in man which makes him man, that whereby he has part in the eternal' (p. 11). While acknowledging that 'to few is granted grace to abide in happy wonder in the eternal and to conceive the rest of life as only a tortuous path to this highest goal' — i.e., to few is granted the grace to dwell on the blissful islands — Scheler nevertheless wanted to 'show how, from those spiritual sources in man where the divine and merely human streams commingle, the thirst of the hour can be satisfied, and the hope of a *nuova vita* restored' (p. 11). Such a demonstration, for Scheler, was part and parcel of what he called Europe's 'cultural reconstruction', and he added:

A man has a poor conception of the eternal if, merely grasping its contrast to the flow of time, he is unable to hear the soft voice of eternity in the most momentary demand which is made on the individual in the hear and now.

> For, rightly, conceived, the eternal is not sealed away from time in a simple
> juxtaposition: it timelessly embraces the content of time and its fulness, per-
> vading each of its moments. (p. 12)

Correspondingly, Scheler explained, the eternal is not 'an *asylum* into which a man
may flee, thinking himself unable to endure any more of history and life', even
if — Scheler is thinking of the 1920s, but his observations apply nearly a century
later — 'considerable numbers of young people today are determined by motives
of escapism' (p. 12). How do these people escape? Some, said Scheler, 'flee to the
mysticism of higher things, things superior to history' (we might think of this as the
New Age form of escapism); some, he said, 'take refuge where history is a flow apart
[*nebenhistorisch*], in the idyll of the naturalist, botanist, astronomer' (we might call
this the escapism of scientific specialism); while others, he added — 'and these are
the least edifying' — 'fly to the subhistorical world of the pleasure of the moment,
this being the antipole of eternity' (we might describe this as the escapism of false
hedonism, the escapism promoted by the popular culture industry and the 'fun'
ethic) (p. 12). Rejecting all of these, Scheler wanted to offer something very different: 'to acknowledge history, to see it in its hard reality — but to revive it with
the water of eternal springs — that is worthier than flight and more fitting to the
age' (p. 12).

If the theme of the eternal in us is an important one for the philosophers, it
is equally important for the poets, too. For instance, in the conclusion to the second text in a sequence of two fragmentary poems, 'The Ego' (*Das Ich*) and 'The
Self'(*Das Selbst*) published in a collection entitled *Gedichte und Reime* in 1797,
Johann Gottfried von Herder (1744–1803) articulates a similar moment of insight
into the eternity of the self as does Schiller:

> Calmly [an unconquerable mind]
> Looked into the abyss — saw the heaven above it,
> And said: "What in me dies, that is not me!
> What lives in me, my most vital part,
> What is eternal in me knows no end."
> [»*Was in mir lebet, mein Lebendigstes,*
> *Mein Ewiges kennet keinen Untergang.*«[67]]

And in arguably the most famous work of German literature, in Goethe's *Faust*,
the final scene in the final act of the work's second part, we see the angels carry
up to heaven Faust's 'immortal part', what a stage instruction in the text calls his
Unsterbliches, as Faust goes on his way to his encounter with the Eternal-Feminine.

Now it is possible, in Schiller's 'The Ideal and Life' and in Goethe's *Faust*, Part
Two, alike, to read this mention of the immortal, to *das Unsterbliche*, in a Platonic or
a Christian sense, as referring to the immortal soul. Yet it can also be read in a different way — and in an aesthetic sense, as referring to the quality that inheres in the
work of art, which, even if it is destroyed, nevertheless remains 'immortal'. It is in

this sense that one might say of Goethe that, during his visit to Italy, he 'discovered God' — when, during his second stay in Rome on 6 September 1787, he remarked as follows on the insight into the equivalence of art and nature he had gained from his exposure to the art of antiquity: 'These masterpieces of man were brought forth in obedience to the same laws as the masterpieces of Nature', he wrote, 'before them, all that is arbitrary and imaginary collapses: *there* is Necessity, *there* is God' (*da ist Notwendigkeit, da ist Gott*).[68]

So we could usefully compare Schiller's conception of the eternal with that found in the work of the aesthetician and novelist, Friedrich Theodor Vischer (1807–1887).[69] Towards the end of the nineteenth century, Vischer achieved considerable fame, thanks to his novel, *Auch Einer* (1879),[70] and in *Memories, Dreams, Reflections*, there is an allusion to the title of this work in the significant context of Jung's secret fear that he might have affinities with Friedrich Nietzsche (*MDR*, 122).

In important respects Vischer's novel, like much of the rest of his work, constitutes a discussion of the problem of idealism. (The role of idealism and realism in Vischer's thought in general and their relation to his aesthetic programme in particular has been discussed in some detail by Birgit Mersmann.[71]) Early on in the novel, the narrator refers to the idea of the novel's central fictional character, known by his initials, A.E.:

> The deeds and activities of the many have carved out something that stands above them, an upper floor, permanent structures, eternal laws, to serve which is to breathe the purest air, because this service lifts the one who serves into timelessness.[72]

Later, in the lengthy concluding section of entries from A.E.'s diary, we read:

> A second world in the world, a second nature above nature, the ethical world [...] rises above time and beyond time, is something unconditioned, truth in itself, one can ignore, for it is irrelevant, that it arose within time — eternal substances, that "hang up there inalienable and unbreakable, like the stars themselves".[73]

In these and in other passages one could regard Vischer as adopting a stance that is entirely consonant with Schiller's idealism, inasmuch as it has practical and pragmatic consequences.[74] It is an idealism that is, so to speak, entirely realistic; as an idealism, it is also (and by that very token) a realism.

Nor should one take the elaborate rhetoric of Schiller's poem, 'The Ideal and Life', as advocating a flight from reality, even when in his third (originally, his fourth stanza) he urges us:

> Would ye soar aloft on her [i.e., form's] strong pinion?
> Fling away all earthly care and strife?
> Up into th' Ideal's [originally: the shadows'] pure dominion

Fly up from this dull, narrow life!
[*Fliehet aus dem engen dumpfen Leben*
In des Ideales Reich! {In der Schönheit Schattenreich!}][75]

It is important not to misunderstand these lines: in them, Schiller is not advising us to flee reality, he is urging us to flee what he called (in his letter to Humboldt of 29 November 1795) *alles Unrat der Wirklichkeit*, 'all the filth of reality' (*NA* 28, 120).

Schiller's meaning becomes clearer if we remember what he told Humboldt about reality in its relation to the ideal (in his discussion about how it is revealed in the idyll). In the idyll, so he argued (as we recalled above) in *On the Naïve and Sentimental in Literature*, we find 'the concept of a conflict completely resolved in the individual man and in society, of a free union of the inclinations with the law, of a nature purified to the highest moral dignity' — or, in other words, 'the ideal of beauty applied to real life' (*das Ideal der Schönheit, auf das wirkliche Leben angewendet*) — note well, *applied to real life* — with the result that 'all conflict between reality and the ideal [...] is completely resolved' (*aller Gegensatz der Wirklichkeit mit dem Ideale [...] vollkommen aufgehoben sei*).[76] Unlike in the elegy and in the satire, in the idyll we find an absence of conflict; but this does not mean that the idyll is not interested in reality, it means that, in the idyll, reality itself is transformed. For the ideal shows us what it is like to apply the *ideal* of beauty to *real* life.

In those stanzas that present the extended metaphor of the statue being sculpted, and in those lines that urge us: 'But press on; the sphere of Beauty gaining! / There find all thy toils remaining / With the matter, they o'ercame, behind' (see above), Schiller is restating his thesis about the transformative power of (aesthetic) form as he had formulated it a couple of years earlier in a letter to C.G. Körner, part of his *Kallias* project, of 28 February 1793: 'It is [...] the form which must win over the matter in artistic depiction' ([*es ist*] *die Form welche in der Kunstdarstellung den Stoff besiegt haben muß*), because 'in an artwork, the *matter* [...] must lose itself in the *form* [...], the *body* in the *idea*, the *reality* in the *appearance*'.[77]

Schiller, no matter what some of his critics might think, is not so naïve as to think that the work of art abolishes reality; and yet he nevertheless believes, and with good reason, that art changes reality — it (literally) trans-*forms* it. As he went on to explain to Körner, when he spoke of 'reality in appearance' (*die Wirklichkeit in der Erscheinung*), reality here means 'the real [*das Reale*], which, in an artwork, can only ever be the material [*die Materie*] and must be set against the formal or the idea [*dem Formalen oder der Idee*] which the artist must effect on the material'. To illustrate his point that 'form in an artwork is mere appearance' (*die Form ist an einem Kunstwerk bloße Erscheinung*), he turned to the example of a statue: 'Marble seems to be a person, but remains, in reality, marble' — although the statue also *is* the god, the man, the woman, or whatever (or whomever) it depicts. Two years later, in *On the Aesthetic Education*, Schiller expanded on this argument and on his definition in the *Kallias* letters of beauty as 'freedom in appearance' (*Freiheit in der Erscheinung*).[78] For in this treatise Schiller makes explicit the link between the *form*-al and the trans-*form*-ative aspects of art:

In a truly successful work of art the contents should effect nothing, the form everything; for only through the form is the whole man affected, through the subject-matter, by contrast, only one or other of his functions. Subject-matter, then, however sublime and all-embracing it may be, always has a limiting effect upon the spirit, and it is only from form that true aesthetic freedom can be looked for. Herein, then, resides the real secret of the master in any art: *that he can make his form consume his material.*[79]

(Letter 22, §5)

Schiller's language here, and in his letter to Körner, contains, it is true, a quality of violence: he speaks of expunging or consuming (*vertilgen*), of form 'winning over' (*besiegen*), of the reality being 'lost' (*verlieren*) in the appearance;[80] so, too, in his poem does he remark that 'only to strong chisel strokes repeated / Will the brittle marble yield'. But this violence is not unfocused or destructive: it is a necessary violence to bring into being something of a higher order, something beautiful; such violence is intimately bound up with the dialectic of creation and destruction,[81] but it is not gratuitous or aggressive, it is (hugely) constructive and (enormously) productive.

In his recent study of ancient Greek philosophy, Bertrand Vergely has insisted on the importance of the ideal for an understanding of reality. According to Vergely, it is a mistake to think that dualism divides reality and that monism offers a unified vision of reality. Rather, he argues, monism divides reality and dualism respects its unity, for if we say that reality is matter and spirit, then even if it is dualist to speak of matter and spirit, one is 'respecting all aspects of reality'; whereas, if one reduces everything to matter, then although one gives the impression of being in a unity, one is 'a dualist in opposing spirit'.[82] (Ultimately, as Vergely recognizes, this is an argument in defence of the sacred. For if one 'reduces the world to the simply visible world of the objects of everyday life' — if, in other words, one 'makes the world *banal*, apart from depriving it of meaning', so that the world no longer corresponds to anything, because there is no longer a translation for it on an invisible level — then one sets up a 'pernicious dualism', which 'reduces everything to the visible and to a banality expressing an implicit opposition to the invisible level'.[83])

Drawing on Plato, Vergely goes on to contend that, in order to understand being, we need to 'go through the ideal'; something, in his view, that artists have always understood. If we look at the paintings of Van Gogh, for instance, we feel that all the trees he paints are the expression of an 'essential tree' (*un arbre fondamental*) that we cannot see; and because all these trees express this invisible tree, we see them — and are struck by them. Creation, then, means 'reintroducing the invisible into the visible, in order to reveal the invisible' — as Plato well understood.[84] Suppose we 'present a tree without linking it to its invisible double', without 'expressing the mystery of its creation', the tree is 'insignificant' — and we do not see it. But if, Vergely suggests, we 'link a visible tree to a unique and unimaginable tree one cannot see, the tree becomes lit up'.[85] (Is such a tree an example of what Goethe meant by the 'primal plant' or *Urpflanze*?)

In the case of Plato's philosophy, Vergely argues, the ideal is placed above reality, thus opposing the intelligible to the sensible, in order to try and show that the former cannot be reduced to the latter. Although Nietzsche reads this as an expression of a hatred life and of nihilism, Vergely disagrees: 'nihilism does not come from the nostalgia' — the *algos* of *nostos*, the 'suffering' for a 'return' — 'for the ideal but rather from the fact that, trying to be the strongest by crushing the world around oneself, one no longer has any ideal nor any nostalgia'.[86] Far from being a nihilist, Vergely continues, Plato's resistance to confusing reality and the ideal is a demonstration of his anti-nihilism, and he points to recent work by two French Marxists, François Châtelet and Alain Badiou, on Plato as a political revolutionary.[87] For Vergely, as for the Neoplatonists before him, Plato can be understood with reference to Homer. In the *Iliad*, and in the desire for conquest embodied by the valiant warrior, Achilles, we see the desire to conquer the world, as well as the vanity of this project; while in the *Odyssey*, and in the desire of Odysseus to return, in his nostalgia for Ithaca (and for the interior native land), we see how philosophy itself is a voyage to Ithaca, distancing itself from the exterior world by means of the interior one.[88]

Back on the Blissful Islands

Nietzsche must have known Schiller's poem 'The Ideal and Life': first, because it is (or was) such a famous text; and second, because Nietzsche playfully alludes to it at one point in his writings.[89] Read in the light of Schiller's poem — correctly understood, that is — Zarathustra's reference to 'the beauty of the superman' coming to him 'as a shadow' can be seen as an example of rhetorical repetition, for the *shadow* (in the Schillerian sense) *is beauty*. 'Ah, my brothers', Zarathustra cries, 'What are the gods to me now!', and what indeed are the gods, after divinity (*die Gottheit*) itself has been subsumed into the human will (*in euren Willen*), transforming this will into the will-to-transform: the will to transform (aesthetically) the block of marble into a beautiful statue, into a 'living form', which is the same as the will to transform (aesthetically) the individual into a beautiful human being — that is to say, into a superman?

For surely in the moment — in the words of Goethe's famous essay on Winckelmann of 1805 — 'when man's nature functions soundly as a whole, when he feels that the world of which he is part is a huge, beautiful, admirable and worthy whole [*einem großen, schönen, würdigen und werten Ganzen*], when this harmony gives him pure and uninhibited delight, then the universe, if it were capable of emotion, would rejoice at having reached its goal [*Ziel*] and admire the crowning glory of its own evolution'.[90] Which in turn poses the question asked by Goethe in this essay:

> For, what purpose would those countless suns and planets and moons serve, those stars and milky ways, comets and nebulae, those created and evolving worlds, if a happy human being did not ultimately emerge to enjoy unconsciously existence [*wenn sich nicht zuletzt ein glücklicher Mensch unbewußt seines Daseins erfreut*]?[91]

At this point on our journey, which so far has led us from the furthest point of the earth and the Blissful Islands to the heights of Mount Olympus; from Plato and Plotinus to the Renaissance Neoplatonism of Michelangelo; and from the German classical aesthetics of Goethe and Schiller to the literary idealism of Friedrich Theodor Vischer, let us pause, look back, and consider whether we have answered those questions posed from the outset by the triumphant conclusion of Zarathustra's discourse, 'On the Blissful Islands'.

In the final lines of that discourse, the beauty of the superman comes to Zarathustra as a shadow, in a reverse parallel to the way in which the 'overshadowing' of Mary by the Holy Spirit betokens the moment of Incarnation and the 'indwelling' of the divine in the believer. In effect, Nietzsche shifts this discourse of 'overshadowing' from the religious to the aesthetic sphere; or, arguably, he returns the religious sphere to the aesthetic for which it is a metaphor. The shadow or the inferior man represents the part of the self that yearns for its own incarnation, actualization, and realization, as part of the totality that — like the divine, as conceived by Jung — contains all things. As the substitute for God *and* the expression of the self, the superman represents this totality — and thus beauty, for beauty *is* totality: it is light *and* dark, good *and* bad.

The complementarity of the opposites is a doctrine that is stated several times by Goethe. In his tribute to Shakespeare of 1771, for instance, Goethe suggested that 'what noble philosophers have said about the world applies to Shakespeare too' — in other words, that 'what we call evil is only the other side of good; evil is necessary for good to exist and is part of the whole, just as the tropics must be torrid and Lapland frigid for there to be a temperate zone'.[92] Likewise, in his review of Sulzer's *The Fine Arts* in 1772, he stated that, in nature, 'beautiful and ugly, good and evil, all exist side by side with equal rights'.[93]

And it is a doctrine that we can also find presented with considerable insistence in the writings of Jung. In *The Relations between the Ego and the Unconscious* (1929), for example, Jung remarks that 'what to contemporary experience and knowledge appears to be evil or at least devoid of meaning and value, can to a higher level of experience and knowledge appear as the source of the best'. Echoing Zarathustra's cry, 'solitary man, you are going the way to yourself! And your way leads past yourself and your seven devils! [...] solitary man, you are going the way of the creator: you want to create a god from your seven devils!',[94] Jung adds, tongue-in-cheek — 'depending on what use one makes of one's seven devils' (*CW* 7 §400). Indeed, Jung goes on to propose in explicit terms the complementarity of good and evil, inviting us to imagine the following dialogue between the conscious mind and the unconscious. Consciousness asks: 'Why is there this terrible conflict between good and evil?' To which the unconscious replies: 'Look more closely — each needs the other; even in the best, precisely in the best, there is the seed of evil, and there is nothing so bad that something good could not proceed from it' (*CW* 7 §289).

Embracing these Goethean and Nietzschean notions of the complementarity of good and evil, Jung argues that to explain (away) our 'seven devils' as meaningless is to rob our personality of its own shadow, without which it would 'lose its shape' (*ihre Gestalt verlieren*). As we have seen, in his *Aesthetic Letters*, Schiller identifies 'living form' (*lebende Gestalt*) with beauty (Letter 15 §2); and, in *Psychological Types*, Jung identifies the living form with the symbol which unites the opposites and enables psychological progress (*CW* 6 §171). That the persona is nothing other than the beginning of the aesthetic formation of the individual is also suggested by Jung's dictum, 'the "living form" needs deep shadow if it is to appear plastic' (*die "lebende Gestalt" bedarf tiefer Schatten, um plastisch zu erscheinen*) (*CW* 7 §400) — or, as one might also translate that phrase, *if it is to appear as a sculpture*.

Of those opposites, none is greater — with the possible exception of the body-mind opposition — than the opposition of freedom and necessity. Yet the tradition of which Goethe and Nietzsche (and, subsequently, Jung) are a part seeks to unite precisely this pair of opposites, Freedom and Necessity. In his journey to Italy, as we have seen, Goethe came to the following astounding conclusion. 'These masterpieces of man were brought forth in obedience to the same laws as the masterpieces of Nature', he wrote, 'before them, all that is arbitrary and imaginary collapses: *there* is Necessity, *there* is God [*da ist Notwendigkeit, da ist Gott*]'. Similarly, in *Dichtung und Wahrheit* (part 3, book 11) Goethe emphasized the extent to which the development of the personality is dependent upon a fruitful, if aporetical, conjunction of necessity and freedom. 'Our lives, like the context in which we live, are an incomprehensible mixture of freedom and necessity', he maintained, 'our desires proclaim in advance what we will do under any set of circumstances'. At the same time, as he recognized, these circumstances 'control us in their own way'. The reflection concludes with the dictum that 'the "what" is within us, the "how" rarely depends on us, the "why" we dare not inquire about, and therefore we are correctly referred to the *quia*'[95] — *quia* here being 'the "because"', what emerges from this conjunction of the individual and his or her circumstances, a 'because' which is more than purely causal.

In his turn, in a passage from *The Gay Science* that must surely be one of the most moving in the whole of his writings, Nietzsche took upon himself the following New Year's resolution in 1882: 'I want to learn more and more to see as beautiful what is necessary in things [*das Notwendige an den Dingen als das Schöne sehen*]', he wrote, and he did so on the understanding that this commitment would have existential implications, for then he would be 'one of those who make things beautiful'.[96] And this beauty would consist in an affirmation of the whole, embodied in the concept of *amor fati*: 'I do not want to wage war against what is ugly', Nietzsche writes, in Jungian terms accepting the ugliest man or the shadow, 'I do not want to accuse; I do not even want to accuse those who accuse', and he added: '*Looking away* shall be my only negation […] some day I wish to be only a Yes-sayer'.[97] Like the figure of Goethe as Nietzsche envisaged it in that remarkable passage of encomium in *Twilight of the Idols*, this view of the world invites us to 'aspire to *totality*', it encourages us to believe the individual should '*create* himself' (or herself), it bestows on us 'the *faith* that only what is separate and individual may be rejected, that in the totality everything is redeemed and affirmed', so that 'a spirit thus *emancipated* stands in the midst of the universe with a joyful and trusting fatalism'.[98] True, this view of the world is described here by Nietzsche as 'realist'; but the counterpoint to such a view is not idealism as such, but 'the unreal'.

What underlines the aesthetics of German classicism, and constitutes the central meeting-point between this tradition and the school of analytical psychology, is the conception of *beauty as wholeness*. As we have seen, in his *Letters on the Aesthetic Education*, Schiller tells us how the material drive (*Stofftrieb*) and the formal drive (*Formtrieb*) give rise, through a process of mutual subordination, to a third drive, the ludic drive (*Spieltrieb*), which in turn, through a synthesis of both drives, brings about beauty. This theory of aesthetics is entirely compatible with the argumentational structure of the alchemical-cum-mystical 'axiom of Maria', as the mutual subordination of the two drives ($2 \times 2 = 4$) gives rise to a third drive ($2 + 1 = 3$) which, combining the two drives ($1 + 1 = 2$), brings forth the one ($1 = 1$), or the unity of beauty.

What Schiller presents in propositional form in his *Aesthetic Letters* is presented by Goethe in poetic-dramatic form. In the concluding Act of *Faust*, Part Two, Goethe reintroduces the mythological figure of Lynceus, the keeper on the watchtower of Faust's palace. We first encounter this figure in Act III, where he is brought, as a bound prisoner, before Helena, accused of having failed to announce her arrival. In other words, he failed to notice the arrival of Beauty (because Helena is the most beautiful woman in the world), and he explains his failure to do so because he was 'blinded' by her: 'For this beauty, which is blinding, / Blinded me, a poor man, quite' (*Diese Schönheit, wie sie blendet, / Blendete mich Armen ganz*).[99]

Now Goethe's source for this figure is the Greek mythological story of the Argonauts, the heroes who accompanied Jason on his quest to find the golden fleece. According to the legend, Lynceus served as watchman because his eyes were so sharp he could even see beneath the earth, and so he became a proverbial figure of penetrating vision.[100] In fact, it is in the sense that 'seeing into the very deeps of the earth' can be understood as talking about 'eyes in the divine' that Plotinus, in his *Ennead* 'On Intellectual Beauty', uses the myth of Lynceus.[101] To contemplate intellectual beauty is, says Plotinus, (using an Homeric expression) to 'live at ease' (cf. *Iliad*, book 6, l. 138) — or, to put it another way, it is to live on the blissful islands. For 'no weariness', so Plotinus maintains, 'overtakes this vision which yet brings no such satiety as would call for its ending'.[102] When, in Act V of *Faust*, Part Two, Lynceus returns, it is his vision of what the aged Faust has achieved that is emphasized: Lynceus sees the setting sun, the ships entering into the harbour, their pennants fluttering, their masts standing proud — 'Good fortune greets you in your latter days' (*Dich grüßt das Glück zur höchsten Zeit*).[103] Later, in the scene set in 'Deep Night', i.e., in darkness, Lynceus sings from his watchtower:

> Born to be seeing,
> Commanded to gaze,
> Sworn to the tower,
> I relish the world.
> I look in the distance,

I look at what is close,
At the moon, at the stars,
At the wood, at the deer.
In all things I see
Th' eternal design
[*Die ewige Zier*],
And as it is pleasing,
It's pleasing to me.
You fortunate eyes,
Whatever you've seen,
Let it be as it may,
It was lovely to me!
[*Es sei, wie es wolle,
Es war doch so schön!*][104]

To the theme of cosmic beauty, *die ewige Zier*, the context of these lines forms a tragic counterpoint: as he gazes out from his tower, Lynceus becomes witness to the destruction of the cottage of the old couple, Philemon and Baucis — and of them along with it. So what this much-cited (and often misunderstood) passage offers is no casual providentialism: the beauty of the world, Goethe is saying, includes ugliness, includes destruction, it includes the darkness in which this scene is set.

This message, which arguably runs throughout the whole of *Faust*, is found earlier in Part Two in two lines which Nietzsche, in his early writings, persistently cites.[105] These are lines spoken by Faust, in an exchange with Chiron the centaur in the Classical Walpurgisnacht of Act II. Desirous of being taken to Manto, a Thessalian sorceress with necromantic powers who will aid him on his descent to Persephone to recover Helena from the realm of the dead, Faust says: 'And shouldn't I, with the most passionate power, / Bring back to life that incomparable figure?' (*Und soll ich nicht, sehnsüchtigster Gewalt, / Ins Leben ziehn die einzigste Gestalt?*).[106] In these lines we find a quotation that links together the key themes of Nietzsche's mature thought, namely *Gewalt* (or the will-to-power), *Gestalt* (or aesthetic form), and *Leben* (or life, vitality).

In a collection of aphorisms in his notebooks for Summer and Autumn 1882, Nietzsche observes, using a vocabulary reminiscent of Goethe's *Selige Sehnsucht*, in one of these fragmentary remarks: 'When scepticism and desire come together in union, mysticism arises' (*Wenn Skepsis und Sehnsucht sich begatten, entsteht die Mystik*).[107] After all he has to say about organised religion, about Platonism, and about Idealism, how can it be at all possible to describe Nietzsche as a mystic? Yet perhaps, in a sense, we can: as Raphaël Enthoven has observed, *Nietzsche est un penseur plotinien, parce que Nietzsche est mystique*.[108] After all, in a study published over a decade ago entitled *Nietzsche — Mystik als Selbstversuch* (2000), Herbert Theierl drew attention to the link between, on the one hand, death and the image of sunset as a return to the elements in *Zarathustra*, and, on the other, the 'naïve' nature mysticism expressed in Hölderlin's *Empedokles* and Goethe's *Selige Sehnsucht*, arguing that Nietzsche's dialectical linking of *Untergang* and *Übermensch* transcends this model and attains 'the hermetic expressive world of speculative mysticism'.[109] For Theierl, we can make a connection from Nietzsche's reference in *The Birth of Tragedy* to 'mystical self-abnegation' (*mystische Selbstentäusserung*)[110] and to Meister Eckhart's declaration in his sermon 'Of Two Ways' that 'the highest delight that can be granted the spirit is to flow again into the nothingness of its primordial image and — as the self — entirely to lose oneself in it' (*die höchste Wonne, die dem Geist zu teil wird, ist, wieder in das Nichts seines Urbildes zu verfließen und — als Selbst — darin völlig verloren zu sein*).[111]

In his discourse 'On the Blissful Islands' there is a remarkable sense of expectation, of potential epiphany, and this sense — which, in a way, pervades the entirety of *Zarathustra*, right from his decision in the Prologue to 'descend' and to 'go down,' in order to proclaim the doctrine of the superman,[112] to his ecstatic declaration at the end of 'The Sign, 'This is *my* morning, *my* day begins: *rise up now, rise up, great noontide!*', and his departure from his cave, 'glowing and strong, like a morning sun emerging from behind dark mountains'[113] — can also be detected later in Part Two, in a discourse entitled 'Of the Sublime Men' (again, with another nod in the direction of a familiar Schillerian theme). Here Zarathustra encourages his listeners by recalling his advice to the 'sublime man', that is to say, 'a solemn man, a penitent of the spirit' — and, by this token, an ugly man: 'oh, how my soul laughed at his ugliness!'.

In a stunning image, Zarathustra brings together the lower and the higher, the bodily and the spiritual, the earthly and the heavenly, when he says: 'To be sure, I love in him the neck of the ox; but now I want to see the eye of the angel, too'.[114] To the various animals found in the menagerie that is *Thus Spoke Zarathustra*, i.e., to the eagle and the serpent, to the camel, the lion, and the child, to the tarantula, to the leech, and to the ass, here another creature is added, the ox: a symbol of 'the earth', of which his 'happiness' should 'smell', although not just any ordinary ox, but a white one — 'a white ox, snorting and bellowing as he goes before the plough: and his bellowing, too, should laud all earthly things!' Like the ox, we should submit to the needs of the earth, that earth to which, in the exhortation from the Prologue, we should remain 'true';[115] but as an ox, we should be white, our thick 'neck' should be accompanied by an angelic 'eye', so that we do not merely 'tame monsters' or 'solve riddles', but we should 'redeem' our monsters and riddles, by 'transform[ing] them into heavenly children'.[116] (After all, according to Pliny the Elder, even the blissful islands are 'plagued with the rotting carcasses of monstrous sea creatures that are constantly being cast ashore by the sea',[117] but can we turn these dead monsters into 'new playthings' and 'new coloured sea-shells'?)[118]

'Still are the depths of my sea', says Zarathustra, and 'who could guess that it hides playful monsters?'[119] Thus Zarathustra begins his discourse on the figure of the *sublime man*, or the man of moral sublimity, a figure whose posture (according to Babette Babich) recalls variously the ancient *kouroi* (or male youths) from the Archaic period of Greece, the Apollo Lyceus, the Apollo Kitharoidos, the Doryphoros (or youth carrying a spear), or the Barberini Faun.[120] For Zarathustra, what the man of moral sublimity must learn to do is to temper his heroism with gracefulness. In other words, however he holds his arm across his head, he must learn to become — like the superman — *beautiful*, and he must learn to emerge, so to speak, *from his shadow*:

> Truly, his longing should be silenced and immersed not in satiety but in beauty! The generosity of the magnanimous man should include gracefulness.
>
> With his arm laid across his head: that is how the hero should rest, that is also how he should overcome his rest.
>
> But it is precisely to the hero that *beauty* is the most difficult of all things. Beauty is unattainable to all violent wills.
>
> A little more, a little less: precisely that is much here, here that is the most of all.[121]

Like the sculptor creating the statue, an uncontrolled and unfocussed violence is no good: we need to extract a little more *here*, add another touch *there*; and these 'little things' add up to a lot, indeed they add up to 'the most of all'. Thus power is not simply a question of *shock and awe*, in fact it has nothing at all to do with *shock and awe*, but it has everything to do with delicacy, with 'grace' (yet another Schillerian term),[122] with 'beauty':

> When power grows gracious and descends into the visible: I call such descending beauty.
>
> And I desire beauty from no one so much as I desire it from you, you man of power: may your goodness be your ultimate self-overpowering.
>
> [...]
>
> You should aspire to the virtue of the pillar: the higher it rises, the fairer and more graceful it grows, but inwardly harder and able to bear more weight.[123]

Thus Zarathustra's advice to the sublime man culminates in the exhortation to emulate a stone pillar and, as it were, to internalize the message of self-sculpting or turning onself into a statue. Reversing the negative image of the mirror found at the beginning of Part Two in 'The Child with the Mirror', where — in a dream — Zarathustra sees his teachings contorted and distorted by his enemies, the sublime man is encouraged to make use of the mirror, to emphasize that he must not only become beautiful but *know* that he is beautiful: 'Yes, you sublime man, you too shall one day be fair and hold the mirror before your own beauty. / Then your soul will shudder with divine desires [...]'. In a final, climactic pronouncement, Zarathustra reveals 'the secret of the soul' and endorses the dream as a means of self-knowledge and self-transformation:

> This indeed is the secret of the soul: only when the hero has deserted the soul does there approach it in dreams — the superhero.[124]

The triumphant apotheosis of Heracles takes place at the moment when he is no longer being heroic: it is not when he is slaying the Nemean lion, or slaying the nine-headed Leraean hydra, not when capturing the golden hind of Artemis or the Erymanthian boar, not when cleaning the Augean stables or slaying the Stymphalian birds, not when capturing the Cretan bull or stealing the mares of Diomedes, not when obtaining the girdle of Hippolyta, the queen of the Amazons, or the cattle of the monster Geryon, not even when stealing the apples of the Hesperides or capturing and bringing back Cerberus — no, Heracles is at his most heroic when he is received into the Hall of Cronion, welcomed by the gods, and greeted by Hebe, his wife-to-be, 'the goddess with the blushing cheeks', who, shyly smiling, hands him a cup filled with nectar.

To enter the underworld, Heracles had to undergo the purification of the Lesser Mysteries of Eleusis, as Proclus had noted — 'Hence Hercules being purified by *sacred initiations*, and enjoying undefiled fruits, obtained at length a perfect establishment among the gods'[125] — and as the Hungarian philologist and mythologist, Carl Kerényi (1897–1973), explored in some detail on the basis of various ancient depictions.[126] Those Mysteries had, according to the translator and commentator Thomas Taylor, been 'designed by the ancient theologists, their founders, to signify occultly the condition of the unpurified soul invested with an earthly body, and enveloped in a material and physical nature';[127] according to another commentator, the Canadian-born historian of mysticism, Manly P. Hall (1901–1990), the Mysteries' 'gloom and depression' had represented 'the agony of the spiritual soul unable to express itself because it has accepted the limitations and illusions of the human environment'.[128] By contrast, when Heracles ascends to Mount Olympus, the only initiation required is the initiation of joy and love. Or does this ascent correspond to the Greater Mysteries of Eleusis, whose ceremonies are said to have 'obscurely intimated, by mystic and splended visions, the felicity of the soul both here and hereafter, when purified from the defilements of a material nature, and constantly elevated to the realities of intellectual [spiritual] vision'?[129] To the stage of the Mysteries where the neophyte, in his initiation, entered a series of chambers whose 'ever-increasing brilliancy' portrayed 'the ascent of the spirit from the lower worlds into the realms of bliss'?[130] Like the journey 'upward to the light even as some as are fabled to have ascended from Hades to the gods' of which Socrates speaks?[131]

For at the end of Schiller's poem 'The Ideal and Life', originally called 'The Realm of the Shadows', Heracles ascends to Mount Olympus, to the realm where dwell the Olympian gods, 'the blessed ones' (*die Seligen*) in a form of life that is 'ever clear, and mirror-pure, and even' (*ewigklar und spiegelrein und eben*) (ll. 1–3). Or, to put it another way, Heracles accedes to the *glückselige Inseln* or to the blissful islands, the traditional resting-place of the heroes. Schiller and Nietzsche, so frequently placed at opposite corners of the intellectual-historical scheme of things, are united in their insistence on the possibility, in the here-and-now, of happiness or joy or *die Freude*, what Schiller in his famous 'Ode to Joy' (or *An die Freude*) called 'the daughter from Elysium' (*Tochter aus Elysium*), using Homer's name for the blissful islands. Yet this is not the Elysium of which, in 'The Artists' (*Die Künstler*), Schiller says that it is some sense unreal: Venus Cypria — his name for what Pausanias in Plato's *Symposium* calls Aphrodite Pandemos (or 'common Aphrodite')[132] — paints it deceptively on the dungeon wall (*malt mit lieblichem Betruge / Elysium auf seine Kerkerwand*). Rather, this is a very real Elysium, a really existing Elysium, i.e., the Elysium of joy. So, in the end, Zarathustra was right: there *are* still blissful islands! And where are they? If, as Voltaire quipped, 'paradise is where I am', then the blissful islands are, to borrow a phrase from Laurie Anderson's definition of paradise, *exactly like where you are right now — only much, much better* …[133]

After all, we should remember Olympiodorus the Younger of Alexandria's remark in his commentary in Plato's *Gorgias* about the blissful islands. The backdrop to his comment is the observation that 'the philosophers liken human life to the sea, because it is disturbed and concerned with begetting and salty and full of toil' (and that is surely true): 'Note that islands rise above the sea, being higher', so 'that constitution which rises above life and over becoming is what they call the Isles of the Blessed', and 'the same thing applies to the Elysian plain', adding: 'And this is also why Heracles performed his final labour in the western regions — he laboured against the dark and earthly life, and finally he lived in the daytime, i.e., in truth and light'.[134] As Thomas Taylor remarked in his treatise on the Eleusinian Mysteries, anyone who, even 'in the present state', 'vanquishes as much as possible a corporeal life, [...] passes in reality into the fortunate islands of the soul, and lives surrounded with the bright splendours of truth and wisdom proceeding from the sun of good'.[135] So where are the blissful islands? *Exactly where you are right now.*

This insight constitutes a lesson that was well understood by the great German Symbolist Stefan George (1868–1933), many of whose poems constitute aesthetic transmutations of events, individuals, or memories from his life. A good example can be found in the twenty-fifth poem in the second book of his cycle, *The Star of the Covenant* (*Der Stern des Bundes*) (1914), in which he recalls an afternoon and an early evening spent in the company of his disciple, Ernst Morwitz (1887–1971), in Bingen, a small town on the Rhein, in the year 1907.[136] After drinking wine together from a silver goblet, George and Morwitz climbed one of the hills surrounding Bingen, and noticed how, on this beautiful late afternoon in spring, the sky suddenly changed from a light green colour to a deep, shining blue, reminiscent of the sea around the coasts of southern Europe. Over the houses and trees of Bingen a rich, golden light was now spread, transforming the landscape before their very eyes. It was as if they were no longer in Germany, but in Greece; it was as if the physical landscape had become 'spiritualized', and as if their shared dream had become reality; it was as if they had suddenly been transported to the realm of 'the Blessed', to those islands on which the gods and heroes of ancient Greece dwell, and, in a way, they had:

> You shared my cup of wine with me the evening
> Before our celebration in the hills.
> We left the river, climbing to the heights,
> And all at once the grassy green of heaven
> Grew limpid blue like southern bays. A halo

Of gold transformed the trees and roofs to dwellings
Of the immortals. Timeless flash of Now,
When landscape turns to spirit, dream to substance.
We trembled in a moment of consummate
Delight that held and crowned our whole existence
And put an end to envy for the longed-for
Sea of the gods, the radiant island-sea.[137]

It was, said Morwitz in his recollection of this experience, 'one of the rare moments' — George uses the old-fashioned expression, *Nu* — 'in which the landscape appears so spiritually transformed, as great painters try to represent it', and yet he insists not just on the *aesthetic quality*, but on the *reality*, of this moment. For George and Morwitz, the moment was real; for us, as readers, it can become real as well, and reading this poem can give us a taste, if only a fleeting one, of what the Blissful Islands are like. The 'Now' of the moment of 'consummate delight', *grösstes Glückes*, is a 'timeless' one, but the sheer physicality of the response — the 'tremble' or *Schauder*, 'shudder' — leaves one in no doubt of its reality. And there is no doubt about it: whatever happened on that evening in 1907, in this poem its protagonists are transported across time and space, setting foot after a journey across 'the sea of the gods', onto the promontory of a territory long-since known to us, emerging from the 'island-sea'. In the end, then, George's poem, like his remarkable poetic œuvre as a whole and the tradition from which it emerges, proves that Zarathustra was right: 'There *are* still blissful islands!'

Notes

1   On Nietzsche's reception and use of Schiller, see N. Martin, *Nietzsche and Schiller: Untimely Aesthetics*, Oxford: Oxford University Press, 1996; and P. Bishop and R.H. Stephenson, *Friedrich Nietzsche and Weimar Classicism*, Rochester, NY: Camden House, 2005.

2   For further discussion of this poem, see P. Carus, 'The Ideal and Life: By Friedrich Schiller', *The Monist*, April 1911, vol. 21, no. 2, 278–284; Schiller, *Selected Poems*, ed. F.M. Fowler, London and New York: Macmillan; St Martin's Press, 1969, pp. 158–162; G. Kaiser, 'Vergötterung und Tod: Die thematische Einheit von Schillers Werk', in *Von Arkadien nach Elysium: Schiller-Studen*, Göttingen: Vandenhoeck, 1978, pp. 11–44; H. Koopmann, 'Mythologische Reise zum Olymp', in W. Segebrecht (ed.), *Gedichte und Interpretationen*, vol. 3, *Klassik und Romantik*, Stuttgart: Reclam, 1984, pp. 83–98; W. Hinderer, 'Das Reich der Schatten', in N. Oellers (ed.), *Interpretationen: Gedichte von Friedrich Schiller*, Stuttgart: Reclam, 1996, pp. 123–148; and J.M. Packer, '"Zwischen Sinnenglück und Seelenfrieden": Chiasmus and Symmetry in Schiller's "Das Ideal und das Leben"', *Colloquia Germanica*, vol. 39 (2006), 257–273.

3   Schiller, *On the Naïve and the Sentimental in Literature*, tr. H. Watanabe-O'Kelly, Manchester: Carcanet New Press, 1981, p. 48.

4   Schiller, *On the Naïve and Sentimental in Literature*, p. 66.

5   Schiller, *On the Naïve and Sentimental in Literature*, p. 66; cf. the reference to the notion of 'endless capacity' in Schiller's letter to Körner of 21 September 1795, cited below.

6   According to another tradition, the Lesser Mysteries in the cult of Demeter at Eleusis were instituted for the purification of Heracles, before he undertook his journey in the opposite direction — to the underworld, in order to capture Cerberus, the three-headed

dog belonging to Hades. For further discussion, see C. Kerényi, *Eleusis: Archetypal Image of Mother and Daughter*, tr. R. Manheim, Princeton, NJ: Princeton University Press, 1967, pp. 52–60.

7 See E. Hamilton, *Mythology: Timeless Tales of Gods and Heroes* [1942], New York: Warner Books, 1999, pp. 166–179; R. Graves, *The Greek Myths* [1955], 2 vols, Harmondsworth: Penguin, 1990, vol. 2, pp. 84–158, 195–207; and M. Leis and P. Weiss, *Mythos Herkules*, Leipzig: Reclam, 2005. For a psychoanalytic interpretation of the twelve labours, see P. Diel, *Le Symbolisme dans la mythologie grecque*, Paris: Petite Bibliothèque Payot, 1970, pp. 206–209. For a detailed account of the depiction of the legend of Heracles in Greek art, see the catalogue of a major exhibition held in the State Collection of Antiquities in Munich in 2003–2004 (R. Wünsche (ed.), *Herakles— Herkules*, Munich: Staatliche Antikensammlungen, 2003).

8 Jung, 'The Concept of the Collective Unconscious' (1936), in *CW* 9/i §93; and 'Religious Ideas in Alchemy' (1937), in *CW* 12 §457.

9 For further discussion, see R. Habel, 'Schiller und die Tradition des Herakles-Mythos', in M. Fuhrmann (ed.), *Terror und Spiel: Probleme der Mythenrezeption* [*Poetik und Hermeneutik*, vol. 4], Munich: Fink, 1971, pp. 265–294; and P.-A. Alt, 'Die Griechen transform-ieren: Schillers moderne Konstruktion der Antike', in W. Hinderer (ed.), *Friedrich Schiller und der Weg in die Moderne*, Würzburg: Königshausen & Neumann, 2006, pp. 339–363.

10 Winckelmann, *The History of Ancient Art*, tr. G.H. Lodge, book 10, chapter 3, in J.J. Winckelmann, *Essays on the Philosophy and History of Art*, ed. C. Bowman, London and New York: Continuum, 2005, vol. 3, p. 264.

11 See 'Description of the Torso in the Belvedere of Rome' (1759), in J.J. Winckelmann, *Johann Joachim Winckelmann on Art, Architecture, and Archaeology*, tr. D. Carter, Rochester, NY: Camden House, 2013, pp. 143–147 (p. 143).

12 Winckelmann, 'Description of the Torso in the Belvedere of Rome', in *Art, Architecture, and Archaeology*, pp. 144–145.

13 Winckelmann, *History of Ancient Art*, tr. G.H. Lodge, book 10, chapter 3, in *Essays on the Philosophy and History of Art*, vol. 3, p. 265.

14 K.P. Moritz, *Götterlehre der Griechen und Römer*, Leipzig: Reclam, 1878, pp. 212–236.

15 Hesiod, *Theogony*, ll. 950–955; in Hesiod, *The Homeric Hymns and Homerica*, tr. H.G. Evelyn-White, Cambridge, MA; London: Harvard University Press; Heinemann, 1982, pp. 149–151.

16 Compare with Socrates's exposition of the allegory of the cave in the *Republic*, where he talks about 'the contemplation of essence and the brightest region of being' (*Republic* 518c; in Plato, *Collected Dialogues*, ed. E. Hamilton and H. Cairns, Princeton, NJ: Princeton University Press, 1989, p. 751; translated by W.H.D. Rouse as 'the sight of being and the most brilliant light of being', in *Great Dialogues of Plato*, ed. E.H. Warmington and P.G. Rouse, New York: Mentor, 1956, p. 317), or those passages in Plotinus where he talks about the experience of the One as pure light and divine radiance, for example, in 'On the Good, or the One': 'Then of it and of itself the soul has all the vision that may be — of itself luminous now, filled with intellectual light, become pure, subtle and weightless. It has become divine, is part of the eternal that is beyond becoming' (*Enneads*, VI.9.9, in *The Essential Plotinus*, ed. and tr. E.O'Brian, Indianapolis, IN: Hackett, 1964, p. 86); or in 'On the Intellectual Beauty', when he writes of the gods in the realm of pure intel-lect (*nous*): 'To "live at ease" is There; and to these divine beings verity is mother and nurse, existence and sustenance; all that is not of process but of authentic being they see, and themselves in all: for all is transparent, nothing dark, nothing resistant; every being is lucid to every other, in breadth and depth; light runs through light' (*Enneads*, V.8.4, in *The Enneads*, tr. S. MacKenna, abridged J. Dillon, Harmondsworth: Penguin, 1991, p. 414). For further discussion of Schiller's relation to Plotinus, see H.F. Müller, 'Plotin und Schiller über die Schönheit', *Philosophische Monatshefte*, 1876, vol. 12, 385–393; H.F. Müller, 'Plotinus über ästhetische Erziehung', *Neue Jahrbücher für das klassische Altertum*, 2 Abt., 1915, vol. 36, no. 2, 69–79; and H.F. Müller, 'Zur Geschichte des Begriffs "schöne

Seele"', *Germanisch-romanische Monatsschrift*, 1915–1919, vol. 7, 236–249; and F. Koch, *Schillers philosophische Schriften und Plotin*, Leipzig: Weber, 1926.

17 *Republic*, 519c; in *CD*, p. 751.

18 Cf. Schiller's poem, 'Ideals' (*Die Ideale*), written in 1795 (the same year as 'The Kingdom of the Shadows') and revised in 1800. Although, for one commentator, in this poem Schiller uses the term *Ideale* 'not in the sense of "realm of the ideal" but in the sense of unrealistic youthful dreams' (Fowler, in Schiller, *Selected Poems*, p. 156), nevertheless the conceptual link between the True and the Good puts a question mark over the sharpness of this distinction, and 'Ideals' stands as an example of an elegaic treatment of a theme which, in Schiller's projected poem in the wake of 'The Kingdom of the Shadows', he envisaged treating as an idyll.

19 See *Republic*, 515a; in *CD*, p. 747.

20 F.G. Klopstock, *Werke und Briefe: Historisch-Kritische Ausgabe*, vol. I.1, *Oden: Texte*, ed. H. Gronemeyer and K. Hurlebach, Berlin and New York: de Gruyter, 2010, p. 23.

21 On Schiller's relationship to the Platonic tradition, see D. Pugh, *Dialectic of Love: Platonism in Schiller's Aesthetics*, Montreal & Kingston, London, Buffalo: McGill-Queen's University Press, 1996. As Pugh remarks in the preface to his extensive study, 'as Schiller sought to turn his early speculations into defensible philosophical positions, it is [...] understandable that he unwittingly developed his arguments in a Platonic framework. Despite the originality of his solutions, the resulting treatises deserve to be viewed in that philosophical tradition, and indeed, their mysteries can be made somewhat less mysterious if we view them in that way' (*Dialectic of Love*, p. xiii).

22 As Paul Redding has suggested, the ludic drive plays the same mediating role between the material and formal drives as does Eros between gods and mortals, beautiful forms and bodily desires, in Diotima's speech in Plato's *Symposium* (202e–203a; in *CD*, p. 555). For further discussion, see P. Redding, 'Self-Surpassing Beauty: Plato's Ambiguous Legacy', *Literature and Aesthetics: The Journal of the Sydney Society of Literature and Aesthetics*, 1997, vol. 7, 94–108.

23 F. Schiller, *On the Aesthetic Education of Man*, ed. and tr. E.M. Wilkinson and L.A. Willoughby, Oxford: Clarendon Press, 1982, p. 215.

24 See Fowler in Schiller, *Selected Poems*, p. 158.

25 See Fowler in Schiller, *Selected Poems*, p. 158.

26 J.W. Goethe, *Briefe*, ed. K.R. Mandelkow, 4 vols, Hamburg: Wegner, 1962–1967, vol. 4, p. 480: for 'the organs of the human being, by means of practice, theory, reflection, success, failure, support and resistance and ever-repeated reflection', Goethe told Humboldt on 17 March 1832, 'link, unconsciously [*ohne Bewußtsein*] and in free activity, the acquired with the inborn, so that the result is a unity which astonishes the world [*so daß es eine Einheit vorbringt, welche die Welt in Erstaunen setzt*]'.

27 See *Select Minor Poems: Translated from the German of Goethe and Schiller*, tr. J.S. Dwight, Boston: Hilliard, Gray, 1839, pp. 294–299 (p. 295).

28 Compare with the use of the concept of *form* in the context of a series of observations on the power of contemplation or reflection in *On the Aesthetic Education*, Letter 25, §2: 'Contemplation (or reflection) is the first liberal relation which man establishes with the universe around him. [...] The necessity of nature, which in the stage of mere sensation ruled him with undivided authority, begins at the stage of reflection to relax its hold upon him. In his senses there results a momentary peace; time itself, the eternally moving, stands still' — compare with the definition of time as 'a moving image of eternity' in the *Timaeus*, 37d (in *CD*, p. 1167) and with the moment of midday presented in 'At Noontide' in *Zarathustra* (in Nietzsche, *Thus Spoke Zarathustra*, tr. R.J. Hollingdale, Harmondsworth: Penguin, 1969, pp. 286–289) — 'and, as the divergent rays of consciousness converge, there is reflected against a background of transcience an image of the infinite, namely *form* [die Form]' (*On the Aesthetic Education*, p. 183). Just as the Neoplatonists did in their interpretations of Homer, Schiller discovers in Greek myth a symbol of psychological development: 'The most primitive poetry speaks of this

great happening in the inner world of man as though it were a revolution in the outer, and symbolizes thought triumphing over the laws of time by the image of *Zeus* putting an end to the reign of Saturn' (*On the Aesthetic Education*, pp. 183–185). Here, Schiller is thinking in a tradition in which Saturn (or, in Greek, Kronos) became confused with Chronos (i.e., Time), or so Wilkinson and Willoughby suggest (*On the Aesthetic Education*, 'Commentary', p. 280).

29 Goethe/Schiller, *Select Minor Poems*, p. 295.
30 Compare with Schiller's playful treatment of this Platonic doctrine in his poem, 'The Secret of Reminiscence' (*Das Geheimniß der Reminiszenz*) (1782), one of a series of odes dedicated to an idealised figure, Laura.
31 Schiller, *On the Aesthetic Education of Mankind*, pp. 101 and 107.
32 Goethe/Schiller, *Select Minor Poems*, p. 296.
33 Schiller, *On the Aesthetic Education*, p. 101.
34 Schiller, *On the Aesthetic Education*, p. 109.
35 Letter 15, §9, in *On the Aesthetic Education*, pp. 107–109.
36 B. Vergely, *Deviens qui tu es: Quand des sages grecs nous aident à vivre*, Paris: Albin Michel, 2014, pp. 77–78.
37 Goethe/Schiller, *Select Minor Poems*, p. 296.
38 For the notion of weight or heaviness implied by the term *die Schwere*, compare with Nietzsche's personification of the concept as 'the spirit of heaviness' (or *der Geist der Schwere*); see, for example, 'Of the Vision and the Riddle', §1, and 'On the Spirit of Gravity', in *Thus Spoke Zarathustra*, pp. 176–178 and 210–213.
39 Goethe/Schiller, *Select Minor Poems*, p. 297.
40 *The Sonnets of Michelangelo*, tr. J.A. Symonds, Plymouth: Vision Press, 1950, pp. 66–67.
41 Goethe/Schiller, *Select Minor Poems*, p. 297.
42 Compare with Schiller's reference in an earlier stanza to *der Menschheit Götterbild* ('Humanity's Ideal', literally 'the divine image of humanity'), recalling a theme from his earlier poems, 'The Gods of Greece' (*Die Götter Griechenlands*) (ll. 191–192) and 'The Artists' (*Die Künstler*) (ll. 260–265).
43 If, in this poem, as in 'Friendship' (*Die Freundschaft*), Schiller is interested in the motif of ascent — 'Lo! arm in arm, thro' every upward grade, / From the rude Mongol to the starry Greek' (*Arm in Arme, höher stets und höher / vom Mongolen bis zum griechischen Seher*) (Schiller, *Poems and Ballads*, tr. E.B. Lytton, New York: Harper, 1887, p. 261) — then in others, such as 'The Triumph of Love' (*Der Triumph der Liebe*), second version — 'Yet he quits the heavenly portals, / Mixes with the herd of mortals' (*Göttern läßt er seine Throne, / Niedert sich zum Erdensohne*) — and in 'The Gods of Greece' (*Die Götter Griechenlands*) — 'Still – Deucalion's favour'd race to visit, / Heavenly powers their starry thrones forsook' (*Zu Deukalions Geschlechte stiegen / Damals noch die Himmlischen herab*) — he depicts a complementary movement of descent from divinity to humanity (*The Minor Poems of Schiller*, tr. J.H. Merivale, London: Pickering, 1844, pp. 189 and 18).
44 Goethe/Schiller, *Select Minor Poems*, p. 298.
45 Schiller, *On the Aesthetic Education of Mankind*, tr. Wilkinson and Willoughby, p. 151.
46 *First Alcibiades*, 133c; in Plato, *Complete Works*, ed. J.M. Cooper, Indianapolis and Cambridge: Hackett, 1997, p. 592.
47 *First Alcibiades*, 133c; in *Complete Works*, p. 592, fn. 30.
48 Proclus, *The Theology of Plato*, book 1, chapter 3; in Proclus, *The Theology of Plato*, tr. T. Taylor [TTS, vol. 8], Westbury: Prometheus Trust, 2009, pp. 57–58. By 'wholes', Taylor notes, Platonic philosophy means 'every incorporeal order of being, and every mundane sphere' ('Additional Notes on the *First Alcibiades*', in Plato, *Works in Five Volumes: Volume I*, tr. T. Taylor and F. Sydenham [TTS, vol. 9], Sturminster Newton: Prometheus Trust, 2006, p. 211, fn.).
49 Proclus, *Theology of Plato*, book 1, chapter 3; in Proclus, *The Theology of Plato*, p. 58; cf. Plato, *Works in Five Volumes: Volume I*, p. 211.
50 Proclus, *Theology of Plato*, book 1, chapter 3; in Proclus, *The Theology of Plato*, p. 58.

51 Porphyry, *On the Life of Plotinus and the Arrangement of his Works*, §2; in M. Edwards (tr.), *Neoplatonic Saints: The Lives of Plotinus and Proclus by their Students*, Liverpool: Liverpool University Press, 2000, p. 4.

52 *Phaedrus*, 247c; in *CD*, p. 494.

53 *Phaedrus*, 247c–e; in *CD*, p. 494.

54 See editorial footnote in Plotinus, *Ennead IV*, tr. A.H. Armstrong, Cambridge, MA, and London: Harvard University Press, 1984, pp. 384–385.

55 Plotinus, *Enneads*, IV.7.10; in Plotinus, *The Enneads*, tr. S. MacKenna, revised B.S. Page, London: Faber and Faber, 1956, p. 354.

56 Spinoza, *Ethics*, part 5, proposition 22, scholium, in *Selections*, ed. J. Wild, London: Scribner, 1928, p. 385.

57 H.A. Wolfson, *The Philosophy of Spinoza: Unfolding the Latent Processes of His Reasoning*, 2 vols in 1, Cambridge, MA, and London: Harvard University Press, 1962, vol. 1, p. 358.

58 Wolfson, *The Philosophy of Spinoza*, vol. 2, pp. 297–298. In the *Ethics*, Spinoza distinguishes between three kinds of knowledge: between (1) knowledge by 'hearsay', sensation, 'vague experience'; (2) knowledge by discursive reason; and (3) knowledge by 'intuition' or *scientia intuitiva*, defined as 'proceed[ing] from an adequate idea of certain attributes of God to an adequate knowledge of the essence of things' (part 5, proposition 25, demonstration; in *Selections*, p. 386). Such intuitive knowledge allows us to attain 'the highest possible peace of mind' (part 5, proposition 27; in *Selections*, p. 386), and ultimately gives rise to 'the intellectual love of God' (part 5, proposition 32, corollary and proposition 33; in *Selections*, pp. 390–391).

59 Wolfson, *The Philosophy of Spinoza*, vol. 2, p. 299.

60 See, for example, *Ethics*, part 2, proposition 44, corollary 2, and part 5, propositions 22, 23, 29 and 30; in *Selections*, pp. 191, 384–385 and 387–389. For further reflections on Jung's part on the eternal, see Jung, *MDR*, p. 327.

61 Schelling, *System of Transcendental Idealism*, tr. P. Heath, Charlottesville: University Press of Virginia, 1978, p. 188; cf. Schelling, *Sämmtliche Werke*, 14 vols, Stuttgart and Augsburg: Cotta, 1856–1861, vol I.3, p. 574.

62 *Philosophical Letters on Dogmatism and Criticism*, Eighth Letter, in F.W.J. Schelling, *The Unconditional in Human Knowledge: Four Early Essays (1794–1796)*, tr. F. Marti, Lewisburg; London: Bucknell University Press; Associated University Presses, 1980, p. 180; cf. *Sämmtliche Werke*, vol. I.1, p. 318.

63 Schelling, *Philosophical Letters*, p. 185; cf. *Sämmtliche Werke*, vol. I.1, p. 325. This phrase, *aus der Zeit in die Ewigkeit*, alludes to the final stanza of the Lutheran hymn, 'O great God, o Lord of time' (*Großer Gott, du Herr der Zeit*) (A. Knapp, *Evangelischer Liederschatz für Kirche und Haus*, vol. 2, Stuttgart and Tübingen, 1837, p. 260).

64 A. Schopenhauer, *The World as Will and Representation*, tr. E.F.J. Payne, 2 vols, New York: Dover, 1966, vol. 2, pp. 477, 478, and 479.

65 M. Scheler, *On the Eternal in Man*, tr. B. Noble [1960], New Brunswick, NJ: Transaction, 2010.

66 M. Scheler, *Formalism in Ethics and Non-Formal Ethics of Values: A New Attempt toward the Foundation of an Ethical Personalism*, tr. M.S. Frings and R.L. Funk, Evanston, IL: Northwestern University Press, 1973.

67 J.G. Herder, *Werke in zehn Bänden*, 10 vols, Frankfurt am Main: Deutscher Klassiker Verlag, 1985–2000, vol. 3, pp. 833–834. For further discussion of this text, see R. Böschenstein, 'Das Ich und seine Teile: Überlegungen zum anthropologischen Gehalt einiger lyrischer Texte', in G. Buhr, F.A. Kittler, and H. Turk (eds), *Das Subjekt der Dichtung: Festschrift für Gerhard Kaiser*, Würzburg: Königshausen & Neumann, 1990, pp. 73–97 (esp. pp. 85–88).

68 Goethe, *Italian Journey*, tr. W.H. Auden and E. Mayer, Harmondsworth: Penguin, 1970, p. 385.

69 For the intellectual background to Vischer, see W. Oelmüller, *Friedrich Theodor Vischer und das Problem des nachhegelschen Ästhetik* [Forschungen zur Kirchen- und Geistesgeschichte, NF, vol. 8], Stuttgart: Kohlhammer, 1959; F. Schlawe, *Friedrich Theodor Vischer,*

Stuttgart: Metzler, 1959; and O. Briese, *Konkurrenzen: Philosophische Kultur in Deutschland 1830–1850: Porträts und Profile*, Würzburg: Königshausen & Neumann, 1998. For evidence of a renewal of interest in Vischer, see B. Potthast and A. Reck (eds), *Friedrich Theodor Vischer: Leben—Werk—Wirkung* [Beiheft zum Euphorion], Heidelberg: Winter, 2011.

70 For further discussion, see H.H. Zißeler, *Beiträge zur Entstehungsgeschichte der Dichtung "Auch Einer" von Friedrich Theodor Vischer*, Göttingen: Dieterich, 1913; F. Feilbogen, *Fr. Th.Vischers "Auch Einer"*, Zurich: Orell Füßli, 1916; R. Heller, 'Auch Einer: The Epitome of F. Th.Vischer's Philosophy of Life', *German Life and Letters*, 1964, vol. 8, 9–18; H.W. Hewtter-Thayer, 'The Road to *Auch Einer*', *Publications of the Modern Language Association*, 1960, vol. 75, 83–96; W.H. Bruford, 'The Idea of "Bildung" in Friedrich Theodor Vischer's "Auch Einer"', in S. Prawer (ed.), *Essays in German Language, Culture and Society*, London: University of London, Institute of Germanic Studies, 1969, pp. 7–17; and I. Oesterle, 'Verübelte Geschichte: Autobiographische Selbstentblößung, komische Selbstentlastung und bedingte zynische Selbstbehauptung in Friedrich Theodor Vischers Roman *Auch Einer*', in R. Grimm and J. Hermand (eds), *Vom Anderen und vom Selbst: Beiträge zu Fragen der Biographie und Autobiographie*, Königstein im Taunus: Athenäum-Verlag, 1982, pp. 71–93.

71 B. Mersmann, 'Friedrich Theodor Vischers ästhetisches Realismusprogramm: Zur Wechselbeziehung zwischen Dichtung und bildender Kunst', in *Literatur im multimedialen Zeitalter: Neue Perspektiven der Germanistik in Asien: Asiatische Germanistentagung 1997* [*KGG- Dokumentationen*, 8/1999], 2 vols, Seoul: Koreanische Gesellschaft für Germanistik, 1998–1999, vol. 2.

72 F.T.Vischer, *Auch Einer: Eine Reisebekanntschaft* [1879], Stuttgart and Leipzig: Deutsche Verlags-Anstalt, 1904, p. 33.

73 Vischer, *Auch Einer*, p. 337, cf. p. 340 und pp. 443–44. The allusion is to Schiller's play, *Wilhelm Tell*, Act 2, Scene 2.

74 For further discussion of Schiller's idealism, see K. Berghahn, *Schiller: Ansichten eines Idealisten*, Frankfurt am Main: Athenäum, 1986; and R. Safranksi, *Schiller oder Die Erfindung des Deutschen Idealismus*, Munich andVienna: Hanser, 2004.

75 Goethe/Schiller, *Select Minor Poems*, p. 295.

76 Schiller, *On the Naïve and Sentimental in Literature*, p. 66; cf. Schiller, *NA* 20, 472.

77 F. Schiller, 'Kallias or Concerning Beauty', in J.M. Bernstein (ed.), *Classic and Romantic German Aesthetics*, Cambridge: Cambridge University Press, 2003, p. 179.

78 Schiller to Körner, 8 February 1793; *Classic and Romantic Aesthetics*, p. 152.

79 Schiller, *On the Aesthetic Education*, pp. 155 and 157.

80 In this rhetoric of violence and in Schiller's focus on 'the inevitable — and morally obligatory — conflict between form and content' rhetoric of violence, David Pugh suggests that Plotinus's description of the sculptor's activity is used as paradigm (D. Pugh, 'Schiller as Platonist', *Colloquia germanica*, 1991, vol. 24, no. 4, 273–295 [p. 280]).

81 For further discussion, see P. Bishop, '"Creation — That Is the Great Redemption from Suffering, and Life's Easement"', Part 1: 'What Do Creation and Destruction Mean in Zarathustra's World?'; Part 2: 'Tragic Affirmation amid the Creation-and-Destruction of Eternal Recurrence', in S. Wirth, I. Meier, and J. Hill (eds), *Destruction & Creation: Facing the Ambiguities of Power*, New Orleans, Louisiana: Spring Journal Books, 2010, pp. 31–43 and 45–58; and P. Bishop, 'The Dialectic of Destruction and Creation in the German Tradition: A Jungian Perspective on Goethe, Nietzsche, Rilke, and George', *Jung Journal: Culture & Psyche*, 2011, vol. 5. no. 4, 60–82.

82 B.Vergely, *Deviens qui tu es: Quand les sages grecs nous aident à vivre*, Paris: Albin Michel, 2014, p. 39.

83 Vergely, *Deviens qui tu es*, pp. 39–40.

84 Similarly, a dialectic of visible and invisible informs the poetology of Rainer Maria Rilke (1875–1926). In a letter of 13 November 1925 to Witold von Hulewicz, the Polish translator of his *Duino Elegies*, Rilke wrote: 'The angel of the *Elegies* is that creature in whom

the transformation of the visible into the invisible, which we are accomplishing, appears already consummated' (*Letters of Rainer Maria Rilke 1910–1926*, tr. J.B. Greene and M.D.H. Norton, New York: Norton, 1969, p. 375). Elsewhere in this letter he asserts: 'It is our task to imprint this temporary, perishable earth into ourselves so deeply, so painfully and passionately, that its essence can rise again "invisibly," inside us. We are the bees of the invisible. We wildly collect the honey of the visible, to store it in the great golden hive of the invisible' (p. 374).

85 Vergely, *Deviens qui tu es*, p. 82.

86 Vergely, *Deviens qui tu es*, p. 84.

87 See F. Chatelet, *Platon*, Paris: Gallimard, 1989; and A. Badiou, *La République de Platon*, Paris: Fayard, 2012.

88 Vergely, *Deviens qui tu es*, p. 85.

89 See *Human, All Too Human*, vol. 2, 'Assorted Opinions and Maxims', §336; in *Human, All Too Human*, tr. R.J. Hollingdale, Cambridge: Cambridge University Press, 1986, p. 290.

90 Goethe, 'Winckelmann and his Age' (1805), in J.W. Goethe, *Essays on Art and Literature*, ed. J. Gearey, tr. E. von Nardroff and E.H. von Nardroff, New York: Suhrkamp, 1986, p. 101 (translation modified).

91 Goethe, 'Winckelmann and his Age', in *Essays on Art and Literature*, p. 101.

92 Goethe, *Essays on Art and Literature*, ed. Gearey, p. 165.

93 Goethe, *Werke* [HA], vol. 12, p. 18.

94 'Of the Way of the Creator', in Nietzsche, *Thus Spake Zarathustra*, tr. R.J. Hollingdale, Harmondsworth: Penguin, 1969, p. 90.

95 Goethe, *From My Life: Poetry and Truth: Parts One to Three*, ed. T.P. Saine and J.L. Sammons, tr. R.R. Heitner, New York: Suhrkamp, 1987, p. 355.

96 *The Gay Science*, §276; in Nietzsche, *The Gay Science*, tr. W. Kaufmann, New York: Vintage, 1974, p. 223.

97 *The Gay Science*, §276; in *The Gay Science*, p. 223.

98 *Twilight of the Idols*, 'Expeditions of an Untimely Man', §49, in Nietzsche, *Twilight of the Idols; The Anti-Christ*, tr. R.J. Hollingdale, Harmondsworth: Penguin, 1968, pp. 102–103.

99 Goethe, *Faust*, Part Two, ll. 9240–9241; in J.W. Goethe, *Faust*, ed. E. Trunz, Munich: Beck, 1972, p. 279.

100 For the legend of Lynceus, see the *Cypria* (fragment 12), in Hesiod, *The Homeric Hymns and Homerica*, tr. H.G. Evelyn-White, Cambridge, MA; London: Harvard University Press; Heinemann, 1982, p. 503; and Apollonius of Rhodes, *Argonautica*, book 1, ll. 151–155, in Apollonius Rhodius, *The Argonautica*, tr. R.C. Seaton, London: Heinemann; New York: Macmillan, 1912, p. 13.

101 Plotinus, *Enneads*, V.8.4; in Plotinus, *The Enneads*, tr. S. MacKenna, abridged J. Dillon, Harmondsworth: Penguin, 1991, p. 414.

102 Plotinus, *Enneads*, V.8.4; in *The Enneads*, tr. MacKenna, p. 415.

103 Goethe, *Faust*, Part Two, ll. 11143–11150; in Goethe, *Faust*, ed. Trunz, p. 336.

104 Goethe, *Faust*, Part Two, ll. 11288–11303; in Goethe, *Faust*, ed. Trunz, p. 340.

105 See *The Birth of Tragedy*, §18 (cf. 'Attempt at a Self-Criticism', §7, and *KSA* 7, 11[1], 357); and *KSA* 7, 5[1], 93, where Nietzsche sketches out a work called 'Tragedy and the Free Spirits'.

106 Goethe, *Faust*, Part Two, ll. 7438–7439; in Goethe, *Faust*, ed. Trunz, p. 227.

107 Nietzsche, *KSA* 10, 3[1] §274, p. 86.

108 Raphaël Enthoven, remark at 49: 40–42 in *Le Gai savoir*, episode entitled 'Plotin: une terrible beauté', broadcast on France Culture on 2 December 2012. Enthoven justifies this remark with a reference to Nietzsche's distinction between the ego and the self.

109 H. Theierl, *Nietzsche: Mystik als Selbstversuch*, Würzburg: Königshausen & Neumann, 2000, p. 13.

110 See *The Birth of Tragedy*, §2 and §5 (in *Basic Writings of Nietzsche*, ed. and tr. W. Kaufmann, New York: Modern Library, 1968, pp. 39 and 50).

111 See 'Von zwei Wegen', in Meister Eckehart, *Schriften und Predigten*, ed. H. Büttner, 2 vols, Jena: Diederichs, 1921, vol. 1, pp. 140–151 (p. 143). The authorship of this text is

disputed, and is sometimes ascribed to Johannes Franke of Cologne; see D. Gottschall, 'Eckhart and the Vernacular Tradition: Pseudo-Eckhart and Eckhart Legends', in J.M. Hackett (ed.), *A Companion to Meister Eckhart*, Leiden: Brill, 2013, pp. 509–551 (pp. 512 and 530). For further discussion of the relation between Nietzsche and Meister Eckhart, see J. Bernhart, *Meister Eckhart und Nietzsche: Ein Vergleich für die Gegenwart*, Berlin: Thomas-Verlag [Greif-Bücherei], 1935; and D. Schoeller-Reisch, 'Die Demut Zarathustras: Ein Versuch zu Nietzsche mit Meister Eckhart', *Nietzsche-Studien*, 1998, vol. 27, 420–439.

112 'Zarathustra's Prologue', §1 and §3; in *Thus Spoke Zarathustra*, pp. 39 and 41.

113 'The Sign', in *Thus Spoke Zarathustra*, p. 336.

114 'Of the Sublime Men', in *Thus Spoke Zarathustra*, p. 140.

115 'Prologue', §3, in *Thus Spoke Zarathustra*, p. 42.

116 'Of the Sublime Men', in *Thus Spoke Zarathustra*, p. 140.

117 Pliny the Elder, *Natural History*, book 6, §37; in Pliny the Elder, *Natural History*, vol. 2, *Libri III-VII*, tr. H. Rackham, Cambridge, MA; London: Harvard University Press; Heinemann, 1941, p. 491.

118 'Of the Virtuous', *Thus Spoke Zarathustra*, p. 120.

119 'Of the Sublime Men', *Thus Spoke Zarathustra*, p. 139; translation modified.

120 See B. Babich, 'Nietzsche and the Sculptural Sublime', in *The Agonist*, vol. 5, no. 1 (Spring 2012). Available online at: www.nietzschecircle.com (accessed 10 May 2013).

121 'Of the Sublime Men', in *Thus Spoke Zarathustra*, p. 141.

122 See Schiller's essay 'On Grace and Dignity' (*Über Anmut und Würde*) of 1793, in J.V. Curran and C. Fricker (eds), *Schiller's "On Grace and Dignity" in Its Cultural Context*, Rochester, NY: Camden House, 2005.

123 'Of the Sublime Men', in *Thus Spoke Zarathustra*, p. 141.

124 'Of the Sublime Men', in *Thus Spoke Zarathustra*, p. 141.

125 Proclus, *Commentary on the Republic of Plato*, cited by Thomas Taylor in *A Dissertation on the Eleusinian and Bacchic Mysteries* [1790], 'On the Eleusinian Mysteries', in *Oracles and Mysteries* [TTS, vol. 7], Frome: Prometheus Trust, 2001, p. 74; cf. 'A History of the Restoration of the Platonic Theology' [1788], in *Oracles and Mysteries*, p. 199. Taylor glosses this remark as follows: 'Well knowing the dreadful condition of his soul while in captivity to a corporeal nature, and purifying himself according to the cathartic virtues, of which certain purifications in the mystic ceremonies were symbolic, he at length fled from the bondage of matter, and ascended beyond the reach of her hands' (p. 74).

126 See C. Kerényi, *Eleusis: Archetypal Image of Mother and Daughter*, tr. R. Manheim, Princeton, NJ: Princeton University Press, 1967, pp. 52–59.

127 Taylor, 'On the Eleusinian Mysteries', in *Oracles and Mysteries*, p. 60.

128 M.P. Hall, *The Secret Teachings of All Ages*, New York: Tarcher/Penguin, 2003, p. 69.

129 Taylor, 'On the Eleusinian Mysteries', in *Oracles and Mysteries*, p. 77.

130 Hall, *Secret Teachings of All Ages*, p. 72.

131 *Republic*, 521c; in *CD*, p. 753. This journey signifies 'a conversion and turning about of the soul from a day whose light is darkness to the veritable day', in other words 'that ascension to reality' which is, Socrates affirms, 'true philosophy'.

132 *Symposium*, 180 d–e; in *CD*, pp. 534–535.

133 The final line of Voltaire's poem *Le Mondain* (1736) reads, 'Le paradis terrestre est où je suis' ('Earthly paradise is where I am'); for Laurie Anderson's 'Language is a Virus', see her album of the same name (1986).

134 Olympiodorus, *Commentary on Plato's "Gorgias"*, tr. R. Jackson, K. Lycos, and H. Tarrant, Leiden: Brill, 1998, p. 302.

135 Taylor, 'On the Eleusinian Mysteries', in *Oracles and Mysteries*, p. 79.

136 E. Morwitz, *Kommentar zu dem Werk Stefan Georges*, Düsseldorf and Munich: Küpper (vormals Bondi), 1969, p. 377.

137 S. George, *The Works of Stefan George rendered into English*, tr. O. Marx and E. Morwitz, Chapel Hill, NC: University of North Carolina, 1949, p. 266; *Werke: Ausgabe in zwei Bänden*, Stuttgart: Klett-Cotta, 1984, vol. 1, pp. 378–379.

4

JOURNEY'S END

Platonic, Nietzschean, and Jungian Attitudes to the Body

> The point of life is life.
>
> (Goethe, letter to Johann Heinrich Meyer, 8 February 1796)

Following the ten sections of the dramatic 'Prologue', the amazing, even stunning, discourse entitled 'Of the Three Metamorphoses' ushers in Part One of *Thus Spoke Zarathustra*. Here the Persian prophet (as re-invented by Nietzsche) tells us how the spirit becomes a camel, then a lion, then a child — 'innocence and forgetfulness, a new beginning, a sport, a self-propelling wheel, a first motion, a sacred *Yes*'.[1] The pattern of transformations in this discourse conforms to Jung's principle of change, the notion of *enantiodromia* (*SNZ* 1, 258). (Jung's embrace of this principle, attributed to the pre-Socratic philosopher Heraclitus, of *enantiodromia* — 'the emergence of the unconscious opposite in the course of time' [*CW* 6 §709],[2] or the mechanism according to which the libido streams back to the source of life, that is, when the libido introverts, and returns to the unconscious[3] — underscores the processual, dynamic character of his approach.) To put it another way, the sequence of camel–lion–child is 'the expression of the process of individuation' (*SNZ* 1, 271).

Almost immediately, however, Zarathustra turns — in a sequence of critical discourses — to a series of sacrilegious *No*'s, the very first of which is an excoriating attack on university philosophers, on 'these lauded wise men of the academic chairs'.[4] On this chapter, Jung commented that Nietzsche had been 'exceedingly sensitive' to 'the spirit of the time',[5] and had 'very clearly' felt that 'we are living now in a time when new values should be discovered, because the old ones are decaying' (*SNZ* 1, 279). For Jung, the crisis of Nietzsche's age — and *a fortiori* the crisis of ours — is a crisis of the symbol: 'Nietzsche felt that, and instantly, naturally, the whole symbolic process that had come to an end outside, began in himself' (*SNZ* 1, 279).

In his following discourses, Zarathustra delivers an equally harsh critique of 'the afterworldsmen', i.e., those who believe in a noumenal or spiritual realm, and 'the despisers of the body', i.e., those who demean and downgrade the value of the material, physical world and the realm of the physiological. Both of these chapters were subjected by Jung to close scrutiny in his seminar on Nietzsche's *Zarathustra* between 1934 and 1939.

In 'Of the Afterworldsmen' Zarathustra presents the following argument:

> It was suffering and impotence — that created all afterworlds; and that brief madness of happiness that only the greatest sufferer experiences.
>
> [...]
>
> Believe me, my brothers! It was the body that despaired of the body — that touched the ultimate walls with the fingers of its deluded spirit.
>
> Believe me, my brothers! It was the body that despaired of the body — that heard the belly of being speak to it.[6]

In this discourse, Jung argued, Zarathustra begins 'to fight the metaphysical idea, the idea of a trans-subjective reality which would be embodied by gods or demons or angels or anything one puts into the beyond' (*SNZ* 1, 287). Once again, Jung detected a universal problem coming into view: when Zarathustra declares that 'nothing of a trans-subjective nature has come to him' and 'recognizes nothing objective in his divine experience', we find an expression (or so Jung believed) of 'the condition which prevails in our actual times' — i.e., in the 1930s, but surely also today, in the twenty-first century — and 'which has been brought about in the course of the last centuries, having begun at the time of the Reformation' (*SNZ* 1, 292). (By contrast, the authenticity of real spiritual experience is said by Jung to be found in the writings of the Swiss hermit St Nicholas of Flüe [1417–1487], St Francis of Assisi [1181/1182–1226], the German mystic Jakob Böhme [1575–1624], or the German mystic poet Johann Scheffler [1624–1677], known as Angelus Silesius.)

In 'Of the Despisers of the Body' Zarathustra follows this critique with an allegory that explains, in a kind of biblical parable (but with a non-biblical message), how there is a soul, but a soul that is subordinate to the body:

> "I am body and soul" — so speaks the child. And why should one not speak like children?
>
> But the awakened, the enlightened man says: I am body entirely, and nothing beside; and soul is only a word for something in the body.
>
> The body is a great intelligence, a multiplicity with one sense, a war and a peace, a herd and a herdsman.
>
> [...]
>
> Sense and spirit are instruments and toys: behind them still lies the Self. The Self seeks with the eyes of the senses, it listens too with the ears of the spirit.[7]

For Jung, by 'the body' Nietzsche means 'the living body', for 'there is an additional secret in the living albumen which science does not know', namely: that 'living body' produces 'something like a psyche', and that 'inasmuch as the living body contains the secret of life, it is an intelligence' (*SNZ* 1, 360). In this discourse, Zarathustra emphasizes the importance of the body, but equally the significance of spirit or *Geist*.

In his seminars, Jung for his part defined *Geist* as 'originally a most effervescent thing, like the opening of a champagne bottle [...], most emotional, really a culmination of life', an interpretation supported by the etymology of the German word (*SNZ* 1, 365).[8] For Jung, this original meaning of *Geist* has to be recovered from the contemporary use of the word:

> Mind and spirit are nowadays so confused that the words are used interchangeably, as in German you use the word *Geist* for simply anything. It also has the connotation of *esprit*, for instance, and one speaks of *esprit de vin*, *Weingeist*, the "spirit of alcohol". Of course, alcohol was called *spiritus* because it is a volatile substance detached from a liquid by distillation, it is the volatile substance which goes over into the alembic. *Geist* is also an expression for a psychological concept, but we have to separate these terms [...].
>
> (*SNZ* 1, 368)

In words that recall our discussion in Chapter 1 of the ancient belief connecting the soul with breath, air, or wind — a belief that persists in the idea of the auricular conception of Christ — Jung says that 'the spirit has always been the creator of life' and that 'the orgiastic madness of antiquity is *prana*, the breath of life', adding: 'A god fills you with his *prana*, or his *pneuma* or wind, and you become an air-being, [...] a ghost or a soul; even body becomes breath. That was the original concept' (*SNZ* 1, 368).

Yet, as Jung is equally at pains to point out, this understanding of *Geist* is in no way opposed to materialism or to Nietzsche's emphasis on the body:

> That we should emphasize the body is Nietzsche's message, and it is also the message of materialism [...]. We should emphasize the body, for thus we give body to concepts, to words. And we should insist on the fact that they are nothing but words since the spirit is gone, that there is no life in them — they are dead things, outside life. We should return to the body in order to create spirit again; without body there is no spirit because spirit is a volatile substance of the body. The body is the alembic, the retort, in which materials are cooked, and out of that process develops the spirit, the effervescent thing that rises.
>
> (*SNZ* 1, 368)

Thus Jung's position could be described as a *vitalist materialism* — or as a materialism that does not exclude the vitality of spirit ... Jung's analysis of the role of *Geist* or spirit in Nietzsche's thought deserves to be taken more seriously than is usually the case. Without citing Jung in detail, this chapter will nevertheless try to develop and to work out the implications of this key Jungian insight into Nietzsche.

Dionysian Spirit

In one of the *Dithyrambs of Dionysos*, 'Amid Birds of Prey' (*Zwischen Raubvögeln*), Jung finds evidence of this developmental process at work in Nietzsche, an experience Jung assimilates to the Nietzschean concept of the Dionysian:

> Nietzsche returned to himself, isolated himself from the whole world, crept into his own retort and underwent this process. Then suddenly he discovered that he was filled with a new orgiastic enthusiasm which he called his experience of Dionysos, the god of wine. [...] In the latter part of *Zarathustra* there is a beautiful poem where Nietzsche describes how he was digging down into himself, working into his own shaft; there you can see how intensely he experienced the going-into-himself, till he suddenly produced the explosion of the most original form of spirit, the Dionysian.
>
> (*SNZ* 1, 368–369)

When writing in *Symbols of Transformation* (1952) about 'Amid Birds of Prey', Jung discerned in this text a remarkable expression of the psychological state he termed 'introversion'. In introversion, the libido sinks, to use a Nietzschean expression, into its 'own depths',[9] where it discovers, 'amid a hundred memories',[10] what Jung calls 'the world of the child, the paradisal state of early infancy, from which we are driven out by the relentless law of time' (*CW* 5 §448). The image of Zarathustra, 'self-excavated, / digging into yourself',[11] — or as Jung puts it, 'sunk in his own depths, he is like one buried in the earth' — is like the image of 'a dead man who has crawled back into the mother', reminiscent (to Jung's mind) of Caeneus,[12] Mithras, or Christ. 'Overtowered by a hundred burdens, / overburdened with yourself', what weighs down Zarathustra (like the cross of Christ, 'or whatever other heavy burden the hero carries'), is '*himself*, or rather *the* self, his wholeness, which is both God and animal — [...] the totality of his being, which is rooted in his animal nature and reaches out beyond the merely human towards the divine' (*CW* 5 §460). Here, as so often, Jung can help explain the curious power of these enigmatic texts, when he suggests that 'what seems like a poetic figure of speech in Nietzsche is really an age-old myth', and that 'it is as if the poet could still sense, beneath the words of contemporary speech and in the images that crowd in upon his imagination, the ghostly presence of bygone spiritual words' — and, above all — 'possessed the capacity to make them come alive again' (*CW* 5 §460).

The chapters of *Thus Spoke Zarathustra* entitled 'Of the Afterworldsmen' and 'Of the Despisers of the Body' are usually read as Nietzsche's reckoning with Platonism and Judeo-Christianity alike, and it is not inaccurate to interpret them in this light.[13] After all, in 1871 Nietzsche described his own philosophy as 'an *inverted*

Platonism: the further something is from true being, the purer, the more beautiful, the better it is', and the goal of this philosophy as 'living in illusion'.[14] And we can find other passages where Nietzsche inveighs in apparently no uncertain terms against Plato.

In 1887, Nietzsche told his friend, the theologian Franz Overbeck (1837–1905),[15] how he had been reading Simplicius of Cilicia's commentary on the *Enchiridion* of Epictetus, and how he found in it the entire philosophical schematic on which Christianity had based itself. Here, he wrote, 'the *falsification* through morality of everything factual stands there in its full glory': its psychology was miserable, the philosopher was reduced to a country parson — 'And all of it is *Plato's* fault! — he *is still* Europe's greatest misfortune!'.[16] And in *Twilight of the Idols*, Nietzsche opposes Sophist to Socratic philosophy, realism to idealism — '*Sophist culture*, by which I mean *realist culture* […] — this invaluable movement in the midst of the morality-and-ideal swindle of the Socratic schools which was then breaking out everywhere'[17] — and presents the historian Thucydides as a counterfoil to Plato: '*Courage* in face of reality ultimately distinguishes such natures as Thucydides and Plato: Plato is a coward in face of reality — consequently he flees into the ideal [folglich *flüchtet er in's Ideal*]; Thucydides has *himself* under control — consequently he retains control over things …'.[18] But to what extent is Nietzsche justified in his attack, or — to put the matter plainly — is Nietzsche right about Plato?

Everybody Needs a Body

What is the Platonic attitude to the body? There are a number of famous passages which provide an answer to this question. In the *Phaedrus*, Socrates speaks of the body as a 'prison house', something in which we are 'fast bound' as 'an oyster in its shell';[19] in the *Cratylus*, Socrates describes the body as 'the grave of the soul', ascribing to the Orphic poets the view that 'the body is an enclosure or prison in which the soul is incarcerated, kept safe, […] until the penalty is paid';[20] and in the *Gorgias*, Socrates glosses a line from Euripides' *Polyeidos*, 'Who knows, if life be death, and death be life?', with the following remark:

> Perhaps we are actually dead, for I once heard one of our wise men say that we are now dead, and that our body is a tomb, and that that part of the soul in which dwell the desires is of a nature to be swayed and to shift to and fro.[21]

In no dialogue is this view more trenchantly expressed than in the *Phaedo*, where Socrates explains that 'despising the body and avoiding it, and endeavouring to become independent' constitutes the task of the philosopher.[22] Indeed, the body is to be regarded here as a source, if not *the* chief source, of evil;[23] and Socrates defines purification as:

> separating the soul as much as possible from the body, and accustoming it to withdraw itself from all contact with the body and concentrate itself by itself,

and to have its dwelling, so far as it can, both now and in the future, alone by itself, freed from the shackles of the body.[24]

Concomitantly, Socrates defines death as precisely this 'freeing and separation of soul from body' and contends that 'the desire to free the soul is found chiefly, or rather only, in the true philosopher'.[25]

These passages would appear to make the case quite clear: Plato hates the body. Yet, as R. T. Wallis has argued, Plato's attitude towards the sensible world might more accurately be described as an equivocal one. Whereas, in the *Phaedo*, a dualistic position is adopted, such that the soul is exhorted to shun the body and made practically a full member of the intelligible order, in the *Timaeus* the soul is regarded as an intermediary between the sensible and the intelligible worlds (and, by that token, as responsible for the organisation of the former).[26] Indeed, in the *Timaeus* the relation between the body and the soul is envisaged as a reciprocal one, 'we should not move the body without the soul or the soul without the body'; the body is to be trained to live in accordance with reason, and vice versa, so that 'the mathematician or anyone else whose thoughts are much absorbed in some intellectual pursuit, must allow his body also to have due exercise, and practise gymnastics', while 'he who is careful to fashion the body should in turn impart to the soul its proper motions and should cultivate the arts and all philosophy'.[27] As the best modes of 'purifying and reuniting the body', Timaeus recommends (and in this order): (1) gymnastics, then (2) sailing or some other form of travel, and (3) purgation (or, more precisely, 'the purgative treatment of physicians', which 'may be of use in a case of extreme necessity, but in any other will be adopted by no man of sense' …).[28] In this same dialogue, Timaeus contends that someone who has a great, mighty soul in a small, weak body is not beautiful, for such a person is lacking in 'the most important of all symmetries' — 'the due proportion of mind and body is the fairest and loveliest of all sights to him who has the seeing eye', as he puts it.[29]

In her attempt, written some twenty years ago, to 'rethink' Plato and Platonism, Cornelia J. de Vogel comes to the following conclusion about the role and place of the body in the philosophy of Plato:

> Plato […] was, in fact, not an over-spiritualist. He did not identify man with the thinking soul or *noûs*; he did hold that the thinking soul was by nature superior to the body and thus had to lead and govern it. But he thought the body an extremely important thing, since it had to serve the soul. Therefore, Plato's whole system of education was built on the principle of equal training of both body and soul, and this was for him the absolute condition to a harmonious life.[30]

To bear out this claim, de Vogel turns to Plato's late works, his *Republic* and his *Laws*. In the *Republic*, Socrates excludes someone lacking in physical training from being a candidate for the study of philosophy.[31] In the *Laws*, the Athenian Stranger ranks an individual's most valuable possessions — after the gods — as first the soul, but second the body, and not 'the comely, nor the strong, nor the swift, no, nor the healthy' body, and not its opposite, but 'the body which displays all these qualities in intermediate degree' is said to be 'by far the most sober, and soundest as well'.[32]

The phrase from the *Phaedo* that philosophers ought to 'hate' the body (67e) has, de Vogel adds, been 'somewhat misused', and she prefers an alternative translation of this passage which renders it as 'their continual quarrel with the body'.[33] When, in the *Phaedo*, the philosophers wish to have the soul 'by itself', this means, de Vogel argues, that 'they feel the body to be a hindrance to reaching knowledge of purely intelligible Being',[34] and in this respect Plato's position is not so different from that held later by Neoplatonism in general and by Plotinus in particular.

What is the Neoplatonic attitude to the body? Again, there are a number of standard passages — some doctrinal, some autobiographical — to which commentators habitually refer. According to Porphyry, Plotinus 'seemed like one who felt ashamed of being in a body',[35] and we are told that he 'kept away from the bath'.[36] In his tractate 'On Happiness' (or 'On Well-Being'), Plotinus himself appears to consider it something of a regrettable distraction that we have to care for the body at all, asking the question, 'health and freedom from pain; which of these has any great charm?', for 'as long as we possess them we set no store upon them'.[37] In this tractate, we find that Plotinus expresses a decided scepticism about the benefits of physical well-being. 'A powerful frame, a healthy constitution, even a happy balance of temperament' — none of these, he contends, brings felicity or well-being, and 'in the excess of these advantages there is, even, the danger that the [individual] be crushed down and forced more and more within their power';[38] one can have, he seems to be saying, too much of a good thing. Indeed, Plotinus goes so far as to argue that 'there must be a sort of counter-pressure in the other direction, towards the noblest', and this means that 'the body must be lessened, reduced, that the veritable may show forth, *the man behind the appearances*'.[39]

At the opening of another tractate, entitled 'The Soul's Descent into the Body', Plotinus makes a unique, and consequently famous, autobiographical remark about how he had often been 'lifted out of the body into myself', 'beholding a marvellous beauty', and 'enacting the noblest life, acquiring identity with the divine', only for then to come 'the moment of descent', in which he asked himself 'how it happens that I can now be descending, and how did the soul ever enter into my body, the soul which, even within the body, is the high thing it has shown itself to be'?[40] Aware of the views of his philosophical predecessors, Plotinus notes that 'in the cavern of Plato and in the cave of Empedocles' — that is, in the cave described in the allegory of book 7 of the *Republic*, and the cave mentioned in the fragment cited by Porphyry in *The Cave of the Nymphs* — we find an image for 'this universe, where the "breaking of the fetters" and the "ascent" from the depths are figures of the wayfaring towards the intellectual realm'.[41]

Plotinus alludes to a wide range of Platonic sources, both the negative view of the soul's descent into the world (the *Phaedo*, the allegory of the cave in the *Republic*, and the *Phaedrus* myth) and the positive view (the *Timaeus*), thus reflecting (as John Dillon notes) a 'tension' in his own attitude.[42] Moreover, Plotinus explicitly observes that, in Plato, 'commerce with the body is repudiated for two only reasons': first, as 'hindering the soul's intellective act', and second, as 'filling it with pleasure, desire, pain'.[43] But neither of these misfortunes, Plotinus adds, can 'befall a soul which has never deeply penetrated into the body, is not a slave but a sovereign ruling a body of such an order as to have no need and no shortcoming', and therefore, he concludes, can 'give ground for neither desire nor fear'.[44] So closer inspection shows that the matter is more complicated than it might at first appear, and somewhat different from how it is commonly presented. As far as Plotinus's tactic of avoiding a bath is concerned, for instance, Pierre Hadot has argued this should not be interpreted as meaning that Plotinus never washed, but rather that he avoided the public baths (*thermae*), and their associated distractions.[45]

And the implications of this explanation can be developed further. Plotinus was a vociferous critic of Gnosticism, and one of his longest tractates (in fact, the concluding section of a single, long treatise divided by Porphyry into four parts) is called 'Against the Gnostics' (II.9), against those who have hatred for the sensory world and for the body. In the context of his polemic against the Gnostics, it is Plotinus who takes *them* to task for their 'hate' for 'the corporeal', based on their misreading of Plato; for instance, in the *Phaedo* (especially 66b–d), where Socrates says that 'the body provides us with innumerable distractions in the pursuit of our necessary sustenance', that the body 'fills us with loves and desires and fears and all sorts of fancies and a great deal of nonsense, with the result that we never get an opportunity to think at all about anything', and that — 'worst of all' — if we do 'obtain any leisure from the body's claims and turn to some line of inquiry, the body intrudes once more into our investigations, interrupting, disturbing, distracting, and preventing us from getting a glimpse of the truth'.[46]

In contrast to the Gnostics, Plotinus praises the beauty of the body, because it contains a trace of the divine: for 'the beauty of things here', he says — alluding to the passage in the *Symposium* where Diotima tells Socrates that 'starting from individual beauties, the quest for the universal beauty must find him ever mounting the heavenly ladder, stepping from rung to rung [...] until at last he comes to know what beauty is'[47] — exist because of the beauty of primary being.[48] For 'even in the world of sense and part, there are things of a loveliness comparable to that of the celestials — forms whose beauty must fill us with veneration for the creator and convince us of their origin in the divine'.[49] In other words, one goes from the beauties of this world to the beauties of the higher world, 'but without insulting these beauties here'.[50]

As R. T. Wallis has pointed out, compared with Manichaean, Gnostic, or even Christian standards, Neoplatonic asceticism is, in fact, remarkably mild. Nor should we, as Wallis suggests, be surprised by this since, in the Platonic view, the material world, while material, is nevertheless the image of its 'ideal archetype'. True, for Plotinus, the world with its basis in sensible matter is inferior to its intelligible archetype.[51] True, for Plotinus, we must not confuse the sensible images of beauty, whether of material objects or noble actions, with that archetypal beauty found only in the intelligible world.[52] Nevertheless, Plotinus also argues that the sage will revere the world in its beauty, for no one can love the intelligible world without also loving its intelligible offspring.[53] Correspondingly, 'the body is not seen as an enemy' and, because 'the keynote remains Hellenic moderation', it was rare for self-discipline to turn into self-torture.[54] For Plotinus, unlike for the Gnostics, the body is not something one should revile, but rather something from which we should patiently await our release at our death, when we shall abandon the body, as does the musician the lyre that has served him well — or the inhabitant the house that has provided him with shelter.[55]

This attitude towards the body had practical implications, too. In his biography of Plotinus, Porphyry notes the remarkable ability possessed by his philosophical master to combine activity in the external world and an inner life of meditation.[56] Even if we ultimately consider the Neoplatonic account of the body to be an inadequate one, we can nevertheless accept its argument for a purification of the spiritual life, rather than turn it into a case for the abolition of such a significant part of human experience;[57] as Pierre Hadot has argued, 'we must consent, with as much courage as Plotinus did, to every dimension of human experience, and to everything within it that is mysterious, inexpressible, and transcendent'.[58]

So in the case of Plotinus, his philosophy is not a philosophy of the 'afterworld' (or *Hinterwelt*), and far from rejecting the body, he is concerned to establish the correct relation to it.[59] (In 'Of the Three Metamorphoses', Zarathustra tells us that 'the spirit sundered from the world now wins *its own* world',[60] and this *neue Welt* is described by Herbert Theierl as being located 'beyond consciousness, and thus in transcendence', a world that is 'not the old paradise of nature to which everyone as a piece of nature belongs, but rather a new, artificial paradise to which only someone has access who succeeds in expanding his ego into a self'.[61] In *Twilight of the Idols*, Nietzsche's trenchant account of 'How the "Real World" at last Became a Myth' concludes with the following sixth and final stage: 'Mid-day; moment of the shortest shadow; end of the longest error; zenith of mankind; INCIPIT ZARATHUSTRA'.[62] Conventionally, this philosophical parody is read as an attack on Platonic dualism — after all, in the preceding section, Plato 'blushes for shame' — and as a celebration of the simulacrum, of a world of appearance and postmodern semblance. Looking more closely at the text, however, this is not at all what Nietzsche proclaims: '*with the real world we have also abolished the apparent world!*' — what Nietzsche is attacking is a dualism of the kind frequently ascribed to Plato, but not the view that there is a distinction to be made between reality and appearance, although both modes of being are inextricably intertwined.[63])

For Plotinus, the correct relation to the body is not one of hatred, but rather one of a certain kind of indifference. For Plotinus, a hatred of the body is a kind of perversion of a love of self, and a distraction from what he saw as the chief philosophical task: to raise the divine in oneself to the divine in the All.[64] In the first of his two tractates on the 'Problems of the Soul', Plotinus insists on the reciprocal relationship between soul and material world, between soul and cosmos: 'The cosmos is ensouled, not by a soul belonging to it, but by one present to it; it is mastered, not master; not possessor, but possessed. The soul bears it up, and it lies within, no fragment of it unsharing'. To explain the relationship between the soul and the cosmos, he uses the image of a net in the sea: 'The cosmos is like a net which takes all its life, as far as ever it stretches, from being wet in the water; it is at the mercy of the sea which spreads out taking the net with it just so far as it will go [...]: the soul is of so far-reaching a nature — a thing unbounded — as to embrace the entire body of the All in the one extension; so far as the universe extends, there soul is'.[65] How then could the body be something bad, bathing as it does in an ocean of soul?

So for Plotinus, the body is not something bad, but what can be bad is an incorrect relation to the body. For him, the correct relation to the body is not one of mortification or of flagellation: rather, it is one of distance and of a certain disinterest. (In Nietzschean terms, it is a relation that expresses the *Pathos der Distanz*, the 'pathos of distance').[66] For to go so far as to hate the body is to attribute to it an exaggerated significance, and hence to fail to recognize it for what it is: for the body is not something of no significance at all, it is rather an image of the intelligible — just as the intellect is the image of the One, and the soul is the image of the intellect, so the world is the sensible image of the intelligible.[67] It is, so to speak, like 'an image sleeping in the stone, the image of my visions' ...

To have a body means to become an individual; it is our point of entrance into the order of ontological necessity. What matters is not the status of the body, but the nature of our relation to it, which should be one of a certain kind of indifference, captured in the image of the musician's attitude towards his lyre, an instance of the great ancient metaphor of the body as an instrument. What matters is to avoid falling into illusion or error, and this task is positively expressed in the injunction that the individual should embark on the task of sculpting one's own statue,[68] and to realize the vision of one's own self. Here lies the existential imperative in Plotinus's philosophy of art: as the artist works away on the work of art, so he (or she) works on himself (or herself), transforming himself (or herself) into a work of art that can, in turn, contribute to and enhance the beauty of the world. The soul must turn away from the body and the material world, in order to discover the principle from which both derive and descend, and then it can appreciate the beauty of the world — and the beauty of the body — for what each really is. Similarly, the sculptor must see the block of marble not just as a block of marble, but also as the statue (be it the Juno Ludovisi, or the Venus of Milo, or whatever) into which — with infinite skill, care, and attention — he (or she) is going to sculpt it.

Nietzsche seems to have understood this message, as is suggested by his reference to *The Birth of Tragedy* as offering an *Artisten-Metaphysik* ('artists' metaphysics'); his call in *The Gay Science* for us to be 'the poets of our life — first of all in the smallest, most everyday matters', and his invitation in that work that we should learn from artists — well, from whom else? — how we can 'make things beautiful, attractive, and desirable for us when they are not'; his illustration in *Ecce Homo* of *Wohlgeratenheit*, or 'having-turned-out-well', by the image of carving oneself out of 'wood at once hard, delicate, and sweet-smelling'; and his cry, in an unpublished note from 1880, '*to make ourselves*, to *shape* a form from all the elements — that is the task! The task of a sculptor! Of a productive human being!'.[69]

Precisely this kind of overlap in discourse prompts one to ask: could Nietzsche and the Neoplatonic tradition be, in fact, much closer than is usually thought to be the case? Might the case of Nietzsche even bear out Thomas Taylor's well-known observation that 'the lyre of true philosophy is no less tuneful in the desert than in the city'; and might Nietzsche's life substantiate Taylor's claim that 'he who knows how to call forth its latent harmony in solitude, will not want the testimony of the multitude to convince him that its melody is ecstatic and divine'?[70]

After all, it is recognized that Neoplatonism advocates a certain kind of ascetic practice, as well as promoting the opportunities for ecstatic experience — this tension between asceticism and ecstasy is, in fact, arguably one of its chief hallmarks. And this tension is one we also find in Nietzsche's writings, which operate with a strikingly similar polarity between asceticism and ecstasy (or, in Nietzsche's terms, between Apollo and Dionysos).

Asceticism ...

In a sense, the whole question of the relation between asceticism and ecstasy was responsible for setting Jung on the train of thought that led him to develop a system of psychology that was, in significant respects, different from Freud's. To the extent that this is so, we can trace the journey undertaken by Jung through its reflection in his correspondence with Freud. In his letter of 8 November 1900, Jung excitedly told Freud how his studies of the history of symbolism, particularly the four volumes of *Symbolism and Mythology of the Ancient Peoples* (1810–1823) by the German philologist Georg Friedrich Creuzer (1771–1858) and *A Discourse on the Worship of Priapus, and its Connection with the Mystic Theology of the Ancients* (2nd edn, 1865) by the English classicist Richard Payne Knight (1750–1824), had revived his interest in archaeology. 'Rich lodes open up', as he put it, 'for the phylogenetic basis of the theory of neurosis'.[71] The sort of thing that had captured Jung's attention is the account of ritual cults of Egypt given in the fifth century BCE by the ancient Greek historian Herodotus, comparing them with Greek traditions.

In his *Histories*, Herodotus tells us what happened at the festival in honour of Artemis at Boubastis (2.60.1–2).[72] (Minus the barge, a number of these customs are still observed on weekend evenings in many British city centres ...) Herodotus also tells us about the festival in honour of Isis at Bousiris, and the cults in honour of Athena, Helios, and Leo at Sais, Heliopolis, and Bouto; but it was the cult of Ares at Papremis that Jung found particularly interesting (2.63.1–3).[73] And Jung found Herodotus's account of the festival of Dionysos especially absorbing. For 'the Egyptians', Herodotus wrote, 'celebrate the festival of Dionysos is nearly the same way as the Hellenes do, except they do not have choral dances' (2.48).[74] 'The dying and resurgent god' — the Orphic mysteries, Thammuz, Osiris, Dionysos, Adonis, etc. — is 'everywhere phallic', Jung triumphantly concluded.[75] Nevertheless, for Jung's tastes, Herodotus was too shy and retiring. 'It's a crying shame,' he told Freud, 'that already with Herodotus prudery puts forth its quaint blossoms', and 'on his own admission he covers up a lot of things "for reasons of decency"', so 'where did the Greeks learn that from so early?'.[76]

In a draft sent to Freud in June 1910, Jung had posed the problem he was grappling with in terms of 'sexuality destroying itself' (*die Sexualität geht an sich selber zugrunde*),[77] a phrase that provoked in Freud 'a vigorous shaking of the head' and which Jung himself described as 'an extremely paradoxical formulation'.[78] Jung chose to frame the debate with reference to the cult of Mithras, the divine figure in an ancient Iranian religion that had been adopted by many in the Roman army.[79] In the central iconography of Mithraism — depicting the god (Mithras) in the act of sacrificing a bull (the tauroctony), while a dog and a snake reach up towards the blood, a scorpion attacks the bull's genitals, a raven flies around the scene, and corns of wheat emerge from the wounded bull — Jung saw something going on that was as problematic as it was intriguing. There is, he argued, 'a *conflict at the heart of sexuality itself*',[80] and the resolution of this conflict leads to an increase in abundance, in fruitfulness, in life.

What we might call an interest in the *ascetic urge* is reflected in the work that emerged from Jung's investigations into mythological symbolism (and marked his shift away from Freud): *Transformations and Symbols of the Libido* (1911–1912), revised (as if to insist on an underlying continuity in Jung's thought) in 1952 as *Symbols of Transformation*. Here Jung noted that asceticism occurs 'whenever the animal instincts are so strong that they need to be violently exterminated' (*CW* 5 §118, fn. 5). It was in order to escape 'the extreme brutality of the decadent Roman civilization', Jung argued, that 'the Desert Fathers mortified themselves through spirituality' and the anchorites built their cities in the desert. Yet asceticism is not simply a negative reaction, it has its own positive content too, and its content is essentially a *symbolic* one:

> If one has any conception of the sexual content of those ancient cults, and if one realizes that the experience of union with God was understood in antiquity as a more or less concrete coitus, then one can no longer pretend that the forces motivating the production of symbols have suddenly become different since the birth of Christ. The fact that primitive Christianity resolutely turned away from nature and the instincts in general, and, through its asceticism, from sex in particular, clearly indicates the source from which its motive forces came.
>
> (*CW* 5 §339)

For Jung, both the pagan 'cult of sex' and the religion of Christianity were different mechanisms by which 'libido' became *transformed*; or, to use another of his favourite terms, 'canalized' (*CW* 5 §204; cf. *CW* 8 §79).

Now a thorough-going critique of asceticism is one of the major themes of Nietzsche's treatise *On the Genealogy of Morals* (1887), particularly its third essay, entitled 'What is the Meaning of Ascetic Ideals?' Read on one level, this essay provides an answer, as Nietzsche summarizes it in *Ecce Homo*, to the question of 'where the tremendous *power* of the ascetic ideal, the priestly ideal, comes from, although it is the *harmful* ideal *par excellence*, a will to the end, a *décadence* ideal'.[81] Read on another level, however, the text is remarkably ambivalent about the effects of asceticism, and precisely half-way through his essay, Nietzsche himself summarizes his case as follows:

> *The ascetic ideal springs from the protective instinct of a degenerating life* which tries by all means to sustain itself and to fight for its existence; it indicates a partial physiological obstruction and exhaustion against which the deepest instincts of life, which have remained intact, continually struggle with new expediences and devices. The ascetic ideal is such an expedient; the case is therefore the opposite of what those who reverence this ideal believe: life wrestles in it and through it with death and *against* death; the ascetic ideal is an artifice for the *preservation* of life.[82]

This leads Nietzsche to the paradoxical conclusion — and this is exactly his point, that the ascetic ideal *is* a paradox — that 'this ascetic priest, this apparent enemy of life, this *denier* — precisely he is among the greatest *conserving* and yes-creating forces of life'.[83] Indeed, in *Beyond Good and Evil* (1886) Nietzsche had described 'asceticism and puritanism' in terms that are positive — well, positive for him — as 'almost indispensable means for educating and ennobling a race that wishes to become master over its origins among the rabble and that works its way up toward future rule'.[84]

(Earlier still, in *Thus Spoke Zarathustra*, where the principle of the will-to-power is announced, Zarathustra creeps in the chapter called 'Of Self-Overcoming' into 'the heart of of life itself and down to the roots of its heart', and there life itself tells Zarathustra a secret: '"Behold," it said, "I am *that which must overcome itself again and again*[…]."'[85] One could well see in Nietzsche's interest in asceticism as a form of the will-to-power a radical extension of a complex and controversial notion found in Goethe, *Entsagung* — usually translated as 'renunciation' or 'resignation', but conceptually related to the idea of self-sacrifice with an aim of greater fruitfulness.)

Early on in the third essay of *On the Genealogy of Morals*, Nietzsche introduces a little-noticed distinction between religious asceticism and philosophical asceticism, noting that philosophers conceive of ascetic ideal as a 'cheerful asceticism', that of 'an animal become fledged and divine, floating above life rather than in repose'.[86] In the same section, he draws a parallel between the desert to which the ancient Pre-Socratic philosopher Heraclitus withdrew — 'the courtyards and colonnades of the great temple of Artemis'[87] — with the modern desert, characterized by 'a voluntary obscurity', 'a dislike of noise', 'a modest […] everyday job', and 'a room in a full, utterly commonplace hotel' (the kind of hotel, he added, where 'one is certain to go unrecognized and can talk to anyone with impunity').[88] Indeed, in the next section, he argues that 'a certain asceticism', which he defines as 'a severe and cheerful continence with the best will', belongs to 'the most favorable conditions of supreme spirituality'.[89]

In *Ecce Homo*, Nietzsche himself embraces a lifestyle that can, without any exaggeration, be described as ascetic: he urges the reader to adopt 'selectivity in nutriment', 'selectivity in climate and place', and 'selectivity in one's kind of recreation'.[90] As far as nutrition is concerned, Nietzsche advocates avoiding heavy cooking, abjures alchohol and tobacco, promotes the drinking of simply water, and has strict rules for the consumption of coffee (none at all), tea (only in the morning), and cocoa (drunk thick and oil-free).[91] As far as place and climate are concerned, Nietzsche recommends places with 'dry air' and a 'clear sky': Paris, Provence, Florence, Jerusalem, and Athens are commended; Naumburg, Thuringia in general and Schulpforta in particular, Leipzig, Basel, and Venice are to be treated with caution.[92] Finally, as far as recreation is concerned, French culture is promoted as vastly superior to German: Pascal, Montaigne; Molière, Corneille and Racine; Paul Bourget, Pierre Loti, Gyp, Meilhac, Anatole France, Jules Lemaitre, and Guy de Maupassant; and Stendhal …[93]

Above all, Nietzsche's asceticism embraces cheerfulness, or *Heiterkeit*, a quality that, so he had argued in *Daybreak*, is all too often slandered. It is people who have been 'deeply injured by life', he argues, who 'discover under every rose a disguised and hidden grave'; those unable to enjoy and appreciate 'festivities, carousels, joyful music' evince a kind of childishness — a childishness 'deriving from that *second childhood* which succeeds old age and is the forerunner of death'.[94]

… and Ecstasy

What is it like to have a mystical experience? For those who have never had one, it is instructive to turn to the description of a 'mystical' experience recorded by the psychologist Havelock Ellis (1859–1939) in his autobiographical work, *The Dance of Life* (1923):

> My self was one with the Not-Self, my will one with the universal will. I seemed to walk in light; my feet scarcely touched the ground; I had entered a new world. The effect of that swift revolution was permanent. At first there was a moment or two of wavering, and then the primary exaltation subsided into an attitude of calm serenity toward all those questions that had once seemed so torturing. […] Neither was I troubled about the existence of any superior being or beings, and I was ready to see that all the words and forms by which men try to picture spiritual realities are mere metaphors and images of an inward experience. […] I had become indifferent to shadows, for I held the substance. I had sacrificed what I held dearest at the call of what seemed to be Truth, and now I was repaid a thousandfold. Henceforth I could face life with confidence and joy, for my heart was at one with the world and whatever might prove to be in harmony with the world could not be out of harmony with me.[95]

As Manly P. Hall notes, similar experiences are recorded in the lives of Meister Eckhart, Emanuel Swedenborg, Dante Alighieri, and Martin Luther; and to this list of those who have experienced what could — with the Canadian psychiatrist Richard Maurice Bucke (1837–1902) — be called *cosmic consciousness*, we might well add Plotinus.[96]

For, according to Porphyry, Plotinus had 'something more by birth when compared to others';[97] what does he mean by this? Elsewhere, Porphyry explains that 'the god who has neither shape nor form, and is set above intellect and all that is intelligible', appeared to Plotinus, 'this daimonic man', as 'time after time he drove himself on towards the first and transcendent god, with his own reflections and according to the ways set forth by Plato in the *Symposium*'.[98] (For his part, Porphyry claimed that he, too, had drawn close to this god and been united with him, albeit only once.) As we have seen, Plotinus himself refers to his numerous experiences of this kind, when he was 'lifted out of the body' into himself.[99] On the Neoplatonic account, *ekstasis* (ecstasy) involves *ektasis* (expansion),[100] the emergence of the soul from its physical surroundings. How is this achieved?

According to Plotinus's account, as explicated by Robert Berchman, such *ekstasis* is achieved by *theoria* (contemplation), and specifically by 'art and the imaginative contemplation of [the soul's] inner beauty', for it is the function of art to erase 'the distinctions between the layers of the soul' and 'to bring the ontologically distant epistemologically present'.[101] Berchman's comments clearly bring out the extent to which aesthetics is involved in Plotinus's thinking: for Berchmann, aesthetics is 'closely tied to the awakening of the soul from its physical nature' and hence to '[the] expansion of the soul to the divine idea', and finally to 'the ascent of the soul to god'.[102]

For, on this account, *aisthesis* (perception) is 'nothing more than the lower soul becoming conscious of what the higher soul eternally beholds', and *phantasia* (imagination) is 'nothing more than the presentation to the lower soul of an apprehension (*antilepsis*), which permits her to identify her empirical self with her pure, true self that transcends the sensible'. Consequently, art itself becomes nothing less than the means to salvation, because it 'serves to heal the disparate self', it 'brings that which is so noetically distant, sensibly present', and it enables 'the joining of heaven and earth in the human soul'. How so? Because:

> The dangerously long distance between being and becoming, consciousness and unconsciousness, is overcome through an aesthetic that stresses the possibility of unanimity between subject and object. Such identification makes the soul conscious of her intelligible beauty. Such consciousness leads the soul upward to divine beauty itself.[103]

In his *Commentary on Alcibiades I*, Proclus explains what is involved in this 'expansion': 'The soul', he says, 'expands in order to get closer to god while god expands to meet the soul, without ever stepping outside, for he always remains inside himself'.[104] One way of stimulating such an ecstatic experience in late antiquity was to enter a holy place — or to view a statue of a god …[105]

Such experiences or doctrines might strike one as being anathema to Nietzsche, yet in his writings we repeatedly come across passages where he discusses, sometimes as a metaphor, sometimes in an explicitly autobiographical context, a similar experience.[106] Writing, for instance, in his notebooks in the summer–autumn of 1873, Nietzsche cries — as if echoing Plotinus's famous allusion to Homer in his tractate 'On Beauty', '"Let us flee to the beloved Fatherland": this is the soundest counsel':[107] — 'O, I so understand this flight, out and across into the peace of the One!'.[108] (Then again, the image of 'the open sea', evoked by Diotima in the *Symposium*'s account of how the philosophical soul 'turn[s] his eyes toward the open sea of beauty'[109] — and used by Plotinus in precisely this context — is a favourite of Nietzsche's: 'Everything is sea, sea, sea!', as he cries out in the concluding aphorism of *Daybreak*; 'We have left behind the land and have embarked [...] Now, little ship, look out! Beside you is the ocean', and 'the sea, *our* sea, lies open again; perhaps there has never yet been such an "open sea"' [*The Gay Science*, §124 and §343], and in 'On the Blissful Islands', Zarathustra's interlocuters are imagined to be 'gaz[ing] out upon distant seas from the midst of superfluity'.[110] This image of the sea is a profoundly Platonic one: which is why David Hume (1711–1776), in his essay called 'The Platonist', chooses to use it in his opening paragraph: 'The divinity is a boundless ocean of bliss and glory: human minds are smaller streams, which, arising at first from this ocean, seek still, amid their wanderings, to return to it, and to lose themselves in that immensity of perfection.')[111]

Or we can turn for another set of examples to the famous preface from 1886, written for *Human, All Too Human* when it was reissued as a two-volume work. Here Nietzsche talks about how 'a spirit in whom the type "free spirit" will one day become ripe and sweet to the point of perfection' will experience 'a *great liberation*'.[112] This 'great liberation' of the *Geist* is further described (among other things) in terms of the soul — 'the youthful soul is all at once convulsed, torn loose, torn away' — of one's metaphysical orientation — 'a desecrating blow and glance *backwards*'[113] — of the will — 'this will to *free* will'[114] — in other words, the great liberation is described, in the same way as the Neoplatonic tradition describes the ascent of the soul, as a mystical experience. As Berchman emphasizes, 'ascent is an important component in Plotinus's philosophical system', and in his comments on the *First Alcibiades* in his *Theology of Plato*, Proclus describes how the soul, 'verging to her own union, and to the centre of all life, laying aside multitude, and the variety of the all manifold powers which she contains', finally 'ascends to the highest watchtower of beings'.[115]

(As Jung points out in *Symbols of Transformation* [*CW* 5 §104, fn. 55], Augustine took up the notion of the ascent to the 'idea' in his *Confessions*, book 10; in chapter 7, Augustine declares: 'By this very soul I will ascend up to [God]; I will soar beyond that faculty of mine, by which I am united unto my body, and by which I fill the whole frame of it with life', and in chapter 8 he asseverates: 'I will soar therefore beyond this faculty of my nature, still rising by degrees unto him who hath made both me and that nature'.[116] Elsewhere in *Symbols of Transformation*, Jung notes the motif of the ascent of the hero, relating it to the motif of the fiery chariot, as found in the ascensions of Elijah, Mithras, or St Francis of Assisi [*CW* 5 §158, fn. 62]; in the legend of Hercules, too, the motif of ascent concludes the life of the hero.[117])

Time and again in his preface to *Human, All Too Human*, Nietzsche emphasizes the experiential aspect of this 'liberation': it is said to consist in a view from
above: 'one lives [...] near or far as one wishes, preferably slipping away, evading,
fluttering off, gone again, again flying aloft; one is spoiled, as everyone is who has at
some time seen a tremendous number of things *beneath* him'[118]; in a kind of mystical eye-opening: 'the free spirit again draws nearer to life [...] It seems to him as
if his eyes are only now open to what is *close at hand* [...] These close and closest
things: how changed they seem! what bloom and magic they have acquired!';[119]
and in a mystical 'shudder': 'Only now does he see himself — and what surprises
he experiences as he does so! What unprecedented shudders! [*Welche unerprobten
Schauder!*] What happiness [*Welches Glück*] [...]!'.[120] As was the case when dealing
with the ancient mysteries, it is important both to recognize the validity of these
experiences — but also to remain silent about them: 'My philosophy advises me to
keep silent and to ask no more questions; especially as in certain cases, as the saying
has it, one *remains* a philosopher only by — keeping silent'.[121]

In other works, Nietzsche approaches the question of ecstatic experience from a
different angle. In *Daybreak*, for instance, he devotes an aphorism to the entire question of 'the many forces that now have to come together in the thinker'. He begins by
recalling how, in the past, to 'abstract oneself from sensory perception, to exalt oneself
to contemplation of abstractions' was felt as *exaltation*; but, he adds, 'we can no longer
quite enter into this feeling'.[122] By revelling in 'pallid images of words and things', by
sporting with 'such invisible, unaudible, impalpable beings', and by feeling 'contempt
for the sensorily tangible, seductive and evil world', one 'lifted oneself upwards'; with
his reference to Plato's dialectic, it is clear which philosophical tradition Nietzsche has
in his sights.[123] And yet, when Nietzsche goes on to say what the real thinker needs —

> imagination, self-uplifting, abstraction, desensualization, invention, presenti-
> ment, induction, dialectics, deduction, the critical faculty, the assemblage of
> material, the impersonal mode of thinking, contemplativeness and compre-
> hensiveness, and not least justice and love for all that exists

— he seems, in this amalgamation of rational and irrational processes, to be echoing the eminently pragmatic, and highly sensory, advice that Plato gives us in his
Seventh Letter:

> The study of virtue and vice must be accompanied by an inquiry into what
> is false and true of existence in general and must be carried on by constant
> practice throughout a long period [...]. Hardly after practising detailed com-
> parisons of names and definitions and visual and other sense perceptions, after
> scrutinizing them in benevolent disputation by the use of question and answer
> without jealousy, at last in a flash understanding of each blazes up, and the
> mind, as it is exerts all its powers to the limit of human capacity, is flooded
> with light.[124]

Further on in *Daybreak*, Nietzsche alludes towards the opening of this letter, where Plato confesses to having cherished 'the hope of entering upon a political career',[125] and he seems to agree with Plato that the philosophical thinker must exist in society as 'the evil principle'. Indeed, Nietzsche compares Plato's ideas with Mohammed's as being eminently '*practical*', and he speculates that 'a couple of accidents more and a couple of other accidents fewer — and the world would have seen the Platonisation of the European south'.[126]

In his notes for May–June 1883, Nietzsche talks about the Dionysian as 'the most accessible side of antiquity' and 'the point of access to the Greeks', juxtaposing this notion with 'a terrible mass of lofty sensations which still lack corresponding thoughts and goals'.[127] As Herbert Theierl has argued, understanding what Nietzsche means when he refers to the Dionysian state (*Zustand*) is central to grasping his thought: it is essentially an ecstatic state of intense delight, in which 'the shattering of the form of consciousness in the mystical unity' is experienced as 'the sudden expansion of perspective and the loss of the ground beneath one's feet', an experience compared by Nietzsche himself to not simply having 'burned our bridges behind us' but having 'gone farther and destroyed the land behind us', and captured in the poem 'Amid Birds of Prey' (a text that so fascinated Jung) in the lines: 'If you love abysses you must have wings …'.[128]

Of all Nietzsche's works, it is his *Zarathustra* that appears, because of its lyrical intensity, to have been the most 'inspired'; this in itself would explain Jung's interest in this work as a manifestation of the unconscious. In *Thus Spoke Zarathustra*, one finds constant references to ecstatic moments when Zarathustra's soul dances,[129] and to metaphors of ascent. (As Manly P. Hall pointed out, dancing formed a key part of the ancient Mystery rituals, and from the second chorale ode in Sophocles's tragedy *Ajax*, addressed to Pan as the director of the dance of the gods, to the round or circle dance performed by Jesus and his apostles at the Last Supper in the apocryphal Acts of John, it is a constant motif in the great Mystery tradition.[130])

To the people assembled in the market-place, Zarathustra declares that 'one must have chaos in one, to give birth to a dancing star',[131] and Jung interprets this image of the dancing star as 'a symbol of individuation', as 'a symbol of the concentration of one living spark, a spark of fire that fell into creation, according to the Gnostic myth' (*SNZ* 1, 106). And to his disciples, Zarathustra confesses that 'I should believe only in a god who understood how to dance' in a discourse that concludes on the ecstatic experience: 'Now I am nimble, now I see myself under myself, now a god dances within me'.[132] On this passage, Jung makes (presumably in an allusion to the Hindu god, Shiva) the following sombre remark: 'We know that god, but he is called the destroyer' and 'his dancing takes place unfortunately in the burial-ground' (*SNZ* 1, 508).

In a letter sent to Overbeck, shortly after the publication of *Beyond Good and Evil* in the summer of 1886, Nietzsche wrote that this latest work was intended to 'throw some explanatory light' on *Thus Spoke Zarathustra*, which he frankly admitted was 'an *incomprehensible* book' — incomprehensible, because it 'draws exclusively on experiences shared with no one else'.[133] What were these experiences? In *Ecce Homo*, where Nietzsche offers an account of the composition of his *Zarathustra*, he has recourse to the ancient discourse of inspiration, echoing the ancient Greek idea of *furor poeticus* when the muses, gods, or goddesses 'breathed into' the poet or artist. (Here again we find the ancient idea, which we met earlier in Chapter 1 in the context of the auricular conception of Christ by the Virgin Mary, that connects the soul with air or wind.) Nietzsche describes the composition of *Zarathustra* as nothing less than a *revelation*:

> The concept of revelation, in the sense that something suddenly, with unspeakable certainty and subtlety, becomes *visible*, audible, something that shakes and overturns one to the depths, simply describes the fact. One hears, one does not seek; one takes, one does not ask who gives; a thought flashes up like lightning, with necessity, unalteringly formed — I have never had any choice.[134]

Here Nietzsche emphasizes that the experience of writing *Zarathustra* was a visible and auditory one: it involved him becoming 'merely incarnation' — incarnation! — 'merely mouthpiece, merely medium of overwhelming forces'. Paradoxically, as the highest experience of a feeling of freedom, it involves an overwhelming sense of necessity. (Is this why Hegel argued that freedom is really insight into necessity, and why he declared that 'the truth of necessity is freedom'?)[135] This sense of necessity is strongly present in the rest of Nietzsche's description of his experience, where he does not shy away from using precisely the terms 'ecstasy', 'absoluteness', and even 'divinity':

> An ecstasy whose tremendous tension sometimes discharges itself in a flood of tears, while one's steps now involuntarily rush along, now involuntarily lag; a complete being-outside-of-oneself with the distinct consciousness of a multitude of subtle shudders and trickles down to one's toes; a depth of happiness in which the most painful and gloomy things appear, not as an antithesis, but as conditioned, demanded, as a *necessary* colour within such a superfluity of light; an instinct for rhythmical relationships [...] Everything is in the highest degree involuntary but takes place as in a tempest of a feeling of freedom, of absoluteness, of power, of divinity ...[136]

Here Nietzsche talks about *Entzückung* (ecstasy) as a feeling of *Außer-sich-sein* (being-outside-of-oneself), and it is instructive to compare this passage from *Ecce Homo* with Plutarch's description of what the soul experiences at the moment of death in terms of what the initiate underwent in the Eleusinian Mysteries, based on the principle that 'the verbs *teleutân* (die) and *teleisthai* (be initiated), and the actions they denote, have a similarity':

> In the beginning there is straying and wandering, the weariness of running this way and that, and nervous journeys through darkness that reach no goal, and then immediately before the consummation every possible terror, shivering

and trembling and sweating and amazement. But after this a marvellous light meets the wanderer, and open country and meadow lands welcome him; and in that place there are voices and dancing and the solemn majesty of sacred music and holy visions. And amidst these, he walks at large in new freedom, now perfect and fully initiated, celebrating the sacred rites, a garland upon his head, and converses with pure and holy men [...].[137]

And we can compare it with what we said earlier about Plotinus, whose experience displays especially strong parallels with Nietzsche's. For Nietzsche talks about an ecstatic experience of being-outside-of-himself, just as Plotinus does in his account of being 'lifted out of the body into myself'; he talks about an excess of light, just as Plotinus does about an experience of pure brilliance, sheer luminosity;[138] and he talks about a feeling of divinity, just as Plotinus makes it his philosophical ambition to raise the god within himself to the divine in the All. Or as Plato himself wrote in the seventh of the letters attributed to him: 'Acquaintance with [knowledge of the subjects to which I devote myself] must come rather after a long period of attendance on instruction in the subject itself and of close companionship, when, suddenly, like a blaze kindled by a leaping spark, it is generated in the soul and at once becomes self-sustaining'.[139] Like a blaze kindled by a leaping spark — or like a bolt of lightning from a dark cloud?

In a shrewd analysis of Diotima's speech about the 'ascent to the forms' in the *Symposium*, the Australian philosopher Paul Redding has argued that Plato and Nietzsche are less far apart than is often understood to be the case. In *The Birth of Tragedy*, and then again in *On the Genealogy of Morals*, Nietzsche is usually read as offering an account of the dissociation of sense and intelligence, conventionally thought of as Platonic. But what, especially in his *Genealogy*, Nietzsche is really doing is offering a critique, not so much of what Platonism considers to be real, as of various processes of idealization: that is to say, of the means by which we arrive at our ideas about the real. Some forms of idealization — the slaves' — are *reactive*, involving logical complements (e.g., good and evil), only one of which possesses any concrete empirical content. Other forms of idealization — the masters' — are *active*, involving polar opposites (e.g., good and bad), allowing for a metaphorical linkage that allows us to transfer a quality from one sphere to another. This transference of a quality from, say, the physical to the spiritual, allows for creativity: in this sense, Nietzsche is arguing a case *for* idealization.

In Diotima's speech in the *Symposium*, the movement of Eros from mortals to gods, from the bodily to the spiritual, is an example of this second kind of idealization, or *active idealization*: the love entertained by the lover of a new, 'higher' object by no means entails his rejection of a 'lower' object. Thus Plato's philosophy, in Redding's words, offers 'a remarkable modern way of conceiving of the developmental continuity of an individual's evaluative experience of the world, with its biologically given constitution, while nevertheless not reducing the former to the latter', and it does so by offering 'a sketch of a process through which these initially somatic desires are metamorphosed or transfigured into something more "ideal" *via* language'.[140] Correspondingly, Redding argues, Nietzsche extends Kant's view that we can know *that* something is beautiful, but not *why* it is so, from the aesthetic realm to the realms of epistemology and practical judgements. All of which prompts the following startling, yet insightful, question: if we can feel 'the compulsion of beauty', acknowledging its demand to be recognized as beautiful without cognizing the ground of this demand, can we experience 'the compulsion of truth and goodness' as well …?[141]

If Redding is right, then Martin Heidegger (1889–1976) was justified when, in his own great lecture course on Nietzsche, he described Nietzsche as 'the *last metaphysician* of the West'.[142] But he is right, not because Nietzsche is 'the thinker of the thought of will to power', but because — in Redding's words — 'against the expectations generated from Platonic metaphysics, Nietzsche's aestheticization of other realms of value are often understood as sanctioning a denial of objectivity, and a relativistic attitude of "anything goes"', whereas in fact it is the case that Nietzsche 'saw it the other way around'.[143] When Nietzsche says 'nothing is true, everything is permitted', he places these words in the mouth, not of Zarathustra, but of Zarathustra's shadow;[144] and, when he cites this phrase in *On the Genealogy of Morals*, he attributes the phrase to the order of the Assassins (or the Hashashin), an Islamic cult founded in the eleventh century shortly before the First Crusade.[145] So can we speak, as Redding does, of Nietzsche's 'aestheticized metaphysics'?

Hierarchy

Let us return then to the question of Nietzsche's relation to Plato. How much did Nietzsche actually know of Plato's works? His engagement with Plato must have begun during his schooldays at Schulpforta, where in 1864 he wrote a short essay entitled 'On the Relation of Alcibiades' Speech to the Other Speeches of Plato's *Symposium*'.[146] Although we know from his notebooks that Nietzsche intended to read the *Apology*, the *Crito*, and the *Euthyphro* in the summer of holidays of 1863, studied the *Symposium* in February 1864, and refers to the *Philebus* in Spring 1864, we know there were other, indirect Platonic influences on Nietzsche. For example, Otto Benndorf (1838–1901), one of the teachers at Schulpforta, noted that 'Nietzsche had the good fortune to have as teacher at Schulpforta the famous Plato translator Steinhart, who, in my opinion, must have influenced him deeply'.[147] This teacher, Karl Steinhart (1801–1872), edited the complete works of Plato and published extensively on Platonism. In October 1864, Steinhart wrote a letter of recommendation for Nietzsche to Carl Schaarschmidt (1822–1909), a professor of philosophy at Bonn, in which he commended his current pupil for having 'a profound, sensible nature, enthusiastic about philosophy, namely the Platonic, into which he is already quite initiated' — Nietzsche as an initiate! — and as someone who, hesitating between theology and classics, would 'gladly turn to philosophy, which is the goal of his innermost drive'.[148] (At the time Schaarschmidt was involved in a major project to distinguish authentic Platonic texts from inauthentic ones, writing *Die Sammlung der Platonischen Schriften: Zur Scheidung der Echten von den Unechten untersucht* [1866].)

As a professor at Basel, Nietzsche regularly taught courses on Plato and Platonism, both at the University and at the Pädagogium. In fact, it has been reckoned that he taught the *Phaido* six times, the *Symposium* twice, and the *Gorgias*, the *Phaedrus*, and the *Laws* each once. So while his preference was for the Presocratics, Plato was a key part of his curriculum, too. Writing in 1868 to the Orientalist and Sanksrit scholar Paul Deussen (1845–1919), Nietzsche rejected the limited approach, as he saw it, of the theologian Friedrich Schleiermacher (1768–1834) or his former teacher, Steinhart, and declared: 'The Platonic question is at the moment a construct of great complexity, a tissue that has grown into itself, an organism [...] it is about psychological insights, it is a question of reconstructing Plato's way of thinking and feeling'.[149] In 1871, writing to another friend, the classicist Erwin Rohde (1845–1898), Nietzsche admitted that he had 'gained a number of fundamental insights through Plato', and he expressed the desire to Rohde that they both 'properly warm up and illuminate from the inside out the history of Greek philosophers, hitherto presented so shabbily and as though it were mummified'.[150]

Other remarks in Nietzsche's correspondence reveal a fundamental ambivalence in Nietzsche's attitude towards Plato. In a letter to Lou von Salomé in 1882, for instance, Nietzsche told her that 'our idea of reducing philosophical systems to the personal deeds of their originators is truly an idea from a "kindred mind": I myself in Basel related the history of ancient philosophy in *this* way', and he chose Plato as an example of this practice: 'I used to like to tell my audience: "This system is refuted and dead — but the *person* behind it is irrefutable, the person always remains immortal" — for instance, Plato'.[151] Thus while, in some sense, Plato's system might be wrong, at the same time, in another sense, Plato *himself* never could be. Then again, in a letter to Franz Overbeck of October 1883, Nietzsche remarks that, while reading a work by a philosopher at Basel, Gustav Teichmüller (1832–1888) — most likely his *The Real and the Apparent World: A New Foundation of Metaphysics* (*Die wirkliche und die scheinbare Welt: Neue Grundlegung der Metaphysik*) (1882), which he had borrowed from Overbeck — he had been struck, or 'increasingly dumbfounded with astonishment', by '*how little* I know Plato and **how much** Zarathustra platonizes'.[152] (Of course, in 1883 Nietzsche was, it would turn out, still only half-way through his *Zarathustra* project: and it is telling that his epic work begins in a cave; an allusion to the famous allegory in book 7 of the *Republic*?)

When, in 1886, Nietzsche added two books of aphorisms to *Human, All Too Human* for its republication in a second edition, he brought the first of them to a close with an aphorism that staged a kind of philosophical *nekyia*. Alluding to book 11 of the *Odyssey*, Nietzsche wrote that he too had been 'in the underworld, like Odysseus, and will often be there again', and had 'sacrificed not only rams to be able to talk with the dead', but had not spared his own blood as well. And who revealed themselves to Nietzsche, 'the sacrificer'? Epicurus and Montaigne, Goethe and Spinoza, Pascal and Schopenhauer, and Rousseau — and Plato.[153] And a year later, writing in 1887 again to Deussen, we find a further restatement of Nietzsche's profoundly ambivalent attitude towards Plato: 'Perhaps this old Plato is my real great *opponent*? But how proud I am to have such an opponent!'.[154] How proud indeed ... or perhaps not: to what extent was Plato really his opponent?

The *differences* between Plato and Nietzsche are manifold and manifest, requiring little further discussion or exposition. (For instance: Plato is seen a philosopher of transcendence, Nietzsche as a philosopher of immanence; Plato rejects the body, Nietzsche embraces it; Plato is invested in a logocentric ontology of Being, Nietzsche nihilistically deconstructs Being and replaces it with Becoming; Plato rejects art, Nietzsche regards life as 'aesthetically justified'; and so on.) At a deeper structural level, however, we can locate the key to the *affinities* between Nietzsche's philosophy and Platonic (and Neoplatonic) thought. This key can be found in a notion that is dear to both traditions — the notion of hierarchy. In Plotinus, for instance, there is a hierarchy of virtues, a hierarchy of beauty, a hierarchy of gods and celestial spirits; in fact, his entire metaphysics is hierarchical, from matter, via the hypostases of soul and intellect, to the ineffable and transcendent One.[155] Although his metaphysical stance rejects the kind of dualism into which such a scheme can be reduced, Nietzsche insists with considerable vigour on the importance of *Rangordnung* (hierarchy). On the one hand, Nietzsche rejects a fundamental tenet of the Platonic and Neoplatonic approach when he writes in *The Gay Science*, §109, with a glance at the Milky Way, that 'the astral order in which we live is an exception', which has made possible 'an exception of exceptions', i.e., 'the formation of the organic'; rather, 'the total character of the world' is 'in all eternity chaos'.[156] Is there a cosmological hierarchy for Nietzsche? Plainly not.

But it is all the more striking that, on the other hand, Nietzsche insists on an ontological hierarchy of another kind. Elsewhere, in his *Nachlass*, Nietzsche asserts: 'My philosophy aims at an ordering of rank: not at an individualistic morality'.[157] As early as in his preface to the second edition of *Human, All Too Human*, we find this theme when the free spirit, questioning the point and purpose of his 'great liberation', is told in reply that he shall see with his own eyes 'the problem of *order of rank*' and 'how power and right and spaciousness of perspective grow into the heights together'.[158] '*The problem of the order of rank*' is declared to be *the* problem for free spirits — a problem that can only be posed 'at the midday of life' (a midday of life conceived elsewhere in that work as a great noontide): 'Here a higher, a deeper, a beneath-us, a tremendous long ordering, an order of rank, which we *see*: here — *our* problem!'.[159]

Nietzsche argues for a hierarchy of greatness,[160] a hierarchy of strengths,[161] a hierarchy of individuals,[162] and above all a hierarchy of values.[163] He affirms the existence of 'the abysmally different order of rank, chasm of rank, between man and man',[164] insisting that 'there is an order of rank between man and man, hence also between morality and morality'.[165] In *The Will to Power*, he underscores that the *Übermensch* or superman, a key element in his strategy to resist 'the dwarfing of mankind' and the 'common economic management of the earth' (in which 'mankind will be able to find its best meaning as a machine in the service of this economy'), is bound up with a resinstatement of hierarchy: the superman 'needs the opposition of the masses, of the "levelled", a feeling of distance from them! he stands on them, he lives off them'.[166]

In *The Anti-Christ*, Nietzsche pushes this argument even further: 'The order of castes, *order of rank*, only formulates the supreme law of life itself'.[167] In line with the Indian treatise known as the Laws of Manu (in Sanskrit, *Manu-smriti* or *Manava-dharma-shastra*) — and in line with Plato's *Republic* — Nietzsche argues for a strict social hierarchy, consisting of an elite, 'the most spiritual human beings'; then, second in rank, 'the guardians of the law, the keepers of order and security; the noble warriors; above all the *king*'; and finally, the mediocre, for whom 'it is happiness to be mediocre'.[168] (Analogously, in the *Republic* Socrates imagines that in Kallipolis, the ideal city-state, there will be three groups: philosopher-kings or rulers, auxiliary guardians or soldiers, and producers or workers.[169]) Note how Nietzsche describes his spiritual elite in terms of self-constraint, of self-mastery, even of asceticism:

> The most spiritual human beings, as the *strongest*, find their happiness where others would find their destruction: in the labyrinth, in severity towards themselves and others, in attempting; their joy lies in self-constraint: with them asceticism becomes nature, need, instinct. They consider the hard task a privilege, to play with vices which overwhelm others a *recreation* … Knowledge — a form of asceticism. [170]

To this higher caste — to these few, to '*the very few*' — belongs the task of representing 'happiness, beauty, benevolence on earth'; consequently, only they are permitted 'beauty, beautiful things', on the basis of a dictum adapted from Horace, *pulchrum est paucorum hominum* ('beauty is for the few').[171] And in these individuals there speaks 'the instinct of the most spiritual', 'the affirmative instinct', which says, in the words from *Zarathustra*'s 'At Noontide', '*The world is perfect*'.[172]

Is the world perfect? The world *is* perfect, even though (as a glance around one will confirm) it isn't: as Nietzsche goes on to say, 'imperfection, everything *beneath* us, distance between man and man, the pathos of this distance, the Chandala themselves' — i.e., the untouchables — 'pertain to this perfection'.[173] Leaving on one side the undoubtedly problematic nature of this passage — its rhetorical difficulty, its contemporary unacceptability, its 'political incorrectness': what is Nietzsche really arguing? He is arguing that the world is perfect, *because it allows us to reorient ourselves*: to discern our priorities, to establish what is important for us, to set up a hierarchy — an order of rank — of what really matters. Because it is only when we have a hierarchy of values, when we prioritize our decisions, when we rank our options — that we can have any kind of meaningful freedom at all.

It is telling that Zarathustra himself confesses that he used to think of the world as imperfect: 'This world, the eternally perfect, the eternal and imperfect image of a contradiction — an intoxicating joy to its imperfect creator', is that how he 'once thought the world'.[174] But later Zarathustra comes to realize that 'this God' which he created was, 'like all gods', mere 'human work and human madness', 'only a phantom […] from my own fire and ashes'.[175] In its place, Nietzsche embraces (in 'On the Blissful Islands') something else, something that is also of his creation — 'the image sleeping in the stone, the image of my visions', 'the beauty of the Superman came to me as a shadow'. Not a phantom, not a shade, not something dead — but a shadow, an aesthetic construct, something very much alive?

This view of the world as something that is perfect is, ultimately, profoundly Platonic. True, in §109 of *The Gay Science* Nietzsche rejects the account of the origin of the world provided by the *Timaeus*. In 'Let us beware', he writes: 'Let us beware of thinking that the world is a living being', for 'we should not reinterpret the exceedingly derivative, late, rare, accidental, that we perceive only on the crust of the earth and make of it something essential, universal, and eternal', which is what 'those people do who call the universe an organism'.[176] So Nietzsche turns his back on what Timaeus tells Socrates about the demiurge: 'When he was framing the universe, he put intelligence in soul, and soul in body, that he might be the creator of a work which was by nature fairest and best', and in this way 'we may say that the world came into being — a living creature truly endowed with soul and intelligence by the providence of God'.[177]

There is much in this part of the dialogue that would have been anathema to Nietzsche: the idea of the creator, the universe as an organism, the providence of God. And yet — it is in the *Timaeus* that Socrates is told that the world is fundamentally, and in its very essence, good:

> [The creator] was good, and the good can never have any jealousy of anything. [...] God desired that all things should be good and nothing bad, so far as this was attainable. Wherefore also finding the whole visible sphere not at rest, but moving in an irregular and disorderly fashion, out of disorder he brought order [...]. Now the deeds of the best could never be or have been other than the fairest [...].[178]

In what does the goodness, the perfection of the world reveal itself? In its *beauty* — or as Nietzsche might say, *the world is justified as an aesthetic phenomenon*.[179] How should we respond to such a world? Well, how did God?

> When the father and creator saw the creature which he had made moving and living, the created image of the eternal gods, he rejoiced.[180]

Nietzsche rejects what he presents as the dual ontology of Platonic thought: but he embraces its hierarchical thought, he admires its sense that the world despite — or because of — all its imperfections, is perfect, and ultimately he shares its attitude of joy. There *is* no eternity, other than the eternity of the present moment; but joy *wants* eternity, or in the words of Zarathustra's Roundelay, the Midnight Song: *But all joy wants eternity, / wants deep, deep eternity!*

In terms of the argument presented by Paul Redding, just as we feel the normativity of the beautiful or the compulsion of beauty — we know *that* something is beautiful but not *why* — so we feel the compulsion of goodness as well. The world is *vollkommen*: perfect *and* good. This insight is one that is capable of bringing us joy; in a Spinozistic sense, that joy is our passage from a less to a greater perfection.[181] And this passage to the greatest possible perfection and the concomitant expression of joy can perhaps explain why, in the proclamation of the great noontide at the conclusion of Part One of *Thus Spoke Zarathustra*, Zarathustra declares that '*all gods are dead*';[182] while, in 'At Noontide', when noontide drinks an ancient brown drop of golden happiness and laughs, Zarathustra tells his soul that 'thus — does a god laugh'.[183]

To this extent, then, Jung was entirely justified in placing Zarathustra's noontide vision in the category of 'immediate experiences', and in describing the contents of the chapter 'At Noontide' as a transcription 'in the form of a spontaneous, ecstatic, or visionary experience' of what, in ancient times, the mystery drama had represented or brought about in the spectator.[184] Equally, at the heart of the project which is Jung's analytical psychology is an entire transformation of the individual's relation to the world; as he put it in *Transformations and Symbols of the Libido*, 'this world is empty to him alone who does not understand how to direct his libido towards objects, and to render them alive and beautiful for himself' — and this is so, because 'beauty does not indeed lie in things, but in the feeling we give to them' (*PU* §284).

After all, the experience of rebirth, which Jung describes as nothing less than an archetype, belongs to one of the most ancient conceptions of philosophy as a divine drama.[185] On this reading, 'At Noontide' is an account of an experience, one moreover that has 'the character of a Dionysian nature myth', for — just 'as classical antiquity saw it' — the Deity appears 'in the garb of nature', and 'the moment of eternity is the noontide hour, sacred to Pan' (*CW* 9/i §210). It is, Jung concludes, 'just as if Nietzsche had been present at a performance of the mysteries' — and if we read *Thus Spoke Zarathustra* (especially its chapters 'On the Blissful Islands' and 'At Noontide') aright, then could the same be said of us? Especially since, as Goethe once told Eckermann,[186] *we all walk in mysteries. We do not know what is stirring in the atmosphere that surrounds us, nor how it is connected with our own spirit.* In Goethe's words, we are all groping among mysteries — and, by that token, among wonders.

Conclusion: *The Red Book*

The final chapter of Part One of *Thus Spoke Zarathustra* is entitled 'Of the Bestowing Virtue', and in return for the gift of his teaching,[187] the disciples give Zarathustra a gift — a staff, on the golden haft of which a serpent is coiled around a sun. Decoding this gift, we may say that, as Zarathustra says, gold signifies 'the highest value', simply and purely because of its sheer beauty, because it is 'uncommon and useless and shining and mellow in lustre; it always bestows itself';[188] indeed, 'the heart of the earth is of gold',[189] and recognizing that the earth is, so to speak, pure gold, is another way of following the injunction to 'remain true' to it;[190] that the sun represents the golden ball[191] (which, at the end of the previous chapter, Zarathustra has thrown to his disciples);[192] and that the serpent here functions, as it did for Goethe, not so much as a 'symbol of eternity', but rather as 'a representation of happiness in time'.[193] At the same time, this gift symbolizes the gift-giving virtue, simply by virtue of what it is: a gift. 'The highest virtue is a bestowing virtue' — thus speaks Zarathustra;[194] and this 'new virtue' — thus he also speaks — is 'power':

> It is power [*Macht*], this new virtue; it is a ruling idea, and around it a subtle soul: a golden sun, and around it the serpent of knowledge.[195]

Etymologically, *Macht* ('power') is related to *machen* ('to do'),[196] and power, as Zarathustra understands it, is not something we have, but something we do: and for Zarathustra, this power is located above all in the will.

Now, the 'will to power' is one of the most famous, and one of the misunderstood, phrases of Nietzsche, but in the context of Zarathustra's final discourse in Part One, it becomes clearer what Nietzsche means by it. For virtue has its 'origin and beginning' — thus speaks Zarathustra — in 'the hour when [our] spirit wants to speak in images [*Gleichnisse*]',[197] that is to say, in 'names of good and evil', for then '[our] body is elevated and lifted up'; or 'when [our] heart surges broad and full like a river'; or when '[we] are exalted above praise and blame'; or when '[our] *will wants to command all things as the will of a lover*' (my emphasis), that is when our virtue has its 'origin and beginning'.[198]

'Virtue', then, is 'power', and the virtuous 'will' is the 'will to power', but the 'will to power' is 'the will of a lover'. For, just as 'the lover loves beyond reward and punishment',[199] so 'whatever is done out of love happens beyond good and evil'.[200] And in 'The Drunken Song' in Part Four, Zarathustra sings of everything in the world being bound up love ('Everything anew, everything eternal, everything chained, entwined together, *everything in love*, O that is how you *loved* the world' — thus sang Zarathustra).[201] Ultimately the will to power is the will to love; and its highest expression is — beauty.

It is entirely characteristic of *The Red Book*'s quirkiness that Jung interrogates the inscription on the crown the white bird has brought him, even while he is hanging, Odin-like yet also Christ-like, 'on the swaying branch of the divine tree, for whose sake the original ancestors could not avoid sin' (*RB*, 326). 'Love never ends' — 'does that mean eternal hanging?', Jung wonders, and realizes: 'I was not wrong to be suspicious when my bird brought the crown, the crown of eternal life, the crown of martyrdom — ominous things that are dangerously ambiguous' (*RB*, 326). Hanging, or rather hanged, between sky and earth, Jung is sceptical: 'Is it really true, shall love never end? If this was a blessed message to them, what is it for me?' (*RB*, 326). As Jung hangs on the tree, a black serpent coils itself around it, and looks at Jung 'with the blinding pearly shimmer of its eyes'. Suddenly, out of the air, a black form condenses itself before him — Satan. Jung, the serpent, the white bird, Salome, and Satan all discuss that quintessentially Jungian idea, 'the reconciliation of opposites'. 'What words', the bird asks Jung, 'did the crown bring you?', and answers its own question: '"Love never ends" — that is the mystery of the crown and the serpent' (*RB*, 326).

In a poetic passage, it appears that Jung reaches some kind of resolution — 'The clouds part, the sky is full of the crimson sunset of the completed third day. The sun sinks into the sea, and I glide with it from the top of the tree toward the earth. Softly and peacefully night falls' — yet, true to the structural dynamic of *The Red Book*,[202] this sense of resolution is soon challenged: 'Fear has befallen me' (*RB*, 326). Recalling the work in the construction of the tower undertaken on his behalf earlier in the *Red Book* by the Kabeiroi (those strange chthonic deities, worshipped on Lemnos, on Samothrace, and at Thebes), Jung moves on to another question:

> The completion of the secret operation approaches. What I saw I described in words to the best of my ability. Words are poor, and beauty does not attend them. But is truth beautiful and beauty true?
>
> (*RB*, 327)

Whatever the answer to the question implied by this allusion to the concluding dictum of John Keats's famous poem, 'Ode to a Grecian Urn' (1819),[203] it is clear that Jung is trying to rearticulate afresh the relation between life and love, and to work out a new kind of *vitalist aesthetics*. Whether he succeeds, is an issue to be addressed on another occasion, but for now, let us conclude — with the knowledge of what, half a century later, Jung will say about 'cosmogonic *love*' in *Memories, Dreams, Reflections* — on his expression of linguistic insufficiency, yet existential balance, in the following paragraph:

> One can speak in beautiful words about love, but about life? And life stands above love. [...] Life should never be forced into love, but love into life. [...] As long as love goes pregnant with life, it should be respected; but if it has given birth to life from itself, it has turned into an empty sheath and expires into transience.
>
> [...]
>
> The word has become heavy for me, and it barely wrestles itself free of the soul. Bronze doors have shut, fires have burned out and sunk into ashes. Wells have been drained and where there were seas there is dry land. My tower stands in the desert. Happy is he who can be a hermit in his own desert. He survives.
>
> (*RB*, 327)

As these powerful words resound in the reader's psyche, an image slowly imposes itself on the mind's eye. Bronze doors, now shut; fires burned out, piles of ashes; a tower in the desert. And, *where there were seas ... dry land ...* An island — of the blessed?

(In the first chapter, we passed over the question of possible links between the classical and pre-classical motif of the blissful islands and the tradition of Buddhism, even though Nietzsche once wrote that he could become the Buddha of Europe,[204] and the relation of Nietzsche to Buddhism, and likewise the relation of analytical psychology to Buddhism,[205] have recently come under close scrutiny. And so we should note here that, in Mahāyāna Buddhism, the tradition centres around a celestial buddha of infinite light and life, known as Amitābha or Amitāyus, who is said to dwell in Sukhāvatī, or in the land of utmost bliss.[206] In the smaller sutra, the Amitāyus buddha describes the land of utmost bliss, also known as the pure land or the Western paradise, to Elder Śāriputra: 'If you travel westward from here, passing a hundred thousand *kotis* of buddha lands, you will come to the land called Utmost Bliss, where there is a buddha called Amitāyus'; 'the beings in that land suffer no pain but only pleasures of various kinds'; 'the Buddha's light shines boundlessly and without hindrance over all the world of the ten directions', and 'it is for this reason that he is called Amitābha'.[207] Maybe the blissful islands are not just at the furthest Western point, but also at the centre of where East meets West …?)

True, Jung goes on to wonder in *The Red Book* whether 'everything' should be 'turned into its opposite', whether there will be 'a sea where ΦΙΛΗΜΩΝ's temple stands', whether 'his shady island' will 'sink' into 'the deepest ground', into 'the whirlpool of the withdrawing flood that earlier swallowed all peoples and lands' (*RB*, 327)? Tellingly, in his *Natural History*, Pliny the Elder records the curious fact that the blissful islands are 'plagued with the rotting carcasses of monstrous sea creatures that are constantly being cast ashore by the sea',[208] and *The Red Book* is replete with monsters of all kinds. So ultimately the image of the blissful islands serves to remind us that happiness, even bliss; and heroism, even idealism, *are* possible ('There still are blissful islands!'), but they remain surrounded by vast seas, in which 'monstrous sea creatures' may be found, whose 'rotting carcasses' are cast ashore … Perhaps these monsters, too, can be 'redeemed' and 'transformed' into 'heavenly children'; perhaps they can be transformed into 'new coloured sea-shells', 'new playthings'; or at least these monsters can be transformed into 'playful monsters', like the ones hidden among the still depths of Zarathustra's sea — depths that are 'imperturbable', but gleam with 'swimming riddles and laughter'.[209] These islands, however blissful, remain 'strange', in the sense that St John of the Cross (1542–1591), commenting on his own stanzas in *The Spiritual Canticle*, says they are:

> Strange islands are surrounded by water and situated across the sea, far withdrawn and cut off from communication with other men. Many things very different from what we have here are born and nurtured in these islands; they are of many strange kinds and powers never before seen by men, and they cause surprise and wonder in anyone who sees them. Thus, because of the wonderful new things and the strange knowledge (far removed from common knowledge) which the soul sees in God, she calls Him "strange islands".[210]

As St John of the Cross notes, 'it is no wonder that God is strange to men who have not seen Him', and by the same token the blissful islands, wherever they are, will be equally strange to those who have never discovered them.

Notes

1 'Of the Three Metamorphoses', in F. Nietzsche, *Thus Spoke Zarathustra*, tr. R.J. Hollingdale, Harmondsworth: Penguin, 1969, p. 55.

2 The actual source of this term in Heraclitus is unclear, but the idea of *Enantiodromie* and *Enantiotropie* as things always having a mutual effect on one another is attributed to Heraclitus in *Meyers Konversations-Lexikon*, 4th edn, Leipzig and Vienna: Verlag des Bibliographischen Instituts, 1885–1892, vol. 5, p. 611.

3 'When the individual stands before a difficult task which he cannot master with the means at his command, a retrograde movement of the libido automatically sets in, i.e., a regression. The libido draws away from the problem of the moment, becomes introverted, and reactivates in the unconscious a more or less primitive analogue of the conscious situation, together with an earlier mode of adaptation' (Jung, *CW* 6 §314).

4 Nietzsche, 'Of the Chairs of Virtue', in *Thus Spoke Zarathustra*, p. 58.

5 Compare with the opposition in Jung's *Red Book* between 'the spirit of the time and 'the spirit of the depths' (Jung, *RB*, p. 229).

6 Nietzsche, 'Of the Afterworldsmen', in *Thus Spoke Zarathustra*, p. 59.

7 Nietzsche, 'Of the Despisers of the Body', pp. 61–62.

8 According to *Wahrig Deutsches Wörterbuch*, the word *Geist* derives from the Indogermanic root *gheis-*, '"aufgebracht, außer Fassung, erregt"; zugrunde liegt wohl die Vorstellung eines (kultisch) erregten Zustands des Menschen').

9 See Nietzsche, *Sämtliche Werke: Kritische Studienausgabe* [*KSA*], ed. G. Colli and M. Montinari, 15 vols, Munich; Berlin and New York: dtv; de Gruyter, 1988, vol. 10, 13[1], p. 427.

10 Nietzsche, *Dithyrambs of Dionysus*, tr. R.J. Hollingdale, London: Anvil Press, 1984, p. 43.

11 Nietzsche, *Dithyrambs of Dionysus*, p. 43.

12 See Ovid, *Metamorphoses*, book 12, ll. 171–209 and 459–525; Pindar, fragments, no. 166 f (147 f).

13 For further discussion of Nietzsche's relation to Plato, which is a vast topic, see for instance R. Wiehl, 'L'antiplatonisme de Nietzsche', in M. Dixsaut (ed.), *Contre Platon, vol. 2, Le platonisme renversé*, Paris: Vrin, 1993, pp. 25–45; M. Dixsaut, 'Nietzsche lecteur de Platon', in A. Neschke-Hentschke, *Images de Platon et lectures de ses œuvres: Les interprétations de Platon à travers des siécles*, Leuven: Peeters, 1997, pp. 295–313; T. Brobjer, 'Nietzsche's Wrestling with Plato and Platonism', in P. Bishop (ed.), *Nietzsche and Antiquity: His Reaction and Response to the Classical Tradition*, Rochester, NY: Camden House, 2004, pp. 241–259; J. Sallis, *Platonic Legacies*, Albany, NY: State University of New York Press, 2004; M. Dixsaut, 'Platon, Nietzsche et les images', in J.-C. Gens and P. Rodrigo (eds), *Puissances de l'image*, Dijon: Editions universitaires de Dijon, 2007, pp. 11–24; T.H. Brobjer, *Nietzsche's Philosophical Context: An Intellectual Biography*, Illinois: University of Illinois Press, 2008, pp. 25–28; and, most recently, M. Anderson, *Plato and Nietzsche: Their Philosophical Art*, London: Bloomsbury, 2014.

14 Nietzsche, *KSA* 7, 7[156], 199; F. Nietzsche, *Writings from the Early Notebooks*, ed. R. Geuss and A. Nehemas, tr. L. Löb, Cambridge: Cambridge University Press, 2009, p. 52.

15 For further information about the relationship between Nietzsche and Overbeck, see K. Meyer and B. von Reibnitz (eds), *Friedrich Nietzsche / Franz und Ida Overbeck: Briefwechsel*, Stuttgart: Metzler, 1999; and F. Overbeck, *Erinnerungen an Friedrich Nietzsche*, Berlin: Berenberg, 2012.

16 Letter of Nietzsche to Franz Overbeck of 8 January 1887; in F. Nietzsche, *Sämtliche Briefe: Kritische Studienausgabe* [henceforth referred to as *KSB*], ed. G. Colli and M. Montinari, 8 vols, Munich; Berlin: dtv; de Gruyter, 1986, vol. 8, p. 9; cf. *KSA* 12, 10[150], 539. Simplicius was a sixth-century Neolatonist who wrote several commentaries on Aristotle and a commentary on the *Manual* by Epictetus, the great Stoic philosopher of the mid-first to second century. His commentaries adopt an anti-Christian stance, particularly towards the Christian Neoplatonist John Philoponus.

17 For further discussion of the Sophist tradition, whose exponents included Protagoras, Gorgias, Prodicus, Hippias, Antiphon, and Critias, see W.H.C. Guthrie, *The Sophists*, Cambridge: Cambridge University Press, 1971; and M. Onfray, *Les sagesses antiques* [*Contre-histoire de la philosophie*, vol. 1], Paris: Grasset, 2006.

18 *Twilight of the Idols*, 'What I Owe to the Greeks', §2; in *Twilight of the Idols; The Anti-Christ*, tr. R.J. Hollingdale, Harmondsworth: Penguin, 1968, p. 107.

19 *Phaedrus*, 250c; in Plato, *The Collected Dialogues*, ed. E. Hamilton and H. Cairns, Princeton, NJ: Princeton University Press, 1989, p. 497.

20 *Cratylus*, 400c; in *CD*, pp. 437–438.

21 *Georgias*, 493a; in *CD*, p. 275. The story of how Polyeidos, a seer from Corinth, saved the life of a young child, Glaucus, after he had fallen into a cask of honey, by resurrecting him from the dead, was the subject of a play, now lost, by the classical Greek tragedian, Euripides.

22 *Phaedo*, 65c–d; in *CD*, p. 48.

23 See *Phaedo*, 66; in *CD*, p. 49.

24 *Phaedo*, 67c–d; in *CD*, p. 50.

25 *Phaedo*, 67e; in *CD*, p. 50.

26 R.T. Wallis, *Neoplatonism*, 2nd edn, London: Bristol Classical Press, 1995, p. 111.

27 *Timaeus*, 88c; in *CD*, p. 1208.

28 *Timaeus*, 89a–b; in *CD*, p. 1208. For further discussion, see 'Physic and Physicians as Depicted in Plato', in W. Osler, *Osler's "A Way of Life" and Other Addresses, with Commentary and Annotations*, ed. S. Hinohara and H. Niki, Durham and London: Duke University Press, 2001, pp. 125–151.

29 *Timaeus*, 87d; in *CD*, p. 1207.

30 C.J. de Vogel, *Rethinking Plato and Platonism*, Leiden: Brill, 1986, p. 230.

31 *Republic*, book 7, 535d; in *CD*, p. 767.

32 *Laws*, book 5, 728 d–e; in *CD*, p. 1315.

33 De Vogel, *Rethinking Plato and Platonism*, p. 230; see *Plato's Phaedo*, tr. R. Hackforth, Cambridge: Cambridge University Press, 1955, p. 53.

34 De Vogel, *Rethinking Plato and Platonism*, p. 230.

35 Porphyry, *On the Life of Plotinus and the Arrangement of his Works*, §1; in M. Edwards (tr.), *Neoplatonic Saints: The Lives of Plotinus and Proclus by their Students*, Liverpool: Liverpool University Press, 2000, p. 1.

36 Porphyry, *On the Life of Plotinus and the Arrangement of his Works*, §2; in *Neoplatonic Saints*, p. 2.

37 Plotinus, *Enneads*, I.4.6; in Plotinus, *The Enneads*, tr. S. MacKenna, Harmondsworth: Penguin, 1991, p. 36; cf. Wallis, *Neoplatonism*, p. 83.

38 Plotinus, *Enneads*, I.4.14; in *The Enneads*, p. 42.

39 Plotinus, *Enneads*, I.4.14; in *The Enneads*, p. 42; my emphasis.

40 Plotinus, *Enneads*, IV.8.1; in *The Enneads*, p. 334.

41 Plotinus, *Enneads*, IV.8.1; in *The Enneads*, p. 335. For further discussion, see Y. Ustinova, *Caves and the Ancient Greek Mind: Descending Underground in the Search for Ultimate Truth*, Oxford and New York: Oxford University Press, 2009.

42 See *The Enneads*, p. 335, fn. 93.

43 Plotinus, *Enneads*, IV.8.2; in *The Enneads*, p. 337; cf. *Phaedo*, 65a and 66c; in *CD*, pp. 47 and 49.

44 Plotinus, *Enneads*, IV.8.2; in *The Enneads*, p. 337.

45 P. Hadot, *Plotinus or The Simplicity of Vision* [1963], tr. M. Chase, Chicago and London: University of Chicago Press, 1993, p. 79. Indeed, Hadot contends: 'As for Plotinian asceticism: there is nothing morbid or unhealthy about it. We find nothing in it which is not in conformity with that philosophical way of life which had, by the time of Plotinus, been traditional for centuries' (p. 78). On the related question of asceticism in the ancient world, and the distinction between the motiviation behind pagan and that behind Christian asceticism, see E.R. Dodds, *Pagan and Christian in an Age of Anxiety: Some Aspects of Religious Experience from Marcus Aurelius to Constantine*, Cambridge: Cambridge University Press, 1965, pp. 29–36.

46 *Phaedo*, 66 b–d; in *CD*, p. 49.

47 *Symposium*, 211c; in *CD*, pp. 562–563.

48 Cf. Plotinus, *Enneads*, II.9.17; in *The Enneads*, p. 130.

49 Plotinus, *Enneads*, II.9.17; in *The Enneads*, p. 130.

50 Plotinus, *Enneads*, II.9.17; in Plotinus, *Enneads: II. 1–9*, tr. A. H. Armstrong, London: Cam bridge: MA: Heinemann; Harvard University Press, 1966, p. 295; cf. de Vogel, *Rethinking Plato and Platonism*, p. 230.

51 Plotinus, *Enneads*, II.9.8; in *The Enneads*, p. 117. Cf. Wallis, *Neoplatonism*, p. 82.

52 Plotinus, *Enneads*, III.5.1 and V.8.2; in *The Enneads*, pp. 175 and 412. Cf Wallis, *Neoplatonism*, p. 84.

53 Plotinus, *Enneads*, II.9.16; in *The Enneads*, p. 129; cf. Wallis, *Neoplatonism*, p. 82.

54 Wallis, *Neoplatonism*, p. 9.

55 Plotinus, *Enneads*, I.4.16. and II.9.18; in *The Enneads*, pp. 44 and 131.

56 Porphyry, *On the Life of Plotinus*, §8 and §9; in *Neoplatonic Saints*, pp. 17 and 18); cf. Wallis, *Neoplatonism*, p. 41.

57 Wallis, *Neoplatonism*, p. 178.

58 Hadot, *Plotinus*, p. 113.

59 Compare with the discussion between Raphaël Enthoven and Gwenaëlle Aubry in 'Plotin ou la sculpture de soi', broadcast in the series *Les vendredis de la philosophie* on France Culture, 26 March 2004.

60 'Of the Three Metamorphoses', in *Thus Spoke Zarathustra*, p. 55.

61 H. Theierl, *Nietzsche — Mystik als Selbstversuch*, Würzburg: Könighausen & Neumann, 2000, p. 90.

62 Nietzsche, *Twilight of the Idols; The Anti-Christ*, p. 41.

63 Although a two-world view is conventionally ascribed to Plato, it would be incorrect to describe Plato's outlook as a dualism: rather, both the ideal realm and the sensory realm stand in a relationship to each other, and the idea of the Good serves as the ultimate ground of Being. Thus there is a relationship not simply of correspondence but also of imitation: the world of ideas and the sensory world relate to each other as the original (*paradeigma*) does to the copy (see H. Ottmann, *Geschichte des politischen Denkens*, vol. 1, *Die Griechen*, part 2, *Von Platon bis zum Hellenismus*, Stuttgart and Weimar: Metzler, 2001, p. 7).

64 See Porphyry, *On the Life of Plotinus*, §2; in *Neoplatonic Saints*, p. 4.

65 Plotinus, *Enneads*, IV.3.9; in *The Enneads*, pp. 262–263.

66 For Nietzsche's notion of the 'pathos of distance', see *Beyond Good and Evil*, §257; and *On the Genealogy of Morals*, Essay II, §2 and Essay III, §14 (in *Basic Writings of Nietzsche*, ed. and tr. W. Kaufmann, New York: The Modern Library, 1968, pp. 391, 461–462, 560–561). For further discussion, see R. Diprose, 'Nietzsche and the Pathos of Distance', in P. Patton (ed.), *Nietzsche, Feminism and Political Theory*, London and New York: Routledge, 1993, pp. 1–26.

67 See Plotinus, *Enneads*, V.8.7; II.9.4; and II.9.8; in *The Enneads*, pp. 417–418, 113, and 117–118.

68 Plotinus, *Enneads*, I.6.9; in *The Enneads*, p. 54.

69 *The Birth of Tragedy*, 'Attempt at a Self-Criticism', §2 and §5; *The Gay Science*, §299; *Ecce Homo*, 'Why I am so Wise', §2; and *KSA* 9, 7[213], 361; in *BW*, pp. 18 and 19; *The Gay Science*, pp. 329–340; and *Ecce Homo: How One Becomes What One Is*, trans. R.J. Hollingdale, Harmondsworth: Penguin, 1992, pp. 10–11.

70 Taylor, conclusion to his essay 'On the History of the Restoration of the Platonic Philosophy', in *Oracles and Mysteries* [TTS, vol. 7], p. 236.

71 S. Freud and C.G. Jung, *The Freud/Jung Letters: The Correspondence between Sigmund Freud and C.G. Jung*, ed. W. McGuire, Cambridge, MA: Harvard University Press, 1988, p. 258.

72 Herodotus, *The Landmark Herodotus: The Histories*, ed. R.B. Strassler, tr. A.L. Purvis, London: Quercus, 2008, p. 144.

73 *The Landmark Herodotus*, p. 145. Why would anybody want to indulge in that kind of behaviour? In *Transformations and Symbols of the Libido*, Jung cited the passage above, and he noted Herodotus's explanation of this custom (2.63.4) (*The Landmark Herodotus*,

p. 145). But Herodotus's explanation is, in turn, in need of an explanation, and Jung believed he could provide it: in this fantasy of the rape of the mother, we see a symbol of a psychological event — the return to the collective unconscious (or the Great Mother) and the rebirth of the heroic individual (Jung, *PU* §397–§398; see also Jung's letter to Freud of 15 November 1909 [*Freud/Jung Letters*, p. 263]).

74 *The Landmark Herodotus*, p. 139.
75 *Freud/Jung Letters*, p. 263.
76 *Freud/Jung Letters*, p. 258. In his *Histories*, Herodotus's discretion is an important topos (see, for example, 2.61.2, 2.65.2, and 2.171–2.172), and at one point (perhaps the passage Jung was thinking of?), he comments that he would 'rather not mention' why Pan is depicted as goatlike (2.46.2) …
77 *Freud/Jung Letters*, p. 334.
78 *Freud.Jung Letters*, p. 335.
79 On the cult of Mithras, see M. Clauss, *The Roman Cult of Mithras: The God and his Mysteries* [1990], tr. R. Gordon, Edinburgh: Edinburgh University Press, 2000; and R. Merkelbach, *Mithras: Ein persisch-römischer Mysterienkult*, Königstein/Taunus: Hain, 1984.
80 *Freud/Jung Letters*, p. 336.
81 *Ecce Homo*, 'On the Genealogy of Morals'; in *Ecce Homo*, p. 84.
82 *On the Genealogy of Morals*, Essay III, §13; in *BW*, p. 556.
83 *On the Genealogy of Morals*, Essay III, §13; in *BW*, pp. 556–557.
84 *Beyond Good and Evil*, §61; in *BW*, p. 263.
85 See 'On Self-Overcoming', in *Thus Spoke Zarathustra*, pp. 137–138.
86 *On the Genealogy of Morals*, Essay III, §8; in *BW*, p. 544.
87 See Diogenes Laertius, *Lives and Opinions of the Ancient Philosophers*, book 9, §2.
88 *On the Genealogy of Morals*, Essay III, §8; in *BW*, p. 545.
89 *On the Genealogy of Morals*, Essay III, §9; in *BW*, p. 548.
90 *Ecce Homo*, 'Why I am so Clever', §3; in *Ecce Homo*, p. 26.
91 *Ecce Homo*, 'Why I am So Clever', §1; in *Ecce Homo*, p. 22–24.
92 *Ecce Homo*, 'Why I am So Clever', §2; in *Ecce Homo*, pp. 24–25.
93 *Ecce Homo*, 'Why I am So Clever', §3; in *Ecce Homo*, p. 27.
94 *Daybreak*, §329; in Nietzsche, *Daybreak*, tr. R.J. Hollingdale, Cambridge: Cambridge University Press, 1982, p. 162.
95 H. Ellis, *The Dance of Life*, London: Constable, p. 201; cited in M.P. Hall, *Lectures on Ancient Philosophy*, New York: Tarcher/Penguin, 2005, pp. 318–319.
96 R.M. Bucke, *Cosmic Consciousness: A Study in the Evolution of the Human Mind*, New York: Dutton, 1901, pp. 121–125. According to Bertrand Vergely, 'cosmic consciousness', defined as 'a vision characterized by the consciousness of belonging to a living Whole', is 'the essence of Greek thought' (B. Vergely, *Deviens qui tu es: Quand des sages grecs nous aident à vivre*, Paris: Albin Michel, 2014, p. 31).
97 Porphyry, *On the Life of Plotinus*, §10; *Neoplatonic Saints*, p. 19.
98 Porphyry, *On the Life of Plotinus*, §23; *Neoplatonic Saints*, p. 44.
99 Plotinus, *Enneads*, IV.8.1; *The Enneads*, p. 334.
100 See Plotinus, 'On the Integral Omnipresence of the Authentic Existent' (1), *Enneads*, VI.4; in *The Enneads*, pp. 439–456.
101 R.M. Berchman, *Porphyry Against the Christians*, Leiden: Brill, 2005, pp. 107–108.
102 Berchman, *Porphyry Against the Christians*, p. 108.
103 Berchman, *Porphyry Against the Christians*, p. 108.
104 Proclus, *Commentary on Alcibdiades I*, §92, cited in Berchman, p. 108; cf. Proclus, *Commentary on the First Alcibiades*, ed. L.G. Westerink, tr. W. O'Neill, Westbury: Prometheus Trust, 2011, pp. 120–122.
105 See Heliodorus, *The Aethiopica*, book 2, §11, where Cnemon complains to Theagenes that the cave in which they have discovered the corpse of Thisbe has not granted him 'the gift of divination, like the Delphic shrine or the cave of Trophonius, which are said to inspire with prophetic frenzy those who enter them' (Heliodorus, *The Aethiopica*, Athens: Athenian Society, 1897, p. 87).

106 Compare with Bruno Hillebrand's observation that Nietzsche 'understood a good deal about mysticism', and his view that, in 'At Noontide', the 'mystical doctrine of eternal return reaches its lyric culmination' (*Ästhetik des Augenblicks: Der Dichter als Überwinder der Zeit — Von Goethe bis heute*, Göttingen: Vandenhoeck & Ruprecht, 1999, pp. 32 and 80).

107 Plotinus, *Enneads*, I.6.8; in *The Enneads*, p. 54. Cf. *Iliad*, book 2, l. 140.

108 Nietzsche *KSA* 7, 29[224], 720; F. Nietzsche, *Writings from the Early Notebooks*, ed. R. Geuss and A. Nehamas, Cambridge: Cambridge University Press, 2009, p. 184; cf. Theierl, *Nietzsche — Selbstversuch als Mystik*, pp. 9–10 and 26.

109 *Symposium*, 210e; in *CD*, p. 562.

110 *Daybreak*, §575; in *Daybreak*, p. 229; *The Gay Science*, §124 and §343; in *The Gay Science*, pp. 180 and 280; and 'On the Blissful Islands', in *Thus Spoke Zarathustra*, p. 109.

111 D. Hume, 'The Platonist', in *Essays Moral and Political* (1741/1742); in *Selected Essays*, ed. S. Copley and A. Edgar, Oxford and New York: Oxford University Press, 1993, pp. 91–99 (p. 92).

112 *Human, All Too Human*, 'Preface', §3; in *Human, All Too Human*, tr. R.J. Hollingdale, Cambridge: Cambridge University Press, 1986, p. 6.

113 This striking phrase caught the attention of Jung, who in *Transformations and Symbols of Libido* glossed it as signifying incest — not, however, in the literal sense, but in the sense of a libidinal investment in the archetypal Mother (*PU* §284–§285).

114 *Human, All Too Human*, 'Preface', §2; in *Human, All Too Human*, p. 7.

115 Berchman, *Porphyry Against the Christians*, p. 108; Proclus, *Theology of Plato*, in TTS, vol. 8, pp. 5–58.

116 Augustine, *Confessions: Book IX-XIII*, tr. W. Watts, Cambridge, MA, and London: Harvard University Press, 1912, p. 93.

117 As Alan Cardew argued in a paper at the 2013 Prometheus Trust Conference, the image of the chariot as the vehicle of the soul's ascent, in Western and Eastern traditions alike, can be found in Parmenides and Plato's *Phaedrus*, in the Book of Ezekiel and in the Jewish notion of Merkabah mysticism, and in the Bhagavad Gita and Mahayana Buddhism. For Cardew, the dynamic and paradoxical image of the chariot links restless haste and utter stillness, passion and reason, earthliness and transcendence.

118 *Human, All Too Human*, 'Preface', §4; in *Human, All Too Human*, p. 8.

119 *Human, All Too Human*, 'Preface', §4; in *Human, All Too Human*, p. 8.

120 *Human, All Too Human*, 'Preface', §5; in *Human, All Too Human*, p. 8. As Nietzsche wrote to Peter Gast (Heinrich Köselitz) from Sils-Maria on 14 August 1881, 'the intensities of my feelings make me shudder and laugh' (*die Intensitäten meines Gefühls machen mich schaudern und lachen*) (Nietzsche, *KSB* 6, 112).

121 *Human, All Too Human*, 'Preface', §8; in *Human, All Too Human*, p. 11. Compare with Nietzsche's allusion in *The Gay Science*, §82, to Martial, *Est res magna tacere* (= it is a big thing to remain silent) (cf. Martial, *Epigrams*, IV, 80.6); *The Gay Science*, p. 136. In *Dawn*, §423, in a section entitled 'In the Great Silence', Nietzsche describes a profound moment of blissful silence, as rich and as significant as the monastic 'great silence' to which its title alludes (*Daybreak*, p. 181). For further discussion of the theme of silence in Nietzsche, see M. Heidegger, 'Tragedy, Satyr-Play, and Telling Silence in Nietzsche's Thought of Eternal Recurrence', tr. D.F. Krell, *boundary 2*, Spring–Autumn 1981, vol. 9/10, 25–39; and C. Crawford, 'Nietzsche's Dionysian Arts: Dance, Song, and Silence', in S. Kemal, I. Gaskell, and D.W. Conway (eds), *Nietzsche, Philosophy and the Arts*, Cambridge: Cambridge University Press, 1998, pp. 310–341, especially her discussion of 'a hierarchy of types of silence' in Nietzsche: first, 'conscious silence'; second, 'silence in which the Self speaks to one'; and third, 'silence as the non-expression of highest experience of oneself and existence' (p. 338).

122 *Daybreak*, §43; in *Daybreak*, p. 30.

123 *Daybreak*, §43; in *Daybreak*, p. 30.

124 *Letter VII*, 344b; in *CD*, p. 1591. See Dixsaut, 'Platon, Nietzsche et les images', p. 22.

125 *Letter VII*, 329b; in *CD*, p. 1574.

126 *Daybreak*, §496; in *Daybreak*, p. 202.

127 Nietzsche, *KSA* 10, 9[29], 354.

128 H. Theierl, *Nietzsche — Mystik als Selbstversuch*, Würzburg: Könighausen & Neumann, 2000, p. 12; *The Gay Science*, §124, in *The Gay Science*, p. 180; and 'Amid Birds of Prey', in Nietzsche, *Dithyrambs of Dionysus*, p. 41.

129 For further discussion of the motif of dance in Nietzsche, see K. King, 'The Dancing Philosopher', *Topoi*, January 2005, vol. 24, no. 1, 103–111; K.L. LaMothe, *Nietzsche's Dancers: Isadora Duncan, Martha Graham, and the Revaluation of Christian Values*, New York: Palgrave Macmillan, 2006; and Crawford, 'Nietzsche's Dionysian Arts', in Kemal, Gaskell, and W. Conway (eds), *Nietzsche, Philosophy and the Arts*, pp. 310–341.

130 See M.P. Hall, *Lectures on Ancient Philosophy*, New York: Tarcher/Penguin, 2005, pp. 369–370; compare with R.P. Knight, *An Inquiry into the Symbolical Language of Ancient Art and Mythology*, London: Black and Armstrong, 1836, pp. 57–58. For the dance performed by Jesus at the Last Supper, see *The Apocryphal New Testament*, ed. J.K. Elliott, Oxford: Clarendon Press, 1993, pp. 318–320: 'Now if you respond to my dancing, see yourself in me who speak; and when you have seen what I do, keep silence about my mysteries! You who dance, perceive what I do; for yours is this passion of mankind which I am to suffer!' (p. 319).

131 'Zarathustra's Prologue', §5; in *Thus Spoke Zarathustra*, p. 46.

132 'Of Reading and Writing', in *Thus Spoke Zarathustra*, pp. 68–69.

133 Letter to Franz Overbeck of 5 August 1886; Nietzsche, *KSB* 7, 223.

134 *Ecce Homo*, 'Thus Spoke Zarathustra', §3; *Ecce Homo*, p. 72.

135 In *The Science of Logic* (*Die Wissenschaft der Logik*, 1812–1816), Hegel writes that '*freedom is the truth of necessity*' (G.W.F. Hegel, *Werke*, ed. E. Moldenhauer and K. Markus Michel, 20 vols, Frankfurt am Main: Suhrkamp, 1986, vol. 6, p. 249; cf. p. 246); and compare with his *Enzyklopädie der philosophischen Wissenschaften im Grundrisse* [1830], I, §158: 'This *truth* of necessity is thus *freedom*' (*Werke*, vol. 8, p. 303).

136 *Ecce Homo*, 'Thus Spoke Zarathustra', §3; in *Ecce Homo*, p. 73.

137 Stobaeus, *Anthologium*, iv. 52.49; in: Plutarch, *Moralia*, vol. 15, *Fragments from Other Named Works*, tr. F.H. Sandbach, Cambridge, MA: Harvard University Press, 1969, pp. 317–319 (Fragment 178). For further discussion, see H.P. Foley (ed.), *The Homeric "Hymn to Demeter": Translation, Commentary, and Interpretive Essays*, Princeton, NJ: Princeton University Press, 1994, pp. 70–75, 'Background: The Eleusinian Mysteries and Women's Rites for Demeter'.

138 See *Ennead* VI.9.9, 'On the Good, or the One' (*The Enneads*, p. 547). For further discussion, see S. Ahbel-Rappe, 'Metaphysics: The Origin of the Becoming and Resolution of Ignorance', in P. Remes and S. Slaveva-Griffin, *The Routledge Handbook of Neoplatonism*, London and New York: Routledge, 2014, pp. 166–181, esp. pp. 168–172, 'Plotinus' Metaphysics of Light'.

139 *Letters VII*, 341c; in *CD*, p. 1589. See Monique Dixsaut, 'Platon, Nietzsche et les images', p. 23.

140 P. Redding, 'Self-Surpassing Beauty: Plato's Ambiguous Legacy', *Literature and Aesthetics: The Journal of the Sydney Society of Literature and Aesthetics*, 1997, vol. 7, 94–108 (pp. 104–105).

141 Redding, 'Self-Surpassing Beauty', p. 106.

142 M. Heidegger, *Nietzsche*, vols 3 and 4, tr. D.F. Krell, New York: HarperCollins, 1991, vol. 3, *The Will to Power as Knowledge and as Metaphysics*, chapter 1, 'Nietzsche as the Thinker of the Consummation of Metaphysics', p. 8.

143 Redding, 'Self-Surpassing Beauty', p. 106.

144 'The Shadow', in *Thus Spoke Zarathustra*, p. 285.

145 *On the Genealogy of Morals*, III, §25; in *BW of Nietzsche*, p. 587.

146 See Nietzsche, *KGW*, vol. I.3, 384–388. For further discussion, see D.N. McNeill, 'On the Relationship of Alcibiades' Speech to Nietzsche's "Problem of Socrates"', in P. Bishop (ed.), *Nietzsche and Antiquity: His Reaction and Response to the Classical Tradition*, Rochester, NY: Camden House, 2004, pp. 260–275.

147 S.L. Gilman (ed.), *Conversations with Nietzsche: A Life in the Words of His Contemporaries*, tr. D.J. Parent, New York and Oxford: Oxford University Press, 1987, p. 17.

148 Nietzsche, *Kritische Gesamtwerkausgabe Briefe*, vol. I.4, p. 338; cited in R.J. Benders and S. Oettermann, *Friedrich Nietzsche: Chronik in Bildern und Texten*, Munich and Vienna: Hanser, 2000, p. 115.

149 Letter of Nietzsche to Paul Deussen of late April/early May 1868; Nietzsche, *KSB* 2, 270.

150 Letter of Nietzsche to Erwin Rohde of 21 December 1871; in Nietzsche, *KSB* 3, 257.

151 Letter to Lou von Salomé of 16 September 1882; in Nietzsche, *KSB* 6, 259.

152 Letter of Nietzsche to Franz Overbeck of 22 October 1883; in Nietzsche, *KSB* 6, 449.

153 *Human, All Too Human*, 'Assorted Opinions and Maxims', §408; in *Human, All Too Human*, p. 299.

154 Postcard of Nietzsche to Deussen of 16 November 1887; in Nietzsche, *KSB* 8, 200.

155 As Dominic J.O'Meara has pointed out, the actual term 'hierarchy' is not found in Plotinus, and he suggests replacing it with the Aristotelian-Platonic term, 'priority'; see 'The Hierarchical Ordering of Reality in Plotinus', in L.P. Gerson (ed.), *The Cambridge Companion to Plotinus*, Cambridge: Cambridge University Press, 2006, pp. 66–81.

156 *The Gay Science*, §109; in *The Gay Science*, p. 168.

157 *The Will to Power*, §287; in *The Will to Power*, ed. W. Kaufmann, tr. W. Kaufmann and R.J. Hollingdale, New York: Vintage, 1968, p. 162.

158 *Human, All Too Human*, Preface, §6; in *Human, All Too Human*, p. 9. For further discussion of the notion of 'free spirit', see P. Bishop, 'Free the Spirit!: Kantian, Jungian and Neoplatonic Resonances in Nietzsche', in R. Bamford (ed.), *Nietzsche's Free Spirit Philosophy*, London and Lanham, ML: Rowman & Littlefield, 2015, pp. 207–232.

159 *Human, All Too Human*, Preface, §7; in *Human, All Too Human*, p. 10.

160 *Daybreak*, §548; in *Daybreak*, p. 221.

161 *The Will to Power*, §55; in *The Will to Power*, p. 38.

162 *The Will to Power*, §911; in *The Will to Power*, p. 482.

163 *On the Genealogy of Morals*, Essay I, §17, fn; in *BW*, p. 492.

164 *Beyond Good and Evil*, §62; in *BW*, p. 266.

165 *Beyond Good and Evil*, §228; in *BW*, p. 347.

166 *The Will to Power*, §866; in *The Will to Power*, pp. 463–464.

167 *The Anti-Christ*, §57; in *Twilight of the Idols; The Anti-Christ*, p. 178.

168 *The Anti-Christ*, §57; in *Twilight of the Idols; The Anti-Christ*, p. 178.

169 Corresponding to these three social classes are three parts of the soul: reason, spirit, and appetite (*The Republic*, book 4, 435d–445e; in *CD*, pp. 677–688).

170 *The Anti-Christ*, §57; in *Twilight of the Idols; The Anti-Christ*, p. 178.

171 *The Anti-Christ*, §57; in *Twilight of the Idols; The Anti-Christ*, p. 177. Compare with Horace, *Satires*, I.9.44: *paucorum hominum et mentis bene sanae* ('a man of few friends and good sense'); Horace, *Satires; Epistles; and Ars Poetica*, tr. H.R. Fairclough, London; Cambridge, MA: Heinemann; Harvard University Press, 1942, p. 109.

172 *The Anti-Christ*, §57; in *Twilight of the Idols; The Anti-Christ*, p. 178; cf. 'At Noontide', in *Thus Spoke Zarathustra*, p. 288: 'What? Has the world not just become perfect?'

173 *The Anti-Christ*, §57; in *Twilight of the Idols; The Anti-Christ*, p. 178.

174 'Of the Afterworldsmen', in *Thus Spoke Zarathustra*, p. 59.

175 'Of the Afterworldsmen', in *Thus Spoke Zarathustra*, p. 59.

176 *The Gay Science*, §109; in *The Gay Science*, tr. Kaufmann, p. 167.

177 *Timaeus*, 30 b–c; in *CD*, p. 1163.

178 *Timaeus*, 29e–30 a; in *CD*, p. 1162.

179 *The Birth of Tragedy*, 'Attempt at a Self-Criticism', §5, cf. §5 and §24; in *BW*, pp. 22, 52 and 141.

180 *Timaeus*, 37d; in *CD*, p. 1167.

181 Spinoza, *Ethics*, part 3, 'The Affects', §2; in Spinoza, *Selections*, ed. J. Wild, London: Scribner, 1928, p. 267.

182 'Of the Bestowing Virtue', §3; in *Thus Spoke Zarathustra*, p. 104.

183 'At Noontide', in *Thus Spoke Zarathustra*, p. 288.

184 Jung, 'Concerning Rebirth'; *CW* 9/i §210.

185 A. Uždavinys, *Philosophy as a Rite of Rebirth: From Ancient Egypt to Neoplatonism*, Westbury: Prometheus Trust, 2008.

186 See Goethe's conversation with Eckermann of 7 October 1827; in J.P. Eckermann, *Conversations of Goethe*, ed. J.K. Moorhead, tr. J. Oxenford, New York: Da Capo Press, 1998, pp. 233–234.

187 'Prologue', §1: 'I should like to give [my wisdom] away and distribute it' (*Thus Spoke Zarathustra*, p. 39); 'Prologue', §2: 'I am bringing mankind a gift' (*Thus Spoke Zarathustra*, p. 40).

188 'Of the Bestowing Virtue', §1; in *Thus Spoke Zarathustra*, p. 100.

189 'Of Great Events', in *Thus Spoke Zarathustra*, p. 155.

190 'Prologue', §3, and 'Of the Bestowing Virtue', §2; in *Thus Spoke Zarathustra*, pp. 42 and 102.

191 Compare with Jung's remarks in his seminar on *Zarathustra*: 'The golden ball [...] symbolizes Nietzsche's [i.e. Nietzsche/Zarathustra's] most important idea, the relation to the earth. [...] The golden ball is the sun, also a divine symbol [...], a reconciling symbol, the symbol that resolves conflicts, that overcomes the oppositions characterizing our lives — a symbol that creates peace and totality. [...] In the hieratic language of the whole world, gold is used to designate something that is valuable [and] when gold appears in dreams it means value. [...] Here we have the reconciling symbol, and a very interesting relation to the alchemistic symbolism: namely, the uncommon gold, the philosophical gold, is the child of the sun and moon, the male and the female' (*SNZ* 2, pp. 788, 792 and 795–796).

192 A significant intertext for this gesture is the throwing of Suleika's passion (*Leidenschaft*) as a ball to her lover, the poet Hafis, in the poem beginning *Die schön geschriebenen* ('These lovely manuscripts') in the Book of Suleika (*Buch Suleika*) of Goethe's *West-Eastern Divan*:

> Joy of existence is great,
> Greater the joy at existence
> When you, Suleika,
> Give joy to me in excess
> When you toss your passion towards me,
> As if a ball
> So that I catch it,
> Casting back again
> Me, my dedicate self;
> That is a moment true!

(J.W. Goethe, *Poems of the West and East: West-Eastern Divan — West-Östlicher Divan: Bi-Lingual Edition of the Complete Poems*, tr. J. Whaley, Bern, Berlin, Frankfurt am Main: Lang, 1998, pp. 274–275).

193 See Goethe's comment in his letter to F.W.H. von Trebra of 5 January 1814: 'People are fond of using, as a symbol of eternity, the snake, which turns into itself in a circle; I, however, like to consider it a representation of happiness in time'. For an alternative (and highly complex) reading of the serpent, in terms of the symbolism of Zarathustra's relation to his disciples, see Jung's comment in his seminar (*SNZ* 2, 794–796): 'If the lonely Zarathustra can be united to a circle of human beings then the golden child, the god, is born, *Hiranyagarbha* [the "golden seed", "golden foetus", "golden womb"]; then the golden ball appears with the serpent' (*SNZ* 2, 796). As one commentator has observed, according to the *Rig Veda* the *Hirnanyagarbha* 'came forth as the first-born of creation from the primeval waters which were created by the first principle,' while in the *Upanishads* it represents 'th[e] conception of the first-born of creation as the original source of all wisdom' (P. Deussen, *The Philosophy of the Upanishads*, tr. A.S. Geden, Edinburgh: T. & T. Clark, 1906, pp. 198–201; cf. *Rig Veda*, 10.121.1: 'In the beginning

the Golden Embryo arose. Once he was born, he was the one lord of creation' (*The Rig Veda*, ed. and tr. W.D. O'Flaherty, Harmondsworth: Penguin, 1981, p. 27), and *Svetasvatara Upanishad*, part 5: 'Brahman [...] is the ONE in whose power are the many sources of creation, and the root and the flower of all things. The Golden Seed, the Creator, was in his mind in the beginning; and he saw him born when time began' (*The Upanishads*, tr. J. Mascaró, Harmondsworth: Penguin, 1965, p. 93).

194 'Of the Bestowing Virtue', §1; in *Thus Spoke Zarathustra*, p. 101.

195 'Of the Bestowing Virtue', §1; in *Thus Spoke Zarathustra*, p. 101.

196 Old High German *maht*, cf. English *might*, from Germanic *mahti-*, cf. Indogermanic *magh-*'[ver]mögen'; Old High German *mahhon*, cf. English *make*, from Germanic *makkon*, cf. Indogermanic *mag-*, cf. *gemach, gemächlich, Gemach, makeln*.

197 For further discussion of *Gleichnis* (metaphor, symbol, allegory, image) as one of Zarathustra's chief rhetorical resources, see P. Bishop and R.H. Stephenson, *Friedrich Nietzsche and Weimar Classicism*, Rochester, NY: Camden House, 2005, p. 125.

198 'Of the Bestowing Virtue, §1; in *Thus Spoke Zarathustra*, p. 101.

199 'Retired from Service', in *Thus Spoke Zarathustra*, p. 273.

200 *Beyond Good and Evil*, §153; in *BW*, p. 280.

201 'The Intoxicated Song', §10; in *Thus Spoke Zarathustra*, p. 332. For further discussion of the theme of love in *Zarathustra*, see *Friedrich Nietzsche and Weimar Classicism*, pp. 113–114.

202 For further discussion, see P. Bishop, 'Jung and the Quest for Beauty: The *Red Book* in Relation to German Classicism', in T. Kirsch and G. Hogenson (eds), *The Red Book: Reflections on C.G. Jung's "Liber Novus"*, London and New York: Routledge, 2014, pp. 11–35.

203 For further discussion, see S. Sikka, 'On the Truth of Beauty: Nietzsche, Heidegger, Keats', *The Heythrop Journal*, July 1998, vol. 39, no. 3, 243–263.

204 In a note from 1883, Nietzsche writes: 'Of all the Europeans who are living and have lived, I have the *most universal* of souls: Plato Voltaire ——— this depends on conditions which are not fully in my power but rather in the "nature of things" — I could be the Buddha of Europe: though admittedly an antipode to the Indian Buddha' (*KSA*, vol. 10, 4[2], p. 109; translated in F. Mistry, *Nietzsche and Buddhism: Prolegomenon to a Comparative Study*, Berlin and New York: de Gruyter, 1981, p. 1). For further discussion, see G. Parkes (ed.), *Nietzsche and Asian Thought*, Chicago: University of Chicago Press, 1991; M. Conche, *Nietzsche et le bouddhisme: édition augmentée*, Paris: encre marine, 2007; R.G. Morrison, *Nietzsche and Buddhism: A Study in Nihilism and Ironic Affinities*, New York: Oxford University Press, 1999; M. Bazzano, *Buddha is Dead: Nietzsche and the Dawn of European Zen*, Eastbourne: Sussex Academic Press, 2006; and A. Panaïoti, *Nietzsche and Buddhist Philosophy*, Cambridge: Cambridge University Press, 2013.

205 See J.M. Spiegelmann, *Buddhism and Jungian Psychology*, Scottsdale, AZ: Falcon Press, 1985; and *Spring: A Journal of Archetype and Culture*, special edition on *Buddhism and Depth Psychology: Redefining the Encounter*, vol. 89 (Spring 2013). Jung himself wrote prefaces to books about Buddhism.

206 See *The Three Pure Land Sutras*, tr. H. Inagaki, Berkeley, CA: Numata Center for Buddhist Translation and Research, 2003, pp. 13 and 131.

207 *The Three Pure Land Sutras*, 346b–347a (p. 92).

208 Pliny the Elder, *Natural History*, book 6, §37; in Pliny the Elder, *Natural History*, vol. 2, *Libri III-VII*, tr. H. Rackham, Cambridge, MA; London: Harvard University Press; Heinemann, 1941, p. 491.

209 'Of the Virtuous', in *Thus Spoke Zarathustra*, p. 120; and 'Of the Sublime Men', pp. 139–140 (translation modified).

210 St John of the Cross, *The Collected Works*, tr. K. Kavanaugh and O. Rodriguez, Washington, CD: Institute of Carmelite Studies, 1979, pp. 464–465.

SELECT BIBLIOGRAPHY

Addey, T., *The Seven Myths of the Soul*, Frome: Prometheus Trust, 2000.

Aeschylus, *Agamenon – Libation-Bearers – Eumenides – Fragments*, tr. H. Weir Smyth, London; New York: Heinemann; Putnam, 1926.

Ahbel-Rappe, S. (ed. and tr.), *Damascius' Problems & Solutions Concerning First Principles*, Oxford and New York: Oxford University Press, 2010.

Ambrose, *Homilies of Saint Ambrose on Psalm 118 (119)*, tr. Í. Ni Riain, Dublin: Halcyon Press, 1998.

Ambrose, *On the Mysteries and the Treatise "On the Sacraments" by an Unknown Author*, ed. J.H. Shrawley, tr. T. Thompson, London; New York: SPCK; Macmillan, 1919.

Ando, C., *The Matter of the Gods: Religion and the Roman Empire*, Berkeley and Los Angeles: University of California Press, 2008.

Anselm of Canterbury, *The Major Works*, ed. B. Davies and G.R. Evans, Oxford: Oxford University Press, 2008.

Ante-Nicene Fathers, vol. 2, *Fathers of the Second Century: Hermas, Tatian, Athenagoras, Theophilus, and Clement of Alexendria*, ed. P. Schaff, New York: Christian Literature Publishing, 1885.

Apollonius Rhodius, *The Argonautica*, tr. R.C. Seaton, London: Heinemann; New York: Macmillan, 1912.

Apuleius, *"Golden Ass" or "The Metamorphosis", and other Philosophical Writings*, tr. T. Taylor [TTS, vol. 14], Frome: Prometheus Trust, 1997.

Aristotle, *Basic Works*, ed. R. McKeon, New York: Random House, 1941

Aristotle, *The Metaphysics of Aristotle*, tr. T. Taylor, London: Davis, Wilks, and Taylor, 1801.

Augustine, *Confessions: Book IX-XIII*, tr. W. Watts, Cambridge, MA, and London: Harvard University Press, 1912.

Augustine, *Letters*, vol. 4, *165–203*, tr. W. Parsons, Washington, DC: Catholic University of America Press, 1955.

Augustine, *Opera Omnia*, vol. 3, part 2 [*Patrologiae cursus completus, Series Latina*, ed. J.-P. Migne, vol. 35], Paris: Migne, 1864.

Babich, B., 'Greek Bronze: On Sculptures, Mirrors, and Life', *Yearbook of the Irish Philosophical Society*, 2006, 1–30.

Babich, B.E., *Words in Blood, Like Flowers: Philosophy and Poetry, Music and Eros in Hölderlin, Nietzsche, and Heidegger*, Albany, NY: State University of New York Press, 2006.

Bachofen, J.J., *Das Mutterecht: Eine Untersuchung über die Gynaikokratie der alten Welt nach ihrer religiösen und rechtlichen Natur*, Stuttgart: Krais & Hoffmann, 1861, p. 163.

Baines, C.A., *A Coptic Gnostic Treatise Contained in the Codex Brucianus — Bruce MS. 96, Bodleian Library, Oxford*, Cambridge: Cambridge University Press, 1933.

Barnes, J., *Early Greek Philosophy*, Harmondsworth: Penguin, 1987.

Barrows, I., *The Usefulness of Mathematical Learning Explained and Demonstrated: Being Mathematical Lectures*, London: Austen, 1734.

Basil the Great, *Opera omnia quæ exstant*, vol. 3 [*Patrologia Graeca*, ed. J.-P. Migne, vol. 31], Paris: Migne, 1885.

Bendres, R.J., and S. Oettermann, *Friedrich Nietzsche: Chronik in Bildern und Texten*, Munich and Vienna: Hanser, 2000.

Bennet, E.A., *Meetings with Jung: Conversations Recorded by E.A. Bennet During the Years 1946–1961*, London: Anchor Press, 1982.

Berchman, R.M., *Porphyry Against the Christians*, Leiden: Brill, 2005.

Berghahn, K., *Schiller: Ansichten eines Idealisten*, Frankfurt am Main: Athenäum, 1986.

Bergson, H., *Œuvres*, Paris: Presses universitaires de France, 1970.

Bernhart, J., *Meister Eckhart und Nietzsche: Ein Vergleich für die Gegenwart*, Berlin: Thomas-Verlag [Greif-Bücherei], 1935.

Bernoulli, C.A., *Franz Overbeck und Friedrich Nietzsche: Eine Freundschaft*, 2 vols, Jena: Diederichs, 1908.

Bernstein, J.M. (ed.), *Classic and Romantic German Aesthetics*, Cambridge: Cambridge University Press, 2003.

Bertram, E., *Nietzsche: Attempt at a Mythology* [1918], tr. R.E. Norton, Urbana and Chicago: University of Illinois Press, 2009.

Bettini, M., *Women and Weasels: Mythologies of Birth in Ancient Greece and Rome*, tr. E. Eisenach, Chicago and London: University of Chicago Press, 2013.

Bishop, P., '"Creation — That Is the Great Redemption from Suffering, and Life's Easement"', Part 1: 'What Do Creation and Destruction Mean in Zarathustra's World?'; Part 2: 'Tragic Affirmation amid the Creation-and-Destruction of Eternal Recurrence', in S. Wirth, I. Meier, and J. Hill (eds), *Destruction & Creation: Facing the Ambiguities of Power*, New Orleans, Louisiana: Spring Journal Books, 2010, pp. 31–43 and 45–58.

Bishop, P., 'Remain True to the Earth: Home and Wandering in Nietzsche', *Spring: A Journal of Archetype and Culture*, Spring 2011, vol. 85, 125–163.

Bishop, P., 'The Dialectic of Destruction and Creation in the German Tradition: A Jungian Perspective on Goethe, Nietzsche, Rilke, and George', *Jung Journal: Culture & Psyche*, 2011, vol. 5. no. 4, 60–82.

Bishop, P., 'The Superman as Salamander: Symbols of Transformation or Transformational Symbols?', *International Journal of Jungian Studies*, March 2011, vol. 3, no. 1, 4–20.

Bishop, P., and R.H. Stephenson, *Friedrich Nietzsche and Weimar Classicism*, Rochester, NY: Camden House, 2005.

Bowden, H., *Mystery Cults in the Ancient World*, London: Thames & Hudson, 2010.

Boyle, N., *Goethe: The Poet and the Age*, vol. 1, *The Poetry of Desire*, Oxford and New York: Oxford University Press, 1991.

Bridget, *The Revelations of St. Birgitta of Sweden*, vol. 3, *Liber Caelestis: Books VI-VII*, tr. D. Searby, New York: Oxford University Press, 2012.

Brooke, R. (ed.), *Pathways into the Jungian World: Phenomenology and Analytical Psychology*, London and New York: Routledge, 2000.

Bruno, G., *The Heroic Frenzies*, tr. P.E. Memmo, Jr., Chapel Hill, NC: University of North Carolina Press, 1965.

Bucke, R.M., *Cosmic Consciousness: A Study in the Evolution of the Human Mind*, New York: Dutton, 1901

Cardew, A., 'Heidegger and Jung: The Greatest Danger and the Saving Power', *Harvest: International Journal for Jungian Studies*, 2004, vol. 50, no. 1, 136–161.

Cardew, A., 'The Archaic and the Sublimity of Origins', in P. Bishop (ed.), *The Archaic: The Past in the Present*, New York and London: Routledge, 2012, pp. 93–146.

Cassirer, E., *The Philosophy of Symbolic Forms*, vol. 4, *The Metaphysics of Symbolic Forms*, ed. J.M. Krois and D.P.Verene, tr. J.M. Krois, New Haven and London: Yale University Press, 1996.

Clark, R.T., *Herder: His Life and Thought*, Berkeley: University of California Press, 1955, p. 88.

Clauss, M., *The Roman Cult of Mithras: The God and his Mysteries* [1990], tr. R. Gordon, Edinburgh: Edinburgh University Press, 2000.

Clement of Alexandria, *Opera quæ exstant omnia*, vol. 1 [*Patrologia Graeca*, ed. J.-P. Migne, vol. 8], Paris: Migne, 1891.

Copenhaver, B P. (ed.), *Hermetica: The Greek Corpus Hermeticum and the Latin Asclepius in a New English Translation, with Notes and Introduction*, Cambridge: Cambridge University Press, 1992.

Curran, J.V., and C. Fricker (eds), *Schiller's "On Grace and Dignity" in Its Cultural Context*, Rochester, NY: Camden House, 2005.

Cyril of Jerusalem, *The Catechetical Lectures of S. Cyril, Archbishop of Jerusalem* [Library of Fathers of the Holy Catholic Church, vol. 2], Oxford: Parker, 1839.

Daniélou, J., 'Grégoire de Nysse et Plotin', in Association Guillaume Budé, *Congrès de Tours et de Poitiers 3–9 Septembre 1953: Actes du congrés*, Paris: Les Belles Lettres, 1954, pp. 259–62.

De Vogel, C.J., *Rethinking Plato and Platonism*, Leiden: Brill, 1986.

Deleuze, G., *Nietzsche and Philosophy* [1962], tr. H. Tomlinson, London and New York: Continuum, 2006.

Diel, P., *Le Symbolisme dans la mythologie grecque*, Paris: Petite Bibliothèque Payot, 1970.

Diogenes Laërtius, *The Lives and Opinions of Eminent Philosophers*, tr. C.D.Yonge, London: Bell, 1895.

Dodds, E.R., *Pagan and Christian in an Age of Anxiety: Some Aspects of Religious Experience from Marcus Aurelius to Constantine*, Cambridge: Cambridge University Press, 1965.

Duncan, B., '"Emilia Galotti lag auf dem Pult aufgeschlagen": Werther as (Mis-) Reader', *Goethe Yearbook*, 1982, vol. 1, 42–50.

Eckermann, J.P., *Conversations of Goethe*, ed. J.K. Moorhead, tr. J. Oxenford, New York: Da Capo Press, 1998.

Edwards, M. (tr.), *Neoplatonic Saints: The Lives of Plotinus and Proclus by their Students*, Liverpool: Liverpool University Press, 2000, p. 4.

Ehrman, B.D. (ed.), *The Apostolic Fathers*, vol. 1, *I Clement; II Clement; Ignatius; Polycarp; Didache*, Cambridge, MA, and London: Harvard University Press, 2003,

Elliott, J.K. (ed.), *The Apocryphal New Testament*, Oxford: Clarendon Press, 1993.

Epictetus/Simplicius, *Epictetus His Morals, with Simplicius His Comment*, tr. G. Stanhope, 2nd edn, London: Sare, 1700.

Evans, E.P., *Animal Symbolism in Ecclesiastical Architecture*, London: Heinemann, 1896, p. 99.

ffytche, M., *The Foundation of the Unconscious: Schelling, Freud and the Birth of the Modern Psyche*, Cambridge: Cambridge University Press, 2012.

Fraser, G., *Redeeming Nietzsche: On the Piety of Unbelief*, London and New York: Routledge, 2002.

Freud, S., *Standard Edition of the Complete Works of Sigmund Freud*, ed. J. Strachey and A. Freud, 18 vols, London: Hogarth Press, 1965–1974.

Freud, S., and C.G. Jung, *The Freud/Jung Letters: The Correspondence between Sigmund Freud and C.G. Jung*, ed. W. McGuire, Cambridge, MA: Harvard University Press, 1988.

Gadamer, H.-G., *The Relevance of Beauty and Other Essays*, Cambridge: Cambridge University Press, 1986.

George, S., *The Works of Stefan George rendered into English*, tr. O. Marx and E. Morwitz, Chapel Hill, NC: University of North Carolina, 1949.

George, S., *Werke: Ausgabe in zwei Bänden*, Stuttgart: Klett-Cotta, 1984.

Gerson, L.P. (ed.), *The Cambridge Companion to Plotinus*, Cambridge: Cambridge University Press, 2006.

Gilman, S.L. (ed.), *Conversations with Nietzsche: A Life in the Words of His Contemporaries*, tr. D.J. Parent, New York and Oxford: Oxford University Press, 1987.

Goethe, J.W. von, *Briefe*, ed. K.R. Mandelkow, 4 vols, Hamburg: Wegner, 1962–1967.

Goethe, J.W. von, *Essays on Art and Literature*, ed. J. Gearey, tr. E. von Nardroff and E.H. von Nardroff, New York: Suhrkamp, 1986.

Goethe, J.W. von, *Faust*, ed. E. Trunz, Munich: Beck, 1972.

Goethe, J.W. von, *From My Life: Poetry and Truth: Parts One to Three*, ed. T.P. Saine and J.L. Sammons, tr. R.R. Heitner, New York: Suhrkamp, 1987.

Goethe, J.W. von, *Gedichte*, ed. E. Trunz, Munich: Beck, 1974.

Goethe, J.W. von, *Italian Journey*, tr. W.H. Auden and E. Mayer, Harmondsworth: Penguin, 1970.

Goethe, J.W. von, *Poems of the West and East: West-Eastern Divan — West-Östlicher Divan: Bi-Lingual Edition of the Complete Poems*, tr. J. Whaley, Bern, Berlin, and Frankfurt am Main: Lang, 1998.

Goethe, J.W. von, *Selected Poems*, tr. J. Whaley, London: Dent, 1998.

Goethe, J.W. von, *Selected Poems*, ed. C. Middleton, Boston, MA: Suhrkamp/Insel Publishers, 1983.

Goethe, J.W. von, *Werke [Hamburger Ausgabe]*, ed. E. Trunz, 14 vols, Hamburg: Wegner, 1948–1960; Munich: Beck, 1981.

Goethe, J.W. von, and F. Schiller, *Select Minor Poems: Translated from the German of Goethe and Schiller*, tr. J.S. Dwight, Boston: Hilliard, Gray, 1839.

Gooding-Williams, R., *Zarathustra's Dionysian Modernism*, Stanford, CA: Stanford University Press, 2001.

Graves, R., *The Greek Myths* [1955], 2 vols, Harmondsworth: Penguin, 1990.

Gregory of Nyssa, *Commentary on the Inscriptions of the Psalms*, tr. C. McCambley, Brookline, MA: Hellenic College Press, 1990.

Gregory of Nyssa, *Commentary on the Song of Songs*, tr. C. MacCambley, Brookline, MA: Hellenic College Press, 1987.

Gregory of Nyssa, *Opera quæ reperiri potuerunt omnia*, vol. 3 [*Patrologia Graeca*, ed. J.-P. Migne, vol. 46], Paris: Migne, 1863.

Gregory of Nyssa, *The Life of Moses*, tr. A.J. Malherbe and E. Ferguson, Mahwah, NJ: Paulist Press, 1978.

Gregory of Nyssa, *The Lord's Prayer; The Beatitudes*, tr. H.C. Graef, Westminster, ML; London: Newman Press; Longmans, Green, 1954.

Gregory the Great, *Morals on the Book of Job* [*Library of Fathers of the Holy Catholic Church*, vols. 35–38], 4 vols, Oxford; London: Parker; Rivington, 1844–1850.

Grimes, P., and R.L. Uliana, *Philosophical Midwifery: A New Paradigm for Understanding Human Problems With Its Validation*, Costa Mesa, CA: Hyparxis, 1998.

Grundlehner, P., *The Poetry of Friedrich Nietzsche*, New York and Oxford: Oxford University Press, 1996.

Guéranger, Abbé P., *The Liturgical Year*, vol. 7, *Paschal Time: Book 1*, tr. L. Shepherd [1949], Great Falls, MT, 2000.

Guthrie, W.K.C., *The Greeks and their Gods*, London: Methuen, 1950.

Hadot, P., *Plotinus or the Simplicity of Vision* [1963], tr. M. Chase, Chicago: Chicago University Press, 1998.

Hall, M.P., *Lectures on Ancient Philosophy*, New York: Tarcher/Penguin, 2005.

Hall, M.P., *The Secret Teachings of All Ages*, New York: Tarcher/Penguin, 2003.

Hamilton, E., *Mythology: Timeless Tales of Gods and Heroes* [1942], New York: Warner Books, 1999, pp. 166–179.

Hattler, C. (ed.), *Imperium der Götter: Isis—Mithras—Christus: Kulte und Religionen im Römischen Reich*, Stuttgart: Theiss, 2013.

Hegel, G.W.F., *Werke*, ed. E. Moldenhauer and K. M. Michel, 20 vols, Frankfurt am Main: Suhrkamp, 1986.

Heidegger, M., 'Art and Space', tr. C.H. Seibert, *Man and World*, February 1973, vol. 6, no. 1, 3–8.

Heidegger, M., *Basic Writings*, ed. D.F. Krell, London: Routledge, 1993.

Heidegger, M., *Being and Time: A Translation of "Sein und Zeit"*, tr. J. Stambaugh, Albany, NY: State University of New York Press, 1996.

Heidegger, M., *Bemerkungen zu Kunst—Plastik—Raum*, ed. H. Heidegger, St Gallen: Erker-Verlag, 1996.

Heidegger, M., *Nietzsche*, vols 3 and 4, tr. D.F. Krell, New York: HarperCollins, 1991.

Heidegger, M., *Pathmarks*, ed. W. McNeil, Cambridge: Cambridge University Press, 1998.

Heidegger, M., *The Basic Problems of Phenomenology*, tr. A. Hofstadter, Bloomington and Indianapolis: Indiana University Press, 1982.

Heidegger, M., *The End of Philosophy*, ed. and tr. J. Stambaugh, New York: Harper & Row, 1973.

Heliodorus, *The Aethiopica*, Athens: Athenian Society, 1897.

Henderson, D., 'The Coincidence of Opposites: C.G. Jung's Reception of Nicholas of Cusa', *Studies in Spirituality*, 2010, vol. 20, 101–113.

Herder, J.G., *Sculpture: Some Observations on Shape and Form from Pygmalion's Creative Dream*, tr. J. Gaiger, Chicago and London: University of Chicago Press, 2002.

Herder, J.G., *Selected Writings on Aesthetics*, ed. and tr. G. Moore, Princeton and Oxford: Princeton University Press, 2006.

Herder, J.G., *Werke in zehn Bänden*, 10 vols, Frankfurt am Main: Deutscher Klassiker Verlag, 1985–2000.

Herodotus, *The Landmark Herodotus: The Histories*, ed. R.B. Strassler, tr. A.L. Purvis, London: Quercus, 2008.

Hesiod, *The Homeric Hymns and Homerica*, tr. H.G. Evelyn-White, Cambridge, MA; London: Harvard University Press; Heinemann, 1982.

Hilary of Poitiers, John of Damascene [*Nicene and Post-Nicene Fathers*, second series, vol. 9], ed. P. Schaff and H. Wallace [1893], New York: Cosimo, 2007.

Hillebrand, B., *Ästhetik des Augenblicks: Der Dichter als Überwinder der Zeit — Von Goethe bis heute*, Göttingen: Vandenhoeck & Ruprecht, 1999.

Hoffmann, E.T.A., *The Best Tales of Hoffmann*, ed. E.F. Bleiler, New York: Dover, 1967.

Hollinrake, R., *Nietzsche, Wagner, and the Philosophy of Pessimism*, London: Allen & Unwin, 1982.

Holmes, S.M. (ed.), *The Fathers on the Sunday Gospels*, Collegeville, MN: Liturgical Press, 2012.

Homer, *The Iliad*, tr. R. Lattimore, Chicago and London: University of Chicago Press, 1951.

Homer, *The Odyssey*, ed. and tr. A. Cook, 2nd edn, New York and London: Norton, 1993.

Horace, *Satires; Epistles; and Ars Poetica*, tr. H.R. Fairclough, London; Cambridge, MA: Heinemann; Harvard University Press, 1942.

Hough, S., *Nietzsche's Noontide Friend: The Self as Metaphoric Double*, University Park, PA: Pennsylvania State University Press, 1997.

Houlgate, S., and M. Baur (eds), *A Companion to Hegel*, Malden, MA and Oxford: Blackwell, 2011.

Hume, D., *Selected Essays*, ed. S. Copley and A. Edgar, Oxford and New York: Oxford University Press, 1993.

Iamblichus, *"On the Mysteries of the Egyptians, Chaldeans, and Assyrians" and "Life of Pythagoras"*, tr. T. Taylor [TTS, vol. 17], Sturminster Newton: Prometheus Trust, 1999.

Jacobi, J., *The Psychology of C. G. Jung*, London: Kegan Paul, Trench, Trubner, 1942.

Jaeger, P., and R. Lüthe (eds), *Distanz und Nähe: Reflexionen und Analysen zur Kunst der Gegenwart*, Würzburg: Königshausen & Neumann, 1983.

Jaffé, A., *Bilder und Symbole aus E. T. A. Hoffmanns Märchen "Der goldne Topf"*, Zurich: Daimon, 1990.

Jankélévitch, V., *Quelque part dans l'inachevé*, Paris: Gallimard, 1978.

John of the Cross, *The Collected Works*, tr. K. Kavanaugh and O. Rodriguez, Washington, CD: Institute of Carmelite Studies, 1979.

Johnson, A. P., *Religion and Identity in Porphyry of Tyre: The Limits of Hellenism in Late Antiquity*, Cambridge: Cambridge University Press, 2013.

Johnston, S. I., 'Animating Statues: A Case Study in Ritual', *Arethusa*, Fall 2008, vol. 41, no. 3, 445–477.

Jones, E., *Essays in Applied Psycho-Analysis*, vol. 2, *Essays in Folklore, Anthropology and Religion*, London: Hogarth Press, 1951.

Jung, C. G., *Collected Works*, ed. Sir H. Read, M. Fordham, G. Adler, and W. McGuire, 20 vols, London: Routledge and Kegan Paul, 1953–1983.

Jung, C. G., *Memories, Dreams, Reflections: Recorded and edited by Aniela Jaffé*, tr. R. and C. Winston, London: Fontana, 1983.

Jung, C. G., *Nietzsche's "Zarathustra": Notes of the Seminar given in 1934–1939*, ed. J. L. Jarrett, 2 vols, London: Routledge, 1988.

Jung, C. G., *Psychology of the Unconscious: A Study of the Transformations and Symbolisms of the Libido: A Contribution to the History of the Evolution of Thought*, tr. B. M. Hinkle, intr. William McGuire, London: Routledge, 1991.

Jung, C. G., *The Red Book: Liber Novus*, ed. S. Shamdasani, tr. M. Kyburz, J. Peck, and S. Shamdasani, New York and London: Norton, 2009.

Jung, C. G., *Visions: Notes of the Seminar given in 1930–1934*, ed. C. Douglas, 2 vols, London: Routledge, 1998.

Jurak, M. (ed.), *Cross-cultural Studies: American, Canadian and European Literatures: 1945–1985*, Ljubljana: Filozofska Fakulteta, 1988.

Juvenal, *The Satires*, tr. N. Rudd, Oxford and New York: Oxford University Press, 1992.

Kariatlis, P., '"Dazzling Darkness": The Mystical or Theophanic Theology of St Gregory of Nyssa', *Phronema*, 2012, vol. 27, no. 2, 99–123.

Kaufmann, W., *Discovering the Mind*, vol. 2, *Nietzsche, Heidegger, and Buber*, New Brunswick and London: Transaction, 1992.

Kayser, J., *Zur Geschichte der Kirchenhymnen* [1881], Bremen: DOGMA in Europäischer Hochschulverlag, 2012.

Kerényi, C., *Eleusis: Archetypal Image of Mother and Daughter*, tr. R. Manheim, Princeton, NJ: Princeton University Press, 1967.

Klages, L., *Sämtliche Werke*, ed. E. Frauchiger, G. Funke, K. J. Groffmann, R. Heiss, and H. E. Schröder, 9 vols, Bonn: Bouvier, 1964–1999.

Klages, L., *The Science of Character*, tr. W. H. Johnston, London: Allen & Unwin, 1929.

Klopstock, F.G., *Werke und Briefe: Historisch-Kritische Ausgabe*, vol. I.1, *Oden: Texte*, ed. H. Gronemeyer and K. Hurlebach, Berlin and New York: de Gruyter, 2010.

Knight, R.P., *An Inquiry into the Symbolical Language of Ancient Art and Mythology*, London: Black and Armstrong, 1836.

Koch, H., 'Das mystische Schauen beim hl. Gregor von Nyssa', *Theologische Quartalschrift*, 1898, vol. 80, 404–427.

Köster, P., *Kontroversen um Nietzsche: Untersuchungen zur theologischen Rezeption*, Zurich: Theologischer Verlag Zürich, 2003.

Lamb, C., and L. Curtius, *Die Tempel von Paestum*, Leipzig: Insel, 1944.

Lampedusa, G.T. di, *The Leopard* [1958], tr. A. Colquhoun, London: Vintage, 2007.

Lampert, L., *Nietzsche's Teaching: An Interpretation of "Thus Spoke Zarathustra"*, New Haven and London: Yale University Press, 1986.

Lapide, C.A, *The Great Commentary: The Holy Gospel According to Saint Mark; The Holy Gospel According to Saint Luke*, tr. T.W. Mossman, revised M. J. Miller, Fitzwilliam, NH: Loreto, 2008.

Lefebvre, H., *Hegel – Marx – Nietzsche: Le royaume des ombres*, Tournai: Castermann, 1975.

Leibniz, *New Essays on Human Understanding*, ed. P. Remnant and J. Bennett, Cambridge: Cambridge University Press, 1996.

Leis, M., and P. Weiss, *Mythos Herkules*, Leipzig: Reclam, 2005.

Linden, S.J., *The Alchemy Reader: From Hermes Trismegistus to Isaac Newton*, Cambridge: Cambridge University Press, 2003.

Livy, *Books XXVIII-XXX*, tr. F.G. Moore, London; New York: Heinemann; Harvard University Press, 1949.

Lucian, *Works*, vol. 3, tr. A.H. Harmon, Cambridge, MA, and London: Harvard University Press, 1921.

McNeill, D.N., 'On the Relationship of Alcibiades' Speech to Nietzsche's "Problem of Socrates"', in P. Bishop (ed.), *Nietzsche and Antiquity: His Reaction and Response to the Classical Tradition*, Rochester, NY: Camden House, 2004, pp. 260–275.

Majercik, R. (ed.), *The Chaldean Oracles*, Westbury: Prometheus Trust, 2013.

Manuel, F.E. and F.P. Manuel, *Utopian Thought in the Western World*, Oxford: Blackwell, 1979.

Markschies, C., 'Die Platonische Metapher vom "inneren Menschen": Eine Brücke zwischen antiker Philosophie und altchristlicher Theologie', Winter 1995, vol. 1, no. 3, 3–18.

Mateo-Seco, L.F., and G. Maspero (eds), *The Brill Dictionary of Gregory of Nyssa*, Leiden: Brill, 2010.

Mattoon, M.A. (ed.), *The Archetype of Shadow in a Split World: Tenth International Congress of Analytical Psychology*, Einsiedeln: Daimon, 1987.

Maximus Tyrius, *The Dissertations of Maximus Tyrius*, ed. and tr. T. Taylor [TTS, vol. 6], Sturminster Newton: Prometheus Trust, 1994.

Meister Eckhart, *Deutsche Predigten und Traktate*, ed. and tr. J. Quint, Munich: Hanser, 1963.

Meister Eck[e]hart, *Schriften und Predigten*, ed. H. Büttner, 2 vols, Jena: Diederichs, 1921.

Meister Eckhart, *Selected Treatises and Sermons*, tr. J.M. Clark and J.V. Skinner, London: Faber and Faber, 1958.

Meister Eckhart, *Sermons & Treatises*, ed. and tr. M.O'C. Walshe, 3 vols, Longmead: Element Books, 1987.

Meister Eckhart, *Teacher and Preacher*, ed. B. McGinn, New York, Mahwah, NJ, Toronto: Paulist Press, 1986.

Meister Eckhart, *The Essential Sermons, Commentaries, Treatises, and Defense*, tr. E. Colledge and B. McGinn, New York, Ramsey, NJ, Toronto: Paulist Press, 1981.

Meister Eckhart, *Werke I*, ed. N. Largier, Frankfurt am Main: Deutscher Klassiker Verlag, 2008.

Merkelbach, R., *Mithras: Ein persisch-römischer Mysterienkult*, Königstein/Taunus: Hain, 1984.

Michelangelo, *Complete Poems and Selected Letters*, ed. R.N. Linscott, tr. C. Gilbert, Princeton, NJ: Princeton University Press, 1980.

Michelangelo, *Life, Letters, and Poetry*, ed. G. Bull, tr. G. Bull and P. Porter, Oxford: Oxford University Press, 1987.

Michelangelo, *The Sonnets of Michelangelo*, tr. J.A. Symonds, Plymouth: Vision Press, 1950.

Mitchell, A.J., *Heidegger Among the Sculptors: Body, Space, and the Art of Dwelling*, Stanford, CA: Stanford University Press, 2010.

Monick, E., *Phallos: Sacred Image of the Masculine*, Toronto, Canada: Inner City Books, 1987.

Morwitz, E., *Kommentar zu dem Werk Stefan Georges*, Düsseldorf and Munich: Küpper (vormals Bondi), 1969.

Nietzsche, F., *Basic Writings of Nietzsche*, ed. and tr. W. Kaufmann, New York: Modern Library, 1968.

Nietzsche, F., *Daybreak*, tr. R.J. Hollingdale, Cambridge: Cambridge University Press, 1982.

Nietzsche, F., *Dithyrambs of Dionysus*, tr. R.J. Hollingdale, London: Anvil Press, 1984.

Nietzsche, F., *Ecce Homo: How One Becomes What One Is*, tr. R.J. Hollingdale, Harmonsworth: Penguin, 1992.

Nietzsche, F., *Human, All Too Human*, tr. R.J. Hollingdale, Cambridge: Cambridge University Press, 1986.

Nietzsche, F., *Sämtliche Briefe: Kritische Studienausgabe*, ed. G. Colli and M. Montinari, 8 vols, Berlin and New York; Munich: de Gruyter; Deutscher Taschenbuch Verlag, 1975–1984.

Nietzsche, F., *Sämtliche Werke: Kritische Studienausgabe*, ed. G. Colli and M. Montinari, 15 vols, Berlin and New York; Munich: de Gruyter; Deutscher Taschenbuch Verlag, 1967–1977 and 1988.

Nietzsche, F., *The Birth of Tragedy and Other Writings*, ed. R. Geuss and R. Speirs, tr. R. Speirs, Cambridge: Cambridge University Press, 1999.

Nietzsche, F., *The Gay Science*, tr. W. Kaufmann, New York: Vintage, 1974.

Nietzsche, F., *The Will to Power*, ed. W. Kaufmann, tr. R.J. Hollingdale and W. Kaufmann, New York: Vintage, 1968.

Nietzsche, F., *Thus Spoke Zarathustra*, tr. R.J. Hollingdale, Harmondsworth: Penguin, 1969.

Nietzsche, F., *Twilight of the Idols; The Anti-Christ*, tr. R.J. Hollingdale, Harmondsworth: Penguin, 1968.

Nietzsche, F., *Writings from the Early Notebooks*, ed. R. Geuss and A. Nehemas, tr. L. Löb, Cambridge: Cambridge University Press, 2009.

Olympiodorus, *Commentary on Plato's "Gorgias"*, tr. R. Jackson, K. Lycos, and H. Tarrant, Leiden: Brill, 1998.

Onfray, M., *La sculpture de soi: La morale esthétique*, Paris: Grasset, 1993.

Onfray, M., *Le crépuscule d'un idole: L'affabulation freudienne*, Paris: Grasset, 2010.

Onfray, M., *Les sagesses antiques* [*Contre-histoire de la philosophie*, vol. 1], Paris: Grasset, 2006.

Origen, *Homilies on Joshua*, ed. C. White and tr. B.J. Bruce, Washington, DC: Catholic University of America Press, 2002.

Origen, *The Song of Songs: Commentary and Homilies*, tr. and annotated R. P. Lawson, Westminster, MD; London: Newman Press; Longmans, Green and Co., 1957.

Ovid, *Fasti*, tr. J.G. Frazer, London; New York: Heinemann; Putnam, 1931.

Panofsky, E., *Idea: A Concept in Art Theory* [1923], tr. J.J.S. Peake, Columbia: University of South Carolina Press, 1968.

Panofsky, E., *Studies in Iconology: Humanistic Themes in the Art of the Renaissance*, New York: Oxford University Press, 1939.

Parkes, G., 'Nietzsche on Rock and Stone: The Dead World, Dance and Flight', *International Journal of Philosophical Studies*, 2013, vol. 21, 20–40.

Pascal, *Œuvres complètes*, ed. L. Lafuma, Paris: Seuil, 1963.

Pascal, *Pensées*, tr. A.J. Krailsheimer, Harmondsworth: Penguin, 1966.

Patton, P. (ed.), *Nietzsche, Feminism and Political Theory*, London and New York: Routledge, 1993.

Pernet, M., 'Friedrich Nietzsche and Pietism', *German Life and Letters*, October 1995, vol. 48, no. 4, 474–486.

Philo, *The Works of Philo: Complete and Unabridged: New Updated Edition*, tr. C.D. Yonge, Peabody, MA: Hendrickson, 1993.

Philostratus, *The Life of Apollonius of Tyana*, vol. 1, tr. F.C. Conybeare, London: Heinemann; New York: Macmillan, 1912.

Pindar, *The Odes of Pindar*, tr. R. Lattimore, Chicago: The University of Chicago Press, 1947.

Plato, *Complete Works*, ed. J.M. Cooper, Indianapolis and Cambridge: Hackett, 1997.

Plato, *Great Dialogues*, ed. E.H. Warmington and P.G. Rouse, tr. W.H.D. Rouse, New York: Mentor, 1956.

Plato, *The Collected Dialogues*, ed. E. Hamilton and H. Cairns, Princeton, NJ: Princeton University Press, 1989.

Plato, *Works in Five Volumes: Volume I*, tr. T. Taylor and F. Sydenham [TTS, vol. 9], Sturminster Newton: Prometheus Trust, 2006.

Plato, *Works in Five Volumes: Volume V*, tr. T. Taylor and F. Sydenham [TTS, vol. 13], Westbury: Prometheus Trust, 1996.

Pliny the Elder, *Natural History*, vol. 2, *Libri III-VII*, tr. H. Rackham, Cambridge, MA; London: Harvard University Press; Heinemann, 1941.

Pliny the Elder, *Natural History*, vol. 9, *Books 33–35*, tr. H. Rackham, Cambridge, MA; London: Harvard University Press; Macmillan, 1961.

Plotinus, *Enneads: II. 1–9*, tr. A.H. Armstrong, London; Cambridge: MA: Heinemann; Harvard University Press, 1966.

Plotinus, *Ennead IV*, tr. A.H. Armstrong, Cambridge, MA and London: Harvard University Press, 1984.

Plotinus, *Ennead V*, tr. A.H. Armstrong, Cambridge, MA, and London: Harvard University Press, 1984.

Plotinus, *The Enneads*, tr. S. MacKenna, abridged J. Dillon, Harmondsworth: Penguin, 1991.

Plotinus, *The Essential Plotinus: Representative Treatises from the Enneads*, ed. and tr. E. O'Brian, Indianapolis, IN: Hackett, 1964.

Plutarch, *Lives*, vol. 8, tr. B. Perrin, London; New York: Heinemann; Putnam, 1919.

Pollitt, J.J., *The Art of Ancient Greece: Sources and Documents*, Cambridge: Cambridge University Press, 1990.

Proclus, *A Commentary on the First Book of Euclid's Elements*, tr. G.R. Morrow, Princeton, NJ: Princeton University Press, 1970.

Proclus, *Commentary on Plato's "Parmenides"*, tr. G.R. Morrow and J.M. Dillon, Princeton, NJ: Princeton University Press, 1987.

Proclus, *Commentary on the First Alcibiades*, ed. L. G. Westerink, tr. W. O'Neill, Westbury: Prometheus Trust, 2011.

Proclus, *Commentary on the "Timaeus" of Plato: Volume I*, tr. T.T. Taylor [TTS, vol.15], Sturminster Newton: Prometheus Trust, 1998.

Proclus, *Commentary on the "Timæus" of Plato: Volume II*, tr. T. Taylor [TTS, vol. 16], Sturminster Newton: Prometheus Trust, 1998.

Proclus, *The Theology of Plato*, tr. T. Taylor [TTS, vol. 8], Westbury: Prometheus Trust, 1995.

Pseudo-Dionysius, *The Complete Works*, tr. C. Luibheid, New York and Mahwah, NJ: Paulist Press, 1987.

[Pseudo]-Dionysius the Areopagite, *Works*, tr. J. Parker, 2 vols, London: Parker, 1897.

Pugh, D., *Dialectic of Love: Platonism in Schiller's Aesthetics*, Montreal & Kingston, London, Buffalo: McGill-Queen's University Press, 1996.

Redding, P., 'Self-Surpassing Beauty: Plato's Ambiguous Legacy', *Literature and Aesthetics: The Journal of the Sydney Society of Literature and Aesthetics*, 1997, vol. 7, 94–108.

Richard of St-Victor, *The Twelve Patriarchs; The Mystical Ark; Book Three of the Trinity*, tr. G.A. Zinn, New York and Mahwah, NJ: Paulist Press, 1979.

Rilke, R.M., *Schriften: Kommentierte Ausgabe*, ed. M. Engel, U. Fülleborn, H. Nalewski, and A. Stahl, 4 vols, Frankfurt am Main and Leipzig: Insel, 1996.

Ritter, J., K. Gründer, and G. Gabriel (eds), *Historisches Wörterbuch der Philosophie*, 13 vols, Basel and Stuttgart: Schwabe, 1971–2007.

Rosen, D., *The Tao of Jung: The Way of Integrity*, New York: Viking Arcana, 1996.

Rosen, S., *The Mask of Enlightenment: Nietzsche's "Zarathustra"*, Cambridge: Cambridge University Press, 1995

Safranksi, R., *Schiller oder Die Erfindung des Deutschen Idealismus*, Munich and Vienna: Hanser, 2004.

Samuels, A., B. Shorter and F. Plaut, *A Critical Dictionary of Jungian Analysis*, London and New York: Routledge, 1986.

Scheler, M., *Formalism in Ethics and Non-Formal Ethics of Values: A New Attempt toward the Foundation of an Ethical Personalism*, tr. M.S. Frings and R.L. Funk, Evanston, IL: Northwestern University Press, 1973.

Scheler, M., *On the Eternal in Man*, tr. B. Noble [1960], New Brunswick, NJ: Transaction, 2010.

Schelling, F.W.J. von, *Sämtliche Werke*, ed. K.F.A. Schelling, 14 vols, Stuttgart and Augsburg: Cotta, 1856–1861.

Schelling, F.W.J., *Schelling's Treatise on "The Deities of Samothrace"*, ed. and tr. R. F. Brown, Missoula, Montana: Scholars Press, 1977.

Schelling, F.W.J., *System of Transcendental Idealism*, tr. P. Heath, Charlottesville: University Press of Virginia, 1978.

Schelling, F.W.J., *The Philosophy of Art: An Oration on the Relation between the Plastic Arts and Nature*, tr. A. Johnson, London: Chapman, 1845.

Schelling, F.W.J., *The Unconditional in Human Knowledge: Four Early Essays (1794–1796)*, tr. F. Marti, Lewisburg; London: Bucknell University Press; Associated University Presses, 1980.

Schiller, F., *On the Aesthetic Education of Man*, ed. and tr. E.M. Wilkinson and L.A. Willoughby, Oxford: Clarendon Press, 1982.

Schiller, F., *On the Naïve and Sentimental in Literature*, tr. H. Watanabe-O'Kelly, Manchester: Carcanet, 1981.

Schiller, F., *Poems and Ballads*, tr. E.B. Lytton, New York: Harper, 1887.

Schiller, F., *Sämtliche Gedichte und Balladen*, ed. G. Kurscheidt, Frankfurt am Main: Insel, 2004.

Schiller, F., *Selected Poems*, ed. F.M. Fowler, London; New York: Macmillan; St Martin's Press, 1969.

Schiller, F., *The Minor Poems of Schiller*, tr. J.H. Merivale, London: Pickering, 1844.

Schiller, F., *Werke: Nationalausgabe*, ed. J. Petersen, G. Fricke, N. Oellers and S. Seidel, in Auftrage des Goethe- und Schiller-Archivs, des Schiller-Nationalmuseums und der Deutschen Akademie, 43 vols, Weimar: Hermann Böhlaus Nachfolger, 1943ff.

Schmitt, G., '*Wahrheit* und *Individuation*: Zum Verlauf von Denklinien bei Heidegger und Jung', in C. Maillard and V. Liard (eds), *Recherches germaniques, hors série No. 9 (2014), Carl Gustav Jung (1875–1961): Pour une réévaluation de l'œuvre / C.G. Jung (1875–1961): Ein neuer Zugang zum Gesamtwerk*, pp. 239–56.

Schoeller-Reisch, D., 'Die Demut Zarathustras: Ein Versuch zu Nietzsche mit Meister Eckhart', *Nietzsche-Studien*, 1998, vol. 27, 420–439.

Schopenhauer, A., *Essays and Aphorisms*, tr. R.J. Hollingdale, Harmondsworth: Penguin, 1970.

Schopenhauer, A., *The World as Will and Representation*, tr. E.F.J. Payne, 2 vols, New York: Dover, 1966.

Schopenhauer, A., *Werke in fünf Bänden*, ed. L. Lütkehaus, 5 + 1 vols, Zurich: Haffmanns, 1988.

Seneca, *Letters from a Stoic*, tr. R. Campbell, Harmondsworth: Penguin, 1969.

Shamdasani, S., '"The Boundless Expanse": Jung's Reflections on Life and Death', *Quadrant: Journal of the C. G. Jung Foundation for Analytical Psychology*, 2008, vol. 38, 9–32.

Shaw, G., *Theurgy and the Soul: The Neoplatonism of Iamblichus*, University Park, PA: Pennsylvania State University Press, 2010.

Sheppard, A., 'Proclus' Attitude to Theurgy', *The Classical Quarterly*, 1982, [NS] vol. 32, no. 1, 212–224.

Smith, A., *Porphyry's Place in the Neoplatonic Tradition: A Study in Post-Plotinian Neoplatonism*, The Hague: Nijoff, 1974.

Spinoza, *Selections*, ed. J. Wild, London: Scribner, 1928.

Spivey, N., *Understanding Greek Sculpture: Ancient Meanings, Modern Readings*, London: Thames and Hudson, 1996.

Spranger, E., *Goethe: Seine geistige Welt*, Tübingen: Rainer Wunderlich Verlag Hermann Leins, 1967

Steebus, J.C., *Coelum Sephiroticum, Hebræorum*, Mainz: Bourgeat, 1679.

Steiner, D.T., *Images in Mind: Statues in Archaic and Classical Greek Literature and Thought*, Princeton, NJ: Princeton University Press, 2001.

Steiner, R., *Geisteswissenschaft als Lebensgut: Zwölf öffentliche Vorträge gehalten zwischem dem 30. Oktober 1913 und 23. April 1914 im Architektenhaus zu Berlin* [Gesamtausgabe, vol. 63], Dornach/Schweiz: Rudolf Steiner Verlag, 1986.

Stockton, A. (ed.), *Art: An Introductory Reader*, Forest Row: Rudolf Steiner Press, 2003.

Strehlow, T.G.H., *Aranda Traditions*, Melbourne: Melbourne University Press, 1947.

Summers, D., *Michelangelo and the Language of Art*, Princeton, NJ: Princeton University Press, 1981.

Tauler, J. *Sermons*, tr. M. Shrady, New York and Mahwah, NJ: Paulist Press, 1985.

Taylor, T. (ed. and tr.), *"Against the Christians" and other Writings* [TTS, vol. 33], Sturminster Newton: Prometheus Trust, 2006.

Taylor, T. (ed. and tr.), *Collected Writings on the Gods and the World* [TTS, vol. 4], Sturminster Newton: Prometheus Trust, 1994.

Taylor, T. (ed. and tr.), *Oracles and Mysteries* [TTS, vol. 7], Frome: Prometheus Trust, 2001.

Sparks, H.F.D. (ed.), *The Apocryphal Old Testament*, Oxford: Clarendon Press, 1984.

Theierl, H., *Netzsche: Mystik als Selbstversuch*, Würzburg: Königshausen & Neumann, 2000.

Thomas Aquinas, *Commentary on Aristotle's "Physics"*, tr. R.J. Blackwell, R.J. Spath, W. E. Thirkell, London: Routledge and Kegan Paul, 1963.

Thomson, A.D., *On Mankind: Their Origin and Destiny*, London: Longmans, Green, 1872.

Tilton, H., *The Quest for the Phoenix: Spiritual Alchemy and Rosicrucianism in the Work of Count Michael Maier (1569–1622)*, Berlin and New York: de Gruyter, 2003.

Turner, D., *The Darkness of God: Negativity in Christian Mysticism*, Cambridge: Cambridge University Press, 1995.

Uždavinys, A., *Philosophy as a Rite of Rebirth: From Ancient Egypt to Neoplatonism*, Westbury: Prometheus Trust, 2008.

Vergely, B., *Deviens qui tu es: Quand des sages grecs nous aident à vivre*, Paris: Albin Michel, 2014.

Vischer, F.T., *Auch Einer: Eine Reisebekanntschaft* [1879], Stuttgart and Leipzig: Deutsche Verlags-Anstalt, 1904.

Vogelweide, W. von der, *Die Gedichte*, ed. K. Lachmann, Berlin: Reimer, 1827.

Wallis Budge, E.A. (ed.), *The Book of Paradise, being the Histories and Sayings of the Monks and Ascetics of the Desert*, 2 vols, London: Drugulin, 1904.

Wallis, R.T., *Neoplatonism*, London: Bristol Classical Press, 1995.

Wiles, M., *Archetypal Heresy: Arianism Through the Centuries*, New York: Oxford University Press, 1996.

Wiles, M. and M. Santer (eds), *Documents in Early Christian Thought*, Cambridge: Cambridge University Press, 1975.

Winckelmann, J.J., *Essays on the Philosophy and History of Art*, ed. C. Bowman, London and New York: Continuum, 2005.

Winckelmann, J.J., *Johann Joachim Winckelmann on Art, Architecture, and Archaeology*, tr. D. Carter, Rochester, NY: Camden House, 2013.

Witte, B. (ed.), *Interpretationen: Gedichte von Johann Wolfgang Goethe*, Stuttgart: Reclam, 1998.

Wolfson, H.A., *The Philosophy of Spinoza: Unfolding the Latent Processes of His Reasoning*, 2 vols in 1, Cambridge, MA, and London: Harvard University Press, 1962.

Wolin, R., *The Seduction of Unreason: The Intellectual Romance with Fascism from Nietzsche to Postmodernism*, Princeton and Oxford: Princeton University Press, 2004.

Wolters, C. (tr.), *The Cloud of Unknowing and Other Works*, Harmondsworth: Penguin, 1978.

Wyndham-Jones, G. and T. Addey, *Beyond the Shadows: The Metaphysics of the Platonic Tradition*, Dilton Marsh, Westbury: Prometheus Trust, 2011.

Zotz, V. *Auf den glückseligen Inseln: Buddhismus in der deutschen Kultur*. Berlin: Theseus Verlag, 2000.

Zweig, C., and J. Abrams (eds), *Meeting the Shadow: The Hidden Power of the Dark Side of Human Nature*, New York: Tarcher/Putnam, 1991.

INDEX

Taylor & Francis eBooks

Helping you to choose the right eBooks for your Library

Add Routledge titles to your library's digital collection today. Taylor and Francis ebooks contains over 50,000 titles in the Humanities, Social Sciences, Behavioural Sciences, Built Environment and Law.

Choose from a range of subject packages or create your own!

Benefits for you

- » Free MARC records
- » COUNTER-compliant usage statistics
- » Flexible purchase and pricing options
- » All titles DRM-free.

Benefits for your user

- » Off-site, anytime access via Athens or referring URL
- » Print or copy pages or chapters
- » Full content search
- » Bookmark, highlight and annotate text
- » Access to thousands of pages of quality research at the click of a button.

> REQUEST YOUR
> **FREE**
> INSTITUTIONAL
> TRIAL TODAY

Free Trials Available
We offer free trials to qualifying academic, corporate and government customers.

eCollections – Choose from over 30 subject eCollections, including:

Archaeology	Language Learning
Architecture	Law
Asian Studies	Literature
Business & Management	Media & Communication
Classical Studies	Middle East Studies
Construction	Music
Creative & Media Arts	Philosophy
Criminology & Criminal Justice	Planning
Economics	Politics
Education	Psychology & Mental Health
Energy	Religion
Engineering	Security
English Language & Linguistics	Social Work
Environment & Sustainability	Sociology
Geography	Sport
Health Studies	Theatre & Performance
History	Tourism, Hospitality & Events

For more information, pricing enquiries or to order a free trial, please contact your local sales team:
www.tandfebooks.com/page/sales

Routledge
Taylor & Francis Group

The home of
Routledge books

www.tandfebooks.com